Clive Hamilton AM is an Australian author and public intellectual. His books include *Growth Fetish, Silencing Dissent* (with Sarah Maddison) and *What Do We Want: The Story of Protest in Australia*. He was for 14 years the executive director of The Australia Institute, a think tank he founded. For some years he has been professor of public ethics at Charles Sturt University in Canberra.

'Anyone keen to understand how China draws other countries into its sphere of influence should start with *Silent Invasion*. This is an important book for the future of Australia. But tug on the threads of China's influence networks in Australia and its global network of influence operations starts to unravel.'

—Professor John Fitzgerald, author of *Big White Lie: Chinese Australians in White Australia*

SILENT INVASION

CHINA'S INFLUENCE IN AUSTRALIA

CLIVE HAMILTON

With research by Alex Joske

hardie grant books

Published in 2018 by Hardie Grant Books,
an imprint of Hardie Grant Publishing

Hardie Grant Books (Melbourne)
Building 1, 658 Church Street
Richmond, Victoria 3121

Hardie Grant Books (London)
5th & 6th Floors
52–54 Southwark Street
London SE1 1UN

hardiegrantbooks.com

A catalogue record for this
book is available from the
National Library of Australia

Silent Invasion
ISBN 978 1 74379 480 7

10 9 8 7 6 5 4 3 2

Cover design by Peter Long
Typeset in 11.5/15 pt Adobe Garamond Pro by Cannon Typesetting
Cover image: Parliament House, Phillip Minnis/Adobe Stock;
Flag, Fstockfoto/Shutterstock
Printed in Canada by Friesens

Contents

Preface

On 24 April 2008, the Olympic torch arrived in Canberra on the last leg of its worldwide relay in preparation for the Beijing Games. I went along to the lawns outside Parliament House to lend quiet support to the Tibetan protesters. I had no idea what I was walking into. Tens of thousands of Chinese students had arrived early and their mood was angry and aggressive. As the torch approached, the pro-Tibet protesters, vastly outnumbered, were mobbed and abused by a sea of Chinese people wielding red flags. Everyday Australians who'd turned up complained later that they were jostled, kicked and punched. Some were told that they had no right to be there. The police presence was too small to maintain order and I feared a riot would break out and people would be severely beaten or worse.

What happened that day left me shocked. Where did all of those people come from? Why were they so frenzied? And I was affronted. How dare they arrive, on the doorstep of our parliament, the symbol of our democracy, and shut down a legitimate protest, leaving me and a few hundred others feeling intimidated for expressing our opinion?

I had no answers, the world moved on and everyone seemed to forget about it. But the incident left a nagging question at the back of my mind. Eight years later, in August 2016, a political storm engulfed Senator Sam Dastyari (which would a year later lead to his exit from parliament). Among the many revelations to emerge over the next couple of weeks was that a handful of very rich Chinese and Chinese-Australian businessmen had become the largest donors to our major political parties. They had bought a lot of influence; our politicians were in bed with them and there were photos to prove it.

China and Australian democracy had collided again. Something big is going on, I thought. I decided to investigate and write a book so that Australians could understand what has been happening to our country.

I had no inkling when I began that publishing this book would prove so challenging. My usual publisher, Allen & Unwin, was enthusiastic about the book when I proposed it and we soon signed a contract. But just as the revised manuscript was about to be sent to be typeset, Allen & Unwin told me they were pulling the plug. They were afraid of retaliation from Beijing, or people in Australia acting on behalf of the Chinese Communist Party. When their withdrawal became public it attracted worldwide media coverage, but it left me without a publisher. Other publishers were scared off. Fortunately, Sandy Grant at Hardie Grant Books took up the challenge. In 1987, Sandy published *Spycatcher*, a book the British government attempted to ban.

• • •

'What about the Yanks?'

When I mentioned to some that I was writing a book about the growing influence of the Chinese party-state in Australia, this was their first response. What about the Pine Gap spying base, they said, and how we slavishly followed the Americans into the Iraq War? We've already given up our independence, haven't we, so what's the big issue with China?

I hope those people will read this book and see that there is a world of difference. Australia may have sacrificed some of its independence, mainly in defence policy, to be in an alliance with the United States, although the degree is open to debate. But after decades of 'American colonialism' do we really feel that our daily lives or democratic freedoms are constrained by this foreign power?

We share the guilt with the United States for the post-2003 disaster in Iraq, but through the decades of the close relationship our big ally has never threatened to take away our freedoms. The United States never had the kind of economic leverage over Australia that China has, nor made threats to damage us if we did not toe its line. It hasn't endangered our democratic system of elected governments, and its government has never used money to buy off our politicians. The United States hasn't attempted to erode the rule of law. Nor has it attempted to mobilise a diaspora to oppose Australian policy. The United States government has never shut down dissenting views in Australia, even ones harshly critical of the USA. Can we imagine a United States government using our laws to frighten publishers into dropping a book criticising it? Within the alliance, the rights of women and gay people have blossomed because of a flourishing civil society, and the rights of minorities have been protected.

When the Berlin Wall fell in 1989, people in the West breathed a sigh of relief because we would no longer have to live under the cloud of Cold War thinking or with the ideological divisions that troubled our societies. Who wants to go back to that? But the Cold War never ended in Asia. In fact, as we will see, the collapse of communism in Eastern Europe gave rise to a fierce intensification of China's ideological war and a consolidation of the Leninist party, especially under President Xi Jinping.

Many in the West, especially after the eclipse of Maoism in the 1980s, have looked upon China as a friendly giant beset by insuperable internal challenges, whose political rhetoric of 'running dogs' and 'imperialist wolves' was a kind of theatre. Now that China is the second-ranked economic power in the world (first by some measures), condescending attitudes towards the Middle Kingdom have become dangerous. They blind us to the deadly seriousness with which Beijing sees its rivalry with the West. The Cold War in Asia may no longer be about communism versus capitalism but it remains just as firmly rooted in the deeper struggle that pitted the West against the Soviet Union—the struggle over who will prevail.

1

Dyeing Australia red

When I began researching this book in late 2016 there were a handful of people who argued that the Chinese Communist Party (CCP) is engaged in a systematic campaign to infiltrate, influence and control the most important institutions in Australia. Its ultimate aim, they said, is to break our alliance with the United States and turn this country into a tribute state. I knew we had a problem, but this seemed far-fetched. As I delved deeply into the problem—including speaking to dozens of experts, specialists and close observers in Australia, China and elsewhere—the evidence for these claims began to seem robust.

According to one person extremely well placed to know about this campaign (named below), it all began in the middle of August 2004 when China brought together its envoys from around the world for a conclave in Beijing. Communist Party Secretary Hu Jintao told the gathering that the party's all-powerful Central Committee had decided that henceforth Australia should be included in China's 'overall periphery'. Looking me in the eye, my informant said: 'This means a lot.' China has always devoted special attention to the countries that have a land border with it—its 'overall periphery'—in order to neutralise them.

The attention devoted to controlling bordering countries arises from China's historical sense of vulnerability. Australia, of course, was always seen as across the ocean and far away. But now Australia was to be treated as a neighbour, within its overall periphery. In China's eyes, its territory now extends far to the south of its land border to encompass almost the entire area of the South China Sea. Its recent occupation of islands, and the building of military bases on them, brings China's southernmost border close to the northwest coast of Borneo.

And so in February 2005 Zhou Wenzhong, a vice-minister in the Ministry of Foreign Affairs, arrived in Canberra to communicate the Central Committee's new strategy to a meeting of senior officials in the Chinese embassy. The first objective of including Australia in its overall periphery, he told them, was to secure Australia as a reliable and stable supply base for China's continued economic growth over the next twenty years. The longer-term goal was to drive a wedge into the America–Australia alliance. Those present were given the task of working out how China could most effectively attain what my informant called 'comprehensive influence over Australia economically, politically, culturally, in all ways'.

The plan would involve frequent meetings between senior leaders from both sides 'to build personal friendships, and exchange personal advice'. China would also use economic measures to force Australia to make concessions on a range of matters, including military affairs and human rights. The combination of close personal relationships, coupled with threats of punishment, is the standard Chinese modus operandi. Beijing hoped to turn Australia into a 'second France', 'a western country that would dare to say "no" to America'.

We know all this because my informant Chen Yonglin, first secretary for political affairs from the Chinese consulate in Sydney, was at the meeting and read the documents.[1] Months later, in June 2005, Chen walked out of the consulate and sought political asylum in Australia. At the time, what he would say about the People's Republic of China's (PRC's) goals and operations in Australia was hard to believe; yet as the years have passed, and evidence has accumulated from a wide variety of sources, his warnings have proven justified.

Chen put it plainly: 'Essentially, in accordance with their fixed strategic plans, the Communist Party of China had begun a structured effort to infiltrate Australia in a systematic way.'[2] Australia (along with

New Zealand) was seen as the 'weak link in the western camp' and has been the site for the Chinese party-state to test its methods of infiltration and subversion. He noted that Australia's openness, relatively small population, large number of Chinese immigrants and commitment to multiculturalism have weakened our capacity to recognise and defend against this threat. In short, we have opened ourselves up to it.

The erosion of Australian sovereignty by Beijing is recognised by a handful of Sinologists, political journalists, strategic analysts and intelligence officers. While some are unwilling to say anything in public for fear of retribution, a few have been sending clear warnings. Those alert to the danger find themselves up against a powerful lobby of overlapping business and political elites who share an outdated and self-serving understanding of China—as a real-world El Dorado to which our economic destiny is tied. These 'panda huggers' are backed by China sympathisers in the media, universities, business lobbies and parliaments who are quick to accuse anyone who rings an alarm bell of being motivated by xenophobia or anti-Chinese sentiment. We will meet many of them.

The rest of this book will describe and document the unfolding process by which we are being robbed of our sovereignty. We have been allowing it to happen under our noses because we are mesmerised by the belief that only China can guarantee our economic prosperity and because we are afraid to stand up to Beijing's bullying. So we must ask the question: What is Australian sovereignty worth? What price do we put on our independence as a nation? In practice, it's a question we are answering every day, and the answer is 'not much'.

I think most Australians will begin to think quite differently, as I did, when they realise that Australian institutions—from our schools, universities and professional associations to our media; from industries like mining, agriculture and tourism to strategic assets like ports and electricity grids; from our local councils and state governments to our political parties in Canberra—are being penetrated and shaped by a complex system of influence and control overseen by agencies serving the Chinese Communist Party.

Huge, swiftly developing, successful at reducing poverty, ideologically rigid, hypersensitive and essentially benign. That has been the conception of China in the Australian public mind. We can add to it the belief (much exaggerated) that only China saved us from the 2008 global recession and has been the main source of our prosperity ever since. It's a view that's been actively promoted by the 'China lobby' in Australia, a loose coalition of businesspeople, politicians, policy advisers, bureaucrats, journalists and commentators.

In recent years, the Australian public has become agitated by perceptions of some negative aspects of our relationship with China. Cashed-up Chinese bidders are taking houses from Australians. The rate of immigration from China is too fast to allow assimilation, so that parts of Sydney no longer feel like Australia. Chinese-heritage (and other Asian) students are monopolising places at highly desirable selective schools. Chinese tourists are buying up infant formula to take home, creating shortages and driving up prices. And Chinese billionaires have bought themselves too much influence over our politicians.

Unfortunately, the term 'Chinese' is often used indiscriminately so that all Australians of Chinese heritage are tarred with the same brush. Among those most alarmed by the growing sway of the Chinese party-state in this country are those Chinese-Australians who see themselves as *Australians*; in other words, those who feel loyal to the country they have made their home. They have watched with dismay and a sense of foreboding as new waves of Chinese have arrived—billionaires with shady histories and tight links to the party, media owners creating Beijing mouthpieces, 'patriotic' students brainwashed from birth (but still seeking residency), and professionals marshalled into pro-Beijing associations set up by the Chinese embassy. And, among many, a pervasive sentiment that 'their hearts lie in the Chinese motherland', as the CCP likes to put it.

In the course of researching this book I have spoken with Australians of Chinese heritage who are deeply worried about the growing influence of the Chinese Communist Party in the million-strong diaspora in this country. They are worried about the coming backlash, when Anglo-Australians wake up to what is happening. They are acutely aware of the anti-Chinese riots that have plagued countries like Indonesia and Malaysia, and can see themselves caught up in the backlash even though they have no love for the Chinese regime and count themselves as loyal

Aussies. As John Hu, the founder of the Australian Values Alliance, an organisation of Chinese-Australians dedicated to resisting Beijing's growing influence, put it to me: 'If we don't stop it, and wait for white people to do it, we will be in trouble.'

For writing this book I will be accused of racism and xenophobia, epithets flung at anyone who raises the alarm about the influence of the Chinese Communist Party in Australia. The accusation can be made only by conflating the CCP with Chinese people so that being anti-CCP must mean being anti-Chinese. (It's exactly what the CCP wants us to think.) It's a cheap accusation, but it serves as an effective silencing device in this country because of the widespread, and quite proper, sensitivity to inflaming racial tensions. However, that sensitivity is exploited by those who do not want attention drawn to what the CCP is doing. They exploit what might be called our xenophobia-phobia, our fear of being accused of racism. There is, nevertheless, a genuine concern that bigots will use this book to vilify all Chinese-Australians. When I expressed this anxiety to a Chinese-Australian friend she told me that we need to confront the ugliness of what the CCP is doing here. 'We *want* you to publish this book. We're in the same boat.'

Chinese-Australians like her and John Hu have learned to prize the freedom, openness and rule of law of this country, and they want all Australians to know that they have no truck with those people of Chinese origin in Australia, whether citizens or not, who put the interests of the People's Republic of China first. They can see that as each year passes the number and influence of Chinese-Australians loyal to Australia are being swamped by the number and influence of Chinese in Australia loyal to Beijing and who regard the PRC motherland as their true home.

You will notice that I wrote 'loyal to Beijing' rather than 'loyal to China'. There is nothing wrong with expatriates anywhere, and their children, feeling affection for the home country. But, as we will see, 'patriotic' Chinese in Australia have been conditioned by decades of propaganda to believe that 'China' and 'Beijing', that is, the Chinese state under the iron rule of the Communist Party, are the same thing. For many new Chinese arrivals in the West, one of the hardest concepts to understand is the distinction, essential to democracies, between the nation and its government. When they do grasp the difference, they are open to becoming critics of the party-state without feeling they are betraying their homeland. They may even become dissidents who love China but hate its government.

When I spoke to John Hu about his compatriots who are 'loyal to Beijing' he corrected me by saying 'loyal to money'. In his view, none of the businessmen who do Beijing's bidding do so because they are committed to the objectives of the Communist Party; they do what they are told because without official backing they cannot do business in China. And unless they serve the party they may well find their business dealings in Australia and in China targeted by the Chinese government, which may 'make trouble' for them, like leaning on others to boycott them.

Apologists for China in Australia know that the Chinese state is repressive. They know it tightly controls the media, suppresses free speech, sanctions abuses of human rights and tolerates no challenge to the party. But they manage to set it all aside, often because they have a material interest in taking an 'optimistic view', focusing instead on the economic opportunities China presents. They rationalise the repression by telling themselves that it's not as bad as people say or that there is nothing they can do about it or that, while regrettable, it doesn't affect us. The last of these is not true and is less true by the day. As we will see, the repressive apparatus of the Chinese state is making itself felt in Australia, and unless Australians begin now to push back and protect our rights and freedoms we will soon find that it is too late. Otherwise our institutions will become so corrupted that we will no longer be able to rely on them to put Australia first when the CCP's interests are involved.

Some still believe that the PRC is on the road to democracy and that the repression is just a stage it is going through. All of the evidence suggests that this is mere wishful thinking. Since their high point in 1989, pro-democracy sentiment and organisation in China have never been weaker. Repression is more deeply entrenched than at any time since the Cultural Revolution and is becoming more severe under President Xi Jinping. Even so, some argue, the dominant fact about modern China is its astounding economic growth which has seen hundreds of millions of people pulled out of poverty and misery. They say that against this achievement (which is undoubtedly of historic significance) repression pales into insignificance. Some actually believe that authoritarian rule has been necessary to achieve it. And so we should be celebrating and profiting from that achievement rather than harping on about Tibetan autonomy or the arrest of human rights lawyers. Even the building of military bases in the South China Sea is out of our control, so let's get on with making money. I hope by the end of this book the reader will understand how dangerous these arguments are to our freedom.

2

How China sees itself in the world

As the 1990s dawned, the Chinese Communist Party (CCP) had to confront the possibility of its imminent demise. After Chairman Mao's death in 1976, the people began to face up to the catastrophes of Mao's Great Leap Forward (1958–62) and the Cultural Revolution (1965–75). As the truth spread and the people became restive, the legitimacy of communism and the Communist Party were shaken. For the party, communism became optional, but giving up power was not. It began to drift, not knowing what it stood for and what its goals should be. In the 1980s the challenge was dubbed the 'Three Belief Crises'—the crises of faith in socialism, of belief in Marxism and of trust in the party. How could the party mobilise the people to support it in the new ideological and spiritual vacuum, one that something else threatened to fill?

When in the late 1970s and early 1980s President Deng Xiaoping discarded many orthodoxies and began to open up the economy to free market reform, Western ideas began to flow into the People's Republic of China (PRC). Some intellectuals and many students called for liberal democratic reform. The burgeoning pro-democracy movement found its peak expression in the 1989 protest movement that centred on Tiananmen Square in central Beijing.

For a party that had lost its mandate to rule in the eyes of the people, pro-democracy thoughts represented a profound threat. As the crisis intensified, a fierce internal struggle racked the party over how to respond. The hardliners under Premier Li Peng, backed by paramount elder statesman Deng Xiaoping, prevailed and the tanks were sent in. The suppression of dissident thought began and has only intensified since. As Stalin is reputed to have said: 'Ideas are more powerful than guns. We would not let our enemies have guns, why should we let them have ideas?'

Yet the leadership knew that after the brutal suppression of the movement it somehow had to regain a mandate to rule if it were to survive. Months after the Tiananmen crackdown, the party leadership was jolted by another shock. When the Berlin Wall fell in November 1989 and the communist regimes of Eastern Europe crumbled, the Soviet Union itself, the great bastion of socialism, disintegrated. In Beijing the message was unmistakable: communism in Europe had collapsed because of its own weakness in permitting *glasnost*, the opening up of government and greater freedom of speech.

But how would the CCP, now desperate, convince the people of its right to rule them? The economic growth and rising prosperity of the 1990s went some way to restoring its legitimacy, but it would not be enough, both because the benefits would take time to spread through the population and because a shared ideology binds a nation together far more powerfully than self-interest. And so in the early 1990s, with remarkable speed, the CCP built a new ideology around a new narrative for the nation. Its essence is captured in the titles of two books: *Never Forget National Humiliation* by Zheng Wang and *The Hundred-Year Marathon* by Michael Pillsbury.[1] The messages of these books, echoed by some of the sharpest China watchers, have the most profound implications for Australia's future.

'Brainwashed'

Children's beliefs can be moulded more easily than those of adults. Education campaigns are more effective than re-education campaigns. And so the CCP set out to create a generation of patriots through the teaching, from kindergarten to university, of the nation's history and its destiny. In 1991, two years after the Tiananmen Square massacre, the Patriotic Education Campaign began in earnest. Party leader Jiang Zemin himself outlined the new master narrative.[2] The basic message was simple: China had suffered a century of humiliation at the hands of foreign powers. For a century after the Opium Wars of the mid-nineteenth century, China was bullied and humiliated by foreigners. Although feudal rulers were corrupt, many brave Chinese people laid down their lives to defend the nation. The CCP led the fight against the imperialists and liberated the nation in 1949, proving that 'the Chinese people cannot be bullied'. (In reality, the Communists left the fight against the Japanese invaders to its rival, the nationalist Kuomintang, and it was the Allies that finally defeated Japan in 1945.) In 1949, the narrative went, the party had set the nation on the path of regaining its past glory as a great nation—indeed, as the world's greatest civilisation.

The new narrative was a radical reinterpretation of China's history. For decades the CCP had woven a story of class struggle against feudal power and the continuing influence of reactionary forces in China who oppressed the people. Now it told a story of struggle against the bullying and humiliation imposed on the nation by foreign powers. It was no longer an internationalist story that united the oppressed of China with the oppressed around the world but a *nationalist* story that set the Chinese people against the rest of the world. If the Tiananmen generation had seen themselves as victims of the CCP, the new generation would see themselves as the victims of colonialism. The new patriots would turn their anger outwards instead of inwards.

And so in August 1991 the powerful PRC National Education Council issued an edict requiring all schools to reform history education to stress that China's purpose is to 'defend against the "peaceful evolution" plot of international hostile powers'. This would be 'the most important mission for schools'. The curriculum guidelines begin: 'Chinese modern history is a history of humiliation in which China gradually degenerated into a semi-colonial and semi-feudal society.' However, the Chinese people under the leadership of the Chinese Communist Party engaged in struggle to achieve independence and social progress. In *Never Forget National Humiliation* Zheng Wang writes: 'Chinese history—"education in national humiliation"—has become one of the most important subjects in the national education system.'[3] It is this belief in China's history of humiliation, and now the 'great rejuvenation of the nation', that is the key to understanding the role of China in the world today.

Through the Patriotic Education Campaign the party set out to unite the nation and 'rally the masses' patriotic passions to the great cause of building socialism with Chinese characteristics'. This was how the party would rebuild its legitimacy in the eyes of the people, by embodying the aspiration of the Chinese people to outgrow but never forget the 'bitterness and shame' of their humiliation and once again become a great nation. No longer victims, they would be victors.

From the early 1990s every child who began school became the subject of an intense and unrelenting program of patriotic education that would continue until they left high school or university. Previously, to gain entry to university, candidates had to pass an exam in politics focusing on Marxism, the thoughts of Chairman Mao and the policies of the CCP. According to one observer, while students had always resisted classes in Marxist doctrine, they proved far more amenable to patriotic education.[4] Zheng Wang concludes his book by noting that the campaign for patriotic education goes a long way towards explaining 'the rapid conversion of China's popular social movements from the internal-oriented, anti-corruption, anti-dictatorship democratic movements of the 1980s to the external-oriented, anti-Western nationalism of the 1990s'.[5]

When I asked intellectuals in China about the younger generation, some said, with a dismissive snort, 'brainwashed'. Others told me that some young people are able to distance themselves from the lifelong propaganda. But they are hard to find. The effectiveness of the Patriotic Education Campaign is the clue to understanding that day in Canberra in April 2008 when, at the Olympic torch event outside Parliament House in Canberra, tens of thousands of Chinese students demonstrated their patriotic feelings for China in such a fervent and belligerent way.

The party is the nation
The campaign of indoctrination, built on a newly shaped sense of Chinese national pride, has enabled the CCP to continue to strengthen

its rule after it jettisoned Marxist notions of revolution, class struggle and proletarian internationalism, while retaining the iron grip of the Leninist party structure. And it has not let up. In 2016, China's education minister, Chen Baosheng, declared that the education system is 'at the forefront of the Party's ideological work' and warned that 'hostile forces' were attempting to 'penetrate' the nation's schools and 'sabotage your future'.[6]

While the campaign aimed at reshaping the Chinese people's narrative of the nation's history has been most intensive in schools, its jingoistic message has gone well beyond the classroom. From the early 1990s it spread into a 'nationwide mobilization'. As Zheng Wang writes: 'Patriotism, along with history and memory, has become the most important subject for ideological education of the party-state system.'[7] In its 1994 planning document, the party declared that patriotic thoughts are to become 'the core themes of our society'.[8] Controlling people's thoughts obviates the need to control their behaviour and the party has striven constantly to implant patriotic thoughts into the minds of the people.

Today, wherever one goes in China there are reminders of the nation's century of humiliation at the hands of the brutal Japanese and the arrogant Westerners, and the resurgence of the Chinese people under the leadership of the Communist Party. Monuments, memorial halls, historical relics and museums have sprouted, all reinforcing the new narrative. And everyone whose job involves advancing the campaign—teachers, military officers and soldiers, and all employees of state agencies—is required to attend regular classes aimed at reinforcing their patriotic enthusiasm.

When the party leadership decided that patriotic education must be made 'the foundation project of the construction of socialist civilization', the audience included overseas Chinese.[9] In Australia, as elsewhere, the new kind of patriotism has become more dangerous as China's economic power and wealth have grown. A powerful sense of national pride built on a belief in historical humiliation, combined with an inability to distinguish between the nation and its government, goes a long way towards explaining why many in the Chinese diaspora, including Chinese-Australian citizens, remain loyal to the PRC and defend its actions even when they conflict with Australia's values and interests.

The shift since the early 1990s from demanding loyalty to the Communist Party to demanding loyalty to the nation has been possible because for the CCP the party is the nation. Reinforcing this identity has been essential to the campaign, but it was not manufactured by it. It skilfully traded on a powerful historical sense of Chinese nationalism and exceptionalism. Zheng Wang writes: 'Many Chinese share a strong collective historical consciousness regarding the country's century of humiliation, and this is a central element in shaping Chinese national identity.'[10] In general, this belief in Chinese exceptionalism and historical destiny is not left behind when its people migrate to other parts of the world. It takes a long time to fade.

The inability to distinguish between nation and government is not universal in China, despite the sustained efforts of the party over some decades. When Chen Xiankui, a party loyalist and professor at Renmin University, wrote an opinion piece proclaiming that 'love of party and love of country are one and the same in modern China', a storm of dissenting voices blew up among netizens.[11] The nationalist tabloid that had published Chen's article, *Global Times*, rounded on the critics with an editorial accusing those who do not equate love of country with love of party of being 'brainwashed public intellectuals'.

Today, in addition to the CCP's iron grip, it is nationalism that holds Chinese society together and justifies the rule of the Communist Party. The party has come to symbolise and represent the Chinese nation. For President Jiang Zemin, those who did not express their patriotism ardently were traitors, 'the scum of a nation'.[12] Jiang's campaign was taken up readily by Xi Jinping when he became president in 2013.

Of course, some reject the party's exploitation of national pride, and none more vehemently than Liu Xiaobo, the Chinese literary critic who was awarded the 2008 Nobel Peace Prize for his eloquent and powerful defence of human rights. He characterised modern Chinese patriotism as 'a complaining, compulsive sort of nationalism, rather like that of a jilted lover'.[13] In the 2000s, he wrote, the regime managed to whip up this kind of 'bellicose, expansionist patriotism' in segments of the population by portraying a long history of humiliation at the hands of foreigners and a popular longing for revenge, all built on a historical feeling of vanity arising from the conviction that China once ruled All Under Heaven. Liu diagnosed a national psychology that alternates between extremes of self-abasement and self-aggrandisement.[14]

Sick man no more

The 2008 Beijing Olympic Games provided the CCP with an irresistible opportunity to reinforce the 'party = nation' identity, and to take the public's commitment to the party-state to a higher level. Winning the right to host the Olympics and then topping the gold-medal tally became a national obsession in which the ugliest forms of national pride were on display. In the words of a party sporting official, 'to win Olympic glory for the Motherland is a sacred mission entrusted to us by Party Central'.[15] Liu Xiaobo saw it differently: 'The gleam of gold can help a dictatorial regime to tighten its grip on power and to fan flames of nationalism that it can use for other purposes.'[16]

The jingoism of the Beijing Olympics had deeper psychological roots, according to Zheng Wang.[17] In the nineteenth century, the Ottoman Empire was described as the 'sick man of Europe' because of its state of decrepitude. When China under foreign pressures was in disarray, someone borrowed the term to label China 'the sick man of Asia'. In the twentieth century, many in China interpreted the phrase as a humiliating insult concerning the poor physiques and ill health of the Chinese people. The Beijing Olympics would be the occasion to prove to the world that the contemptuous epithet is wrong, that the Chinese people could compete physically with the best in the world. The Beijing Olympic Organising Committee even published an article entitled 'From "sick man of East Asia" to "sports big power"'. So much was riding on Chinese success at the Olympics that failure was unthinkable. When the Chinese body triumphed, the historic shame would be wiped away in a surge of national honour. The passions of the Olympic torch event in Canberra leading up to the 2008 games become explicable when we understand that the students who arrived to give vent to their patriotic rage had been the subjects of a campaign of mass brainwashing in which they learned that even their bodies had been regarded as a source of shame.

When China topped the medal tally, the wave of patriotic elation that broke was visceral in origin. Eight years later, Australian swimmer Mack Horton had no idea of this cultural history when at the 2016 Rio games he dismissed his PRC rival, Sun Yang, as a drug cheat. (In 2014 the Chinese champion had served a three-month doping ban.) The backlash against Mack Horton was instant and brutal as China's army of online trolls launched a frenzy of ultranationalist abuse and threats, much of it on his Facebook and Twitter accounts. Horton is reported to have received over 243,000 angry comments on his Weibo account (similar to Twitter).[18] One hoped he'd be killed by a kangaroo; another wished him luck at the 2020 Paralympics. It's believed that many of the hostile comments came from ethnic Chinese living in Australia. He became the target of what Liu Xiaobo had described as the 'thuggish language that unabashedly celebrates violence, race hatred and warmongering passion [that] now haunts the Chinese Internet'. For its part, the state tabloid *Global Times* attacked the southern land as one that had been settled by 'the UK's unwanted criminals' and was now stained by 'white supremacism' and a 'tinge of barbarism'.[19]

In addition to the Horton–Sun affair, patriotic Chinese watching the 2016 Rio Olympic coverage in Australia found much to complain about. When Channel Seven's coverage of the opening ceremony cut to an ad break as the Chinese team entered the stadium, patriots with a chip on the shoulder took to social media complaining of racism and the insult to the nation. Anti-China conspiracy theories went into overdrive when a technician accidentally put Chile's flag next to China's name on the tally board. (If Channel Seven had mistakenly put Austria's flag next to Australia's name, Australians would have greeted it with amused ridicule.)

One of the oddest protests ever seen in Sydney was staged in reaction to Channel Seven's slip-ups. Half a dozen members of the Construction, Forestry, Mining and Energy Union (CFMEU) turned up outside the station's studio brandishing a Chinese flag and demanding an apology. A union statement quoted CFMEU organiser Yu Lei Zhou as saying that Channel Seven's actions were ignorant and discriminatory.[20] Why, one might ask, would Australia's major construction union bother itself with a glitch in a TV broadcast? As we'll see, trade unions number among the organisations in this country targeted for infiltration by the CCP's agencies.[21]

Noticing these stories of misguided patriotism, Chinese writers have argued that some Chinese people are driven by a powerful but hidden fear of their own inferiority, one that can only be salved by the approval of the rest of the world. 'If the approval is not granted,' writes Zheng Wang, 'or is granted only with qualifications, initial pride can suddenly morph into resentment, anger, and deepened insecurity.'[22] Uncontrolled, such passions can threaten the CCP too.

'Twisted patriotism'

In creating the surge of patriotism, the CCP has found that it is riding a tiger. After twenty-five years of patriotic education through every medium that Chinese people have access to, segments of the public have absorbed an acute sense of victimhood and nationalist rage, causing them to overreact to any slight from foreigners. Online, 'red bloggers' have launched unapproved but coordinated attacks on Taiwanese websites whenever Taiwan looks as if it has taken a step towards independence.[23] In 2012, in response to an escalation of tensions with Japan over the Senkaku Islands, nationalist protesters went on rampages in dozens of Chinese cities.[24] Although the protests seem to have been officially sanctioned, Japanese restaurants and supermarkets were smashed up, Japanese vehicles were damaged and a Panasonic factory was set alight. The police had trouble controlling the mobs, with one group climbing onto the roof of a hotel in Guangzhou to wave the flag, sing the national anthem and chant 'Japan, get the hell out of China'.

The government had lost control and cracked down. But the popular anger also forced its hand so that party leaders had to show greater determination to resist 'Japanese imperialism' than they might have. President Xi Jinping, who has fanned the flame of nationalism, has to live up to his rhetoric and be seen to be responsive to its demands, which means a more assertive China for other nations to contend with.

In anticipation of unauthorised protests following the 2016 ruling by the international arbitration tribunal on the South China Sea, the official media warned the public against planned protests outside KFC restaurants. Already some protesters had harangued KFC customers for being 'unpatriotic'. A *China Daily* editorial distinguished between rightful patriotism and 'jingoism that does a disservice to the ... nation'.[25] Young people who posted online photos of themselves smashing iPhones were described, with no sense of irony, as 'angry youth' fed on aggressive nationalism from birth. Perhaps anticipating further disorder as Beijing pushed its expansionist agenda more aggressively, in early 2017 the party announced that public outbursts would be nipped in the bud so as to 'properly handle the relationship between the people's patriotism and social stability'.[26]

Even the hypernationalist *Global Times* has found the need to hose down the patriotic belligerence it has done so much to inflame. When in December 2016 an anti-Japanese protester was prosecuted, it warned of the dangers of 'twisted patriotism'.[27]

In nations like Australia where parts of the Chinese community retain their loyalty to the PRC, these dangerous sentiments of paranoia and wounded national pride are acted out. As a senior academic commentator in Shanghai expressed it to me: 'If they are patriotic, Chinese think they can do anything.'

The great rejuvenation

The Australian journalist Philip Wen tells the story of a boozy banquet he attended at which the brother of a billionaire confided, 'In time, this world will be China's.'[28] The billionaire in question now controls the Port of Darwin through his company Landbridge Group. This kind of sentiment is not uncommon in China. It captures an ambition beyond a simple assertion of patriotism. The century of humiliation that ended in 1949 was succeeded by a hundred-year marathon in which China will resume its place at the centre of the world. Jiang Zemin, president from 1993 to 2003, developed a new catchphrase, 'the great rejuvenation of the Chinese nation', conjuring up the historical memory of China as a great power in the world.[29] President Hu Jintao would take up the 'historic cause', reminding the people about foreign bullying and declaring that 'the great rejuvenation of the Chinese nation has become the unswerving goal that each Chinese generation has striven to realise'. But Hu's strategy, following the ancient advice of *The Art of War* and that of his predecessor Deng Xiaoping, was to keep the ambition under wraps and bide one's time until China was strong enough to act on its intention, a strategy that became known as 'hide and bide'.

After he'd been anointed the next president in late 2012, Xi Jinping announced that achieving the China Dream of 'the great rejuvenation of the Chinese nation' would be his grand ambition. China would no longer hide and bide but assert the nation's newfound power for all to see. While Xi himself has not spelled out his China Dream, scholars understand it to mean the 'revival of Chinese glories of the past', including economic dominance, and making China the world's dominant power.[30]

Xi is thought to have borrowed the phrase 'China Dream' from a famous military hawk, the retired People's Liberation Army (PLA) colonel and military academic Liu Mingfu. Liu's book—published in English as *The China Dream: Great power thinking and strategic posture in the Post-American era*—'defines a national strategy to restore China to its historical glory and take the United States' place as world leader'.[31] In the first decades of the twenty-first century China must aim to surpass the United States 'to become the world's No. 1 power'.[32] Liu's 2010 book became a nationwide bestseller in China, appealing to a public ready to embrace a global master narrative in which the revival of the Middle Kingdom would restore China to its proper place as the centre of the world, and from where it would spread harmony through its culture, language and values, an empire that, in the words of another scholar, 'values order over freedom, ethics over law, and elite governance over democracy and human rights'.[33]

Veteran US strategic thinker Michael Pillsbury argues that Xi, who has long and deep links with the PLA and who arranged for himself to be appointed as commander-in-chief, 'is closely connected to the nationalist "super-hawks" in the Chinese military'.[34] His China Dream singles out a 'strong army dream'. The influence of the hawks is seriously underestimated in the West. They have become dominant under Xi, in whom they find a leader sympathetic to their understanding of Chinese history as the Hundred-Year Marathon that began in 1949 and through which China will avenge its previous century of humiliation by eclipsing the United Sates as the dominant economic, political and, eventually, military power.

The rise of Xi Jinping has given confidence to those who favour this imperial interpretation, justifying China's global domination with the traditional notion of *tianxia*. Although open to differing interpretations, *tianxia* or 'all under the heavens' describes the world ruled over by the Chinese emperor and around which all else revolves. It is not just an archaic notion, for as Zheng Wang observes, 'the Chinese feel a strong sense of chosenness and are extremely proud of their ancient and modern achievements'.[35, 36]

These appear to be the sources of Xi's 'China Dream', and it is not too difficult to see this grand vision guiding China's more assertive intervention in the world, from the vast investment program of the One Belt, One Road Initiative, to the infiltration of CCP values in Western institutions, to the rapid expansion of the PLA Navy, and to the aggressive annexation of the South China Sea. Although perhaps part braggadocio, Liu Mingfu himself claimed in 2015 that the 'sleeping lion' of China has been awakened and 'Xi Jinping is the leading lion of the lion packs, who dare to fight anytime'.[37] The more hawkish of the elites believe that the 2008 financial crisis in the United States, brought on by its own institutional decay, marked the turning point beyond which a 'Chinese-led world order' became unstoppable. They may be right. The Hundred-Year Marathon may take only eighty years to complete.

All of this has been obvious to one of Asia's most longstanding and acute observers, the late Singapore president Lee Kuan Yew. 'It is China's intention to be the greatest power in the world,' Lee said.[38] China is pursuing a long-term 'peaceful rise' strategy, but this is not commonly understood in the West. It means that China aims to achieve global dominance not by direct military confrontation with the United States but by pursuing economic domination, via what Liu calls a 'non-conquering civilization', which in time will give it the same result.[39] Beijing's judgement is that it's better not to deplete one's own resources by attempting to match the vast sums spent by the US on maintaining its bloated military forces. Pillsbury describes China's strategy to defeat the United States militarily by other means. Even so, China's military spending has been growing quickly, with emphasis on dominating the seas. Pressure on its neighbours is being ratcheted up daily.

The CCP leadership is aware that announcing its longer-term ambition would provoke resistance and so it conceals its deep strategy behind a story of peaceful economic development and engagement with the world. Every now and then, however, the secret leaks out. In 2015 the deputy director of the Overseas Chinese Affairs Office (OCAO), He Yafei, gave a speech to senior cadres.[40] As we'll see, the OCAO is a leading organ of the State Council, the PRC's chief administrative authority, with the primary task of mobilising the Chinese diaspora to serve Beijing's goals. A report of the speech (in Chinese) somehow made its way onto the website of the State Council Information Office. He Yafei's theme was the need to propagate 'China's voice' throughout the world. The first of six areas he covered was the domination of international public opinion by Western media groups and the need 'to carve out a bloody path and smash the West's monopoly and public opinion hegemony'. He then set out the need to replace with 'China's value system' important ideas invented by America and the West like 'soft power' and the 'clash of civilisations' as well as ideas like 'freedom, democracy [and] equal human rights'.

The lumping of academic inventions like soft power together with fundamental rights into a single category of 'Western ideas' to be replaced with Chinese ones is disturbing enough. But what is truly revealing in He Yafei's speech is his caution to senior cadres about the 'shortcomings and contaminations' of overseas audiences: 'If we simply stress our own dominance … then we will find it difficult to achieve good results in our external propaganda'. Can we just dismiss this revelation by such a senior CCP leader—He Yafei previously served as deputy foreign minister—as one man's aberrant patriotic enthusiasm? Or has he given the game away? The evidence that he expressed the true ambitions of at least the dominant faction of the CCP is overwhelming, and is set out further in the subsequent chapters of this book.[41]

Yet here in Australia some of our most senior figures have fallen completely for the propaganda. One, former Labor prime minister Paul Keating, reassured us: 'Unlike the Soviet Union before it, China is not an ideological power seeking to propagate an international ideology. It is a great nation-state but it seeks fundamentally to live within its own precinct.'[42] Tell that to the nations that wake up to find the Chinese military occupying islands in their traditional waters, like Vietnam and the Philippines, or the Tibetans whose territory has been occupied. As we'll see, Keating frequently echoes CCP propaganda.

Unlike the 'friends of China' in the West, some scholars in China have serious misgivings about the emerging triumphalism of China under Xi Jinping, as one of the more acute and well-informed China analysts David Kelly points out.[43] In necessarily veiled criticism, they argue that China is not sufficiently mature to assume a world leadership role and the triumphalism of the party and the media is dangerous. One compares it to German triumphalism in the 1930s. Instead of posing as the 'saviour of the world', China should focus on domestic development. Kelly argues that their 'realistic' stance is 'a more sustainable big power strategy in the current situation'.

Yet the hawks are in the ascendant. The Chinese are 'the finest people on earth', declares Liu Mingfu, and with its greater civilisation China will become 'the world's leading nation', 'the uncontested global leader'.[44] A great unknown of this century is raised by China watcher Jamil Anderlini:

> The logic of China's great rejuvenation is essentially revanchist [revenge-seeking] and assumes the country is still a long way from regaining its rightful level of power, influence and even territory. The dangerous question for the rest of the world is at what point China will feel it has reached peak rejuvenation and what that will look like for everyone who is not included in the great family of the Chinese race.[45]

China's claim to Australia

Soon after his first meeting with Xi Jinping, Donald Trump told a journalist that the Chinese president had told him that 'Korea actually used to be part of China'. Trump's gullibility is unsurprising, but the Koreans knew what Xi was up to. Korea has never been part of China. A scathing editorial in the respected and widely read *Chosun* newspaper noted that 'at the root of this nonsense lies a powerful hegemonic nationalism' traceable to the days of the tribute system.[46] The PRC's pressure on South Korea is 'motivated by nothing more than a bully's belief that Korea somehow owes it obeisance'.

Other Asian nations are well aware of the highly dubious and confected 'historical rights' China says it has to the South China Sea and the islands in it. It claims to have discovered, named, explored and exploited the whole of the South China Sea some 2000 years ago. This is the basis for its sovereignty, which it reclaimed by hand-drawing the nine-dash line around most of it in 1947. Reviewing the situation, one expert concludes that 'such a claim not only has no basis in international law, but also no basis in China's own history. It is nonsense.'[47] Historical nonsense, however, is no deterrent to China's hawks. And so they dismissed the ruling of the Arbitral Tribunal in The Hague, which concluded that even if China's historical claims about fishing in the sea were valid, they are irrelevant to any claim to the islands in the sea.[48]

Professor John Fitzgerald, one of Australia's leading Sinologists and president of the Australian Academy of the Humanities, has summed up the CCP's thinking as follows:

> In laying claim to disputed territories, Beijing reaches back centuries to establish historical ownership over land and maritime territories that can then be forcefully 'reclaimed' as its own. A country can never invade itself, and so China's leaders believe that by claiming to be recovering 'lost' territories they can never be accused of invading anyone.[49]

It would be a mistake for Australians to believe that spurious historical claims to justify territorial ambitions are confined to China's traditional sphere of influence. China is using fake history to position itself to make a future claim over Australia. When in 2003 President Hu Jintao addressed the Australian parliament, he began with a piece of outrageous historical revisionism.

> The Chinese people have all along cherished amicable feelings about the Australian people. Back in the 1420s, the expeditionary fleets of China's Ming Dynasty reached Australian shores. For centuries,

the Chinese sailed across vast seas and settled down in what they called Southern Land, or today's Australia. They brought Chinese culture to this land and lived harmoniously with the local people, contributing their proud share to Australia's economy, society and its thriving pluralistic culture.[50]

Hu's claims may have been based on the junk history penned by Englishman Gavin Menzies in his book *1421: The year China discovered the world*, which claimed a fleet led by Admiral Zhou Man sailed the world, stopping off at all major continents where the Chinese sailors mixed with the natives, including in Eden, New South Wales. The evidentiary holes in Menzies' claims began to be pointed out even before his book was published,[51] and in 2006 an ABC *Four Corners* program eviscerated Menzies and his history.[52] Maps that Menzies has produced to prove his propositions have been shown to be fakes. Chinese scholars have been as assiduous in their testing and debunking of Menzies' historical claims as Western ones.[53] In short, there is no evidence that a Ming Chinese fleet came anywhere near Australia. (Having wrung all he could out of the 1421 story, Menzies moved on, discovering the lost city of Atlantis.)

A commentary published by the Australian Parliamentary Library in 2008 noted that, while President Hu Jintao did not use the word 'discovery', he was putting forward a counter-narrative of Australian history, one in which history began when the Chinese reached Australian shores and engaged in the symbolically meaningful and, in CCP thinking, legally significant acts of naming, mapping and settling the land.[54]

Hu's intervention worked on some. Carried away by feelings of harmonious cooperation, Liberal Senator David Johnston proposed a few days later that the history books be rewritten to acknowledge the Chinese admiral's 'monumental voyages of exploration and discovery' and to 'concur with President Hu Jintao's statement that the Chinese fleets of 1421 did in fact visit our shores'.[55]

Although Menzies' 'history' had been thoroughly debunked, two years after President Hu's address to parliament the Chinese ambassador Fu Ying told the National Press Club that 'Australia has always been on China's map of world voyage'.[56] In the same year, a Central

Office of Foreign Propaganda website claimed that it is likely Admiral Zheng He's fleet arrived in northwest Australia centuries before Captain James Cook or Abel Tasman.[57] In case we thought the Chinese claim to have found Australia had faded away, in 2016 former foreign minister Li Zhaoxing arrived at the Australian National University (ANU) to give a speech in which he claimed an explorer in the time of the Yuan dynasty (the thirteenth and fourteenth centuries) discovered Australia. No one challenged this fabrication of Australian history.

3

Qiaowu and the Chinese diaspora

'As the standing of overseas Chinese rises abroad, and as their ethnic consciousness awakens, they will have the desire as well as the ability to collect their power in order to push forward the development and advancement of China …'.[1]

Mobilising overseas Chinese

With these words the deputy chief of the Overseas Chinese Affairs Office (OCAO), He Yafei, revealed the vital role expected of overseas Chinese in fulfilling the Communist Party's ambitions of global ascendancy. Tentatively from the year 2000, and totally since 2011, the party revised its attitude towards overseas Chinese—from distancing itself to the 'embracing of every foreigner of Chinese descent as one'.[2]

To mobilise the vast Chinese global diaspora, numbering over fifty million people, the CCP has developed a highly sophisticated, multi-faceted plan, implemented by several well-resourced agencies targeting overseas Chinese, including over one million residing in Australia.

The history, goals, plans and tactics of this program have been laid out in detail by James Jiann Hua To, a New Zealand academic of Chinese ethnicity, in an important study based on a painstakingly thorough doctoral dissertation.[3] It is indispensable for understanding what is taking place in Australia. James To could describe in intimate detail the CCP's policies and practices towards 'Overseas Chinese' (OC) only after managing to obtain access to a large trove of secret documents in Beijing.[4] Overseas Chinese management is known as *qiaowu* (pronounced *chiow-wu*), literally translated as 'Overseas Chinese affairs', and can be described as 'a massive operation involving incorporation and cooptation of the OC at every level of society, and managing their behaviour and perceptions through incentives or disincentives to suit the situation and structural circumstances that the CCP desires'.[5]

While reading James To's eye-opening account, I realised I had not fully understood the CCP's overseas objectives. I had assumed that the primary objective of the various programs devoted to infiltrating and guiding ethnic Chinese in Australia was to counter and eliminate dissident and critical voices. But this 'negative' goal has a positive counterpart—to use the diaspora to transform Australian society in a way that makes us all sympathetic to China and easy for Beijing to control. Australia will then assist China to become the hegemonic power in Asia and eventually the world.

The *qiaowu* program provides the context in which we should understand, for example, the influence of wealthy Chinese businessmen in our political system through donations and networking. The documents reveal that, in the longer term, *qiaowu* work involves mobilising ethnic Chinese as voting blocs and placing Chinese candidates loyal to the PRC in parliaments and senior public positions.[6]

In fact, Beijing sees Australia, along with New Zealand, as the 'weak link' in the Western world and the ideal place for testing its strategies for breaking up the global reach of the United States and so helping to realise Xi Jinping's China Dream. It's for this reason that, in complete contrast to the policies before the 2000s, the CCP now *promotes* emigration of Chinese nationals.[7] And it helps explain why Beijing so vigorously presses countries like Australia to relax labour market regulation as part of its free trade agreements. The more Chinese loyal to Beijing that live in Australia, the more influence the CCP will have over Canberra.

A 2006 internal State Council document noted that there are more migrants leaving China illegally than legally.[8] China 'makes some efforts to combat illegal migration' (including pursuit of corrupt or allegedly corrupt officials and businessmen), although some claim PRC authorities turn a blind eye.[9] For example, James To reports that in the early 2000s there were 'at least forty "Chinese only" brothels in Suva, Fiji, staffed by Chinese on visitor or student visas working on the side while trying to gain entry into Australia'.[10] (In 2017, seventy-seven Chinese nationals, said to be prostitutes, were deported from Fiji.[11] When Chinese police took the hooded victims from their houses and put them on a plane, questions were raised about the violation of Fijian sovereignty.) After studying his cache of documents, To concludes that Beijing is relaxed about illegal emigration. Although there is some anxiety about the poor ethics and values of 'lower-class, uneducated' illegal migrants, party cadres are urged to tend to the needs of illegal migrants because in a decade or two they will become an accepted part of the diaspora and thus useful to the party.

Before looking at *qiaowu* activities in detail, it's worth briefly revisiting a slice of Australian history for the light it sheds on the problem we now confront.

Bob Hawke's gift

No one could have foreseen the profound effects that the crushing of the 1989 protests centred on Tiananmen Square would have on Australia. As we will see, they have been immense. Let's begin, though, with one of the immediate consequences of the decision to send tanks to crush the students.

When Prime Minister Bob Hawke, deeply shaken by the images of brutality, tearfully told Chinese students in Australia that they would not be sent home, his decision led to 42,000 Chinese obtaining permanent residence rights and, with close family members following, some 100,000 Chinese immigrants. Like me, most Australians regarded this act in benevolent terms—after all, who would want to be responsible for sending those students back to a place where their fellow students had been killed or jailed?

The reality was not as it appeared. Hawke's unilateral decision, taken against strong advice from officials, continues to reverberate through the nation. Some of the hidden history was explained to me by a former public servant who was close to the action at the time. For a start, three-quarters of the students were not studying at universities but were here for short-term language training of a few months.[12] They were permitted to work up to twenty hours a week but there was virtually no enforcement, and many worked full-time.

Immigration department officials regarded the expansion of Chinese arrivals—seen as a cash cow by education providers—as a means for thousands of Chinese to come to Australia to work, for the price of enrolling in a language course. The department wanted tougher entry tests for short-term language students but was outgunned by education bureaucrats who only saw a pot of gold. Nearly half of the students had overstayed their visas.

After Hawke had granted temporary visas to stay, the immigration department was flooded with thousands of applications for refugee status. The applicants wanted permanent residency and ultimately citizenship. With a system set up to cope with only a couple of hundred asylum applications a year, the department was overwhelmed. Anecdotal evidence from members of the Chinese community suggests that to support their applications some of the students, who'd never before been active, began joining pro-democracy groups, attending protests and waving placards while their friends took photographic evidence. The department had to find ways of rubber stamping most applications.

Why did Bob Hawke along with most of us believe that all of the Chinese students in Australia on 4 June 1989 were pro-democracy activists who faced persecution if they returned home when their visas expired? In fact, pro-democracy activists, or even supporters, were less likely to have been let out of China to study abroad. It's been estimated that among Chinese students in North America at the time only ten per cent were actively anti-CCP.[13] Yet there, as in Australia, virtually all of them were allowed to become permanent residents because it seemed inhumane to send them back. In truth, most were economic migrants.

Among the thousands granted asylum some were genuine pro-democracy supporters who needed protection, and of those some today continue to resist PRC influence in Australia. But Bob Hawke's decision after Tiananmen was a windfall for many who were granted what would otherwise have been denied to them. While some stepped up their anti-CCP activism, many others allowed to stay either backed the crackdown or were indifferent to it. I have been told by some who have witnessed it that each year on 4 June groups of Chinese-Australians get together to drink a toast to the Tiananmen Square crackdown for getting them permanent residency. The CCP soon realised that these overseas Chinese had not turned against the party and could be made into allies serving the motherland from abroad. A few of those granted political asylum would become some of the most effective agents of influence in Beijing's campaign to transform Australia into a tribute state.

While some, like Hawke's education minister, John Dawkins, saw the post-Tiananmen influx as 'a bit of quick intellectual improvement' of Australia's skill base, and others, like migration advocate James Jupp, welcomed it as a way of forcing 'a whole new middle class' onto the 'musty and limited' Australian middle class, the real long-term effect of Hawke's decision was to lay the foundations for Beijing's plans to have Australia conform to its wishes.[14] How it has been doing this is explored later. First, we have to understand what is driving modern China and what its true ambitions are.

The United Front in Australia

Much of the *qiaowu* work is conducted by the United Front Work Department (UFWD) of the CCP Central Committee and 'is based upon Marxist-Leninist mass line tactics, techniques and strategies'.[15] The UFWD targets Chinese social organisations, Chinese-language media, student associations, professional associations and business elites. While the UFWD is a party organ, all government agencies are expected to pursue *qiaowu* objectives.[16] The Overseas Chinese Affairs Office (a government agency as opposed to a party one) is responsible for drafting *qiaowu* policy and planning, and implementing overseas Chinese policy. The Propaganda Department of the CCP (whose overseas functions are explained by China scholar Anne-Marie Brady[17]) is also central to the campaign.[18] Already at the centre of power, the UFWD has grown in importance under President Xi Jinping, who described United Front work as a 'magic weapon' in the great rejuvenation of the Chinese people.[19] A full account of United Front and related activity in Australia would need a book in itself, so this chapter can only point out some of the more significant activities. Anne-Marie Brady has provided an extensive account of United Front activities in New Zealand, which in some respects are more advanced than in Australia and are meeting less resistance.[20]

Along with Chinese-language media, Chinese-Australian social and professional organisations are the primary means of guiding people of Chinese origin and promoting China's 'soft power'. The China Council for the Promotion of Peaceful National Reunification (CCPPNR) is a central organ of the United Front Work Department.[21] The Australian arm of the council is the Australian Council for the Promotion of Peaceful Reunification of China (ACPPRC), the peak body of dozens of overseas Chinese organisations in Australia.[22] The council's executive positions are filled by people the embassy trusts to advance the interests of the PRC. When the ACPPRC was founded in 2000 as part of the CCP's renewed United Front effort, its aim was to eclipse the older Chinese social organisations run by ethnic Chinese whose loyalty to Beijing was questionable. The old groups had been created by what *qiaowu* analysts disparagingly called the 'Three Knives', poorly educated Chinese migrants who worked in restaurants, market gardens and the garment industry.[23] The 'Three Knives' would be pushed out by the 'Six Masters'—lawyers, engineers, doctors, accountants, professors and scientists—who, united by the new organisations, would spread China's new vitality.

The billionaire political donors Chau Chak Wing and Huang Xiangmo have held senior positions in the ACPPRC, but its inaugural president in 2000 was William Chiu. Chiu was a radical Maoist as a student, persecuted in his Malaysian homeland, who would become an eminent citizen of New South Wales and an important Liberal Party political donor who hobnobbed with the state's great and good. He was also a loyal Chinese Communist Party cadre. When he died in 2015, Liberal Party grandee Philip Ruddock spoke at his funeral and delivered a eulogy in federal parliament. New South Wales premier Barry O'Farrell laid a wreath. Chiu's ashes were laid to rest at the Babaoshan Revolutionary Cemetery in Beijing, reserved for revolutionary heroes and top officials, including Xi Jinping's father. His corpse was draped with the flag of the ACPPRC, brought from Australia. Comrade Yu Zhengsheng, one of the seven members of the Standing Committee of the Politburo, chairman of the China Council for the Promotion of Peaceful National Reunification and chairman of the Chinese People's Political Consultative Conference, sent flowers to the ceremony. Senior cadres from the United Front Work Department and the Overseas Chinese Affairs Office also paid their respects. The *People's Daily* hailed William Chiu as a 'great China patriot'.[24]

The PRC does not necessarily exercise direct control over the dozens of United Front organisations in Australia. It prefers to guide and assist them with money, embassy support and links to the homeland. These tasks occupy the time of cultural and educational attachés at the embassy in Canberra and the consulates in the capital cities.[25] They practise psychological and social techniques developed over decades that usually obviate the need for explicit coercion. As a result, writes To, *qiaowu* work is 'an effective tool for intensive behavioural control and manipulation, yet *qiaowu* appears benign, benevolent and helpful'.[26] Groups that cannot be persuaded in these ways, like Falun Gong practitioners and Tibetan autonomy supporters, are subject to aggressive and coercive methods, including denunciations, blacklisting, cyber operations and harassment.

In Australia, United Front organisations like the ACPPRC do Beijing's work, allowing the CCP to conceal its guiding hand and present a friendly public face. As a result, many prominent politicians have been happy to associate themselves with them, accepting honorary positions, attending functions and so on, access that allows their ears to be filled with subtle Beijing propaganda.

Patrons of the ACPPRC have included Gough Whitlam, Malcolm Fraser and Bob Hawke. Honorary advisers have included the ALP federal minister and now China lobbyist Nick Bolkus, New South Wales Labor luminary Meredith Burgmann, and a collection of state and federal MPs from both major parties. Ernest Wong, the key link between the New South Wales Labor Party and Chinese billionaires,[27] who was nominated by the party to fill a seat in the New South Wales Legislative Council, is an honorary adviser to the ACPPRC and seems to be heavily involved with the body. Chris Bowen, Labor's federal shadow treasurer from the New South Wales Right, is a patron of the ACPPRC, or was until the 2016 Sam Dastyari affair (discussed later) when his name was removed from the website. Bowen has so far managed to fly under the radar but his Chinese links are wide and deep.[28]

Among ACPPRC activities are the teaching of 'Chinese culture' to children, partnering in multicultural events, and in 2015 organising, in collaboration with the Sydney consulate, a celebration of 'China's victory over Japan'. (Actually, it was American atom bombs that defeated Japan in 1945, but that does not fit well with the PRC narrative.)[29] Former New South Wales premier Mike Baird often turned up to the council's events and in 2015 the council persuaded his government to allow it to celebrate Chinese New Year by lighting up the Sydney Opera House in a shade of bright red matching that of the PRC flag. As Australians congratulated themselves on our multicultural openness, the symbolism was not missed by the *People's Daily*. 'Sydney Opera House was draped in red with Chinese characteristics', it announced, quoting a pleased consul-general on how Chinese culture is being absorbed by Australians.[30]

The annual celebration of Chinese New Year was renamed from Lunar New Year by the Sydney City Council, thereby expropriating it from other Asian cultures that have lunar calendars, including Vietnam's and Korea's. It has become a high-profile event in United Front work in Australia. The use of traditional festivals for propaganda and networking purposes is recommended in the secret OCAO documents uncovered by James To, not least as a means of bringing older Chinese expatriates suspicious of Beijing into the fold so that they can together promote the interests of the PRC.[31] Under President Xi's leadership, money and manpower have poured into building China's soft power, spearheaded by the Ministry of Culture, which has successfully multiplied Chinese New Year events around the world from 65 in 2010 to 900 in 119 nations in 2015.[32]

Recent Chinese New Year celebrations in Australia, featuring the traditional dragons, fireworks, dumplings and red gift envelopes, have been funded by the OCAO in Beijing through a payment of millions of dollars made through the Sydney-based media group Nanhai Media, as revealed by Fairfax journalist Philip Wen.[33] Breaking out of the confines of Sydney's Chinatown, they are now held in every capital city, with Sydney staging eight across the metropolis and Melbourne five in 2017.[34]

What was for decades a celebration of popular East Asian culture and the contribution of the Chinese-Australian community has been turned into a propaganda display for the Chinese Communist Party and an opportunity for its proxies in Sydney to gain greater influence over our political leaders, who turn out in droves, usually led by the prime minister. If politicians turning up to Chinese New Year celebrations are now unwitting dupes, corporate Australia has joined the bandwagon, proving its multicultural credentials and appealing to the million-strong Chinese-Australian market. In 2017 ABC television carried scores of plugs for the Chinese New Year between programs, playing perfectly into the hands of the OCAO.

In April 2016 a group named the Australian Action Committee for Protecting Peace and Justice called a meeting of sixty community leaders 'to bring together [in Sydney] forces which could protect the core interests of the Chinese nation', namely, Beijing's claim to islands in the South China Sea.[35] The committee's head, Sydney-based businessman Qian Qiguo, is active in various United Front bodies.[36]

When in 2016 Prime Minister Turnbull was making his first official trip to China, Chinese 'community leaders' got together and urged him to 'firmly safeguard the sovereign rights of China in the South China Sea'.[37] A spokesperson, Lin Bin, warned darkly of the risks of antagonising the homeland. According to Philip Wen, one of the best-informed observers, the community leaders were affiliated with Huang Xiangmo's ACPPRC and the Chinese embassy. Its pressure on Turnbull was amplified by Chinese-language newspapers like *Sydney Today* and Chau Chak Wing's *Australian New Express Daily*.[38]

In Melbourne one of the dominant groups is the Federation of Chinese Associations (FCA) (Victoria), which is unapologetic about its aims:

> While propagating Chinese culture the FCA will also not forget to protect the Ancestral Nation's dignity and interests, promptly organising many kinds of meetings in order to strike back against anti-China

groups and behaviours. Even though we're far away, our devoted hearts remember the nation with passion from beginning to end.[39]

FCA members hold Australian passports yet their ardent patriotic feelings are directed towards another country. The FCA has received delegations from the Overseas Chinese Affairs Offices of Shanghai and Guangdong and often refers to its contacts with the Melbourne consulate in organising patriotic events, like the one in 2016 celebrating the 'War of Resistance against Japanese Aggression' where those present could 'commemorate martyrs and never forget the national humiliation'.[40] As we saw, feelings of national humiliation have been stoked by the CCP for its own purposes.

The FCA's president is Su Junxi. When in 2016 she ran (unsuccessfully) for deputy mayor of Melbourne (on the Phil Cleary team), she nominated Melbourne's previous ethnic-Chinese mayor and deputy mayor as her models.[41] The federation is 'a base for fostering' political leaders, she said, noting that the previous two mayors 'came out of the Chinese Association'.[42] Su's speech at a July 2016 march against the Hague tribunal's ruling on the South China Sea was quoted approvingly by the *People's Daily*: 'all the islands of the South China Sea are inherently China's territory, and China has always had the right to administer these islands, history cannot be overthrown.'[43]

At the Melbourne rally at which Su Junxi spoke, some 3000 overseas Chinese demonstrated in support of Beijing. They waved Chinese flags and called for 'peace'. With only a couple of days' notice, the demonstration was said to have been organised by '169 associations of overseas Chinese in Melbourne'.[44] As we'd expect, the protest organisers sought and obtained permission from the Chinese embassy.[45] The organisers declared that the Hague ruling 'makes the Chinese people filled with righteous indignation!'—except that many were Australian citizens.

Chinese-Australians resist

In September 2016, United Front groups planned to stage concerts glorifying 'the charming personality and heroism of Mao Zedong'. Some Chinese-Australians took strong exception to the celebration of the 'most fearful Chinese tyrant'. For them, celebrating Mao was opposed to what they love about Australia. The concerts were booked to be staged in the Sydney and Melbourne town halls but were cancelled after an online petition and planned protests foreshadowed trouble.

In February 2017 anti-Communist Chinese-Australians mounted protests against the planned performance of a ballet named *The Red Detachment of Women*. The ballet glorifies the Red Army and romanticises the Communist Party. Carrillo Gantner, speaking for the sponsor, the Sidney Myer Fund, said that the ballet had 'lost its propaganda power'. For those Chinese-Australians who retain vivid memories of 'the nightmares of the past' it hadn't.[46] Nor has it for Xi Jinping, who has instructed the party to spread Chinese culture abroad as a form of soft power. Protest organiser Qi Jiazhen, an author and former political prisoner, said that the ballet promotes hatred and preaches slaughter. She warned that China is using cultural exchanges to infiltrate Western societies.[47] The protests failed to stop the performances.

The creeping and almost complete takeover of Chinese organisations in Australia by people loyal to Beijing has caused alarm in the traditional Chinese-Australian community. Those who migrated to escape persecution or simply to live freely are feeling outnumbered. But they are not yet defeated. A new 'pro-Australia' movement of Chinese-Australians who abhor the growing influence of the Chinese party-state was launched in September 2016. The Australian Values Alliance believes that if someone decides they want to live in this country then 'you should agree to the values of Australia', in the words of its founder, John Hu.[48] Hu stands firmly against the aims of the *qiaowu* program and the way it conflates 'China' and the CCP: 'if you don't like this country's values, and think constantly of another place as your country, then go back there.'

These are strong words, and make some of us feel uncomfortable. So for me it was fascinating to spend an hour and a half listening to John Hu talk about the Chinese community in Australia. We met in the café at the Museum of Contemporary Art, looking across Circular Quay to the Sydney Opera House. Among other roles, Hu was at the time a Liberal Party member of the City of Parramatta Council. He described to me the kinds of activities the PRC consulate in Sydney engages in to manipulate overseas Chinese, and how wealthy Chinese businessmen do the consulate's bidding because it's profitable for them.

Intriguingly, when I asked about big donations by those businessmen to Australia's political parties he said: 'There is no such thing as a private donation.' One way or another the consulate is mixed up in them.

After numerous meetings with Chinese-Australians I began to understand that the community is pervaded by a constant low-level fear. Loyalty to 'China' is expected by powerful people who can punish them. Australians are used to being able to turn up to a demonstration without having any concern about what might happen to them. But for Chinese-Australians, to attend a public protest against a Beijing policy requires courage and a decision to accept the possible consequences. They know they may be photographed, identified and have their name sent to the Chinese embassy. They may receive phone calls from 'powerful people' issuing warnings. They may be denied a visa to visit their sick mother. Or their brother's business in China might be raided by the police. Their name, personal details and activities will stay on a list somewhere and could come up at any time.

When I asked John Hu if the takeover of Australia by forces loyal to Beijing already has too much momentum he replied, 'It is stoppable.' But, he believes, Anglo-Australians have to wake up to what is happening in their country. With a handful of others, he had formed the alliance to show that there is no single 'Chinese community' in Australia, and to give 'white Australians' the jolt they need.

Contesting Chineseness

The party documents seen by James To distinguish between Chinese citizens living overseas (known as *huaqiao*) and ethnic Chinese with foreign citizenship (*huaren*). Yet all are regarded as Chinese with their first duty to the motherland, and so the party has developed methods to strengthen the 'Chineseness' and ethnic affinity of all ethnic Chinese living abroad.[49] The CCP leadership is sensitive to the perception that it is manipulating the loyalties of overseas Chinese,[50] and so the true objectives of the *qiaowu* program are, in James To's words, 'carefully shrouded in secrecy'.[51]

The CCP takes special interest in younger Chinese whose education or business endeavours have taken them abroad. Compared to earlier emigrants, they often have a much stronger affinity and ties to the 'ancestral home', seeing themselves not as a minority cut off from the motherland but as a part of China in another country.[52] They are perfect recruits to the CCP's international goals, even more so if they have high-level capacities in business or science and technology.

The China correspondent of the *Financial Times*, Jamil Anderlini, has argued that a more accurate translation of Xi Jinping's favourite phrase is 'the great rejuvenation of the Chinese race'.[53] That is what Chinese people, Han and non-Han, hear. (On the mainland, ninety-two per cent of the population is ethnically Han.) Some China scholars believe this is not accurate, and the best rendering is 'the great rejuvenation of the Chinese people'. Geoff Wade argues that the idea of *Zhonghua minzu* (the Chinese nation) was invented in the twentieth century 'to validate Chinese domination and control of other peoples across Eurasia' including Tibet and Xinjiang, and often encompassing overseas Chinese too.[54] Even so, *minzu* can mean a nationality, a people, an ethnic group or a race, depending on the context. Beijing is promoting the notion of a Chinese people to justify Han rule over non-Han regions.

Whatever the translation, most would agree with China scholar Daniel Bell when he writes of the view deeply ingrained in contemporary China that 'to be Chinese is to belong to a race'.[55] Senior leaders, like Premier Li Keqiang, are making troubling references to how love of the motherland is 'infused in the blood' of all people of Chinese ethnicity.[56] And when Xi Jinping spoke of there being no DNA for aggression in 'Chinese blood',[57] it was a statement with a worrying undertone of racial essentialism.

Further evidence for the CCP's expectation that the first loyalty of ethnic Chinese in Australia is to the motherland despite their Australian citizenship came in a revealing article in the Chinese-language edition of the *Global Times* in June 2017.[58] It reported domestic intelligence sources accusing Australia of attempting to persuade Chinese overseas to 'defect' (more specifically, to switch sides and spy for Australia). It used the word *huaren*, meaning all people of Chinese ethnicity. So Beijing is worried that Australian citizens will defect to Australia.

First-generation migrants living abroad and their children, even if they do not speak Mandarin and know little about China, are targeted for recruitment. Even Chinese babies adopted and raised by Western families become natural targets for enlistment to the cause of the China Dream.[59] On weekends some ethnic Chinese children in Australia attend Chinese schools that teach a CCP view of the world. Free summer camps take teenagers back to China for two weeks of subtle reinforcement of their Chineseness and indoctrination in party views.

While other developing nations have lamented the departure of their best and brightest as a brain drain, as early as the 1980s the CCP began to view it differently. While the brains may stay abroad there is no reason why the products of those brains, especially in the science and technology area, should not contribute to the homeland. With access to better labs, colleagues and resources, those brains can do a lot more than at home. So why not, as CCP general secretary Zhao Ziyang put it, 'store brain power overseas'?[60] In 2001 the CCP formalised the policy of 'serving the nation from abroad'. As James To writes: 'By contributing to China from abroad, because of certain innate Chinese moral qualities and loyalty to China, migrants represent a new quintessential mobile modernity of "Chineseness"'.[61] (In Chapters 9 and 10 we will see how this is working in Australia.)

The trick is to keep Chinese brains abroad patriotic. It's not so hard when those brains have since kindergarten been subjected to the systematic brainwashing of the Patriotic Education Campaign. Against the liberal expectation that Chinese students will have their minds opened by studying abroad, the evidence shows that those returning from abroad are 'no less jingoistic than those who have never gone abroad'.[62] President Xi Jinping was therefore confident in telling a 2015 conference of United Front cadres that it is no problem if Chinese students studying overseas decide to stay abroad. From there, he said, they can 'serve the country in multiple other ways'.[63]

Chinese law forbids dual citizenship, demanding the undivided loyalty of its citizens. The law, however, is inconsistent with the CCP's aim of keeping and strengthening the ties of overseas Chinese to the motherland. So in practice large numbers of Chinese who carry Australian, American and other passports retain their PRC passports, allowing unimpeded travel between the ancestral homeland and the new country of citizenship. The CCP's aim is to persuade or induce overseas Chinese to owe allegiance to Beijing. As more Chinese-Australians enter politics (which in itself is to be welcomed), section 44 of the Australian Constitution (the cause of so much parliamentary angst in 2017) will become increasingly germane. It renders ineligible for federal parliament anyone who owes 'allegiance, obedience, or adherence to a foreign power, or is a subject or a citizen or entitled to the rights or privileges of a subject or citizen of a foreign power'.

In recent decades, Chineseness has been reconstructed by the CCP power elite as a way of strengthening its incumbency, as well as its global reach. It does so by promoting a 'common ethnic consciousness' based on biology, culture and nostalgia, one that overseas Chinese are increasingly identifying with.[64] The hugely popular song 'Descendants of the Dragon', a karaoke favourite approved by the party, exalts those with 'black hair, black eyes, yellow skin'. *Qiaowu* work, writes James To, 'seeks to penetrate OC communities and individuals, and instil amongst them nationalistic, patriotic, or ethnographic sentiment that converge with Beijing's political identity'.[65] This proved much easier with the new waves of Chinese migrants in the 1990s and 2000s who came not to escape political oppression, as earlier waves often did, but to get ahead in the world while retaining links to the motherland.

After the 1989 Tiananmen Square massacre, *qiaowu* work received much greater emphasis and much better resourcing. The party leadership felt threatened by the surge of pro-democracy sentiment and activity in the diaspora. It immediately began planning how to deal with the students. Amnesties would be provided to those who had engaged in anti-CCP protests but wanted to return to China. Those who stayed in Australia would not be regarded as enemies but as a valuable resource that could be mobilised to advance China's interests. Intractable elements would be attacked and marginalised.[66] The extraordinary success of the strategy of winning over the diaspora in Australia is apparent when we compare its rebellious mood in 1989 with the massive outpouring of nationalist and pro-party sentiment in the lead-up to the 2008 Olympic Games.

The vigorous promotion of a single national Chinese identity that 'gathers a nation' across borders works against Australia's multicultural policy of integrating new migrant groups into the Australian community while recognising cultural diversity. New citizens are required to pledge their loyalty to Australia, yet the Chinese Communist Party is successfully working at securing the loyalty of many Chinese-Australians for China. As long as it is allowed to continue in this way, the integration of Chinese-Australians into a diverse but unified Australian society will likely fail.

Chinese Hansonism

In a conversation with a Chinese-Australian loyal to Australia, I was astonished when he said that, among those he mixes with, there is a lot of sympathy for right-wing populist Pauline Hanson. I reminded him that she made her name in the 1990s by warning darkly of Australia being swamped by Asians, sparking a spate of racial abuse against people of Asian appearance. Yet for some Chinese-Australians Hanson's blunt defence of 'Australian values' is appealing.

'The Chinese,' I have been told several times, 'are the most racist people in the world.' There was sympathy for the Chinese café owner in Kings Cross who was pilloried in the press for refusing to employ a black man. He hasn't yet learned that you can't do that kind of thing in Australia. And Chinese historically have seen themselves as superior to other Asian people. They have no sympathy for Muslims, and Hanson's strident attacks are appreciated. Although few would vote for her, Hanson's calls for unpatriotic residents to be kicked out of the country ring true for those anti-Communists who would like to see Beijing's agents, operatives and supporters in Australia put on the next plane back to their motherland.

For these Chinese-Australians, 'the Communists' are much more powerful than Muslim radicals, and they have a long-term plan to gradually exert their power. For them, this hostile power is a greater threat than racist outbreaks sparked by Hansonism. They are more afraid of the consulate than of being hassled in the street. There's a bit more to it though. In the late 1990s the Sydney consulate used the Hanson threat to try to *unite* the Chinese community under the consulate's influence.

Controlling the news

Should a foreign government be permitted to secretly own radio stations in Australia that broadcast Communist Party propaganda? It's illegal in the United States—the businesspeople who own radio stations are required to register as 'foreign agents'. A 2015 Reuters investigation uncovered a global network of radio stations across fourteen countries including Australia that are majority owned by the state-run China Radio International, which Sinologist John Fitzgerald describes as 'the Central Propaganda Bureau's international media arm'.[67]

The documents uncovered by James To reveal that the takeover of Chinese-language media in the West has been a carefully planned component of the broader strategy of controlling overseas Chinese, a 'core goal' of *qiaowu* work that has gained greater importance in recent times with President Xi Jinping's call to increase China's 'soft power'.[68] Media companies are offered inducements to adopt a pro–Communist Party position, including 'subsidies, cash injection, content sharing, infrastructural, technological and resource support'.[69] Those that refuse are subjected to an aggressive campaign to win them over or close them down, including regular threats to advertisers and distributors of media outlets that refuse to buckle.

James To reports that the consul general in Melbourne called Chinese media leaders to a meeting in 2000 where he issued strong warnings against publishing anything sympathetic to Falun Gong, the Chinese spiritual practice suppressed by the CCP.[70] Journalists who don't toe the party line are blacklisted from official events and pro-PRC functions. If officials expect an anti-CCP event to be held they may stage their own to divert attention, such as the 'spectacular' held at the Sydney Opera House to coincide with the seventeenth anniversary of the 4 June Tiananmen Square massacre. When the president of the Tibetan government-in-exile visited Canberra in August 2017, many of the seats at his ANU event were booked out by Chinese students who then failed to turn up, leaving the room half empty.

Independent Chinese-language media have to be particularly determined and well resourced to resist the intense and unrelenting pressure. Virtually none has been. The only substantial newspaper the PRC has failed to take over or run out of business is the Falun Gong–backed *Epoch Times*, now a thorn in Beijing's side and subject to frequent cyber attacks. In the United States, journalists with *The Epoch Times* have been physically attacked and had their computers destroyed.[71] It's alleged that in 2010, CCP supporters were responsible for a drive-by shooting at the newspaper's offices in Brisbane.[72]

Australia is now covered by a network of Chinese-language radio stations that never broadcast any criticism of China and carry stories following the party line on everything from the South China Sea to pro-democracy protests in Hong Kong and the Dalai Lama. The stations are owned by a Melbourne-based company, CAMG Media Group, which is controlled through a company owned by China Radio International and is probably heavily subsidised by it.[73] CAMG is active in New Zealand too, and consulate officials are even more brazen in their manipulation of Chinese-language media.[74]

The man behind CAMG is Tommy Jiang. Jiang arrived in Australia in 1988 (and probably benefited from Bob Hawke's invitation to Chinese students to stay).[75] He set up Australia's first 24-hour Chinese radio station, 3CW, in 1999 and built a Chinese-language media empire, including eight newspapers and a number of radio stations.[76] Jiang has since become a prominent Chinese-Australian, receiving a Multicultural Award for Excellence from the Victorian government in 2007.[77]

Yet he maintains strong connections with the ancestral homeland. A 2004 *Xinhuanet* article described an 'Overseas Chinese Association' delegation including Jiang visiting Jilin province to attend an event organised by the United Front Work Department.[78] In 2006, he attended a gathering in Beijing of overseas Chinese media groups to commemorate the first anniversary of China's controversial anti-secession law, which mandates that if Taiwan should attempt to secede then the mainland will go to war against it.[79] *Xinhuanet* reported Jiang, together with three other Chinese-Australian representatives, declaring that 'they will firmly uphold the "anti-secession law", earnestly longing for the early unification of the Ancestral Country'.[80]

In 2016, at another event for patriotic overseas Chinese titled 'Tell China's story well, spread China's voice well', Tommy Jiang said that to tell China's story well one must 'base oneself on China's perspective, China's attitude and China's position'.[81] He said that Chinese-language media like his in Australia 'had the resources to compete with international media on the same platform, and should fully display their overseas dominance'.

Some say China is just doing what other countries do in projecting a national image abroad. Yet as John Fitzgerald notes, this is a false equivalence: 'The BBC doesn't seek monopoly control of information, it doesn't intimidate, extort, and silence critics, and it doesn't operate clandestinely through deception and subterfuge.'[82] As in China, patriotic media groups in Australia take their cues on what is acceptable and what is prohibited from the official Xinhua News Agency. Some Chinese language radio stations allow China Radio International to vet its guests for their political acceptability. 'In Melbourne,' Fitzgerald writes, 'a CRI staff member from Beijing sits in the background on radio talkback programs and intervenes if callers start veering in a wayward political direction.'[83]

Chinese-language radio in Australia and almost all Chinese-language newspapers have their news and editorial comment written, sometimes literally, in Beijing. An editor at one of the pro-Beijing publications admitted that 'almost all the Australian Chinese newspapers only publish what the Chinese government wants them to'.[84] Loyalty is rewarded by granting patriotic media owners preferential access to business opportunities.

Those media outlets in Australia that do not toe the party line come under intense pressure. The consulate leans on Chinese-owned businesses to withdraw advertising. Businesses and community organisations are threatened if they stock noncompliant publications, including threats to their families in China.[85] And this is true not only of Chinese-owned businesses. The Sofitel hotel in Sydney was pressured by the Sydney consulate to stop supplying its guests with *The Epoch Times*.[86]

It should be said that while the supply of pro-Beijing news media in Australia has grown, so has the demand for it among Chinese-Australians, for whom reading newspapers often plays a larger role in daily life than for other Australians. While some find the proliferation of CCP propaganda in Australia galling, others welcome it as a counterpoint to Western reporting on Chinese politics. They like to read about China's rising power and its increasingly nationalistic presence around the world. Western criticism of the PRC's abuse of human rights and aggressive stance on Taiwan annoys them.

In Australia as elsewhere, CCP propaganda spread by Chinese-language media keeps patriotic expatriates informed about Beijing's positions on various issues and guides their thinking and activities. University of Technology Sydney media expert Wanning Sun argues that there is 'little clear evidence that such "localised" propaganda has a direct impact on Chinese-speaking audiences',[87] yet the effect on Australian society is to consolidate and expand the perception of a large group of citizens whose understanding of the world is shaped in Beijing and whose first loyalty lies with the PRC. The authorities in China see a politically mobilised diaspora as vital to the nation's assertion of influence around the world.

Wanning Sun and John Fitzgerald consider what might be done to limit Beijing's 'authority over Australian conversations' on Australian soil, which Fitzgerald calls 'a potentially grievous challenge to Australian sovereignty by a foreign power'.[88] A legal challenge to social media platforms that restrict free speech is possible. Sun argues that the mainstream media should try harder at reflecting Chinese (and other) points of view, but this only turns the blame away from Beijing. After all, Beijing is in a position to pressure the mainstream media too. Fairfax Media has derived a chunk of badly needed revenue from monthly inserts from the *China Daily*. *Media Watch* reported that the ABC has been censoring its news in order to gain access to Chinese consumers.[89] Fitzgerald put it bluntly: 'the ABC has offered tacit support for China's repressive media strategy at home and abroad. The national broadcaster's dealings with China signal to the world that our commitment to values and core interests is negotiable.'[90]

SBS is supposed to provide 'balanced and impartial' news to Australia's various ethnic communities. I have spoken with a number of Chinese-Australians who say that several SBS Mandarin radio presenters admit to being members of the Chinese Communist Party. They complain that the station's political position is pro-PRC, sometimes carrying news items taken unedited from Chinese state media. Li Weiguo, for ten years a reporter and presenter at SBS Mandarin radio, is chairman of the Youth Committee of the leading United

Front body ACPPRC.[91] He now works as a producer at the ABC's Radio Australia.[92]

Chinese voices

Chinese-Australians opposed to Communist Party rule of China have watched the expanding influence of *qiaowu* work in this country with dismay. I met three of them in the heart of the Sydney Chinese community in Ashfield, at a restaurant that looked grungy from the outside but served delicious food once we were through the door and up the stairs. John Hu had booked a private room and we were joined by two of his friends.

Jingping Cheng is a quietly spoken public servant who decided to 'come out' by joining the protest against the *Red Detachment of Women* performance. He had been the president of the Chinese Professionals Club of Australia until a few years ago when a new group of pro-Beijing members suddenly joined up, then proceeded to vote out the old committee and install a new one with links to the consulate. The consulate, he said, is always set on controlling any Chinese organisation, and this kind of political ambush has befallen many long-standing Chinese community groups. Few independent ones are left. As Jingping put it, 'They are using democracy to destroy democracy.'

John Zhang Xiaogang told me that he was now taking a public stand because the Communists are 'coming to my home', Australia. After he began speaking out, he was refused a visa to visit his sick mother in China. He too confirmed what I had seen and heard across the community: 'People are afraid of the consulate.'

For a clear-eyed view of Beijing's methods we can do no better than listen to Anson Chan, who served as chief secretary of Hong Kong from 1993 to 2001, before and after the handover of the British territory to China in 1997. The first ethnic Chinese to head its civil service, she became known as the 'Iron Lady'. She stayed on in her position after the handover because she was confident that Beijing would respect the independence of Hong Kong guaranteed by the 'One China, Two Systems' agreement.

Over breakfast in the exclusive surroundings of the Hong Kong Club, Anson Chan told me she had been naïve to expect the CCP to allow the citizens of Hong Kong their autonomy. She described in detail the strategies used by Beijing to infiltrate, pressure and coerce Hong Kong's institutions, from using money to control NGOs to suppressing dissident voices, placing sympathisers on university boards, setting up clan associations, controlling the media and pressuring businesses. Beijing looks upon Hong Kongers as renegades who refuse to accept China's rule. And it is becoming impatient. Chan has become a thorn in their side. She will not travel to the mainland because of the risk of being abducted and made to disappear. The 2015 abduction and psychological torture of five Hong Kong booksellers (one a Swedish citizen) by Chinese state security sent shockwaves through pro-democracy activist circles.[93] She knows she is not safe in Hong Kong from a regime that has no regard for human rights or the law.

But what would Anson Chan know? In 2017 John Brumby, former Victorian premier and chairman of the Australia China Business Council and a frequent advocate for closer ties, told *Xinhuanet* that Hong Kong's return to China has been a resounding success and there is 'much to celebrate'.[94]

In October 2016 Chan, with Hong Kong lawyer and fellow pro-democracy leader Martin Lee, travelled to Australia to send us a warning. The Chinese embassy in Canberra did not succeed in its efforts to pressure ministers and MPs to refuse to meet them. Interviewed by journalist Peter Hartcher, Anson Chan warned that China is infiltrating Australia, and that Australians do not understand 'the designs of the one-party state'.[95] She could see how the CCP was subverting social organisations, NGOs, the media and the government itself. It was establishing Confucius Institutes, controlling Chinese-language media and buying off political candidates. We should have no illusions: China under the CCP has a 'well-thought-through, long-term strategy to dominate'.

After meeting Australian MPs and the foreign minister, Anson Chan and Martin Lee travelled to New Zealand for their pre-arranged meeting with Deputy Prime Minister Bill English.[96] However, the night before the meeting English cancelled it, saying it was 'diplomatically sensitive', code for caving in to pressure from the Chinese embassy. New Zealand has shown itself to be more responsive to Beijing's demands than Australia. As far back as 2002, Auckland International Airport gave in to pressure to remove a billboard ad paid for by Falun Gong practitioners. And the University of Auckland cancelled a visit by Uyghur leader Rebiya Kadeer, only reversing the decision after a public outcry.[97] According to China scholar Anne-Marie Brady, China no longer has 'to pressure New Zealand to accept its soft power activities and political influence. The New Zealand government has actively courted it'.[98]

The long arm of China's law

China's Ministry of State Security has been caught sending agents to Australia to intimidate suspects.[99] This violates Australian law. The ministry also kidnaps foreigners and renders them to secret prisons in China, as it did in 1993 with the Australian James Peng Jiandong, who was abducted in Macau then taken to the mainland and jailed on trumped-up charges.[100] He had run afoul of a company linked to a niece of Deng Xiaoping. A Hong Kong court later ruled that he was innocent and had been robbed of $800 million.[101]

The ministry is also known to pay, or otherwise reward, triad gangs to do its dirty work. In 2014 and again in 2017 pro-democracy protesters in Taiwan were attacked by thugs led by the criminal 'White Wolf', variously described as a 'notorious gangster' and 'a tool of China's united front policy'.[102] The CCP has a long history of links with criminal gangs. Deng Xiaoping once said that some triad gangs are patriotic, while another senior official called for the CCP to join forces with them.[103] *The South China Morning Post* used to carry reports of the CCP's use of criminals for political purposes in Hong Kong. James To notes that PRC diplomats are said to cultivate links with criminals to spy on and infiltrate community groups.[104] Triads are well established in Australia but there is no evidence they have links to the Chinese consulates.

The CCP adopts a cynical attitude towards international law—use it when convenient, ignore it or denounce it otherwise. Adopting the former approach, in 2017 Beijing asked Interpol to issue a red notice against the Chinese billionaire Guo Wengui, who, after taking refuge in the United States, made sensational claims of corruption reaching high into the Politburo. The Interpol notice, which allows law enforcement bodies to cooperate, was issued three days after Guo's claims were reported in *The New York Times*. But Interpol's intervention immediately raised suspicions because in November 2016 the position of Interpol president had been filled for the first time by a Chinese security official, Meng Hongwei, formerly vice-minister for public security. As one observer put it, Interpol 'is in danger of becoming an extension of the increasingly long reach of the Chinese state … [a means to] extend its influence over unruly citizens abroad'.[105]

Despite the reassurances of those pushing for it, the ratification of Australia's extradition treaty with China would extend that long reach into this country. In 2017 the government's mishandling of the plan to ratify the extradition treaty revealed some of the fault lines in the larger Australian debate. The treaty was signed by the Howard government in 2007 and lay on the table until the Turnbull cabinet decided in March 2017 to put it to parliament for ratification (or, technically, for possible disallowal). It was intended as a sign of good faith to the visiting PRC premier, Li Keqiang. Two weeks earlier, I had asked a senior official why the government was pushing for ratification and he replied that he didn't know why Australia had agreed to such a treaty in the first place but we should ratify it 'because it's there'. It was a piece of housekeeping. Besides, an Australian attorney-general would not be obliged to agree to any extradition request, so plenty of safeguards would remain.

The foreign minister, Julie Bishop, assumed it would cruise through parliament, and was annoyed when right-wing senator Cory Bernardi, who'd recently left the Liberal Party to form his own conservative party, moved a disallowance motion. After testing views in caucus, the Labor leadership decided it would back the Bernardi resolution. The Greens and other independents agreed. Their stance drew on advice from the Law Council of Australia, which noted that China's legal system, always subject to political interference and corruption, was becoming worse.[106] More alarming for the government, some of its own members had indicated they would cross the floor to oppose ratification. Tony Abbott, who as prime minister had decided not to pursue ratification, was one of them.

Acutely embarrassed with Premier Li in the country, the government faced defeat and withdrew the treaty. It was duly castigated by the

Chinese ambassador. Julie Bishop promised to keep trying. But China's case was seriously dented when, as Li's visit began, security officials in China refused to allow a visiting academic from the University of Technology Sydney, Feng Chongyi, to leave China. Associate Professor Feng, an Australian permanent resident with a wife and daughter holding Australian citizenship, had written articles critical of the growing influence of China in Australia. When he was allowed to return home, after two weeks of interrogation, he declared that ratifying the treaty would be a 'fatal mistake'.[107] It would encourage the Chinese state to invent charges to get their hands on dissidents in Australia.

· · ·

Left and right of the political spectrum agree that China's legal system is not independent but a tool of the state. Justice cannot be assured, torture is not uncommon and judges are often bribed or instructed on their verdicts. In China's court system the conviction rate is ninety-nine per cent. (It's around eighty-seven per cent in Australian criminal courts.[108]) China's Supreme Court has rejected the principle of independence of the courts from the political system as 'erroneous western thought'.[109] The courts have imprisoned tens of thousands of Chinese people for the meditation practice of Falun Gong. In prison many have been drugged and had their vital organs surgically removed for sale to Chinese hospitals with wealthy patients needing transplants.[110] After hearing evidence from some campaigners and victims in 2013, the Australian Senate passed a resolution condemning human organ harvesting. In 2016 it was reported that Queensland's two major organ transplant hospitals were refusing to train Chinese surgeons because of organ harvesting in their homeland.[111]

Most China apologists and appeasers sit in the soft centre of Australian politics. Although prone to be dazzled by the economic promise, the right is more consistent in its scepticism towards China. The right has always held a knee-jerk hostility to anything that has the word 'communist' attached to it. Although it's hard to identify anything collectivist in post-Deng China, the right's belief that communism is inherently dictatorial and oppressive receives plenty of vindication from modern-day China, which has refined the Leninist party-state beyond anything achieved in the Soviet Union, and even more so under Xi Jinping.

Some on the left retain a romantic attachment to the idea of the Chinese Revolution, despite the horrors of Maoist excess, not to mention the fierce repression of 1989 that continues to this day. This attachment spills over into an unexamined sympathy for the post-Mao regimes. One of the more unrepentant is journalist and film-maker John Pilger in his 2016 film *The Coming War on China*, which paints China as an innocent victim of American aggression. That may have been an accurate characterisation thirty or forty years ago, but in the last twenty years the United States has worked hard at facilitating China's rise through integration into the global economic system, including its membership of the World Trade Organization. Pilger even repeats the CCP line that economic progress trumps abuses of human rights.[112] The kind of strident anti-Americanism that many shared in the 1970s and 1980s now does nothing more than provide cover for the PRC's bullying of its neighbours and extending its new form of imperialism in places like Africa.

• • •

The ratification fiasco revealed the hypersensitivity of Australia's elites to the Mao-style hysterics that issue from the Chinese government and media whenever it does not get its way. As journalist Fleur Anderson observed, although they adopted different views on ratification, both the current Coalition government and Labor 'were at pains to avoid explicitly referencing concerns about China's legal system in order to avoid any possible breakdown in diplomatic relations'.[113] Curiously, a 2014 briefing paper from the prime minister's department advised against ratification partly on the grounds that raising the issue would prompt critical commentary from Australians concerned about China's legal system, reproaches that would upset Beijing.[114]

This 'don't talk about the war' attitude has underpinned the relationship, keeping it on the safe terrain of mutual economic interests. Our politicians claim that they have 'robust' exchanges with the Chinese, but in truth the manufactured tantrums and appeals to 'the hurt feelings of the Chinese people' have mostly cowed them into silence on all issues involving human rights abuses and the outrageous incursions of the Chinese party-state into our society. When dissident writer Liu Xiaobo died in a Chinese prison hospital, the censors launched a blitz against any expression of grief or anger, even using image recognition software to block drawings of empty chairs like the one at Liu's Nobel Prize award ceremony in 2010. There was no need to censor the Australian government's tepid reaction because it had censored itself, speaking out only after his death and then merely to express regret. Of course, this restraint and respect for national feelings is not reciprocated, with party-controlled media frequently loosing volleys of harsh criticism and abuse directed at our government and the moral faults of Australian people in general.

An extradition treaty would be for China just another means of exerting pressure on Australia. Each time the attorney-general considered refusing a request, he or she would be assailed with Chinese histrionics and economic threats. Beijing sympathisers in the Australian business community would be mobilised to pressure the government to hand over whoever Beijing wanted, including political critics facing trumped-up charges and automatic jail sentences.

In fact, China already has its own means of repatriating those it wants. It has methods of encouraging people to return to China 'voluntarily'. The Chinese police speak of their 'persuasion work', with one saying: 'A fugitive is like a kite, the body is overseas but the thread is inside China. Through family and friends, we can always find them.'[115] In 2015, Chinese police blindsided Australian authorities by arriving unannounced and unlawfully to persuade Dong Feng, a bus driver and Falun Gong practitioner, to return to China to face embezzlement charges. It was reported that his elderly parents in China were being pressured by the authorities.[116]

In 2016, Australian permanent resident and grandmother Zhou Shiqin was charged with corruption by a Dalian court. She strongly disputed the charges, claiming they were a tactic in a political quarrel; in Chinese business disputes it's not uncommon for a rival to bribe a judge to issue an arrest warrant.[117] But after Zhou's sister's assets in China were frozen and her own face was splashed across Chinese media as a criminal, the psychological pressure on her became 'extraordinary', according to her lawyer, and she went back to China. As Philip Wen observed, the 'case underlines the pervasive pressure tactics employed by Chinese authorities outside the bounds of bilateral law enforcement cooperation'.[118]

'They can do anything. They don't care.'

Is it any wonder that Australian politicians of conscience, on the left and the right, had grave misgivings about signing an extradition treaty with the PRC? These misgivings can only deepen with the passage in July 2017 of China's new National Intelligence Law. Although typically vague in its wording, wrote Beijing correspondent Rowan Callick, it indicates that Chinese intelligence operations in Australia will be legally authorised.[119] While it's well known that state-owned enterprises operating abroad have party committees, the new law imposes an obligation on those companies to provide cover posts for spies.[120] The legislation calls on all Chinese people to work with the nation's intelligence services. Since the PRC regards all people of Chinese heritage to be 'Chinese', no matter what their passports say, it raises the possibility that Chinese-Australians will be expected to assist Beijing's spying here.

In modern times no group in China has been more severely and tirelessly persecuted than Falun Gong. For outsiders it is strange that a loose organisation promoting a spiritual practice, one based firmly on traditional Chinese *qi gong* (the slow-flowing moving meditation) and with no political aims, should have provoked such a ruthless crackdown. But CCP leaders felt threatened by a movement with more members than the party and attracting greater devotion, and so in 1999 declared it illegal. To pursue practitioners who have fled the country, the Central Committee of the CCP established the 610 Office to coordinate the persecution. This includes monitoring their activities, confiscating their passports, destroying their families' businesses in China, pressuring news outlets not to report on them, and phoning local, state and federal politicians to strong-arm them into withdrawing any kind of support for Falun Gong.[121] Chinese students abroad are pressed to stage rowdy protests against the 'evil cult'.

The embassy in Canberra actively works to suppress free speech in Australia when that speech makes for uncomfortable listening. Reacting to pressure, in 2002 foreign minister Alexander Downer forced Falun Gong practitioners to scale back their long-running peaceful protest outside the Chinese embassy. Beijing's campaign has been effective, suppressing the voice of Falun Gong in Australia and marginalising it from public discourse. In the meantime, the continued inflow of pro-Beijing migrants from China swells the ranks of overseas Chinese that the embassy can rely on to come out in support when called upon.

In summing up his meticulous study of *qiaowu* work, James To warns that the growing populations of overseas Chinese in Australia, New Zealand and elsewhere 'serve as a financial and skilled resource, and increasingly, as a ready supply of soft power to advance or support Beijing's outreach throughout the world'.[122] The overseas Chinese 'have the potential to become politicized and mobilized as a highly coordinated ethno-nationalist force with transnational loyalties to influence political, economic, diplomatic, and military outcomes'.[123]

The Bennelong by-election in December 2017 saw Beijing pulling the various levers at its disposal in order to defeat the sitting Liberal Party member John Alexander. It was a way of punishing the Turnbull government for introducing new foreign interference laws. If Labor's high-profile candidate Kristina Keneally were to win, the government would lose its majority in the House of Representatives, so the by-election became a focus for intense United Front activity. Bennelong, on Sydney's north shore, is especially well suited to CCP operations because it is the electorate with the highest percentage of ethnically Chinese residents, some twenty per cent. And they tend to be more recent arrivals, and therefore more pro-Beijing.

The levers included mobilising Chinese-language media (traditional and social) to launch a virulent attack on the government for its 'racist' and 'anti-China' stance.[124] A 1700-word anonymous letter, widely circulated on Mandarin social media, described the Liberal Party as being 'against China, against Chinese, against ethnic-Chinese migrants and against Chinese international students', calling on 'we Chinese to take down this far-right Liberal Party ruling party'.[125] (The letter was circulated by a United Front operative and may have been composed by the Sydney consulate.) The 'anti-China' message gained traction, leading the Labor Party to sing the CCP's tune by accusing the government of 'China-phobia'. On election day, in the suburbs with the highest ethnic Chinese vote the swing to Labor was over ten per cent, although Alexander retained the seat.[126]

No one is more alarmed by these developments than those Chinese-Australians who are loyal first and foremost to Australia. When I met with dissident writer Qi Jiazhen in Melbourne, her friend told me that wherever you go the party wants to control you. 'They can do anything. They don't care … You never have peace.' His blunt message to his fellow Chinese-Australians is this: 'You chose this place as your home. If you go out and protest and support the Communist Party then Australia should send you back to China.'

Professor John Fitzgerald, often named as the most authoritative expert on China in Australia, writes that the Chinese party-state is 'massive, capable, authoritarian, indifferent to the rights of individuals, resentful of the liberal West, jealous of its own standing, and here to stay'.[127] For a quiet and thoughtful academic, Fitzgerald has lately been ringing the alarm bells loudly. 'Beijing seeks to penetrate and influence Australia's small, open and inclusive society,' he writes. 'It seeks to restrict Australia's freedoms of speech, religion and assembly. It threatens social harmony. Where it succeeds, it breaches Australian sovereignty and security'.[128]

When I met him one morning in a hot and crowded café in one of Melbourne's famous lanes, it was as if his life's work now had to be put to a much larger use than advancing China scholarship. He had warned of the silencing effect of Beijing's propaganda and security systems which 'have migrated and settled comfortably in Australia'. When I left the laneway I felt fearful, afraid for Australia's future being stolen from us by an overwhelmingly powerful force. And, if I'm honest, I felt nervous about my own future, given the reach and ruthlessness of China's security apparatus.

4

Dark money

Huang Xiangmo in China

On his walls and websites, billionaire Huang Xiangmo proudly displays photographs of himself smiling and talking to the most powerful politicians in Australia, including all recent prime ministers. There is only one way to get that kind of access—buy it. In little more than four or five years the new arrival to Australia had become a dominant figure in the Chinese community, the largest donor to Australia's political parties and a significant player in New South Wales and national politics. As early as December 2012 he was meeting with former and soon-to-be-again prime minister Kevin Rudd, a chat perhaps arranged by another Labor powerbroker present at the meeting, New South Wales branch general secretary Sam Dastyari.

Huang sits at the centre of a web of influence that extends throughout politics, business and the media in Australia. Any doubt about his importance to the CCP is dispelled by the fact that he was chosen to give the speech at the farewell banquet for the Chinese ambassador to Australia in 2016, and was one of the handful of representatives of the Chinese-Australian community at the banquet when President Xi Jinping made a state visit in 2014. These great honours sent an unmistakable message to the Chinese community in Australia.

Understanding how Huang Xiangmo became rich in China, what led to his apparently hurried departure, and the way he set about building influence in Australia powerfully illustrates how ill-prepared the nation is to protect itself from the PRC.

Huang was born in 1969 in the village of Yuhu (meaning 'Jade Lake') in the Chaozhou region of Guangdong province. (Chaozhou is also the ancestral home of Chau Chak Wing, whom we'll meet later.) He took Yuhu as the name of his company. In interviews he has said that he came from a humble family and his father died when he was very young.[1] According to a story in the Chinese press, he was too poor to continue his schooling and dropped out to work.[2] However, other reports say that he studied economics at the Guangdong Academy of Social Sciences, which is unlikely as it is an institute for research and graduate study. At some stage he moved to the prefecture of Jieyang, a large, nondescript city that underwent a remarkable real estate and development boom in the 2000s. Jieyang is also in the Chaozhou region and Huang has retained a network of business associates there, although some have moved to Australia. In Jieyang he worked his way into senior management positions in the China Railway Group.

One way or another Huang acquired some capital, business nous and influential contacts through, it seems, real estate and development deals. Little is on the public record. The company website and a government company database say he established his Yuhu company in 2006, but in an interview with journalist Primrose Riordan he said he founded the company in 2001 (aged thirty-two). 'Over the following decade in Jieyang,' wrote Riordan, 'Huang's business prospered. In 2009 he even gave 150 million yuan ($32 million) towards a monumental, pagoda-style city gate that was the pet project of his friend, Communist Party secretary Chen Hongping.'[3]

According to Hurun, a Chinese company that publishes lists of wealth and philanthropy, Huang's wealth in 2016 amounted to RMB 6.2 billion yuan ($1.25 billion).[4] While he was still in China in 2011 he was reported to have donated a total of RMB 300 million yuan ($60 million) to various causes.[5] In 2011 Hurun ranked him as China's tenth most generous philanthropist and twenty-second in 2012.[6] Huang has spoken humbly of his giving, insisting that he has never made donations in order to secure business transactions. His only motive is compassion and 'giving back to society'. His aim is 'to enrich the masses',[7] although in Jieyang, instead of giving to hospitals or schools for the poor, he preferred to donate to a grand city gateway that happened to be the passion of the city's party secretary, the town's most powerful person, more powerful than the mayor.

The Jieyang tower corruption scandal is too complicated to set out here, and much remains shrouded in mystery. For our purposes, a short version runs like this. In 2008 Huang Xiangmo met with Jieyang party secretary Chen Hongping. Chen was obsessed with giving Jieyang a monumental city entrance. Huang agreed to give 150 million yuan, a very large sum.[8] It's not clear whether all of the funds were actually spent on the gate or found their way into someone's pocket, with public funds used instead. Another prominent Jieyang businessman Huang Hongming (no relation) was also persuaded to make a large donation to the project (and perhaps to another, the Rongjiang Guanyin Pavilion).

Chen is a superstitious man with a strong belief in feng shui and so spent tens of millions of yuan acquiring a rhyolite boulder from Mount Tai, 1600 kilometres distant, and surrounding it with nine spires. The *People's Daily* would later criticise him for 'believing in spirits and ghosts'. Huang Xiangmo seems to share the superstition: in 2012 he shelled out $12.8 million on a mansion on top of the hill at Beauty Point in the Sydney harbourside suburb of Mosman; according to real estate agents, the area is said to have excellent feng shui.[9] After waiting for Huang to settle on his house, several of his Chinese business associates bought houses nearby, but all lower down the hill and of lesser quality.

The Jieyang Tower was completed in mid-2009 (with the devoted hard work of city deputy secretary Zheng Songbiao) and photos show Secretary Chen smiling broadly as he stood beside Huang Xiangmo at its opening. But soon everything would begin to unravel in a frightening way. In July 2012 Secretary Chen Hongping was taken into the *shuanggui* process, the CCP's extra-legal anti-corruption interrogation process often accused of using torture to extract confessions. It was reported that the anti-corruption body had received dozens of letters accusing Chen of soliciting bribes and other offences. Almost all of those caught up in *shuanggui* are subsequently charged, convicted and punished for serious crimes. Under interrogation, Chen implicated the Jieyang senior deputy mayor, Liu Shengfa, who was also mixed up in the tower scandal. In February 2013 the city's deputy mayor, Zheng Songbiao, also came under suspicion for taking bribes. Both Zheng and Liu were expelled from the party and Liu was charged with bribery.

In November 2013 Huang Xiangmo's business associate Huang Hongming was arrested and charged with bribing Chen Hongping. Chen had confessed to being bribed by Huang Hongming and tearfully appealed to the court to show leniency towards him.

Huang Xiangmo was not publicly named as being under investigation and has not been charged with any offence. According to a report on a Chinese news site, at least seven businesses were involved in Jieyang's corruption.[10] One senior official in Jieyang, speaking anonymously, was quoted as saying that '2006 to 2011 was the period when collusion between businessmen and the officials of Jieyang was at its peak'.[11]

Huang Hongming was also close to the previous Jieyang party secretary, Wan Qingliang, who held the post from 2004 to 2008 before being promoted to the powerful and lucrative position of Guangzhou party secretary. Wan too came under investigation for bribery, as did his deputy in both Jieyang and Guangdong, Luo Ou. Wan Qingliang and Chen Hongping are believed to have been partners in criminal activity for years, heading a network of corruption in Jieyang that would eventually lead to the fall of 'a string of Guangdong officials who had earlier worked together in Jieyang'.[12]

In September 2016 the most powerful official, Wan Qingliang, was sentenced to life imprisonment for soliciting bribes while mayor of Jieyang. In June 2017 Chen Hongping received a suspended death sentence and is expected to spend his life in prison.[13] The case was heavily publicised in the local press, including colourful details of the excesses of Wan and Chen, such as their sharing the same mistress. Fairfax Media noted: 'There is no suggestion Mr Huang's contribution toward the Jieyang Tower should be construed as a bribe.'[14]

In February 2017, Huang Hongming was convicted of bribing Chen Hongping and sentenced to two years and eleven months' imprisonment. Fairfax reporters Philip Wen and Lucy Macken wrote that sources close to the corruption case say that Huang Xiangmo fled

China after being tipped off that a 'close political patron would be investigated for graft'.[15]

It's important to put the Jieyang scandals in a broader context because few Australians understand just how corrupt the Chinese system is. The typical view is that China is such an authoritarian society that corruption could not flourish except in the gaps within the system. In fact, the opposite is the case: the entire system is rotten with corruption and it is only in the gaps that honesty clings on.

China's crony capitalism

The most systematic and thorough study of the emergence of endemic corruption in China in the post-Tiananmen era is *China's Crony Capitalism* by the highly regarded scholar Minxin Pei.[16] From late 2012 attempts to stamp out corruption intensified with new president Xi Jinping's elevation. Xi saw endemic corruption as undermining the authority of the regime and jeopardising the stability of the economy. Yet, writes Pei, 'the lurid details of looting, debauchery, and utter lawlessness that have emerged during the campaign only confirm … that … modernization under one-party rule has produced a form of rapacious crony capitalism'.[17]

Just how deep-rooted corruption has become was revealed by Xi himself when he launched his campaign with a remarkably candid speech. Systemic corruption reaches from the lowest administrative level in the counties right into the top leadership of the nation, that is, the seven-member Standing Committee of the Politburo, equivalent to an inner cabinet. When he was arrested the public learned that Zhou Yongkang, the Standing Committee member responsible for China's internal security, had built a network of corrupt officials, businessmen and at least one murderous mafia boss that he used to amass vast sums for himself and his family members.[18]

The system of endemic corruption emerged in the 1990s and, the data show, gained special virulence in the 2000s with the rise of new forms that involved several or even dozens of officials all engaged in collusive corruption within and across agencies.[19] According to Pei, it has been virtually impossible to do business in China and become rich without encountering it. It was no longer the odd rotten apple in an otherwise healthy barrel. In some large jurisdictions the networks of corrupt senior officials, businessmen and, at times, crime bosses, often all overseen by the local party secretary, have been so extensive that they are referred to as 'collapse-style corruption'.[20] Minxin Pei describes the case of the Guangdong prefecture of Maoming where in 2015 over 200 officials were punished, including three successive party chiefs, two mayors, the police chief and the head of the party's discipline inspection committee, whose job it was to root out corruption.[21]

One of the most pervasive forms of corruption is the selling of positions within officialdom and the party hierarchy, known as *maiguan maiguan*. Many provincial and county party secretaries have bought their positions. For any position obtained through bribery, the price depends on the extent to which the position can be monetised, either through selling state assets cheaply, allocating contracts to preferred businessmen, embezzlement, turning a blind eye to environmental pollution or by using one's seniority to sell appointments to more junior officials. Mayors and party secretaries have been known to spill all jobs in order to sell them again to the highest bidder. Those who bribe their way into positions are henceforth the captive of their sponsor and have a strong interest in covering up other corrupt activities. Often corrupt networks are broken only with the arrest and torture of one official who then implicates others. The first arrest is often made following tip-offs from 'the masses',[22] who might include applicants outbid for promotion or aggrieved mistresses.

When announcing his crackdown, President Xi noted that '*Guanxi* networks of all kinds have grown tighter and denser', providing more incentives and opportunities for officials and businessmen to collude.[23] Every businessman in China understands, in Pei's words, that 'private wealth unconnected with political power is inherently insecure under a predatory regime'.[24] The risk is that one's political protection may evaporate overnight if one's patron comes under suspicion. Unless one has an even more powerful protector, it may be time to get out before the investigation spreads to them. As the saying goes, 'Monkeys scatter when the tree falls.'

Rather than go into business themselves, corrupt officials retain their positions and use them to enrich their family members. Many officials have mistresses who serve the same function of looking after one's business interests, although they have been known to dob in their exes when jilted.[25] Businessmen typically build these lucrative *guanxi* networks step by step, often setting out to befriend their targets by inviting them to expensive restaurants, offering gifts and picking up the tab for services like foot massages and access to brothels.[26] They might then offer a smallish envelope of cash, preferably at Chinese New Year when gift-giving is customary.

No institution is free of corruption's corrosive influence. Networks of bribery have been exposed in the judiciary, including the highest courts in the country. One businessman, Ding Haiyu, had twenty-five judges on his payroll. He sued on spurious grounds most of the companies he did business with and had favourable judgements awarded by his crooked judges. One senior judge helped him fabricate evidence.[27] Ding 'turned his company into a virtual slush fund' for judges and court officers who would come to him for reimbursements for various expenses.[28]

All journalists in China are reminded of their patriotic duty to serve the party, and are quickly brought into line should they deviate. At times the media have been allowed to investigate and expose the malfeasance of medium-sized and large companies, including cases of deadly environmental pollution. But the staff at the *People's Daily* and its online offshoot have for years been using the material they gather through their investigations for a different purpose—blackmailing the companies into paying to keep them quiet. Jun Mei Wu, a journalist who defected to Australia, said she had engaged in these investigations in the heavily polluted city of Wuhan: 'At the end of every month, each reporter received an envelope stuffed with 10,000 to 20,000 yuan. That was the norm.'[29] Dozens of complaints from local people about poisons being dumped in the river would be used as evidence for the blackmail. One of the worst-offending companies paid the news outlet US$119,000 in hush money each year. It's also rumoured that newspaper editors and journalists at the central newspapers—the ones read by Xi Jinping, members of the Politburo and other powerful figures—accept payments to publish articles praising them.

In the military, the buying and selling of promotions is widespread. Indeed, corruption in the PLA is judged to be of 'epidemic proportions'.[30] In March 2015 *Xinhuanet* reported that fourteen generals had been convicted or were being investigated for corruption.[31] One of China's most powerful generals, Xu Caihou, was among the generals arrested, now totalling some three dozen since the start of Xi's crackdown. A member of the Politburo, Xu enriched himself by demanding huge payments from subordinates seeking promotion.[32] When he was arrested in 2014, several trucks were needed to carry away the loot he had stockpiled in his house. In early 2015 Guo Boxiong, who for ten years until 2012 was one of the two vice-chairmen of the Central Military Commission and so second-in-command in the military hierarchy, underwent the *shuanggui* process.[33] Linked to former president Jiang Zemin, Guo was said to have sold promotions, with the rank of major general priced at five million yuan (about $1 million) and lieutenant general at ten million yuan.

Due to the spread of corrupt practices, rising through the ranks of the PLA has penalised merit and honesty and favoured those willing to pay bribes for promotions and to demand bribes from those below them in their turn. As a result, Western military strategists judge that China's armed forces would perform less well than might be expected in a hot conflict. Perhaps recognising this, and in the context of China's expanding international military engagements, the PLA has recently been attempting to improve its fighting capability by reforming its rank and grade systems.[34]

Xi's corruption crackdown

Since his accession to China's presidency in November 2012, Xi Jinping has prosecuted a fierce campaign against corruption. The kind of grubby conspiracies to defraud the public in Jieyang have been exposed in scores of cities across the nation. At the same time, Xi has undertaken a ruthless crackdown on all forms of dissent, including jailing many human rights lawyers and arresting the family members of critics abroad.

Although the campaign has reached up to the most senior levels of the party, with even a number of Politburo members purged, some of the most powerful cadres and princelings have been protected, not least the family of the president himself. Xi's family, along with seven other members or former members of the Politburo, were all exposed as owning secret offshore bank accounts in the Panama Papers, the trove of financial documents leaked in 2015 from a Panamanian law firm. His sister and her husband have amassed fortunes, although there is no evidence that Xi used his positions to help them.[35] All mention of Chinese officials in the Panama Papers was suppressed in the Chinese media. When Bloomberg published a long exposé of Xi's family wealth, the company's reporters were banned from China. Bloomberg later agreed to play by Beijing's rules.

The immunity of certain senior officials (mainly the political supporters of Xi) also confers some protection on those businessmen and officials closest to them, although all live in fear that the political winds might change. Moreover, the campaign has had the additional objective of weakening the influence of the former Chinese leader Jiang Zemin, whose faction vies with Xi's hold on power. Senior cadres in Hong Kong, a bulwark of the Jiang Zemin faction, are said to have been heavily targeted.[36] Targets include wealthy Hong Kongers who bribed their way onto the Chinese People's Political Consultative Conference (CPPCC), membership of which attracts VIP treatment and access to top officials.[37] Some are said to have gone into hiding. Chinese billionaires routinely pay bribes to be appointed to the CPPCC.[38] Membership provides an unrivalled forum for extending one's *guanxi* to the highest levels. While we think of *guanxi* as networking with Chinese characteristics, it is better understood as cronyism.

Has President Xi's crackdown succeeded? The official figures are eye-popping. *China Daily* reported that in 2016 there were 734,000 corruption investigations with 410,000 officials punished for 'disciplinary infractions or illegal activity', including seventy-six at the ministerial level.[39] Some of the most serious offenders have been executed. Some corruption investigators are themselves tied into corrupt networks. The campaign has garnered strong support among the public (though not among the anxious elites). According to one well-placed observer, low-level officials have become more circumspect while higher-level officials have put up their prices as the risks of detection increase, to the chagrin of the businesspeople who must pay them.[40] And more creative ways of paying bribes have been invented, such as direct foreign currency payments into overseas bank accounts.

One ingenious businessman hired an American card shark to lose big-time to targeted party bosses. The tactic had the collateral benefit for the bosses of added 'face' from beating a professional player.[41]

Minxin Pei argues that combining supreme Leninist party-state power with a market economy inevitably generates corruption, which is why periodic crackdowns have largely failed to quash the crony networks.[42] 'If a market economy is to be combined with reasonably non-corrupt government,' writes Martin Wolf, 'economic agents need legal rights protected by independent courts. But that is precisely what a Leninist party-state cannot provide, since it is, by definition, above the law.'[43] In any town or city, the party secretary wields more power than the mayor, the chief judge and the police chief. The cause is not helped by the fact that Xi is using the anti-corruption drive to target his political foes.

Fearful of being prosecuted for corruption or other crimes, many Chinese businessmen who have acquired fortunes over the last two decades have created boltholes abroad, shifting assets, buying property, sending their children to be educated and seeking visas or passports. The preferred destinations are the United States, Canada, New Zealand and Australia, in part because those countries do not have extradition treaties with China.

In Australia it is impolite to mention the systemic nature of corruption in China; it can be construed as racist, even though it is the system that is rotten and no one resents it more than the Chinese people who live under it. For those who deal with China's business or political elites, acknowledging the dirty secret behind the polite façade causes discomfort, even moral doubt, so it's better to suppress the thought while toasting the latest deal.

Huang in Australia

Huang Xiangmo seems to have begun setting himself up in Australia around 2011.[44] His Yuhu Group was incorporated here in 2012. He appears to have left China permanently in 2013.[45] He immediately went about using his wealth to build his status in the Chinese-Australian community and to cultivate broader political influence.

The Yuhu Group website tracks how he quickly came to dominate the Chinese-Australian community.[46] By 2014 he was chairman of the

Australian Council for the Promotion of Peaceful Reunification of China (ACPPRC), an unmistakable sign of his new influence. The ACPPRC is the foremost Beijing-controlled Chinese organisation in Australia. Only those endorsed by the embassy in Canberra or the Sydney consulate can occupy its senior ranks. The ACPPRC is a member of an international network of more than eighty councils around the world controlled by the China Council for the Promotion of Peaceful National Reunification, until recently headed by Yu Zhengsheng, a member of the Politburo Standing Committee and so one of the most powerful leaders in China.[47] The Australian arm is therefore at the centre of China's United Front work in this country.[48]

Huang occupies a string of other executive positions in influential overseas Chinese organisations in the country. One is the presidency of the Australian Fellowship of China Guangdong Associations. In a speech at its launch in September 2013, Huang said it was supported by the Guangdong Overseas Chinese Affairs Office, which (as we saw) is the kind of province-level organisation prosecuting the CCP's *qiaowu* program.[49] (The Labor Party operative and Sam Dastyari staffer Paul Han has held positions in both organisations.)

Any Chinese-Australian appointed to a senior role at the ACPPRC ipso facto has the trust of Beijing and can be relied upon to act in a patriotic way (although the true motive may be pecuniary). The relentlessly pro-Beijing stance of the council and its consistent criticism of Australia's bipartisan position on issues like the South China Sea show that it serves as a reliable Beijing mouthpiece in the Australian public debate.

According to the ACPPRC article introducing Huang as chairman, he had to be implored to take on the role. It notes that he 'has extensive influence, appeal and high prestige in the Australian overseas community, political circles, business circles and academic circles', reporting that he had donated a total of RMB 378 million yuan ($75 million) over the years. In his various meetings with luminaries from the prime minister down, it says, 'Huang Xiangmo always stressed … that the sons and daughters of China, both at home and overseas, are of one heart and mind, united as one'.[50] In fact, in Australia the diaspora is deeply divided.

In an important move to build his *guanxi* or network of relationships in his new country, Huang recruited the former New South Wales Labor treasurer Eric Roozendaal. From 1999 until he entered New South Wales parliament's upper house in 2004, Roozendaal had been general secretary of the New South Wales branch of the Labor Party (located in Sussex Street, in Sydney's Chinatown, as it happens). In addition to being the party's chief fundraiser, he ran election campaigns for New South Wales Labor and was in charge of the state's federal election campaigns. His contact book among Labor heavyweights was unrivalled, except by that of Sam Dastyari (on whom more soon). Huang was not deterred by Roozendaal's own brush with corruption allegations involving jailbird Eddie Obeid and his son Moses, allegations he was cleared of by the Independent Commission Against Corruption.

In November 2012 Huang donated $150,000 to the New South Wales branch of the Australian Labor Party (ALP). Over the next four years his generosity would see $1.78 million going into the New South Wales ALP bank account, some from Huang's companies, employees, family members or close associates.[51] Huang's employees and associates are recorded as making large political donations.[52] One came from an otherwise unidentified Meijuan (Anna) Wu, who turned out to be Yuhu's company secretary.[53] (Before joining Yuhu and making her $50,000 donation she worked as a barista at the Max Brenner chocolate bar chain.[54]) In March 2014, the New South Wales ALP received $60,000 from Su Zhaokai, whose contact is given as a Gmail address and a flat in the Sydney suburb of Rhodes.[55] Mr Su was in fact an office manager at Yuhu.[56] (The declaration form indicated the money was earmarked for 'Sam Dastyari'.)

In March 2013 Roozendaal, while still a member of the Legislative Council, paid a visit to Yuhu's Australian headquarters. The company's website announced that he was invited to visit by Huang Xiangmo in order to improve relations between Yuhu and the Australian government.[57] In the same month, at Huang's invitation, he toured Yuhu's projects in China.[58] The company website said that the parliamentarian had agreed to 'promote … cooperation between Yuhu Group and Australian government'. Roozendaal had become a lobbyist for Yuhu. He quit parliament in May 2013 and in February 2014 began in his new job as Yuhu Australia's vice-chairman.[59] In 2016 he was promoted to chief executive officer.

When Roozendaal resigned his plum seat in the New South Wales Legislative Council with six years still to run, New South Wales Labor gifted it to Ernest Wong. Wong, a former mayor of Burwood, appears to be the most important link between Labor and Chinese money.[60] He is close to Huang Xiangmo.

Huang quickly built ties with Labor prime ministers Julia Gillard and Kevin Rudd. His first reported meeting with an Australian federal politician was with Rudd in December 2012 (Rudd was then plotting his return to the prime ministership). In attendance was the general secretary of the New South Wales ALP, Sam Dastyari, whose questionable connections with Chinese businessmen would four years later stall his political career and in December 2017 end it.

Yuhu's website would claim that the meeting was organised by Hong Yongyu, president of the Hokkien Huay Kuan Association since 2002.[61] Hong (also known as Eng Joo Ang) has been a senior figure in the Chinese-Australian business community with strong connections to the embassy since at least 2002.[62] Hong, as Eng Joo Ang, gave $110,000 to New South Wales Labor in 2014–15 (a donation he later said he couldn't recall making)[63] and was an executive vice-president of the ACPPRC.[64] Hong Yongyu assisted Huang Xiangmo to build his *guanxi* in Australia.[65] He was standing beside Huang when he shook hands with Liu Yandong, a Politburo member visiting Australia, at a Chinese community leaders event in December 2012.[66]

In March 2013, Huang was seated between Kevin Rudd and one of his backers, Chris Bowen, at a lantern festival event hosted by the Chaozhou and Fujian associations (Huang had acquired honorary positions in both), in the Fujian Association's hall. Also present were Bob Carr, Hong Yongyu, the founding chairman of the ACPPRC and 'great China patriot' William Chiu, and Zhou Guangming, the president of the Australian Chinese Teo Chew Association. Within months of settling in Australia, Huang had succeeded in making himself a prominent member of the Chinese community.[67]

In an opinion piece published in Chinese by the nationalistic *Global Times* (and reported in *The Australian* by Rowan Callick), Huang wrote that 'overseas Chinese should accumulate strength in politics' and wrote of the soft power of money. 'Money is the milk for politics.'[68] He lamented that overseas Chinese have not pushed hard enough to enter and influence politics in Australia. He clearly had an agenda to work on.

In addition to the goals of status and business advancement common to all kinds of political donors, Huang Xiangmo's donations please Beijing insofar as they help advance the policies and objectives of the PRC. Research has shown that successful entrepreneurs in China 'are highly sympathetic' to the political values of the Communist Party; after all, it is the CCP system that enabled them to accumulate wealth and influence.[69]

Huang's rapid trajectory is easy to measure. He began to be mentioned often in articles on the Sydney consulate's website, appearing in photos with the consul general on many occasions. Seven articles from 2016 mention him compared to only two from 2014 and three from 2015. As this suggests, in 2013 his relationship with the embassy and the consulate seems to have been minimal. Except for the ceremony for his donation to Westmead Hospital, which the then ambassador Ma Zhaoxu attended, there are no reported links in 2013.[70] In February 2014 he opened the ceremony for Chinese New Year in Sydney, together with other community leaders (including Hong Yongyu), consular officials and the usual bevy of Australian politicians.[71] In 2016 he was selected by the embassy to represent the Chinese community by welcoming the new ambassador Cheng Jingye.[72] Huang had made it.

In March 2014, he was interviewed by the CCP's main organ, the *People's Daily*, on the topics of the Chinese National People's Congress and the China-Australia Free Trade Agreement, then being negotiated. Using President Xi's catchphrase he declared that, 'My "China Dream" is that the motherland will continuously grow greater, that it can reinforce the people's self-confidence, and I hope that the motherland can be peacefully reunited and prosperously grow.'[73]

Bipartisan *guanxi*

Huang Xiangmo arrived in Australia to settle in 2012 or 2013 after making what was reported to be a hasty departure from China, where he had been caught up in a corruption scandal. Huang disputes this account of his exit, but whatever the truth he immediately went about using his wealth to build his status in the Chinese-Australian community and cultivate networks among politicians. As we saw, in 2014 he became chairman of the Australian Council for the Promotion of Peaceful Reunification of China (ACPPRC), the peak United Front organisation in Australia. According to China scholar Anne-Marie Brady, the ACPPRC's counterpart in New Zealand is controlled by the Central Committee of the Chinese Communist Party and is organised, supported and subsidised by the Chinese government.[74]

Despite Huang Xiangmo's protestations that he and ACPPRC are not connected with Beijing or the CCP, four ACPPRC officer bearers participated in the 14th Conference of Overseas Peaceful Reunification Promotion Committees, convened in Beijing by the China Council for the Promotion of Peaceful National Reunification (CCPPNR) in September 2016, at which the Australian Council's Tian Fei (Victor Tian), an Executive Vice President of the Council, gave a speech on behalf of Mr Huang.[75] In March 2017, Mr Huang hosted and fêted a CCPPNR delegation to Australia led by Sun Lingyan, the deputy secretary of the organisation.[76] In the same month, Mr Huang hosted Qiu Yuanping, the Director of the PRC's Overseas Chinese Affairs Office.[77] The ACPPRC also organised public displays of support during the 2017 visit to Australia of PRC Premier Li Keqiang.[78]

The unification councils are the most influential 'non-government' agencies of the Chinese state abroad, and Australia is no exception. Their role is to aid the Chinese state in mobilising and controlling ethnic Chinese people in their respective countries, a task shared with the PRC's Overseas Chinese Affairs Office of the State Council.[79]

Some prominent Australians have been wholly misled by the public face of the ACPPRC. In particular, Bob Carr has written:

For Coalition and Labor politicians who have attended [ACPPRC] annual dinners, [the Council] has functioned as a charitable organisation (raising funds to send Australian eye surgeons into Tibet, for example) and an umbrella organisation for the Chinese community. Whether its links with China's United Front Work Department are vestigial or active, they are now a distraction.[80]

This is a complete misunderstanding of the function and operations of the ACPPRC; its charitable activities have always been a cover for its political role. The ACPPRC is a creature of the United Front Work Department and the involvement of senior Australian politicians has always been a means of gaining influence for the PRC.

Huang Xiangmo has eclectic political tastes. Since arriving in Australia he and his companies have donated $1.3 million to the Labor and Liberal parties. Adding in donations by family, employees and his close associates, the total comes to almost $2.9 million, $1.8 million to Labor and $1.1 million to the Liberal Party.[81]

Having secured the services of Labor powerbroker Eric Roozendaal, in 2015 he employed the former New South Wales deputy premier and National Party leader Andrew Stoner, a few months after he left parliament.[82] Stoner would provide advice on investments in agri-business, including the $2 billion fund Huang had formed to invest in Australian agriculture.

Huang had also developed a close relationship with federal trade minister Andrew Robb. After Robb left parliament to work for various Chinese firms, Huang hired his former press secretary Cameron Hill to look after Yuhu's media relations.[83]

When foreign minister Julie Bishop gave a twenty-minute speech at the opening ceremony of Huang's Australia-China Relations Institute (ACRI) at the University of Technology Sydney (UTS), it was a sign of the billionaire's deep links in the government ranks. Huang boasted that he personally chose Bob Carr to be ACRI's director.

UTS was so grateful that it gave Huang the right to call himself 'professor' and the *People's Daily* was soon referring to him as an 'Australian scholar'.[84] He was, of course, photographed smiling with the foreign minister. In August 2013 Yuhu donated $230,000 to her West Australian branch of the Liberal Party, despite the fact Huang has no business or any other apparent links with the western state.[85]

Bishop said she was particularly delighted to see Mr Huang at the event, going on to speak of China as a force for good, noting that in addition to being our largest trading partner, China is 'our largest source of immigrants, our largest source of overseas students and our largest source of international tourists'.[86]

Judging by her firm comments in 2016 calling on China to recognise international law in the South China Sea, Julie Bishop seems to have resisted becoming the captive of Chinese money. If Bishop begins to change her tune it will signal a huge step forward in Beijing's plan to shift Australia away from the US alliance, but that now seems unlikely.

Huang was photographed with Tony Abbott when he was prime minister. When Malcolm Turnbull took over in September 2015 the new top leader needed to be schmoozed. It didn't take long: in February 2016 Huang and Turnbull were snapped at the Chinese New Year celebrations in Sydney.

However, it is the businessman's relationship with another senior minister that raises more questions. In April 2014, Huang convened a meeting in Hong Kong with trade minister Andrew Robb, along with representatives from the Australian consulate in Hong Kong, to discuss the China-Australia Free Trade Agreement.

In addition to Huang and his company staff, Yuhu had invited representatives from two Chinese companies. One was the China National Agricultural Development Group, the other known as China Aidi Group.[87] The five remaining members of the Chinese side of the table were from Yuhu. A few months later, in a speech to the dairy industry, Robb singled out Yuhu's agricultural investment fund for praise.[88]

Yuhu's report on the meeting noted that 'Robb … looked forward to the two countries being able to complete negotiations about the free trade agreement by the end of the year and finally sign the agreement, putting a satisfactory full stop on eight years of discussion'. Robb then listened to and recorded Huang's thoughts about problems Chinese businesses have when investing in Australia, not least their difficulties with working visas.[89]

The last is particularly interesting because the main criticism of the trade agreement had been the provisions it contained for importing workers from China. Robb would attack calls by the unions to introduce market testing for labour shortages as 'dishonest, vile and racist' and the Labor Party as 'xenophobic'.[90]

The meeting wound up satisfactorily. Huang would soon organise large sums of money to be channelled into the Victorian Liberal Party

(Robb's base) as well as his personal election fund in his Goldstein electorate. As Fairfax Media revealed in May 2016, 'Yuhu Group executives donated $100,000 to then trade minister Andrew Robb's fundraising entity [the Bayside Forum], including $50,000 on the day the China-Australia Free Trade Agreement was settled.'[91]

It hasn't been all business. In 2013 Robb was Huang's guest at the Melbourne Cup, including ticket and hospitality.[92] Huang has made himself an important figure in the racing industry, presenting the winner's cups at the Melbourne Cup Carnival.[93]

In February 2015 Robb, among other smiling politicians, turned up for Huang's publicity-intensive 'giving day' at which the tycoon and his business friends wrote fat cheques for charities like children's medical research. Along with Labor Party leader Bill Shorten, Andrew Robb is thought to have been an honoured guest at the wedding of Huang's daughter, Carina, in January 2016.

By 2016 Huang was certainly being looked on favourably by Beijing. Only the most reliable are allowed to write opinion pieces for the party mouthpiece the *People's Daily*, as he did in July. Communist Party culture, he wrote, 'is a common gene that enables over 60 million overseas Chinese compatriots "to breathe together, to share in a common fortune".'[94]

A month earlier the chairman of ACRI gained access to the opinion pages of the *Australian Financial Review*, where Huang echoed Beijing's threat that Australian support for US freedom of navigation exercises in the South China Sea 'would have been very harshly viewed by China'.[95] It would have been 'folly' that 'Australia may end up regretting'.

He went on to hold up the 'pragmatic' approach to China of the new Philippines president, Rodrigo Duterte, as an example Australia should emulate. Beijing could hardly believe its luck when in May 2016 the Philippines elected the gun-toting vigilante.[96] Beijing had been urging Australia to take the same 'pragmatic approach' and it found a compliant voice in Sam Dastyari, who, at his infamous press conference for Chinese media, spoke the words Beijing wanted to hear.

Huang Xiangmo may have fallen out of favour in Beijing after the damaging publicity generated by the first Dastyari affair in September

2016. After 2016 his name stopped appearing so often on the Sydney consulate's website. Embroiled in the second Dastyari affair in November 2017—leading Prime Minister Turnbull to describe him as a foreign national 'very very close indeed' to the Chinese government[97]—Huang Xiangmo resigned as president of the ACPPRC.[98]

At the February 2017 Chinese New Year celebrations in Sydney, now effectively controlled by the consulate, Huang looked on from the sidelines while the task of hosting the prime minister was assigned to Xue Shuihe. A Chinese national with extensive property developments in Australia, Xue Shuihe seems to have made his money in construction, textile and food businesses in Fujian and Sichuan.[99] As well as a long list of other honorary positions in Chinese associations (including senior honorary president of Huang's ACPPRC), Xue chairs the Australia China Economics, Trade and Culture Association (ACETCA), a United Front body with the standard list of noble objectives involving culture, youth, harmony and peace.[100] Xue Shuihe's brothers, Xue Shuihua and Xue Yeguang, are also honorary chairmen of ACETCA. On his profile Xue Shuihua declares: 'We need to grow the seeds of Chinese values and spread them overseas'.[101]

Chau Chak Wing

Wealthy Chinese businessmen are not the only or the most powerful network of businesspeople with influence in state and federal parliaments. Taken together, they come nowhere near rivalling the power of the mining companies or the media conglomerates, for example. But greater profits are all that mining and media companies seek. As the influence of the Chinese party-state in the most important Australian institutions expands, those concerned about the growth of money politics ought to be alert to the possibility of networks of Chinese businesspeople and their amenable politicians becoming embedded in the Australian political and economic systems. If traditional business lobbies only aim to protect their profits and promote corporate growth, some wealthy Chinese businessmen use their political connections to promote the objectives of the Chinese Communist Party.

Although a consummate networker, Chau Chak Wing is publicity shy (in China keeping a low profile is known as *di diao*) but his $20 million donation to the University of Technology Sydney to build the Frank Gehry–designed business school edifice was always going to attract attention. (Gehry said it looked like a 'brown paper bag'.) To persuade Chau to open his wallet so widely, the university's vice-chancellor, Ross Milbourne, had a cunning plan. Realising that Chau's son Eric was studying architecture at UTS, Milbourne asked the undergraduate if he would like to fly to Los Angeles for a private meeting with the world's most famous architect, Frank Gehry.[102]

In 2009 Chau's impressive donations to the Liberal, Labor and National parties had drawn media attention. As far as we know, since 2007 he has given $4.6 million to the main political parties ($2.9 million to the Liberals and $1.7 million to Labor).[103] His generosity coincides with federal election years. The money has kept flowing. In 2007–08 he donated almost $1.4 million and the same amount in 2013–14.[104] In 2015–16 he donated $860,000, mainly to the Liberal Party, including $200,000 to Julie Bishop's West Australian branch.[105] No Chinese businessman, and perhaps no businessman, has been more generous with our political parties.[106] If money talks, in Australia it increasingly does so in Mandarin.

Chau is an Australian citizen but lives in his vast luxury estate in Guangzhou. In 2015 he paid an Australian record of $70 million for gambling mogul James Packer's Vaucluse mansion La Mer, and then knocked it down. The story of how the billionaire, a self-described 'small businessman', acquired his wealth in the Chaozhou real estate and development game remains opaque and he is reluctant to speak of it, despite the best efforts over some years of Fairfax journalist John Garnaut.[107] Garnaut reports an acquaintance of Chau's observing that his 'star began to rise when Xie Fei, a Chaozhou neighbour, rose to the Guangdong Communist Party secretaryship in 1991', where he stayed for eight years. Chau's star rose higher when Lin Shusen, a protégé of former premier Zhu Rongji, was appointed mayor of Guangzhou in 1998 and promoted to party secretary in 2003.[108] After his friend Lin was shifted to Guizhou, Chau 'had uncharacteristic difficulties acquiring a huge land parcel'.[109]

He certainly has not had any difficulties gaining access to Australian politicians, from prime ministers down. He even manages to befriend those on the fast track to becoming famous. As three *Age* journalists noted in 2009: 'In 2004 and 2005 he partially funded trips to China for the future prime minister, Kevin Rudd, the future treasurer, Wayne Swan, the future foreign affairs minister, Stephen Smith, and the future agriculture minister, Tony Burke.'[110] He's described by Juwai.com (the top real estate website for wealthy Chinese) as 'an A-grade schmoozer [who] has made a practice of entertaining some of Australia's top politicians at his luxurious home in Conghua, just north of Guangzhou'.[111] When Chau agreed to a rare interview with Garnaut, the journalist found he was met on the airbridge, escorted through a tunnel beneath Guangzhou's Baiyun airport, and ushered into a Bentley that was waiting to take him to Chau's estate (which his staff call 'the Castle'). At the end of the interview, Chau offered Garnaut a family holiday, some fine French wine, and a job.[112] Garnaut declined it all, explaining to his colleagues at the time that he thought Chau was setting a reciprocity trap and that if he accepted the gifts Chau would believe he 'owned' him. (After another of Garnaut's articles was published in 2016, Chau sued Fairfax Media for defamation, a case still before the courts at the time of publication.)

Curiously, Chau seems to have little to do with Huang Xiangmo's forces. Although he was an honorary chairman of ACPPRC in the early 2000s, Chau held no formal position when Huang ran it (until November 2017).

Chau became especially close to senior figures in the New South Wales branch of the ALP. In 2006 Bob Carr became the sole honorary president of Chau's Association of Australia China Friendship and Exchange.[113] The organisation is a close partner of the Chinese People's Association for Friendship with Foreign Countries, a well-known United Front group headed by Li Xiaolin, daughter of Li Xiannian, former PRC president and chairman of the Chinese People's Political Consultative Conference.

In 2004 Carr was so impressed with Chau's daughter, Winky, that he took her on as an intern in his office. She stayed on in the premier's office when Morris Iemma succeeded Carr, and later set up a consulting business with Iemma after he left politics. Winky Chow's job nowadays is running the Chinese-language newspaper Chau set up in Sydney. The *Australian New Express Daily* is the Australian version of the Guangzhou newspaper he bought in 2001 in a partnership with the Yangcheng Evening News Group.[114] Of the parent paper Chau has said: 'The Government has found this newspaper very commendable, because we never have had any negative reporting.'[115] In preparation for the 2008 mass rally of patriotic Chinese students in Canberra to defend the Olympic torch and 'dye Australia red', Chau's *Australian New Express Daily* did a rush order to import a thousand Chinese flags.[116]

The Australian version of the paper, launched by Bob Carr in 2004, also keeps faithfully to the Beijing line. John Garnaut wonders how it is that a foreign citizen can run a newspaper in China, but of course he knows the answer. Chau holds prominent positions in a number of party-sponsored associations in China, such as the Guangzhou Chamber of Commerce for Overseas Chinese Enterprises. He was appointed to the Tianhe District Chinese People's Political Consultative Conference, 'a patriotic united front organisation of the Chinese people',[117] and has been praised as a 'representative individual' by the Shantou United Front Work Department.[118] As we saw, under President Xi the activities of the United Front Work Department have taken on a renewed importance. United Front cadres are expected to promote the party's views in their circles of influence and report back, in exchange for enhanced status and material reward.[119]

A joint Fairfax Media and *Four Corners* investigation into PRC influence culminated in June 2017 with a program on the ABC and feature articles in Fairfax newspapers. These claimed that Chau is associated with United Front organisations and explored his links to a US bribery scandal. Chau hired bull-terrier defamation lawyer Mark O'Brien and launched defamation actions against the ABC, Fairfax Media and the journalist Nick McKenzie, claiming that he 'has been greatly injured and his business, personal and professional reputation has been and will be brought into public disrepute, odium, ridicule and contempt'.[120] At the time of publication the case was still before the courts.

The program and the news stories, according to Chau's statement of claim, imputed that Chau 'betrayed his country, Australia, and its interests in order to serve the interests of a foreign power, China, and the Chinese Communist Party'. Chau appears to have taken exception to the imputation that he is a member of the CCP and of the Chinese People's Political Consultative Conference and 'as such, carries out the work of a secret lobbying arm of the Chinese Communist Party, the United Front Work Department'. Chau went to Simon Benson at the *The Australian*, who wrote a soft story publicising the aggrieved billionaire's side of the story. He rejected the ASIO assessment of him on which he believes the Fairfax/*Four Corners* allegations are based.[121]

In immediate response to Chau's claim that 'I have no idea' what the United Front Work Department (UFWD) is, Fairfax published a demolition of this claim by Nick McKenzie and Richard Baker. They referred to many instances of Chau's meetings with UFWD cadres, UFWD publications featuring him and Chinese government documents naming him as a member of UFWD-aligned organisations.[122] And they had come across, via WikiLeaks, a 'sensitive' report written by a United States diplomat in 2007 stating that Zhou Zerong, as Chau is known in Mandarin, had said he is the leader of a new organisation called the Guangdong Overseas Chinese Businessmen's Association. The diplomat judged that the new organisation led by Chau is 'part of the party's United Front strategy'.

In suing the ABC and Fairfax, Chau was keen to repudiate the suggestion that he employed 'a corrupt espionage agent of the Chinese government' and paid a $200,000 bribe to the president of the General Assembly of the United Nations. In 2015 Chau Chak Wing was mixed up in a nasty bribery scandal. Prominent Sydney socialite Sheri Yan, an American citizen, was arrested in New York by the FBI for allegedly paying $200,000 to the president of the UN General Assembly, John Ashe, for Ashe to make an official appearance at Chau's lavish Guangzhou resort.[123] Sheri Yan is married to Roger Uren, a former senior Australian intelligence analyst and diplomat in Beijing and Washington, and later at the Office of National Assessments.[124]

At one stage Uren was tipped to become Australia's ambassador to China. He is now vice-president at Phoenix Satellite Television, a pro-Beijing broadcaster in Hong Kong, and a collector of Chinese erotica.

The United Nations is reported to have launched an investigation into Chau's involvement in bribing Ashe.[125] Chau insisted he knew nothing of the transactions between Yan and Ashe. In July 2016 Sheri Yan pleaded guilty to paying Ashe a total of US$800,000 in bribes, including US$200,000 to attend a private conference in China 'hosted by a Chinese real estate developer identified as "CC-3" in the Complaint'.[126] She was sentenced to twenty months in prison. When asked about Chau's links to the scandal, his daughter Winky said: 'The whole thing is a misunderstanding.'[127]

John Ashe was charged with tax fraud associated with the bribes. He was reported to be still engaged in a plea bargain a few days before he was to appear in court in June 2016, at which he would presumably spill the beans. But he had an unfortunate accident and died. Initially his lawyer said he'd suffered a heart attack, but a coroner later concluded that while he was working out at home a barbell had accidentally fallen onto his neck, crushing his windpipe.[128]

In their defence against Chau Chak Wing's statement of claim, the ABC and Fairfax Media told the court there are reasonable grounds to believe that Chau Chak Wing 'betrayed his country, Australia, in order to serve the interests of a foreign power, China, and the Chinese Communist Party by engaging in espionage on their behalf.'[129] The news organisations further pleaded that there are reasonable grounds to believe Chau is a member of a body that 'carries out the work of a secret lobbying arm of the Chinese Communist Party, the United Front Work Department … [and] donated enormous sums of money to Australian political parties as bribes intended to influence politicians to make decisions to advance the interests of the People's Republic of China, the Chinese government and the Chinese Communist Party.'

The defence case went on to argue that there are reasonable grounds to believe that Chau is CC-3 and paid a '$200,000 bribe to the President of the United Nations, John Ashe' and was therefore 'knowingly involved in a corrupt scheme to bribe the President of the General Assembly of the United Nations.'

Finally, the ABC and Fairfax Media pleaded that 'there are reasonable grounds to believe that the Applicant broke the pledge of loyalty he took to Australia on becoming an Australian citizen by secretly advancing the interests of a foreign power at the expense of the interests of Australia.'

Zhu Minshen

Few people noticed, but the fishy smell around Zhu Minshen's Top Education Institute was noticeable a few years before it began wafting from the front pages of the newspapers. In 2013 Primrose Riordan reported in the *Australian Financial Review* that China had given the private for-profit Sydney college official endorsement, a status very hard to obtain for private colleges.[130] Zhu said he was not sure why others were not included; one thing is certain, though: he is very well connected in China, with pictures adorning his website showing him with various top government officials, from Premier Li Keqiang down.

His photos with leading Australian politicians are easier to explain. He gave them money. Zhu had donated over $230,000 to the major parties up to 2014–15, and an extra $72,000 in 2015–16, mostly to the New South Wales Liberals.[131] These are the contributions as far as we know them.[132] The obligatory photos show him meeting Malcolm Turnbull, Tony Abbott, Kevin Rudd, Julia Gillard, Julie Bishop, Bob Carr, Kim Carr and his successor as education minister, Christopher Pyne.

Unlike Huang and Chau, who have spent large sums and been rewarded with honorary degrees, Zhu is a genuine scholar, specialising in ancient Chinese characters. His father and grandfather, both intellectuals, were branded reactionary and counter-revolutionary and persecuted during the Cultural Revolution. The experience does not seem to have alienated him from Communist Party rule.[133] He arrived in Australia in 1984 to study for a PhD in calligraphy at the Australian National University (ANU), duly awarded in 1989.[134] After being knocked back for various academic jobs he moved to Sydney and set up a garment factory, drawing, he says, on the ten years he worked in a Shanghai cotton factory during the Cultural Revolution. He is an Australian citizen.

In the early 1990s he formed some kind of partnership with the huge state-owned investment company CITIC Group to help it sell clothing into Australia.[135] It was an odd venture for this massive investment vehicle owned by the Ministry of Finance and set up as a United Front vehicle to be the party's 'window to the outside world'.[136] Zhu must have had some important connections. He became a manager of the company CITIC established, which had an annual turnover of over $50 million. He made a lot of money and with it, in 1996, he set up a property development company that made him tens of millions of dollars.[137]

In the same year, now a rich man, Zhu established the *Australian Chinese Times*, the first pro-CCP newspaper in Australia—not counting, of course, *Vanguard*, the monthly newspaper still published by the militantly Maoist Communist Party of Australia (Marxist–Leninist).[138] Zhu said later he was moved to found the paper after the existing Chinese-language papers refused to publish his articles, which were 'too pro-Communist Party'.[139] His newspaper, he declared, would be resolute in fighting 'anti-China forces' and was established after he decided to dedicate himself to writing 'positive propaganda about the ancestral nation'.[140] Among other articles it published were many exposing the 'evil cult' Falun Gong, and proclaiming that 'the great undertaking of Chinese reunification cannot be hindered'.

Dr Zhu was true to his word, maintaining unstinting support for and close connections with the Chinese state. According to Chen Yonglin, the defector who once headed the Sydney consulate's political department, the *Australian Chinese Times* was paid by Beijing to reprint content from mainland newspapers.[141] At a conference in Nanjing in 2003, organised by the official Xinhua News Agency, Zhu Minshen spoke of how he republished articles from official newspapers, many of them demonising Falun Gong.[142] Zhu's work for the Communist state was rewarded in September 1999 when he was picked to be one of the handful of Chinese community representatives to sit on the rostrum with visiting President Jiang Zemin at the banquet in his honour.[143] Jiang Zemin reserved a particular hatred of Falun Gong, and consulates around the world devoted enormous resources to tracking, defaming and disrupting its members overseas.

In his 2001 speech in Nanjing, Zhu made much of the difference between the new and old generations of Chinese migrants to Australia. It was the old generation that found his pro-Communist views unpalatable, while the new immigrants have 'deep feelings for their ancestral home'. He spoke of the 'struggle' the *Australian Chinese Times* had to endure in its early years, but he was convinced that 'the power of new Chinese migrants will grow stronger and stronger'.[144] He found a home as an adviser to the ACPPRC in the early 2000s [145]

Zhu always saw himself as a scholar and so in 2001 he combined his intellectual interests with his business acumen to found Top Education Institute ('Top' is a translation of the Chinese word meaning 'elite'). It has flourished into a lucrative business. Of the college's 1000 students, 98.5 per cent are from overseas, mostly China. The private provider received a big boost in 2016 when Christopher Pyne awarded it access to the streamlined visa program, one of only a handful granted to private colleges. Labor's Kim Carr said that when he was minister for higher education in 2013 he had rejected Top Education's application because the immigration department had advised him there was a 'very high level of risk', presumably of Chinese coming over to 'study' but actually just intending to work.[146] Zhu Minshen's entities had donated $44,275 to the Liberal Party in 2014–15.

Zhu and the Olympic torch

Zhu Minshen is on the board of the Confucius Institute at the University of Sydney and he is well connected with the prestigious Fudan University in Shanghai. He is also an overseas delegate to the Chinese People's Political Consultative Conference (CPPCC), which, as we saw, is 'a patriotic united front organisation', in the words of one of its leaders. Membership is prized by Chinese billionaires and those looking to spread their *guanxi* networks into the highest reaches of the CCP. Members are ushered to the front of airport queues and find limousines waiting for them at flight's end.

Although an Australian citizen, Zhu appears to have played a significant role in organising the Chinese student protest at the Olympic torch relay in Canberra in 2008. When approached by some Chinese students from Canberra, Zhu readily provided financial help. It would be a day, he wrote, he'd 'not forget for the rest of his life'.[147] Zhu estimated that 30,000 students turned up and mentioned the organising role of the Chinese embassy and of how, at a get-together after the event, Ambassador Zhang Junsai 'spoke emotively' of the patriotic actions of the students. Zhu singled out for praise the overseas Chinese students from the University of New England. He was the dean of its International Institute in the 2000s.[148] According to his account, the university had fewer than a hundred Chinese students but forty-two of them drove for twelve hours to attend the torch relay.

Zhu was also proud of the ninety students from his own Top Education Institute who turned up at the demonstration. In fact, he chartered buses and made it a school activity 'that counts towards assessment' (making it perhaps the only accredited degree program in Australia that counts agitating for a foreign power towards its qualifications). He personally took along a hundred small Chinese flags, twenty large ones, and a specially made thirty-square-metre flag. Arriving in Canberra with his students, he saw that they were 'full of vigour as they waved their red flags'.

After standing with the students at the torch relay, he later waxed lyrical about the chants of 'One China forever' and 'Go China' that 'resounded across the sky'.[149] The voices of the troublemakers 'were drowned out as if in a great sea'. It was, he gushed, 'my unforgettable April 24, 2008!'.

> After the welcoming event finished, the students said to me, 'Principal Zhu, this event has such significance. Why don't you give the national flags to us so we can keep them as a memento?' And just like that, the international students, fully treasuring them, took with them all the flags.

Zhu Minshen's role in organising a menacing and at times violent mass demonstration by foreign students in the heart of Australia's democracy had no repercussions for him. According to a well-connected journalist I spoke to, ASIO 'shat themselves'; but Australia's supine political leaders looked on benignly, none wondering how their counterparts in Beijing would react if the Australian ambassador took it into her head to organise a rowdy protest by thousands of angry flag-waving Australians in Tiananmen Square. Quite the reverse. In 2012 Australia's newly minted foreign minister, Bob Carr, appointed Zhu to the federal Chinese Ministerial Consultative Committee. The photo shows him flanked by Carr and Prime Minister Julia Gillard.[150] It does not seem to have struck anyone as odd that Zhu should serve simultaneously on high-level advisory panels for both the Chinese and Australian governments.

Zhu's role in Dastyari's downfall

In April 2015 the federal Department of Finance sent the rising Labor star Senator Sam Dastyari a bill for $1670.82 to cover an overspend on his annual travel budget of $95,279.63. Instead of paying it, Dastyari forwarded the invoice to Zhu's Top Education Institute, which settled the account. When the facts were reported by Latika Bourke in *The Sydney Morning Herald* on 30 August 2016, all hell broke loose.[151] What was most galling to the public, and most revealing about the relationship between the NSW Labor Party and wealthy Chinese donors, was the casual way Dastyari asked a rich mate to bail him out. Dastyari seems to have regarded Top Education as a convenient fund he could dip into when needed. Huang Xiangmo's Yuhu Group was another. When in 2014 he was presented with a legal bill for $5000, Dastyari asked Huang to pay it for him, and Huang was happy to oblige.[152] Handing out money to politicians is standard practice in China.

Before he was placed by the Labor Party on the Senate ticket, Sam Dastyari was the party's chief organiser and fundraiser in New South Wales at party headquarters, which he moved from its notorious Sussex Street HQ to Parramatta. In early 2014 he was flown to China by the Chinese People's Institute of Foreign Affairs, and took the time to visit Huang's Yuhu headquarters as well as Huawei, the telecommunications behemoth that (as we'll see) has worked assiduously to spread its influence in Australia. In January 2016 he was flown to China by the Australian Guangdong Chamber of Commerce (run by Huang Xiangmo). The trip was also supported by the International Department of the CCP. Huang plied him with expensive bottles of wine. It seems like a long time ago that influential figures from the Labor

Right were flown to the United States by the CIA to attend workshops on how to resist communist influence.[153] In a wonderful irony, in 2016 the outgoing US ambassador, whose predecessors had meddled in Australian politics for decades, issued a public warning about the dangers of foreign interference in our political process.[154] Even so, compared to the PRC's 'full court press', American meddling has been child's play.

Dastyari attempted to make up for his sins by paying the $1670.82 Zhu had given him to an Indigenous foundation. Why he thought that would make the perception that he is in bed with rich donors go away is a mystery. He just didn't get it. The foundation did though, and returned the money to him. And his sins were compounding. Primrose Riordan reported that in the parallel world of wooing Chinese-Australian voters, Dastyari, standing next to benefactor Huang Xiangmo, had directly contradicted ALP policy on the South China Sea dispute. He soothed his Chinese-speaking listeners with words his speechwriter might have lifted from the *People's Daily*: 'The South China Sea is China's own affair. On this issue, Australia should remain neutral and respect China's decision.'[155] It seemed like a propaganda coup for Beijing and Dastyari's intervention was reported triumphantly in the official Chinese press. The *People's Daily* elevated him to the status of a key international supporter of China.[156] Journalists in Canberra dug up Hansard records showing Dastyari grilling defence and foreign affairs officials about the advice they were providing to the government on Australia's stance on the South China Sea.[157] (In 2010, as a reformist NSW Labor Party secretary general, Dastyari told a branch meeting: 'We need to end the practice where seven people meeting in a Chinese restaurant decide everything'.[158])

Dastyari had used his position at other times to advance the interests of Beijing over those of his country of citizenship. In 2014 he argued that Australia should not oppose China's aggressive and illegal imposition of an 'Air Defense Identification Zone' over islands in the East China Sea claimed by Japan. These are the pro-Beijing efforts of Dastyari that have come to light.

When Prime Minister Turnbull accused Dastyari of taking 'cash for comment' the senator was offended.[159] How it must have pained him when his billionaire donor Huang Xiangmo withdrew an enormous promised donation of $400,000 before the 2016 election because Labor would not change its policy on the South China Sea, an astonishing attempt at cash-for-policy uncovered by Nick McKenzie for his *Four Corners*/Fairfax investigation.[160]

The Dastyari affair exposed the rot at the heart of Australian democracy. As Rory Medcalf, head of the National Security College at the ANU, observed: 'Imagine how Beijing would react if entities linked to a powerful foreign government were paying travel and legal bills for rising stars in the Chinese polity'.[161] Labor leader Bill Shorten did not ask for Dastyari's resignation. Instead, defending the hyperactive senator as an asset to the Opposition, he gave him a slap on the wrist. With the government piling on the pressure, and the media targeting the senator for his hypocrisy in calling for financial malfeasance to be rooted out of the banking sector, Dastyari was eventually forced to step down. Yet within months he was being rehabilitated. In February 2017 he was appointed a deputy whip and in June Melbourne University Press helped out by publishing a memoir, which the ABC promoted with a soft-focus profile on *Australian Story*. Medcalf wrote that the affair is 'a priceless lesson in the vulnerability of Australian democracy to foreign influence in a contested Asia'.

In the end, it was Dastyari's relationship with Huang Xiangmo that killed off his political career. In late November 2017, Fairfax journalists Nick McKenzie, James Massola and Richard Baker reported that some weeks after the Dastyari affair broke, the senator travelled to his benefactor's Mosman mansion to warn him that his phone was probably being tapped by intelligence agencies.[162] On the same day a tape recording was aired of Dastyari's infamous press conference at which he contradicted the Labor Party's policy on the South China Sea. His comments were carefully scripted, and not off the cuff as he would claim. Prime Minister Turnbull pointedly asked why a parliamentarian would be giving counter-surveillance advice to a foreign national who is close to a foreign government. 'Whose side is Sam on? Not Australia's it would seem.'[163] The pressure was too much for Labor leader Bill Shorten and he sacked Dastyari.

It was left to Nick O'Malley, Philip Wen and Michael Koziol to make the larger point. Dastyari, they wrote, 'is just a minor cog in a far-larger machine of political gift-giving and influence-peddling that China has built' to advance its influence in Australia and across the globe.[164] Medcalf suggested that the affair 'could be the moment when the expensive tapestry of China's "soft power" influence in Australia ... begins to unravel'.[165] Perhaps, but there is a long way to go.

When the Australian media were full of stories about wealthy Chinese influencing Australian politics and apparently winning over politicians to a pro-Beijing view, the *Global Times* editorialised about anti-Chinese paranoia and 'hyping up the alarm toward China', a line adopted by some commentators in Australia. Taking its usual bullying tone, it warned us that talk is one thing but if Australia 'resorts to real actions to hurt China's security such as sending warships to the South China Sea, it is bound to pay a heavy price'.[166]

In July 2016 the jingoistic tabloid that often gives vent to the more uninhibited feelings of the leadership had scolded Australia when our government called for the international arbitration ruling on the South China Sea to be respected, reminding us of our 'inglorious history' as an offshore prison, charging us with hypocrisy over our claims to the Antarctic, accusing us of sucking up to China when our economic interests call for it, saying, 'China must take revenge' on Australia, and finishing with a flourish by dismissing us as 'not even a "paper tiger"'. Australia is only a 'paper cat at best', a paper cat that will not last.[167] This kind of nationalist hyperventilation from the CCP's id is amusing, until one understands the expansionist aggression at the highest levels of the state that is behind such hyperbole.

Political plants[168]
Donations to political parties are the most obvious potential channel of influence for the CCP in Australian politics. However, a small but growing number of Chinese-Australians with close links to the CCP now occupy influential roles in this country's political structures. It's a trend that goes to the heart of concerns about the undisclosed sway of Beijing's agents of influence in Australian politics. The New South Wales Labor Party is the epicentre of PRC influence in Australian

politics. Mapping the byzantine links would take a book in itself but it's worth noting here that the state party's current leader, Luke Foley, seems to have been won over to a point of view pleasing to Beijing. In September 2017, standing next to Ernest Wong (the upper house MP close to Huang Xiangmo), Foley denounced Australia's reluctance to sign up to One Belt, One Road (OBOR), Xi Jinping's grand strategic vision to use China's surplus capital to fund infrastructure development around the world.[169] Borrowing CCP language, which he may have picked up on a trip to China organised by Wong, he said a 'Cold War mentality' was harming our friendship with China. Australia should follow New Zealand's lead and sign up to OBOR without delay.

Foley's colleague Chris Minns, a rising Labor star and potential party leader, employs James Zhou on his staff. Zhou is an executive vice-president of the ACPPRC and close to Huang Xiangmo.[170] (Zhou also operates an export business to China with the wife of Chris Minns.) Minns has paid tribute to Ernest Wong and travelled to China in 2015 as a guest of the CCP and another of Huang's United Front organisations. He was accompanied by federal Labor's shadow treasurer Chris Bowen, who in September 2017 gave a landmark speech indicating that a Labor government would link the northern Australia infrastructure fund to OBOR.

If the Labor Party in New South Wales is the epicentre of Communist Party influence, the Liberal Party is not far behind. On the night of the 2016 federal election, a beaming Craig Laundy was photographed surrounded by two dozen campaign supporters who had helped him retain the seat of Reid for the Liberal Party. Laundy had snatched the inner-western Sydney seat from Labor three years earlier. In the photograph the MP has his arm draped around the shoulders of a man in the middle of the group. His name is Yang Dongdong and he claims to be a 'community adviser' to Laundy. He is also a conduit to the large Chinese-Australian community in his electorate.

In response to inquiries, the Liberal MP disavowed Yang's claims about the pair's closeness and dismissed the assertion that Yang has worked as an adviser, despite one of Laundy's own staffers, when asked about the connection, saying that Yang is a 'consultant' and is 'quite close' to him.[171] Whatever the precise nature of the relationship between the pair, it is clear that Yang has sought to stay close to Laundy throughout the Liberal MP's political ascension. All the while, Yang Dongdong has nurtured his intimate and long-standing links to the Chinese consulate in Sydney and, according to Yang himself, sought to advance the objectives of the CCP.

Before coming to Australia at the end of 1989, Yang was deputy secretary of a branch of the Chinese Communist Youth League in Shanghai. Yang proudly reminisces on social media about his time in the party hierarchy, sharing old photos of himself at party meetings. In 1988 his name was inscribed on the Chinese Communist Youth League honour roll. He was named 'Shanghai New Long March Shock Trooper' for his work as a cadre devoted to the Youth League's mission of promoting the party.[172]

Arriving in Sydney not long after the Tiananmen Square massacre, Yang appeared 'desperate' to establish his eligibility for the visas being offered to Chinese students, according to Qin Jin, a prominent member of the Sydney anti-CCP group Federation for a Democratic China.[173] Yang joined the federation and attended protests. He also claimed to have been an underground Christian in Shanghai, a ruse used by some migrants from countries like China that ban religious freedoms to bolster their case for protection or residency. Eventually, he was granted permanent residency and then citizenship.

There are few traces of Yang's early Australian pro-democracy activities in his more recent dealings. Yang now promotes himself as one of the strongest supporters of the CCP in Australia. His old friend Qin Jin believes Yang's first loyalty is to Beijing. He is a member of the Overseas Committee of the All-China Federation of Returned Overseas Chinese as well as its subsidiary, the Shanghai Federation of Returned Overseas Chinese. In one of Yang's company profiles, the groups are described as part of the CCP's United Front Work Department.[174]

Yang's 2014 application letter to be admitted to the Overseas Committee of the Shanghai Federation of Returned Overseas Chinese—which he posted temporarily online—details his activities on behalf of the Chinese government. At the end of the document he refers officials who wish to make further inquiries about him to the Chinese consulate in Sydney or the embassy in Canberra.[175]

Yang, whose business activities have included a Sydney telecommunications shop, also claims in the application that he has supplied phone services to visiting Chinese presidents, the Chinese Olympic Committee, Chinese diplomats and even the Chinese navy when in Australia.[176] Former diplomat Chen Yonglin confirms these claims, which suggest Yang had somehow acquired a high level of trust from Chinese officials at the consulate and the embassy, and within China's intelligence services.

Yang was trusted to provide phones to consulate staff from his Ashfield phone shop. Chen says Yang once reported to the consulate that ASIO had approached him to provide information about these phones. ASIO's policy of not commenting on operational matters means that this cannot be verified.[177]

At the 2008 Olympic torch relay in Canberra, Yang was the leader of two 'order maintenance corps'.[178] He had earlier told a Chinese state media outlet that he would protect the torch from Tibetan independence activists.[179] Inspired by what he saw, he penned an article titled 'This evening by the lake we did not sleep—a record of Australia protecting the Olympic flame'.

Yang organised a number of anti–Dalai Lama protests to disrupt the Tibetan leader's visits, including one in 2015.[180] And he is also an honorary president of the Sydney Council for the Promotion of Peaceful Reunification of China, aligned with the United Front Work Department and easily confused with the Australian Council for the Promotion of the Peaceful Reunification of China, headed by Huang Xiangmo.

Via several Australian organisations with an ostensible focus on business development, including the Australia China Business Summit, Yang has gathered contacts in the Liberal Party. In 2015, then prime minister Tony Abbott wrote to him ('Dear Dong Dong'), thanking him for his hospitality. In 2016 he was snapped joining a toast with Prime Minister Malcolm Turnbull and China's ambassador, Ma Zhaoxu. He has been photographed with a range of Liberal Party heavyweights including Andrew Robb and New South Wales premier Gladys Berejiklian (who with Liberal powerbroker John Sidoti handed him a community service award).[181] His closest contact, though, is the Member for Reid.

When Craig Laundy, who is heir to one of the largest pub empires in Australia and lives in an $8 million mansion in Hunters Hill, won the federal seat of Reid for the Liberal Party in 2013, it was the first time the Liberals had held it since its creation in 1922. The seat of Reid is centred on Burwood, Drummoyne and parts of Strathfield in Sydney's inner west. Around ten per cent of its voters were born in China.[182] After his election, Laundy was promoted to the front bench as assistant minister for multicultural affairs. Now serving as assistant minister for industry and science, the Turnbull ally has been earmarked as a future cabinet minister.

Laundy's election campaign in 2016 received energetic support from Yang, who is also a founder of the Liberal Party's Chinese Council.[183] The Labor Party was blindsided by a highly effective Chinese-language media campaign,[184] with Yang writing an article praising Laundy and rallying dozens of Chinese-Australians to take to the streets to campaign for the Liberal Party candidate.[185] Laundy has become one of federal politics' most vigorous promoters of the China–Australia friendship. He's candid about his desire to work with the Chinese consulate in Sydney. In 2016, Yang's business group arranged for him to meet China's consul general, Gu Xiaojie. The consulate later reported that during this meeting, the MP expressed his willingness to 'closely cooperate with the Consulate … and to deepen practical cooperation [between the two countries]'.[186]

When Laundy met the billionaire donor Huang Xiangmo in December 2015, the ACPPRC reported that the Liberal MP 'highly praised how the ACPPRC under Huang Xiangmo's leadership had done much work for Australia and China'. He 'expressed his admiration for Huang's penetrating opinions on Australia's culture, economy, history, and so on, and expressed appreciation for the contributions of Huang's compassionate philanthropic services'.

When Yang organised a protest against the visit by Japan's prime minister, Shinzo Abe, to the Yasukuni Shrine in March 2014, Laundy appeared alongside Yang waving Chinese and Korean flags. Laundy also promised to deliver a petition from the protesters to the foreign minister, the prime minister and parliament, and to call on them to support the protest.[187] He wasn't going against the government's position, but his spear-carrying on an issue cranked up by Beijing's propaganda machine raised eyebrows among China watchers.

Yang claims in his application to the Overseas Committee of the Shanghai Federation of Returned Overseas Chinese that he 'had a federal parliamentarian make a speech in parliament opposing Abe's veneration of spirits'. It must have been Laundy because a *People's Daily* article—headlined 'Voices of opposition to Abe's visiting Yasukuni Shrine appear in the Australian parliament for the first time'—triumphantly reported on Laundy's and fellow Liberal backbencher David Coleman's criticism of Abe.[188] In July 2015, when Tibetans staged a protest outside China's Sydney consulate in Camperdown, Yang's business group claimed on social media that Craig Laundy had issued a statement 'strongly condemning the conduct of the thugs who attacked the Chinese Consulate in Sydney'.[189] In his media release, Laundy wrote that after talking to 'Reid's local Chinese-Australian community' he condemned the 'violence' of the protesters. They had, in fact, done no more than take down the Chinese flag. He made no mention of the cause of the protest, the death in a Chinese prison of a prominent Tibetan monk.

After mining magnate Clive Palmer made insulting remarks about Chinese people, Yang Dongdong led the anti-Palmer protests. Laundy turned up too, along with Sam Dastyari. In his application Yang claims to have lobbied parliamentarians and the government to put pressure on Palmer, finally leading to Palmer offering a 'most genuine and sincere apology'.[190]

Noting his consistently pro-Beijing stances, China's state-run media treat Laundy as a go-to man for comment. The MP has been quoted in several CCP-controlled newspapers praising China's contribution to Australia, and has featured on the cover of *BQ Weekly*, the inflight magazine of China Southern Airlines and Air China, under the headline 'Chinese migrants represent the Australian dream: In an exclusive interview federal MP Laundy says no to anti-Chinese people'.[191]

Laundy is confident his pro-Beijing comments and relationship with Yang don't raise any serious questions about whether he has been the target of a campaign of influence. Yet he applied a different judgement to Senator Sam Dastyari's Chinese connections. In September 2016, Laundy described Dastyari as 'at best wilfully reckless'.[192]

Two days after the story broke about Yang Dongdong's extensive CCP connections, it was reported that, after a meeting with Liberal Party powerbrokers, Yang had withdrawn his name from the party's list of candidates for the Burwood Council elections.[193] Placed second on the ticket, he was a certainty to be elected. Liberal Party sources had seen Yang as a godsend: well connected, a proven fundraiser and a vote-winner among some Chinese-heritage residents. They must have calculated that the ninety per cent of non-Chinese constituents would have no sympathy for putting a man so close to the CCP on their local council.

There are numerous other people close to the CCP actively involved in Australian politics, including elected representatives, more often from the Labor Party. A couple of dozen Chinese-Australians stood for election to local councils in New South Wales in September 2017. Around half a dozen of those elected are linked to United Front organisations.

5

'Beijing Bob'

The 'China-Whatever' research institute

By 2015 Huang Xiangmo had graduated to semi-official commentator on China's political affairs, acting as a representative of the Chinese-Australian business community in his comments on free trade. Perhaps inspired by Chau Chak Wing's links to the university world, in May 2014 Huang donated $1.8 million to the University of Technology Sydney (UTS) to establish the Australia-China Relations Institute (ACRI). He now moved in the big league. And he would have won plaudits in Beijing, which had recently announced it would be making a large investment in think tanks at home and abroad.

To run the new centre he recruited the previous Labor Party foreign minister and former New South Wales premier Bob Carr, whose inexperience in the academic world was more than made up for by his friendships with powerful people in Australia and abroad.[1] The incumbent foreign minister, Julie Bishop, accepted the invitation to launch the centre. At the opening ceremony, Huang sat next to the Chinese ambassador, Ma Zhaoxu, and perhaps reflected on how much he had achieved in such a short time.[2] If Huang retained any doubts, they would be swept away six months later when he was invited by the ambassador to be his guest at a grand dinner at Parliament House in Canberra for the visiting president, Xi Jinping.[3] Whatever dark thoughts Beijing may once have harboured for the Jieyang developer, it was now smiling on him.

Measured by the greater prominence of Beijing's worldview in Australian public debate, Huang's $1.8 million investment in ACRI has paid off in spades. In 2016 the vigilant Primrose Riordan reported that ACRI's reports had been quoted in federal parliament as authoritative sources for defending the benefits of the China-Australia Free Trade Agreement.[4] They were used especially to ridicule the anxieties of Labor and the trade unions about the migrant worker provisions of the agreement. Bob Carr may have been a stalwart of the Labor Party but a range of conservative MPs gleefully used the China-funded think tank's work to excoriate the Labor Party for its scepticism about the terms of the deal. In parliament, Andrew Robb cited ACRI's work in praising Australia's decision to join the Asian Infrastructure Investment Bank, Beijing's challenger to the World Bank. The institute's economist and deputy director James Laurenceson had been singing the praises of deeper trade links with China. Now, even Beijing's friends in the Pakistani media go to Laurenceson to 'hail China's commitment to an open, global economy'.[5]

Ensconced at ACRI, Bob Carr declared that 'we take an unabashedly positive and optimistic view of the Australia-China relationship'.[6] It was a long way from the stance he took in 1989 when, as New South Wales Opposition leader, he addressed a rally in Sydney Square two days after the Tiananmen Square massacre on 4 June. Denouncing the single Marxist–Leninist party as a 'ludicrously outdated notion', he told the 10,000 mourning protesters that only a multi-party democracy in China could guarantee there would be no more bloodshed.[7] As late as 2012 the foreign minister was criticising Australia's 'pro-China lobby'.[8] How things change.

At ACRI, Carr would soon be talking up the role of his new institute in pushing the China-Australia Free Trade Agreement through parliament in the face of union criticism of its labour provisions.[9] He attacked those who believe Australia is being supine towards China as governed by 'Cold War instincts'. His approach is 'pragmatic' while theirs is 'heavily ideological'. Senior Labor sources say that Carr has been pushing an aggressive pro-China position in Labor caucuses, and especially within the New South Wales Right faction.[10]

UTS abuts Chinatown and hosts large numbers of PRC students (5500 in 2015, or over forty per cent of all international students[11]). As we'll see, it has also cultivated extensive links with Chinese universities.[12] Although it was a modest donation compared to the $20 million Chau Chak Wing had given the university for its landmark Frank Gehry building, the university readily agreed to take Huang's $1.8 million.[13] It made Huang an adjunct professor and appointed him chairman of its board. The billionaire boasted that he 'personally appointed' Bob Carr as ACRI's executive director.[14] When I asked UTS deputy vice-chancellors Glenn Wightwick and Bill Purcell in person about this, it was an awkward moment, but they confirmed that Huang had asked for Carr. In their written reply they dodged my question. Professor Huang, as he is now referred to in China, confided to a journalist that he had someone else in mind, 'an even more influential figure from politics' (which, if true, could only have been Kevin Rudd), but settled on Carr because 'I consider him to be a very good academic'.[15]

In response to written questions from me, UTS said it had carried out rigorous due diligence on Huang Xiangmo, does not see its association with him as a liability and made him an adjunct professor because of his 'outstanding achievements as a business leader and contributor to international relations'. In November 2017, when it was revealed that Senator Sam Dastyari had visited Huang at his home and warned him about his phone being tapped, Prime Minister Turnbull said that Dastyari was assisting a foreign government and that Huang Xiangmo is 'a foreign national with close links to a foreign government'.[16]

ACRI under pressure

For anyone who comprehends academic freedom and intellectual independence, ACRI was stained from the outset. The Chinese Communist Party condemns academic freedom as a 'polluting' Western idea,[17] but any university worth its salt would have insisted that a donor have no influence on the appointment of university staff. But, like so many Australian universities today with their sights on a pile of cash, UTS seems not to have cared too much about the niceties of tradition.

The institute insists that it 'has a fully independent, academically rigorous and transparent research agenda'.[18] Beyond the initial $1.8 million donation, its funding situation has been opaque, although the university said in 2017 that it would be publishing a full statement of its finances.[19] Some UTS academics, who have watched the whole affair with dismay, have their doubts, with one characterising the institute's seminars and publications as resembling 'party propaganda of the Chinese Government'.[20] Another Australian China expert, James Leibold of La Trobe University, put it more bluntly, saying UTS had made a mistake by allowing Huang to chair the ACRI board: 'It becomes a backdoor propaganda vehicle for the Chinese Communist Party among the Chinese Australian community.'[21] Bob Carr and the university reject this characterisation.

The launch ceremony in May 2014 was a grand affair. China's ambassador, Ma Zhaoxu, welcomed the institute as 'a big step forward in the China–Australia relations studies', going so far as to hail it as 'a historic event in our bilateral relationship'. Stepping up to the podium, our foreign minister agreed with the ambassador that no two countries enjoyed the same degree of 'interdependence and complementary ties'.

The ambassador could be confident that he would not be later embarrassed by any of ACRI's work. Any kind of sharp criticism of China—for its human rights abuses, for example, or its persecution of dissidents or its bullying of neighbours—would be *verboten*. The institute's research is expressly based on 'a positive and optimistic view of Australia-China relations'.[22] An optimistic view is, according to the dictionaries, one disposed to hope for the best or tending to look on the bright side of things. Carr has claimed that the institute would 'not shy away from thorny dimensions of the relationship such as human rights'. To date ACRI has not got around to publishing anything on China's human rights record, even though it has become more oppressive and brutal. Questioned by me about this, Bob Carr listed a number of statements and publications he said were 'critical' of China.[23] To me, they read more like advice to Beijing about how to avoid mis-steps in spreading its influence.

For his advocacy of pro-Beijing positions within the New South Wales and federal Labor Party, Carr has been nicknamed 'Beijing Bob'.

It seemed apt when in September 2015 a photo appeared in the *People's Daily* depicting Carr hosting a Sydney meeting with Zhu Weiqun, former deputy head of the United Front Work Department and chair of the Ethnic and Religious Affairs Committee, one of whose tasks is to denounce the Dalai Lama and the 'Tibet separatist clique'.[24] Next to Carr, dressed in a golden robe, stood the 'living Buddha' Tudeng Kezhu, a party flunky who goes to Beijing to 'represent' the Tibetan people. Carr's praise for China's historical claim to Tibet (invaded by the PLA against armed resistance in 1950) and his hostility to the Dalai Lama predate his appointment as foreign minister. In a 2011 blog post titled 'Don't meet this cunning monk', Carr urged Prime Minister Gillard to shun the spiritual leader with a 'mischievous agenda in pursuit of theocratic power', whose aim is to create ill feeling between Australia and China.[25] The post was deleted before he took up his role as foreign minister. When I asked him about his hostility to the Dalai Lama he replied that his 'approach to Tibet is that of the Australian government'.[26]

Carr and UTS now downplay Huang's role and highlight the 'mix of sources' of funding. (Carr has said he does not see the Huang funding as a liability and would welcome another donation from him.[27]) Huang's $1.8 million donation to UTS for ACRI was soon augmented by another $1 million from Zhou Chulong.[28] Who is Zhou Chulong? For someone able to make million-dollar donations it's extraordinarily difficult to find out anything about him, and it's curious that the university and ACRI usually omit any mention of him.[29] All that we know from accessible public records is that he is the CEO of a property company in Shenzhen named Zhiwei Group, and an honorary president of the ACPPRC.[30] Zhiwei and Huang's Yuhu Group are both members of the Shenzhen Chaoshan Chamber of Commerce. In October 2013 Zhou bought a $5.6 million house in the same Mosman street that Huang Xiangmo lives in (but lower down).[31]

UTS has claimed that it carried out 'due diligence' on Huang Xiangmo and could not find 'any impropriety'.[32] The deputy vice-chancellors told me that UTS pays an external company to conduct due diligence assessments against various 'risk parameters'. (I wondered whether the company in question is able to access Chinese-language documents.) They were not sure whether a due diligence had been carried out on Zhou Chulong.

There is a worrying backstory to the establishment of the institute.[33] In 2005 the university had come under direct pressure from the Chinese government over a student union art exhibition that referenced Falun Gong. Consular officials expressed their displeasure and insisted that the material be taken down. The university did not comply and soon after found that its website in China had been blocked, depriving it of its prime means of recruiting Chinese students. Enrolments from China collapsed causing 'very major damage', according to vice-chancellor Ross Milbourne. Other universities were reported as having been targeted and the sector had 'gone to ground'. UTS's website was blocked again after it was reported that Milbourne said UTS would have to suffer losses in order to take a principled stand. The Chinese government never admitted any connection. John Fitzgerald said the incident sent a clear message: 'free and open critical inquiry is not necessary, perhaps even not wise, for a university planning to deepen its engagements with China'.[34]

By bankrolling ACRI Huang gained the opportunity to rub shoulders with Julie Bishop, Labor frontbencher Tanya Plibersek, the Chinese ambassador, Ma Zhaoxu, and various other luminaries. An unanticipated bonus arrived in February 2016 when Brian Wilson took over as the university's interim chancellor. Wilson was then chair of the Foreign Investment Review Board, which had been ordered by the treasurer to crack down on illegal purchases of prestige properties by wealthy Chinese.

The Sydney Morning Herald argued that Carr had used his position at ACRI to become 'one of Australia's most strident pro-China commentators'.[35] In perhaps the most withering put-down, John Fitzgerald wrote of 'the monotony of Carr's China-Whatever comments'.[36] Never one to take criticism lying down, Carr hit back, describing his critics—including Australia's first ambassador to Beijing, Stephen FitzGerald, who said he would not have taken Huang's money—as 'people on the cold warrior fringe of Australian politics' who harbour resentments.[37]

In September 2016, under intense media scrutiny, UTS deputy vice-chancellor Glenn Wightwick was bravely defending the institute's 'high quality and extremely important research'.[38] If the board of a research institute oversees the quality and direction of its research, what were the qualifications of chairman Huang for that role? Three weeks after the Dastyari affair broke Huang stepped down, citing too much public attention on 'supposed Chinese influence'. Liberal Party grandee Philip Ruddock, who headed the Australia–China Parliamentary Friendship Group, was asked to chair the board. (Ruddock's daughter Caitlin works as the head of corporate relations at UTS.[39]) But the university knew it was on a hiding to nothing and announced a review of its governance.[40] It decided to abolish ACRI's board. Primrose Riordan wrote: 'ACRI was subjected to a major governance review, which will now result in the board Mr Huang chaired being dissolved and the institute coming under a new management committee headed by deputy vice-chancellor Professor Bill Purcell, UTS confirmed.'[41]

Joining the deputy vice-chancellor on ACRI's new management committee was the university's Director of International, Leo Mian Liu.[42] Liu oversees the university's international matters; he's also its Vice-President, Global Partnerships.[43] In Chinese media he's consistently referred to as the 'executive director of ACRI'. The ACPPRC describes him as ACRI's 'executive dean'.[44] In the early 2000s Leo Mian Liu was a diplomat at the Chinese consulate in Sydney. The defector Chen Yonglin knew him, and has said Liu was responsible for managing the consul general's itinerary.[45] Liu has maintained deep links with the PRC and United Front organisations in Australia, not least as an adviser to the ACPPRC.[46] He encouraged members of the council's Youth Committee to become actively involved in politics and demonstrate their strength in Australian political circles. A May 2015 meeting of the Youth Committee, attended by Huang Xiangmo and his deputy Simon Zhou, was addressed by NSW Liberal member of the Legislative Council Mark Coure, who offered the young members some tips on how to enter politics.[47] Federal Liberal MP David Coleman helped by explaining the structure of Australian politics and the personal qualities needed by future parliamentarians.

Leo Mian Liu is also the president of the recently established Beijing Foreign Studies University (BFSU) Alumni Association of Australia.[48] The BFSU is one of the main Ministry of Foreign Affairs universities.

The vice-minister for foreign affairs (and former ambassador in Canberra) Fu Ying sent him a congratulatory message for the occasion. According to the *People's Daily*, Leo Mian Liu was standing on the Tiananmen Square viewing stage during the 2015 military parade commemorating the defeat of Japan seventy years earlier.[49] The platforms, which flank the Gate of Heavenly Peace, are only accessible by official invitation. Liu told the *People's Daily*: 'As an overseas Chinese person, I vividly experienced the might of the Ancestral Nation'.

In place of a board ACRI now has a Chairman's Council consisting entirely of corporate sponsors. When I asked about the chairman I was told there isn't one.[50] When I asked who chairs the Chairman's Council I was told no one chairs it. Bob Carr says it does not hold meetings, although he does discuss ACRI's research plans with its members.[51] In 2016 Huang told the *Australian Financial Review* that 'Yuhu would also withdraw from ACRI's Chairman's Council', and in July 2017 Bob Carr said that ACRI no longer receives funds from Huang Xiangmo. In July 2017 Yuhu was still listed as a paid-up member, as was Zhou Chulong's company, Zhiwei Group.

A true friend of China

On its opening, deputy director James Laurenceson expressed his hope that 'ACRI will become the main go-to source for comment' on China.[52] Some journalists are helping him out. On the other hand, Carr's star in China has never shone brighter (although he says he has no influence there).[53] In the official Communist Party media he has become the go-to man for the real story on Australia–China affairs. In late 2014, *China Daily* was quoting the director of ACRI praising the benefits of the free trade agreement, and reassuring the masses that Australia respects 'core Chinese interests'.[54] Throughout 2015 readers would see the 'former FM' arguing that 'the United States had to accept China's new status', praising the 'brilliantly successful' reforms of Deng Xiaoping, admiring China's 'strength as a civilization', urging Australians to work harder at understanding China's 'different political values', and attacking the 'racist lie' spread in Australia about the free trade agreement's generous labour import provisions.

In 2016 Carr was reported in the stridently nationalistic *Global Times* (part of the *People's Daily* stable of newspapers) as proclaiming that our relationship with China is 'the best thing Australia has going for it over the next 15 years', declaring that critics of China were guilty of a 'McCarthyist indictment' driven by a Cold War rage, and dismissing concerns about Chinese investment in strategic assets as an 'anti-China panic' and 'hysteria'.[55] He warned his compatriots not to see China 'through US eyes'.

When in August 2016 treasurer Scott Morrison decided on the basis of security advice to prevent a Chinese state-owned enterprise buying the New South Wales electricity distributor Ausgrid, the *People's Daily* went to Bob Carr to explain it. In the article, titled 'UTS ACRI: Australian government's blind xenophobia', Carr said the decision would damage our economic relationship with China. He reassured his Chinese readers that Morrison's decision 'does not represent the Australian people's views'.[56] Carr, it seems, keeps his finger on the pulse of the Australian people.

In yet another exclusive interview with the *People's Daily* soon after the launch of ACRI, Carr revealed that his greatest achievement as foreign minister was to deepen Australia–China bilateral relations. 'I believe that Australia and China should cooperate more in drawing up foreign policy—the cooperation of our two countries on national security will be strengthened—and this is also [ACRI's] current research direction.'[57] In words that could have been penned by the Chinese newspaper's editorial writers, he added: 'Australia and China have common interests. We both seek peace, we both hope to avoid territorial disputes, and to carefully deal with disputes.'[58]

In 2017, at the same time that the PRC was building military facilities in their traditional waters, Bob Carr was arguing that China would not attempt to bully its Southeast Asian neighbours.[59] Asian leaders have recognised the new strategic situation and have got on board, he wrote. This represents China's 'regional success'—a 'positive and optimistic view' if ever there was one.

In an earlier interview, Carr had stressed that Australia should always remain neutral: 'From the beginning I've thought it extremely important that Australia should in any situation express and reiterate its neutral position, especially regarding the China-Japan dispute in the East China Sea.'[60] He then demanded foreign minister Julie Bishop 'explain her comments' after she said 'China doesn't respect weakness'. Carr had fallen into the trap of telling the leadership in Beijing what it wanted to hear.

When Donald Trump, famous for his criticisms of China's predatory economic policies, was elected to the White House, Carr took the opportunity to drive home his vision for an Australian pivot to China. Trump, he wrote, talks with 'sneering contempt about democracy itself—prosecuting his opponent, not accepting the election outcome'. Who would want to align with a nation where that kind of thing happens? Unaware of the hole he'd dug for himself, Carr argued that Australia must leave behind our 'sentimentality' for the US alliance, reduce our ties with an America in decline and focus on the enormous importance of China to the Australian economy.[61]

Carr's deputy, James Laurenceson, soon followed him into print, warning against anti-Chinese populism in Australia.[62] If any country is a drag on Australia's economy, it's the United States rather than China, he argued. China promises a kind of golden future, with much more scope for further trade, investment and flows of workers from our northern neighbour.

Perhaps inspired by Carr and Laurenceson, Huang Xiangmo too picked up his pen. On a Chinese-language website he wrote that with the election of Donald Trump Australians will be 'slaughtered' like sheep unless we strengthen our ties with China. The patriotic property developer informed us that it is now in our interest to cooperate with China more than ever.[63] In a 2015 article following the seventieth anniversary parade to mark the defeat of Japanese aggression, the *People's Daily* published an article under the heading 'Australian political figures: China is a core force in safeguarding world peace'. The journalist had interviewed three politicians, all of whom expressed their appreciation for China's role in the resistance to fascism. They were Bob Carr and his two amigos, Sam Dastyari and Ernest Wong.[64]

The *guanxi* among them has been tight. It was Sam who hatched the plan to parachute Bob into the Senate vacancy, and persuaded

Julia Gillard to make him foreign minister.[65] Bob had backed Sam to succeed Eric Roozendaal as New South Wales party boss. Ernest linked Sam to the Chinese donors.[66] Sam backed Ernest to be elevated to the Legislative Council. Huang Xiangmo boasted of appointing Bob to run ACRI. Huang paid Sam's bills. Eric now works for Huang. Ernest works with Huang at the ACPPRC. Huang helps fund the Labor Party.

Media deals

In May 2016, without any fanfare, a high-ranking Communist Party leader arrived in Australia. Liu Qibao heads the Chinese Communist Party Central Committee Propaganda Department, and as a member of the Politburo is among the nation's top twenty-five leaders.[67] The Propaganda Department is responsible for the Patriotic Education Campaign in China that has deeply transformed the country over the last twenty-five years. It is also responsible for media censorship, including instructing editors at compulsory weekly meetings on what can and can't be said. Abroad, it prosecutes China's program of 'political warfare'; its methods include influencing foreign business, university and media elites, who are courted through visits, exchanges and joint research projects.[68]

In a development that seasoned journalists still find hard to fathom, Liu was in Australia to sign six agreements with the major Australian media outlets, under which, in exchange for money from the PRC, they would publish Chinese propaganda supplied by outlets like Xinhua News Agency, the *People's Daily* and *China Daily*. Fairfax and Sky News (part-owned by Murdoch) agreed to publish or broadcast Chinese news stories.[69] *The Sydney Morning Herald, The Age* and the *Australian Financial Review* agreed to carry monthly eight-page lift-outs supplied by *China Daily*.

The visit was approvingly overseen by the acting secretary of the Department of Foreign Affairs and Trade, Gary Quinlan. The media agreements represented a coup for China's external propaganda campaign, which is believed to be backed by a $10 billion budget.[70] Although it went largely unremarked in Australia (after all, each of the major media outlets took the money), John Fitzgerald noticed that in China 'the party would trumpet the deal as a victory for its overseas propaganda to change world opinion'.[71] Fairfax carried a news story about the deal by its Beijing correspondent Philip Wen.[72] After all, it could not fail to report it.

Fitzgerald and Wanning Sun, two of Australia's best-informed China media analysts commented: 'Leninist propaganda systems work not by persuading people through what they say but by intimidating or embarrassing others into not reporting things that matter.'[73] The deals were a striking instance of China exploiting the openness of a Western system—and the parlous financial state of the mainstream media. The fact that there was no outcry about the deal—in which a powerful nation, ranking 176 out of 180 on the press freedom index, is given leverage over our media—is a sign of the fragility of the institutions on which we rely.

In November 2015 in Beijing, Bob Carr met with Sun Zhijun, assistant minister of the Central Propaganda Department.[74] A Chinese report on the meeting noted that '[b]oth parties consolidated the friendly relationship between Chinese and Australian media, deepening bilateral cooperation and exchange'. They also 'exchanged ideas on promoting relations between the two countries and other topics'. In addition to 'relevant comrades' from the Propaganda Department, senior executives from the All-China Journalists Association were also present.

Credulous journos

One of the deals signed in May 2016 was a memorandum of understanding (MOU) between Bob Carr's ACRI and Xinhua News Agency, the PRC's official news agency. ACRI was soon organising Australian journalists to undertake study tours to China. It is impossible for foreign journalists to visit China as journalists, unless they go through the process of official accreditation with an approved media outlet. So for Australia-domiciled journalists Bob Carr could offer something unique: a one-off, officially approved trip to China to write some news stories.

Carr emailed a number of senior Australian journalists inviting them on a five-day, all-expenses-paid 'fact-finding tour' of China. The itinerary showed that the components of the tour would be organised either by ACRI or Xinhua. Chaperones would be provided by the

All-China Journalists Association, a party organisation whose guide-lines stipulate that all journalists 'must learn to master Marxist news values'.[75] A number of Australia's most respected journalists took up the invitation, and in July 2016 Ross Gittins of *The Sydney Morning Herald*, Brian Toohey and Andrew Clark from the *Australian Financial Review*, Glenda Korporaal from *The Australian* and Shane Wright from *The West Australian* flew out for China.

The Central Propaganda Department's strategy seems to have paid off. In a series of articles, Ross Gittins gushed about China's amazing economic performance, its decisive decision-making, and its determination to become rich.[76] 'Sorry if I sound wide-eyed', he began, 'but I was mightily impressed when I visited China … Those guys are going places.' China is bold and impatient to build a better future, while we in Australia are fearful, riding our luck and hoping China will remain our gold mine. We are too timid to sign up to Beijing's grand One Belt, One Road strategy, Gittins told us, but the Japanese and South Koreans 'will be happy to eat the Chinese lunch we don't fancy'.

Andrew Clark was dazzled by the scale of China's 'breathtaking' transformation.[77] 'China is amazing,' he wrote. In the New China 'people seem taller, more animated, healthier, louder and happier'. (In fact, the evidence shows they are less happy.[78]) He did not pick up 'any sense of an Orwellian 1984 … emerging'. Besides, as there are so many new freedoms to enjoy with a decent standard of living, some political repression, he implies, is justified. The tour visited only the most exciting cities and the most gleaming corporate headquarters. Clark was impressed by Chengdu with its massive buildings and the world's busiest Louis Vuitton store. China is following its own path 'powered by the unique, ever-adaptable Chinese mind, with its unmatched ability to focus on the task at hand'. Yet, he warned his readers darkly, if Australians don't go along with its demands we might be scapegoated by China. Refusing to accept China's claims to the South China Sea, for instance, could see China 'giving the Australian kangaroo a proverbial clip over the ears'. China's rise is a fact of life and our prosperity depends on it.

Brian Toohey began filing stories before he got back from China. Perhaps spooked by the sabre-rattling of the *Global Times*, Toohey laid out one of the most bizarre pieces of strategic analysis I have seen.[79] The gist of it is that, because John Howard joined the Iraq invasion without good justification and so got us into a mess, Australia should just accept China's conquest of the South China Sea. If we, with the United States and other allies, were to challenge China's annexation we could certainly defeat China militarily (while crashing the global economy) but we could keep China down only by invading and occupying the Chinese mainland and then waging 'a protracted guerrilla war against millions of patriotic Chinese'. And so we should do whatever we have to do to avoid war. The choice is: acquiesce or mobilise the armed forces and end up in another Iraq.

This is the kind of appeasement advocacy Beijing is hoping for. But what really impressed Toohey on his tour was the massive investment in futuristic technology, which he witnessed in Shenzhen. He reproduced amazing statistics for Huawei, BYD and BGI (as it happens, the very same companies the other journalists were impressed by). Toohey too sees Australia as a 'frightened country', increasingly xenophobic about China's intentions. Banning Chinese ownership of Ausgrid's electricity network made no sense because there is no way China would risk damaging itself economically by engaging in spying. Besides, if they did, our spies would detect it and we would take the asset back.

The gleaming glass towers and new superhighways of Shenzhen seem to have had less impact on Glenda Korporaal than a scary briefing from a Chinese foreign affairs official. The official stressed how 'very disappointed' the Chinese government was when Australia supported the ruling of the arbitral tribunal in The Hague backing the Philippines against his country's claim to the South China Sea. Korporaal amplified the routine threats by talking up the prospect of war unless Australia changes its tune.[80] China, she reported, only wants peace and stability. Bob Carr was also at the briefing and urged China not to take Australia's talk about the importance of international law too seriously. The official, perhaps mollified, then urged Australia to accept more Chinese investment.

Some days later, Korporaal followed up with an article explaining how resisting China would damage our economic interests, which could be avoided if we stopped speaking out. She highlighted the official's threat: 'China hopes Australia does nothing to harm regional peace and stability.'

Shane Wright's report for *The West Australian* also operated as a megaphone for Beijing's bullying, repeating the official's threat that, should Australia back any US freedom-of-navigation exercises near the disputed islands, China will take 'very serious countermeasures' against us.[81]

What marks out the stories by these journalists, published in Australia's leading serious newspapers, is their lack of scepticism about what they saw and heard on this carefully planned and supervised exercise in influence. Two weeks after they left China an article from the All-China Journalists Association was published through *Xinhua*. Titled 'Impressions from visiting China: Why Australian journalists were moved to say their "expectations were exceeded"', it included short interviews with each of the journalists, who all talk about how impressed they were by China's economic and technological development.[82] The journalists had gone back to Australia, readers were told, and 'related to Australian society the historical opportunity that China's economic development gives to Australia, and impartially conveyed "China's voice".'

It's worth noting here that the All-China Journalists Association has other means of reaching into Australia. It is one of the funding partners of the Asia Pacific Journalism Centre (APJC), a not-for-profit organisation in Melbourne that aims to promote quality journalism in Asia. The APJC teams up with the All-China Journalists Association to arrange study tours to China for Australian journalists, with the help of China's official media. The centre's director, John Wallace, tells me no money changes hands. The exchange programs focus on the economic relationship, he says, suggesting that human rights and press freedom are off limits.

After the June 2016 Fairfax–ABC *Four Corners* investigation of Chinese money in Australian politics, John Wallace took to the keyboard to defend Chau Chak Wing.[83] The stories were motivated by racism, he suggested, and lacking hard evidence of Chau's links to the CCP. He presented the billionaire as an innocent victim of poor journalism. Wallace claimed that, compared with the treatment given to Chau,

Rupert Murdoch's political activities are accepted as normal. In truth, the powerful American media tycoon has been subject to frequent and harsh criticism for his political interventions by authors and commentators in the United States and Australia. Wallace makes no comment on the state of China's media landscape, where a program like that aired by *Four Corners* is impossible. Wallace told me he wrote the article for the 'Chinese in our communities who were voicing concerns over aspects of the coverage'. Of course, there are other Chinese voices in Australia who cheered the program; for them it was a sign that we are at last waking up to what is happening here.

Perhaps surprised by how well the study tour had worked, Bob Carr took another delegation of the nation's journalists to China in March and April 2017. The visit coincided with the detention and interrogation of UTS academic Feng Chongyi by the Tianjin State Security Bureau. Judging by the stories filed by Malcolm Farr and Troy Bramston (each in China 'as a guest of ACRI'), Carr freed Feng single-handedly.[84] While some back in Australia may have puzzled over Carr's public silence, wrote Farr, the ACRI boss was pulling strings behind the scenes. Carr had been told by 'a Chinese official' that China does not appreciate megaphone diplomacy (of course it doesn't). 'China likes to settle issues in a quiet way' (which is true when they screw up as badly as this). The only source mentioned for the story was the hero of it. The headline on Farr's piece read: 'Bob Carr's backroom manouevering ends Chinese nightmare for Sydney academic'.

For his part, Troy Bramston wrote that he could 'reveal' that Carr 'made private representations to senior Chinese officials'. He too echoed Beijing's message—'we don't like megaphone diplomacy'. It's true that Beijing is unhappy when the rest of the world criticises it for its violation of human rights, like detaining academics who dare to interview human rights lawyers.

Others involved in the saga saw it differently. After his return, Feng Chongyi was asked about Carr's role in having him released. He denied that backroom negotiations played any role. He said that Malcolm Farr's claim that a softly, softly approach is best is 'absolute rubbish'.[85] If you do anything 'under the table' and keep it secret, then it gives the authorities absolute control, and they can do anything.[86]

Let's call the Australia-China Relations Institute for what it is: a Beijing-backed propaganda outfit disguised as a legitimate research institute, whose ultimate objective is to advance the CCP's influence in Australian policy and political circles; an organisation hosted by a university whose commitment to academic freedom and proper practice is clouded by money hunger, and directed by an ex-politician suffering from relevance deprivation syndrome who cannot see what a valuable asset he has become for Beijing.

At least, he was a valuable asset until his pro-Beijing stance attracted so much criticism and ridicule that he lost much of his credibility as a public voice. His more recent actions indicate a bunker mentality. In January 2018 he was tweeting from Berlin that an exhibition he'd seen of Ming and Qing dynasty portraits could not be staged in Australia because we are 'locked in [a] McCarthyist anti-China panic' and museums would be too nervous.

6
Trade, invest, control

'Economic ties serve political goals.'[1]

In Australia, exports of goods and services account for nineteen per cent of our GDP.[2] The share is the same for China. In Germany it is forty-six per cent, in Korea forty-two per cent and in the Philippines twenty-eight per cent. In the United States it is twelve per cent.[3] Around a third of our exports go to China. They have risen quickly in the last several years, increasing our exposure, but as a share they may well have reached their peak.[4] While our export exposure to China is high, the overall risk is lowered because the share of exports in our GDP is modest.[5]

Yet according to some business commentators, if China were to sneeze, Australia would contract pleural pneumonia, so we must do nothing to upset the northern giant. Yet, if we are as vulnerable as they tell us, isn't the answer to look for ways of reducing our exposure, rather than accepting it as a fact of life?

How dependent are we?
ANU strategic studies professor Rory Medcalf points out that China is unlikely to use our biggest export, iron ore, to put pressure on us because the PRC relies on Australia for sixty per cent of its iron ore imports.[6] For other Australian exports, like coal, tourism and education, China has alternatives and would suffer less if it decided to punish us by buying elsewhere. We examine economic coercion in the next chapter,

but I suggest here that the Australian government and export producers should be analysing our vulnerabilities and taking measures to eliminate them. Instead we have trade ministers and state governments who seem willing to do anything China wants in order to increase our exposure.

The 2015 China-Australia Free Trade Agreement will make a small difference to our exports to China. But it was not really about trade; it was about investment. It explicitly agreed to treat Chinese investments no differently to investments by Australians in Australia.[7] (This provision in article 9.3 was ostensibly reciprocated but only an innocent would believe that reciprocity will prevail. While the agreement will be enforced in this country by the courts, Australian investors in China have no guarantees at all.) The threshold at which the Foreign Investment Review Board (FIRB) must screen investments was lifted to a much higher level (from $252 million to $1094 million, although lower for certain sensitive sectors).[8] And it's the flood of Chinese capital into Australia that is the real threat to our sovereignty.

To assuage public anxiety, China's friends like to compare the total amount of Chinese ownership of Australian assets with the substantially larger amount owned by American and Japanese companies. But the Americans have been buying for a century and the Japanese for five decades. The last decade has seen a huge surge in Chinese investment, one that is expected to continue at ever-higher rates for many years to come.

The figure that should have Australians sitting up and taking notice is this. Globally, Australia ranks second behind the United States as a destination for the massive capital outflow from China, but only just. According to a KPMG analysis, since 2007 the United States has received US$100 billion of accumulated new Chinese investment while Australia has accepted US$90 billion.[9] Given that our economy is only one thirteenth the size of the USA's, this means that proportionately twelve times more Chinese capital has poured into Australia than into the United States.

China's friends in the business community keep telling us that there is no reason to worry about these capital flows because we need all the foreign investment we can get. Happily for them, 2016 was a record year for Chinese investment in Australia—a record number of deals, record investment in Australian infrastructure, record investment in agriculture, and a record year for investment in Tasmania (on which more later).[10]

In the financial year 2016/17, Chinese ownership of agricultural land surged, increasing ten-fold to place China just behind the United Kingdom as the largest owner, each holding around a quarter of foreign-owned land in Australia.[11] With China's planners focused on overcoming the nation's growing 'animal protein deficit' this surge in PRC interest in Australian agriculture is set to continue. China's annual average meat consumption is on a trajectory to equal that of Taiwan (from 60 up to 76 kg per person per year), which 'will require an additional 15 million hectares of agricultural land—an area the size of England and Wales—which China simply does not have'.[12] While a number of countries (such as Brazil and Argentina) have taken measures to stop Chinese firms buying up their arable land, Australia's free trade agreement with China is removing barriers and global banks are lining up to facilitate the buy-up.[13]

Measured by bids for Australian assets emanating from greater China, investment proposals leapt from $9 billion in 2015–16 to $20.5 billion in 2016–17, accounting for fifty-four per cent of the value of all foreign investment proposals.[14] Over eighty per cent by value were targeted at energy, mining and utilities.

Reflecting the profound misunderstanding of China that pervades Australian elite thinking, former prime minister John Howard said: 'We can't apply a different standard to Chinese investment to investment from Japan or America.'[15] After spending pages trying to make out that state-owned enterprises (SOEs) are not controlled by the Chinese government, the Drysdale report—a report written jointly by ANU economists and a party think tank in Beijing, considered in the next chapter—makes the same mistake: 'There is no logical basis for treating the vast bulk of Chinese SOEs ... any differently from other potential investors in Australia'.[16] Claims that the new owner of the Port of Darwin, Landbridge, has close links to Beijing have no foundation, we are told, because 1.63 million private companies in China have party committees; it's just 'a natural result of China's political system' and nothing to be alarmed about. Even those claiming China expertise, like Linda Jakobson and Andrew Parker of the China Matters consultancy, make this naïve claim: 'Saying you don't want Chinese investment if it's connected to the

Communist Party is the same as saying you don't want Chinese investment at all.'[17] The major sponsors of China Matters are corporations with strong commercial interests in China, including Rio Tinto, PwC, Aurizon, Westpac and James Packer's Star casino group.[18]

But Chinese investment *is* different. Whatever their faults, American companies are not prone to act in ways dictated by Washington to suit America's strategic interests. And if they are tempted to do so, they must contend with a vigorous American civil society and an inquisitive media holding them to account. And of course US corporations have been prosecuted and fined heavily for engaging in bribery overseas. Howard's historical equivalence between anxiety over Japanese investment in the 1970s and Chinese investment today does not stack up. Discomfort with foreign influence is indeed part of the Australian character. But suspicion of Chinese investment is grounded in a political truth: it is subject to manipulation by a totalitarian regime bent on dominating Australia. That is entirely new.

The fact is we can and should apply a different standard to Chinese investment, one appropriate to the non-commercial goals often at stake. Responding to Jakobson and Parker's apologia for the CCP, a less innocent analyst, Geoff Wade, pointed out that China is 'openly utilising its financial clout globally to facilitate expanded strategic leverage. Chinese capital is, without doubt, being employed as a strategic tool.'[19] British, American and Japanese investors do not hail from one-party states that habitually use overseas trade and investment to pressure and coerce other countries into policy positions sympathetic to their strategic interests. For them the guiding principle is not 'economic ties serve political goals'. Nor do they bring modes of operating that are secretive, deceptive and frequently corrupt, and whose important decisions are often made by political cadres embedded in companies and answerable to a totalitarian party at home. Only when the Chinese state no longer operates in these ways should we treat Chinese investment like any other.

The party-corporate conglomerate

In December 2016, the industrialised nations of the world refused to grant China the status of 'market economy', something that Beijing badly wanted both for its practical benefits and its political value. The list of China's infractions of the standards of free market behaviour is long, from manipulating the currency to killing off competitors by dumping subsidised goods like steel on the world market, from misusing health rules to punish imports for political reasons to imposing a range of obstacles to foreign companies that Chinese investors do not face in the United States or Australia.

The problem is not that the government in Beijing interferes in the operation of the market. It goes far beyond that. The state and the market cannot be separated. The Chinese Communist Party is present in all major enterprises in China and manipulates or directly controls their decisions to achieve political and strategic aims. Australian businesspeople know that the Chinese companies they deal with have party committees but they dismiss these as relics of the past that have no bearing on their operation. Nothing could be further from the truth—and yet for Beijing, nothing could be more convenient to have foreigners believe.

Writing in the current affairs magazine *The Diplomat*, China analyst Greg Levesque notes that the CCP's policies of 'civil-military integration' and One Belt, One Road set out to deploy commercial actors to advance the party-state's global objectives.[20] SOEs are being strengthened and the CCP is exercising greater control over them. President Xi declared in 2016 that they should 'become important forces to implement' the party's decisions. Company boards are now expected to take guidance from the party committee before making major decisions.[21]

Party control is not confined to the SOEs which produce thirty per cent of China's industrial output.[22] In the words of one close observer, Yi-Zheng Lian, the CCP 'has systematically infiltrated China's expanding private sector and now operates inside more than half of all non-state firms; it can manipulate or even control these companies, especially bigger ones, and some foreign ones, too. The modern Chinese economy is *a party-corporate conglomerate*' [emphasis added].[23]

It's a mistake to think of party committees as political bodies that at times meddle in company management. They are in fact closely integrated into the management structure. The party secretary can often appoint and dismiss senior managers and nominate board members. He or she may chair the board or hold an executive position. In late 2016 the respected Caixin finance news group reported the 'growing number of Chinese state-owned enterprises that are merging the two roles' of chairman and party secretary.[24] A detailed study of the role of party secretaries in listed firms found that in ninety per cent of firms surveyed, the party 'heavily influenced strategy and policy because the senior managers were also CPC members … the role of party secretaries in the private sector is strong and influential'.[25] Larger firms (both private and state-owned) are more likely to have powerful party secretaries.

This mostly reflects the desire of the CCP to maintain control, but it is also true that having a powerful party secretary can be instrumental to the success of the firm because a secretary with strong political ties can bring business and clear paths through corrupt bureaucracies. (The same is true of China's universities, where the party head sits above the academic head of the university to ensure that the institutions serve party-state needs.)

Even so, in some SOEs tensions have emerged between the business direction preferred by the company board and the priorities of the party. And so in December 2016 it was announced that henceforth the secretary of the party committee and the chairman of the board must be the same person.[26] The reforms mean 'SOEs should strengthen the Party's leadership and at the same time improve the corporate governance structure'.

From the early 2000s the Communist Party adopted a policy of drawing capitalists and corporate executives into the party apparatus, such as through appointment to the Chinese People's Political Consultative Conference, and subjecting them to the party's chain of command in exchange for party favours. Billionaires, bankers and chief executives were encouraged to join the party. The methods available to persuade them to abide by the wishes of Beijing were hard to resist. Even a superstar entrepreneur like Jack Ma has been forced to succumb to Beijing's wishes when the state has a political or strategic favour to ask, saying, for example, that sending the tanks in against the students in Tiananmen Square was the 'correct decision'.[27]

Beijing's Australia strategy

China plans to dominate the world, and has been using Australia and New Zealand as a testing ground for its tactics to assert its ascendancy in the West. Two years ago I would have regarded such a claim as fantastic. But now, despite Beijing's determined attempts to conceal its ambitions and plans, so much evidence has accumulated that the conclusion seems irresistible.

According to historians, the ambition has lain dormant in the Chinese consciousness for a long time. It's been rekindled by the Patriotic Education Campaign described in Chapter 2. The campaign has embellished and given substance to the old idea of China as the Middle Kingdom, the centre of the world that rules the entire *tianxia* (All Under Heaven) in a harmonious universe of order. Whatever the historical accuracy of this idea, the old dream quickly became a believable ambition from the early 2000s as China's economic power expanded, and especially after the financial crisis of 2008, which seemed to expose the inherent weakness of the West and the superiority of China's unique development path. As one former Australian leader now very close to Beijing explained it, the panic on Wall Street shocked China's leaders. 'It demonstrated to China the days of their belief in the US running the financial system were coming to an end. And it was the financial crisis with Lehman Brothers and Wall Street which tipped the Chinese to moving away from a policy of "caution, understatement and reservation" to a policy of "clarity, assertion and ambition".'[28]

We saw in Chapter 1 that in 2004 president Hu Jintao and the Politburo decided to designate Australia as part of China's 'overall periphery' and asked the embassy in Canberra to formulate a strategy to subdue us. As we become aware of the regional and global strategies covering economic control, diplomatic pressure and military expansion actually being prosecuted by the Chinese party-state, we begin to see that, left unchecked, the internal subversion of our institutions and the relentless external pressures from Beijing, coupled with our own weakening commitment to democratic values, would see Australia become a tribute state of the resurgent Middle Kingdom.

Trade politics

When Andrew Robb was appointed Australian trade minister in September 2013, he made it clear to his officials that Australia would sign the free trade agreement with China without further delay. The officials had been in tough negotiations for ten years, resisting Chinese bluffs and pressures and slowly working towards a document that, they hoped, would reflect some kind of parity. After all, China is notorious for its use of sneaky ploys to damage competitors. And so the officials despaired when Robb swept in and said we're signing no matter what.

While experienced Australian public servants have worked out how to manage the system of flattery, courtship, pressure, manipulation and subtle threats of Chinese negotiators, Chinese officials have been running rings around our politicians for years. The 'can do' types are the easiest to hoodwink, especially those who believe they know it all because they have been 'doing business in China for years'. As journalist John Garnaut pointed out, the Chinese have a whole section, the PLA's Liaison Department, devoted to 'planning and executing external influence'.[29] Its effective motto is 'make the foreign serve China'.

One technique is to win over 'caring friends' who then serve your interests. The uncomplicated mining billionaire Andrew Forrest became such a friend, and then began attacking Australian politicians for not appreciating what the Chinese were offering us. Australia's hesitation to sign up immediately to China's Asian Infrastructure Investment Bank (AIIB) attracted a tongue-lashing from Forrest, whose words echoed Beijing's more or less precisely: 'Australia needs to be independent in this part of the world. We don't need to treat China as the enemy.'[30] It was left to John Garnaut to point out to this innocent abroad that his good friend and regular host in China, Xing Yunming, had all along been a lieutenant-general in the PLA's Liaison Department.[31]

Having decided to give the Chinese what they wanted, Andrew Robb had to get the free trade deal through the Senate. He took to the airwaves with a blunt warning: it's 'five minutes to midnight', he thundered. And if there was any more delay 'China will walk away and the biggest deal we have ever had with any country' will fall over. (More seasoned hands know that the second last move in any bargaining game is to start to walk away.)

The Australian Council of Trade Unions (ACTU) was worried about jobs; after all, the draft agreement would give Chinese companies special migration arrangements for large projects. The ACTU wanted stronger tests to make sure there were no Australian workers left unemployed by cheap imported labour. Unlike other trade agreements, this one would permit importation of semi- and low-skilled workers, probably under 457 visas. Although the immigration department was giving mixed messages, Chinese companies would not have to show that there were no Australians who could do the job.[32]

The Labor Party expressed reservations but in the end was not willing to make a fight of it. Its views were influenced by Bob Carr's ACRI, and by the commitment by the New South Wales Right faction—which had been 'bought and paid for by Chinese money'—to see the deal go through.[33]

The protections for local workers were weak, labour market experts concluded. But taking 'a positive and optimistic view', James Laurenceson at Bob Carr's China-funded think tank insisted that the protections were perfectly adequate.[34] The agreement would be 'a coup for Australia'. It was only a year earlier, before he joined ACRI, that in an article titled 'Why an Australian FTA with China has never stacked up' Laurenceson set out all the reasons why the free trade agreement with China is a bad idea.[35] Meanwhile in Beijing, the president of the Export-Import Bank of China, Li Ruogu, had been saying Australian labour costs were too high and we could solve our problem by opening up to larger flows of Chinese workers.[36]

The agreement was pushed through parliament. Article 10.4.3 of the binding treaty explicitly commits parties (read Australia) to ruling out any limit on the number of workers who could arrive from China and bans any 'labour market testing'.[37] We lost. Soon after his FTA triumph Andrew Robb left politics to work for Chinese companies, including Landbridge, the lessee of Darwin Port, which paid him $880,000 a year (including GST).[38]

Business analyst Ian Verrender would later observe that Minister Robb 'launched into a tirade whenever there was even a hint of scepticism about his FTA frenzy'.[39] In parliament Robb had gone low, accusing the Opposition of 'xenophobic racist activities', to which Labor spokeswoman Senator Penny Wong responded by saying local jobs should be safeguarded. Accusing China critics of racism and xenophobia is an effective tactic because it builds on white Australia's deplorable history, including anti-Chinese sentiment going back to the goldfields. Official media in China and pro-Beijing Chinese-Australians resort to the tactic often. Serious critics, of course, are motivated not by fear of foreigners but by fear of a ruthless dictatorship.

Independent analysis concluded that the benefits of the trade deal, touted as the greatest thing since the invention of the harbourside mansion, would flow almost entirely to China, and that Australia would lose from it. It was opposed, for example, by the hard-nosed, free-market economists at the Productivity Commission, which is especially critical of the legal rights that bilateral agreements grant to foreign investors.[40]

The Australian debate over our agreement with China reflected the usual blinkered, short-term perspective. We missed completely how it was understood in Beijing. As Geoff Wade put it, the agreement 'constitutes a key plank in China's global strategic aspirations'.[41] The latest stage in Xi Jinping's China Dream is the export of hundreds of billions of Chinese dollars around the world, targeting infrastructure as well as resources, energy and food industries. Opening economies up to these investment flows, and thereby gradually obtaining political leverage over them, is essential to the strategy. The agreement with China was not so much a trade agreement as an investment agreement, one heavily favouring China, and which reinforces the other elements of this grand plan: One Belt, One Road and the AIIB.

Most of China's recent trade agreements, Wade points out, are with allies of the United States: ASEAN, New Zealand, Singapore, Korea and Australia, with an EU agreement on the cards. The aim is to prise these nations or blocs away from the United States by making them more dependent on decisions in Beijing. Breaking up the US alliances is Beijing's foremost strategic aim.

In February 2017 state media in China was filled with the news that President Xi Jinping had vowed that China would lead a 'new world order' and 'guide' the international community to this end.[42] It was interpreted broadly as a response to the apparent withdrawal from global leadership of the United States under Donald Trump and the approaching end of the world order shaped by the West since the eighteenth century. Xi's speech followed one month after his appearance at the World Economic Forum in Davos where he claimed for China the mantle of world leader in 'economic globalisation' (the 'economic' ruling out leadership in human rights).

The reactions of netizens to a *Global Times* story about the passing of the China-Australia Free Trade Agreement were revealing:[43] 'While China continues to work with and trade with people of all nations for mutual benefits and a more peaceful earth, by contrast, the war mongering USA Government focuses all its energy and resources on instigating wars ... [and] supporting and arming ISIS terrorists'; 'China will do all that it can to show Australia its peaceful rise and not a threat to any country. China must wean Australia off Uncle Sam's tit'; 'no need to wean as this kangaroo will hop to where there's plenty'.

Assets for sale

For some years Australia has innocently welcomed all kinds of invest-ment from China. Public anxieties have been scorned as xenophobia. Warnings from intelligence agencies have been dismissed as Cold War thinking. Presenting ourselves as the most open economy had become holy writ among the economic, business and political elites. The United States government has learned to be more guarded. It has noticed, for example, Chinese companies attempting to buy land, ports and indus-trial facilities in close proximity to military installations. One wanted to build a wind farm next to a US naval weapons system training base.[44] We, on the other hand, are relaxed about a PLA-linked company buying the port that is vital to protecting Australia from any aggression from the north.

However, in 2016 the Turnbull government seems to have realised that Australia has a problem. The warnings of a handful of well-informed sources that the Chinese acquisition of certain assets was endangering the national interest seemed to be getting through. Turnbull had been persuaded by intelligence briefings. One of the government's first acts was to beef up the somnolent Foreign Investment Review Board (FIRB), which for years had been failing to effectively fulfil its mandate. American objections to the sale of the Port of Darwin to a Chinese company had rung an alarm bell.

The government appointed former ASIO chief and Beijing ambassador David Irvine to the board, with instructions that security considerations must be given a greater priority. To reinforce the point, in April 2017 Irvine replaced Brian Wilson as chair of the board. Wilson had been criticised for accepting, while FIRB chair, a position with a private equity firm specialising in Asian buyouts.[45]

In January 2017 the government also created a new body known as the Critical Infrastructure Centre, drawn from various agencies including ASIO and Treasury, to create a register of sensitive assets like power, ports and water facilities that may be in the sights of overseas buyers. It will provide a quick reference point for the FIRB.

Whether these new or beefed-up institutions have the resources and the resolve to tackle the problem is yet to be seen. And the same can be said of the federal government itself. After all, the two main political parties have been severely compromised by their links to Chinese benefactors and their infiltration by people whose loyalties lie in Beijing.

Several horses have already bolted. The penetration of Australia by China's 'party-corporate conglomerate' through ownership of important assets is deeper than most people recognise. A thorough review is impossible here—not least because no agency has kept track of it—but a few examples will give a flavour of it.[46]

Energy assets

The Chinese government-owned State Grid Corporation owns large chunks of our energy network, including part-ownership of three of Victoria's five electricity distributors and the transmitting network in South Australia. The giant Hong Kong–based Cheung Kong Infrastructure (owned by tycoon Li Ka Shing) owns other segments. EnergyAustralia, one of the big three electricity retailers with nearly three million customers in the eastern states, is wholly owned by China Light and Power, based in Hong Kong and close to Beijing.[47] Alinta Energy, one of Australia's largest energy infrastructure companies, was sold for $4 billion to Chow Tai Fook Enterprises, a Hong Kong jewellery retailer that had been 'scouring Australia for assets'.[48]

Electricity distribution is now combining telecommunications services, so ownership gives access to Australian internet and telephone messaging. In the case of TransGrid, for example, strategic policy expert Peter Jennings has pointed out that it 'supplies Australia's defence and intelligence facilities in NSW and the ACT and operates the third largest telecoms network in the country'.[49]

When in August 2016 the federal government blocked New South Wales from selling a 99-year lease on its power utility Ausgrid to either State Grid or Cheung Kong Infrastructure, pro-Beijing lobbyists complained that it was inconsistent. For them, Australia should continue making the same mistake in order to be consistent. Following its practice of waving through Chinese purchases of energy assets, the FIRB had given it a tick. When the treasurer said there were security concerns with Chinese corporations owning so much of our essential infrastructure, Bob Carr rushed into print declaring that Scott Morrison had succumbed to 'the witches' Sabbath of xenophobia and economic nationalism'.[50] *Xinhua* reproduced his words in an article criticising Australia's new concerns about Chinese investment.[51]

Strangely, in April 2017 the new security-conscious FIRB approved a $7.48 billion takeover of the big energy utility operator DUET by a consortium led by Cheung Kong Infrastructure. DUET owns a number of major energy assets including the strategically important gas pipeline from Bunbury to Dampier and a substantial portion of Victoria's electricity distribution infrastructure, giving it the dominant position in that state.[52] The same consortium already owned the gas distribution network in Victoria. This makes no sense.

Why should we be worried? One reason is the enhanced risk of spying, confirmed by the Australian Cyber Security Centre 2017 threat report: 'Foreign investment in the Australian private sector is creating new motivations and opportunities for adversaries to conduct cyber espionage against Australian interests.'[53] Another is simply that it gives Chinese companies a great deal of political leverage, and the ability to turn off the lights in a conflict situation. David Irvine has warned that Chinese hackers could already shut down our power grid.[54] So why are we making it easier rather than building protections?

If Australia became involved in a hot conflict between the United States and China, Beijing's capacity to shut down its enemy's power network would be a formidable weapon, one it would not hesitate to use if the stakes were high enough. We have now handed Beijing this weapon. In the United States, the electricity networks' control systems are already the target of serious cyber intrusion, perhaps by hostile powers looking for ways to shut them down should conflict break out.[55] Chinese owners of Australia's energy networks will not need to hack into the systems—they'll own them. The first hours of a modern war would be all cyber.

The penetration of China-linked corporations into Australia's energy infrastructure has a further worrying consequence. Energy Networks Australia is the peak body representing the companies that own this country's electricity and gas distribution networks. Half of those who sit on the board of Energy Networks Australia represent two Beijing-controlled or -linked corporations, State Grid and Cheung Kong Infrastructure.[56] In 2016 the peak body teamed up with the Commonwealth Scientific and Industrial Research Organisation (CSIRO) to publish a detailed roadmap for the transformation of Australia's electricity networks over the next decade.[57] There is nothing about Australia's energy networks and how they will evolve in the future that is not known in Beijing.

Ports and airports

A 99-year lease of Darwin Port was sold to a Chinese company with close links to the CCP in 2015. In 2014 China Merchants, a state-controlled conglomerate,[58] paid $1.75 billion to buy the Port of Newcastle, the world's biggest coal export port and close to the air force base at Williamtown. When the Port of Melbourne was sold to a consortium of investors in 2016, the Chinese state-owned sovereign wealth fund CIC Capital grabbed a twenty per cent share.

Chinese interests have had their eye on regional port facilities in Australia for some time. Townsville is the kind of area in which Chinese groups are trying to gain a foothold—poorer regions that see themselves as ignored by the metropolitan centre and are thirsting for funds (like Greece in Europe). Tasmania has been another target. Townsville is far-north Queensland's export hub, mainly for minerals and agricultural produce. Development sites in north Queensland, especially for tourism, have attracted a great deal of Chinese interest.

In March 2015 a delegation arrived in Townsville from government agencies in the southern Chinese cities of Guangzhou and Huizhou to explore investment opportunities as part of China's 'Maritime Silk Road initiative'.[59] According to the Queensland government, Townsville 'has been highlighted as a key possible partner in this project due to its port and the live cattle market in the region'.[60] The delegation signed an MOU with the Port of Townsville to cooperate on a plan to develop shipping between Townsville and Huizhou.

In 2013 Townsville mayor Jenny Hill warned that the port could be taken over by Chinese interests if it were privatised.[61] She was accused of 'dog whistling'. Perhaps she was aware that Townsville also hosts two of Australia's most important military bases, the air force base and the army's Lavarack Barracks, which houses, among other units, the Combat Signals Regiment. And Singapore, which the PRC has not been able to subdue, has signed an agreement with Australia for a very large program of military exercises in the Townsville Field Training Area.

In May 2017 it emerged that China is interested in building the new international airport at Badgerys Creek to the west of Sydney.[62] Alarm bells should be ringing. The airport will become the foremost departure and arrival point for travel to Australia and therefore a high-value target for close monitoring and tracking of the movements of all kinds of people of interest to the Chinese government—businesspeople, political leaders, dissidents, spies. With a comprehensive system of video surveillance combined with sophisticated face-recognition technology (now being rolled out across China), or simply access to airline booking systems, the entire traffic could be covertly monitored from Beijing.

This is not speculation. If a Chinese company built the airport I believe all of this is virtually certain to be attempted, no matter who then operated it. Would it, for example, be equipped with dozens of security cameras made by Hikvision, the world's largest CCTV manufacturer with links to the Chinese military? A 24-hour video surveillance system is being planned by Beijing for cities in Pakistan from Peshawar to Karachi as part of the massive China–Pakistan Economic Corridor project.[63] In China itself, the CCP is in the process of transforming the entire country into a kind of modern panopticon with every street, road and building under constant CCTV surveillance, and with masses of data, including facial images, being collected and analysed in a highly sophisticated computer system using cutting-edge artificial intelligence technology. Already there are 179 million CCTV cameras in operation, one for every seven citizens, and that figure is growing rapidly.[64]

One Belt, One Road

One Belt, One Road (OBOR)—also known as the Belt & Road Initiative (BRI)—is a grand strategic agenda designed to link China more closely with larger Eurasia as well as Africa and Oceania.[65] Inspired by the ancient Silk Road, and first mentioned by President Xi Jinping in 2013, it now has two routes, one over land and one across the seas. The driving force behind the strategic initiative is the vast sums of cash China has in reserve for investment and foreign aid. One powerful motive is to sustain China's economic expansion by sending Chinese money, businesses and labour overseas, with a view to diversifying energy supplies, stimulating underperforming home provinces, and cultivating outlets to fill China's huge industrial over-capacity for steel and other building materials. Yet its ambitions go well beyond economic ones.

Most of OBOR's emphasis is on building or acquiring infrastructure: ports, railways, roads, energy networks and telecommunications, all to promote 'connectivity'. To date there has been a particular emphasis on the construction or acquisition of port facilities—five dozen foreign ports, according to a 2017 Chinese state television report.[66] And while most emphasis has been on the westward land bridges to Pakistan, and through Central Asia to Western Europe and Russia, the sea route down through Indochina and Southeast Asia to Australia is of growing importance. It aims at 'building smooth, secure and efficient transport routes connecting major sea ports along the belt and road'.[67] Chinese companies, both private and state-owned, will be at the front line of the OBOR offensive.

The vital role of state corporations in OBOR was confirmed by the boss of the SOE supervisory commission, Xiao Yaqing, who wrote that SOEs contributed sixty per cent of China's outbound investment in 2016. The ten million CCP members who work at SOEs form 'the most solid and reliable class foundation' for CCP rule.[68]

OBOR was the brainchild of new president Xi Jinping and has acquired enormous political momentum in China. While sold as a new

phase of globalisation, beneath the lure of cheap money for development, OBOR is the practical manifestation of Xi's 'China Dream' of
restoring China to its rightful place, not through military conquest but
through economic domination. Xi's idea is a crystallisation of trends
that had been underway for some time, and feeds into other planning
efforts emerging from the new economic superpower keen to create a
world in which China can assume its rightful place, captured in the
phrase repeated ad nauseam 'the great rejuvenation of the Chinese
nation', the endpoint of the Hundred-Year Marathon. It therefore has
geostrategic as well as economic objectives. In the summary words of
one close observer:

> There is little doubt that President Xi views OBOR as the signature
> foreign policy theme of his leadership tenure and the practical
> embodiment of his 'China Dream' for promoting national rejuvena-
> tion and cementing the country's place as a leading world power.[69]

Some foreign observers seem mesmerised by the rise of China, charac-
terising OBOR as the defining trend of the twenty-first century and
echoing Beijing's benign story of 'win-win' cooperation. ('After colonialism, imperialism and hegemonism', one Chinese academic has
now dubbed China's new theory of global governance 'win-winism'.[70]
The CCP has turned a vapid American business slogan into its
state ideology.)

The funding of OBOR projects from China's vast reserves is taking
place through China's state-owned banks. China is also directing the
Asian Infrastructure Investment Bank—Beijing's multilateral bank,
endorsed and funded by Australia and many other countries, designed to
push out the World Bank—to fund OBOR projects.[71] In fact, as Wade
notes, the AIIB was created in order to fund projects under OBOR.

One Belt, One Road is a grand strategy to multiply China's economic
clout, including making the renminbi the main trading and investment
currency of those countries drawn into it.[72] Many nations have welcomed the promises of financial flows into development projects. But
some projects have run into trouble. When the Sri Lankan government announced it would sell the port of Hambantota to the China

Merchants shipping company (which owns the Port of Newcastle), the community rioted; the huge new industrial park promised as part of the Silk Road development would have dispossessed local farmers.[73] Local politicians said they did not want to become a 'Chinese colony'. At the industrial zone's opening the Chinese ambassador promised $5 billion and 100,000 jobs while local citizens including Buddhist monks fought police nearby.[74] The ambassador did not mention that the Hambantota port is strategically important to China's projection of naval power in the Indian Ocean. In July 2017, Sri Lanka found it necessary to sell a seventy per cent stake in the port to China in a bid to recover from the heavy burden of repaying a Chinese loan obtained to build the facility. The creation of crippling indebtedness is a powerful Chinese tool under OBOR.[75]

Other nations, particularly those with a history of conflict with China, like Vietnam and India, are far more sceptical, seeing the New Silk Road as a formidable means for China to advance its strategic as well as its economic dominance. An Indian scholar has argued that China is using OBOR as 'the silk glove for China's iron fist'.[76]

China already dominates some small and poor nations in Southeast Asia (such as Cambodia and Myanmar) and Africa (Namibia, Angola). Its growing influence in Latin America prompted the head of Mexico's trade agency to say, 'We do not want to be China's next Africa'.[77] The PRC exercises great leverage through its provision of credit, control of infrastructure and ownership of natural resources. OBOR will intensify that process. Already, state-owned and state-linked operators are investing in infrastructure all over Southeast Asia, including ports, airports, railways, energy networks and dams. Ports are particularly valued because of China's dependence on sea trade and for their strategic functions in times of peace and conflict.

It would be naïve to try to separate the flow of OBOR investment funds to countries like Malaysia and Indonesia from China's commitment to controlling the South China Sea. Resistance to its efforts to compel all nations to accept its de facto annexation of this vital economic and strategic zone will weaken as its economic influence expands, not least through the explicit plan to connect up the infrastructure of ports, roads and railways across the region.

More alarmingly, the role of the PLA in protecting Chinese assets and citizens along the OBOR chain is under active discussion among military strategists.[78] There appears to be an emerging consensus that the PLA should be deployed to protect Chinese interests along the Belt and Road, but varying opinions about whether the PLA has the capability. One expert reviewing the debates concludes that the PLA 'pays great attention to the One Belt One Road' and that 'the relationship between the protection of Chinese overseas interests and the use of the PLA in time of peace is growing stronger'.[79]

A 2017 Pentagon report anticipated a growing global PLA footprint to match the spread of China's economic assets, noting that China's naval base in Djibouti on the Gulf of Aden will see the PLA Navy stationed permanently abroad for the first time. And it mentions the Chinese maritime militia, a vast reserve army of military-trained civilians working in the fishing industry and ports. Its tasks include intelligence gathering and 'rights protection', including intimidation of rival fishers in places like the South China Sea.[80] Andrew Erickson, a professor of strategy at the US Naval War College, wrote that under PLA direction 'China's maritime militia plays a central role in maritime activities designed to overwhelm or coerce an opponent through activities that cannot be easily countered without escalating to war'.[81] The militia has received renewed support under President Xi. Based on the company's own documents, Geoff Wade pointed out that the new Chinese owner of the Port of Darwin, Landbridge, operates a unit of the maritime militia.[82]

We need to project ourselves forward ten or fifteen years, when Chinese investment in infrastructure abroad approaches the expected scale so that China's continued economic health and global influence are dependent on highly valuable but far-off assets. If control over those assets is jeopardised by a local revolt, a blockade or nationalisation, then it would be only a matter of time before China sent its armed forces abroad to protect Chinese-owned facilities and Chinese citizens. Military strategists are already discussing how the PLA could be used to protect assets built under OBOR schemes.[83]

Isn't that precisely what the United States did for decades in Central and South America? Is it far-fetched to envisage circumstances in which the PLA or its maritime militia is mobilised to protect Chinese assets in Australia from any attempt to take them back?

The defence and intelligence establishment in Canberra, who see OBOR as another means to buttress China's global ambitions, is now divided against the economic departments and DFAT, for whom the economy rules.[84] Yet when investments are mostly led by state-owned enterprises and are responding to a strategic plan worked out in Beijing, thinking only about the economic returns to Australia becomes a form of wilful blindness.

The Australian OBOR connection

Beijing has its eye on Australia's north. As early as November 2014 Australia was being linked to OBOR by none other than Xi Jinping in his address to the Parliament of Australia. 'Oceania is a natural extension of the ancient maritime silk road', he said, 'and China holds an open attitude towards Australian participation in the 21st century maritime silk road.'[85] He explicitly focused on Australia's north, saying that 'China supports Australia's implementation of the northern development plan'. (The northern development plan's greatest advocate has been Gina Rinehart, who funded a major lobbying campaign through the Institute of Public Affairs resulting in the Liberal Party adopting it before the 2013 election.) A year later at the G20 summit the Chinese president returned to the theme: 'China is willing to align its Belt and Road initiative with Australia's northern development plan, and encourage Chinese companies to participate in infrastructure construction in northern Australia.'[86]

Between the two speeches, in August 2015 treasurer Joe Hockey and the trade minister, Andrew Robb, talked up OBOR when they met with the head of China's powerful National Development and Reform Commission, Xu Shaoshi. The *People's Daily* enthused:

Both sides recognised that China's OBOR initiative and international production capacity cooperation have a lot of points in common with Australia's northern development initiative and the national infrastructure development plan. Both sides were willing to increase the breadth and level of cooperation between their countries by linking up their development strategies.[87]

The Chinese embassy in Canberra was fully briefed to begin promoting the integration. The day after, 14 August 2015, ambassador Ma Zhaoxu gave a speech at the ANU in which he spoke of:

> how China and Australia could jointly build the '21 [sic] Century Maritime Silk Road'. Australia is highly relevant to the initiative. The Maritime Silk Road will connect China's eastern coastal cities, across the South China Sea into the South Pacific. Australia is a major country at the end of this route.[88]

China's anxiety about its long-term food security has led it to designate agricultural developments in northern Australia as eligible for state-backed investments.[89] By the middle of 2016 some 900 potential OBOR projects in Australia had already been identified.[90] In November 2016 Beijing dispatched former foreign minister Li Zhaoxing to Canberra to give a public speech talking up OBOR,[91] and in February 2017 the foreign minister, Wang Yi, arrived to reiterate China's willingness to align the belt and road initiative with our northern development plan. (He also said that China wanted to link OBOR to Australia's National Innovation and Science Agenda.)[92]

Since then it has been all systems go for the Australian government. In February 2017 new trade minister Steve Ciobo was boosting OBOR, with the head of the National Development and Reform Commission, Xu Shaoshi, noting how the new Critical Infrastructure Centre, which will list sectors that require automatic scrutiny, would remove obstacles for Chinese investors.[93]

Needless to say, Australia's business and political elites have fallen over themselves to embrace OBOR and encourage its spread across Australia. Andrew Robb is perhaps its most enthusiastic spruiker.[94] BHP director and chairman of Orica Malcolm Broomhead is also a fan. Both have been enticed onto the board of the Australia-China Belt & Road Initiative (ACBRI), an outfit fronted by three little-known people with no obvious connection to OBOR but set up by the National Development and Reform Commission in Beijing.[95] ACBRI describes itself as 'an engagement platform that enables Australian and Chinese industry leaders to articulate clear business opportunities' available through OBOR.

Among other objectives, ACBRI aims to 'facilitate the interconnectivity of China's infrastructure construction plans with the rest of Asia'. Despite its likely Chinese government provenance, DFAT supported it with a grant of $20,000. Under its auspices Andrew Robb led a delegation of twenty senior Australian business executives to China to explore business opportunities in the Belt and Road project pipeline.

OBOR has found more immediate acceptance in New Zealand, with the National Party government willingly signing up to it. The New Zealand OBOR Council has brought together pro-China elements including Johanna Coughlan, who is the sister-in-law of former prime minister Bill English and chairs both the Council and the so-called OBOR Think Tank. The OBOR lobby has generated a stream of opinion pieces aimed at stimulating public support, even though there appears to be little political resistance, other than from Winston Peters, who opposed New Zealand joining OBOR and often warned of the dangers of PRC domination.[96] Since becoming New Zealand's foreign minister at the end of 2017 Peters has performed a *volte face*, praising the PRC, suggesting it has much to teach us and chiding those who harp on about 'the romance of freedom'.[97] What happened?

Consistent with its strategy of spending money to win over academics and opinion makers, the Chinese state is funding seminars and conferences to explain and promote OBOR in Australia, with the University of Queensland and the University of Sydney at the forefront. The support of some Australian academics can be bought quite cheaply. In 2015 Premier Li Keqiang made it clear that overseas Chinese are expected to help advance the OBOR agenda by using their 'advantages in capital, technology, management, and business networks'.[98]

In December 2016 the official Xinhua News Agency reported that a meeting of Confucius Institutes around the world agreed to advocate for OBOR. As well as offering language training for all of the local workers employed by Chinese companies, the Confucius Institutes could act as 'think tanks', so authorising them to expand their operations in nations like Australia.[99]

China's northern Australia strategy is not mere talk. In January 2016, a *People's Daily* report on the joining up of OBOR and northern Australia noted that 'Australia's northern gateway', Darwin, is only a five-hour flight from China's southern coast.[100] The vexed issue of the sale of the Port of Darwin lease is a perfect case study of the extent to which the misunderstanding of China reaches to the very top of Australia's political and military establishment.

China's propagandists have launched an online campaign using cartoons showing adorable Western children singing the praises of Xi's One Belt, One Road—'everyone can make friends', they trill—and a loving father reads a bedtime story to his little girl extolling the wonders of this great 'opportunity to move globalisation forward'.[101] The videos are probably made by the secretive Fuxing Road Studio, responsible for a bizarre 2015 video in which American-accented cartoon characters sing ditties praising the Thirteenth Five-Year Plan.[102] The cute Anglo kids present China as the new bastion of free trade and international cooperation. One expert familiar with China's continued restrictions on trade and investment describes the campaign as 'beyond ironic'. None of this raises any suspicions of Chinese intentions for Australian strategic thinker Hugh White, who advises that it is in Australia's interest to sign up.[103]

However, by March 2017 others in Canberra were pouring cold water on the hype. During the visit of Premier Li Keqiang, it was made clear that Australia would not be signing a memorandum linking OBOR to the Northern Australia Infrastructure Facility. DFAT was keen on signing, while Defence was nervous. At the top, the feeling was that we ought not to sign up to something we don't understand. From Beijing, Australian business consultant and former ambassador to China Geoff Raby lamented the influence of the defence/security establishment which, he said, was placing too much emphasis on 'values' rather than economics. Yes, those old softies at ASIO and the Department of Defence were at it again. Down the road from Raby's Beijing office, Renmin University professor of international relations

Graham Tidy/Fairfax Syndication

After the Tiananmen Square massacre on 4 June 1989, Prime Minister
Bob Hawke announced that Chinese students in Australia would be allowed to
stay in the country. It turned out that few of them were pro-democracy activists,
although many more pretended to be.

Outside Parliament House at the 2008 Olympic Torch relay in Canberra, Tibetan autonomy supporters were outnumbered and roughed up by thousands of angry Chinese students bussed in from all over Australia by the Chinese Embassy.

Beijing's United Front strategy aims at silencing all criticism of the Chinese Communist Party (CCP) in Australia. Pro-democracy activists, Falun Gong practitioners, and supporters of Tibetan autonomy have been in its sights. These groups are hardly heard nowadays.

'Sydney Opera House was draped in red with Chinese characteristics,' bragged the *People's Daily* in 2016, after the NSW Government approved a plan by a front organisation of the CCP to turn the Sydney Opera House red as a Chinese New Year stunt.

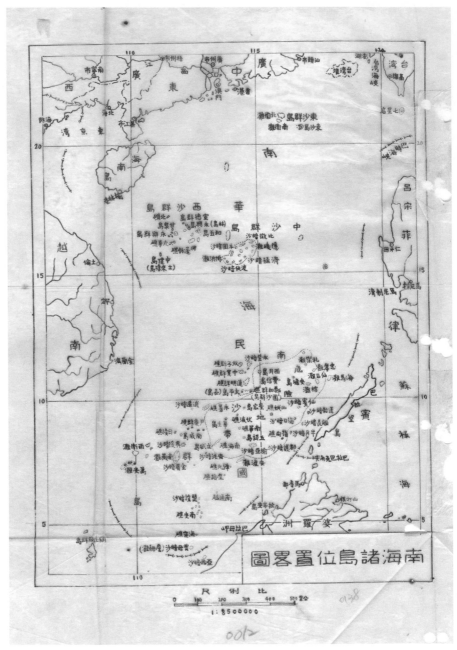

This is the original map showing the 'nine-dash line' drawn by hand in 1947, two years before the CCP took power in China. It's the basis for China's occupation of islands in the South China Sea. In July 2016 an international tribunal in The Hague ruled that China's claim to 'historic rights' within the defined area has no legal basis. China attacked the ruling and continued to build navy bases on reclaimed islands.

Prime Minister Malcolm Turnbull, businessman Huang Xiangmo, Liberal MP Craig Laundy and his 'consultant' Yang Dongdong at a Chinese New Year celebration in 2016. Yang Dongdong was exposed as having close links to the CCP.

In 2017 Labor leader Bill Shorten condemned Julie Bishop in federal parliament for associating with Huang Xiangmo after Labor Senator Sam Dastyari was criticised by the government for having improper dealings with the wealthy donor. Dastyari would later be forced to resign from the Senate when accused of giving 'counter-surveillance advice' to Huang at a visit to his Mosman home.

Bill Shorten photographed with Huang Xiangmo before the first Dastyari affair in September 2016. According to a Fairfax–ABC investigation, ASIO advised both major parties not to accept donations from Huang Xiangmo or Chau Chak Wing because they are suspected of being conduits for interference in Australian politics by the CCP. They have denied that they operate on behalf of the CCP.

Huang Xiangmo with Prime Minister Turnbull and Phillip Ruddock in 2016. Craig Laundy is obscured behind Huang. Chinese New Year events have become propaganda exercises operated by groups guided by the CCP and with funds from Beijing.

Australian National University Vice-Chancellor Brian Schmidt flies the flag with ANU PhD student and Chinese Communist Youth League propagandist Lei Xiying. While studying at ANU, Lei produced a virulently patriotic video, with martial music and goose-stepping troops, which went viral in China. On his social media account, he wrote about 'dumb c**t Aussies'.

In 2016 the 'Australian Eighth Corps' of the People's Liberation Army (PLA) (aka the Australia Chinese Ex-services Association) dressed in PLA uniforms and held a variety show in Sydney's Hurstville. The former Chinese soldiers wanted to 'revive the life of the barracks'. At its 2017 Congress, the CCP reaffirmed that the party 'shall uphold its absolute leadership' over the PLA.

A note from the Department of Defence's assessment of the national security implications of granting a 99-year lease over the Port of Darwin to a company linked to China's military. It reads: 'Chris, I held a telecom with the Landbridge CEO (at his request and recommended by Treasury). This is a private company, Australian managed, and operated with a significant degree of autonomy by Australian based people. You will see that they intend to employ an Australian management team also for the Darwin Port.' Beijing has been running rings around us, and Defence is no exception.

Shi Yinhong was closer to the mark: '[O]n the Maritime Silk Road project, Australia has been hesitant because of a fundamental disagreement over the South China Sea.'[104] Yet in September 2017 Labor's shadow treasurer Mark Butler announced that a Labor government would link the $5 billion Northern Australia Infrastructure Facility to OBOR.

7

Seduction and coercion

In August 2002 the media jubilantly reported that an Australia-based consortium had just won, against fierce competition, a contract to supply natural gas to Guangdong province. Then prime minister John Howard declared that winning the bidding for the $25 billion gas supply was 'a gold medal performance' and the fruit of close engagement with China.[1] To press the Australian case, Howard had met President Jiang Zemin more times than any other world leader. It was a close-run thing, with Australia's chances of beating Qatar, Malaysia, Russia and Indonesia looking poor only two weeks before the contract was agreed. Yet Australia pulled it off, and in business circles Howard has been surrounded by the aura of a commercial winner ever since.

The *People's Daily* reported, perhaps with a suppressed smile, that the 'Australian side expressed its excitement over its largest single export order'.[2] While Australians congratulated themselves, in fact we had been played by Beijing, and in a way that has been paying off for China ever since. Chen Yonglin, who at the time was a political officer in the Chinese consulate in Sydney and had been following events closely from the inside, later revealed that the Guangdong government was about to award the contract to Indonesia, which tendered the lowest price, until the CCP's Central Committee in Beijing ordered it be given to Australia. 'They thought that Australia was really important,' said Chen, 'and that at the time Australia had totally turned towards America, so they thought we should use economic means to bring Australia back.'[3]

Aware of how quickly Australia jumps when an economic string is pulled, from then on Beijing would 'use economic measures to guide Australia'. After all, Prime Minister Howard had refused to meet the Dalai Lama while Beijing dangled the carrot of the $25 billion deal.[4] A month after the deal was struck, the chairman of the National People's Congress, Li Peng, made a visit to Australia to congratulate Howard on winning the contract and to 'enhance mutual trust, broaden common ground and deepen cooperation' between the two countries.[5] The 2002 gas deal was the starting gun for the 'China is our future' craze that now dominates elite thinking in this country, exactly as Beijing planned it. Chau Chak Wing is said to have played a pivotal role in the negotiations and made enduring friendships, not least with John Howard, who has been a guest at Chau's 'imperial palace' a number of times.[6]

China's fifth column in Australia

One of China's most effective instruments of economic statecraft is the making of dire but vague threats of economic harm to a country that displeases it. It works because governments believe the threats. As we will see, China is willing to make countries suffer. In Australia, China's threats are amplified by a corporate fifth column that has grown around the bilateral economic relationship, a business elite unwittingly beholden to a foreign master and undermining Australian sovereignty from within. This cohort of business leaders and their advisers shuttle between the two countries doing deals and making 'friends' (with people whose backgrounds and motives they only think they know).

The fifth columnists include many of the most powerful corporate figures in the land, those whose phone calls the prime minister and the treasurer answer. They are convinced they 'know China' and take it as given that Australia's future depends above all on deepening the economic relationship and not allowing politics and differences of 'values' to get in the way. They present themselves as operating in the 'national interest', but it is no coincidence that our 'national interest' always happens to coincide with China's. Their understanding of the options available has been narrowed by their enthrallment to Beijing.

Apart from the sway of China's powerful friends, there is a more diffuse reason for our sensitivity to economic pressure: the enormous influence of free-market thinking whose unspoken assumption is that the economy must come before everything else, including our freedom. China apologists repeatedly downplay or evade the importance of freedom and the threats to it. Or they insist that economic growth is the best way to guarantee freedom, as if money can *buy* the rule of law rather than corrupt it. In their globalist commercial worldview, national sovereignty is increasingly a relic of the past. As one senior Australian official sardonically put it to me, 'Who cares about the blood?'

'China is our destiny'

China is vital to Australia's future because of our economic dependence on it. Or so it is said. It's truer to say that the *perception* of our economic dependence gives China immense influence over Australia. It's widely believed, for example, that only our close economic relationship with China saved us from the 2008 global crash. Even though China did nothing for Australia other than continue to buy from us the iron ore and other resources it needed to fuel its growth, there is a widespread view that Australia should be *grateful* to China for saving us, that we owe China. Many Chinese believe this too. When a difference of view emerges, over the South China Sea, for instance, it is not uncommon for China's netizens to berate Australia for our *ingratitude* (often coupled with comments on how uncivilised we are). Instead of pushing back and turning the argument around—you should thank us for agreeing to fuel your boom with our resources—our commentators and politicians echo the view that we are somehow indebted to China.

Perceptions of our vulnerability to China's whims weaken our resolve to resist the growing penetration of the CCP's influence in Australia. Sensing this, Beijing repeatedly reminds us that a continued healthy economic relationship depends on a harmonious political relationship, with harmony guaranteed when Australia conforms to Beijing's wishes. As the head of ANU's National Security College, Rory Medcalf, writes: 'Essentially, Beijing wants from its commercial partners the same deal it has with its own people—economic benefits in return for acquiescence on politics and security.'[7]

In Chapter 12 we will consider the positions of some of China's chief apologists in Australia, but it's worth commenting here on how the 'China is our destiny' argument has played out in the public debate.

Linda Jakobson of China Matters—a non-profit company founded to 'stimulate a realistic and nuanced discussion of China'—bemoans the 'emotional outcry' over certain Chinese investments. It's true, she admits, that 'every senior business person in China is closely connected to the party', but, hey, that's how it is in China, so what are people worried about? If we could have a 'grown-up debate', Jakobson asserts, we'd realise that without Chinese investment we would spend less on hospitals and schools, so let's not have any more 'public spats' and just get on with it.[8]

A more sceptical commentator, Geoff Wade, shreds this kind of apologetics, showing the contradiction between party influence in Chinese corporations and the belief that those companies are only interested in profits. 'Capital … goes where the Chinese state wants it to go.'[9] So if state-directed Chinese capital is buying up Australian energy infrastructure, telecommunications and ports, having a 'public spat' over it is more grown-up than burying one's head in the sand.

In her 2017 book with Bates Gill, Jakobson argues that China and Australia–China relations are complex and subtle, so much so that it is hard for the authors to give a clear answer to any question.[10] They confess that when they migrated to Australia they were surprised at the level of ignorance about China in this country. Misconceptions, missteps and blunders are frequent in Australia's dealings. The public, and even many of the so-called experts, cannot grasp the complexity and subtlety, and so commentary and advice are best left to those, like them, who know China and truly understand.

The belief that 'China is our destiny' is in fact an exaggeration created by business interests and people who make their living from China, amplified by the media. Like former ambassador and China buff Stephen FitzGerald, they believe 'we are living in a Chinese world'.[11] Our only sensible response is to gain a deeper understanding of China and learn how to engage it with more sensitivity and skill. The latter is undoubtedly true; a greater understanding of China is the objective of this book. But it is a trap to believe that we now live in a Chinese world.

We don't. We live in a complex, multipolar world. We will live in a Chinese world only if we choose to.

Stephen FitzGerald argues that Chinese influence in Australia is mostly benign and welcome. He then sets out the various ways the CCP is interfering in Australian society and politics, and comments on how it is undermining our values.[12] How should we respond? He argues we must become so close to China that 'we can be a frequent, sought and heeded voice in Beijing'. Good luck with that. In effect, FitzGerald tells us that the only way for Australia to survive is to disentangle ourselves from the United States and make ourselves a 'friend at court' in Beijing—in other words, a client state. China has no strategic partners, but FitzGerald, spooked by Donald Trump, says we should become its first. Some of us are not yet willing to give up our national sovereignty, but FitzGerald wants big business in Australia to mobilise to support his vision and praises the Drysdale report (considered below), which neatly laid out and argued for Beijing's entire economic agenda as if it were our own.

We are inclined to see China's official propaganda as crude, sometimes laughable, and yet the extent to which Beijing has shaped the way we in the West view it is extraordinary. Even those who regard themselves as having a sophisticated understanding of China can be dupes. While wide-eyed businessmen like Andrew Forrest see nothing beneath the veneer created by Chinese officials, we expect more from our academics and economic advisers. For an example of this intellectual naivety we can't go past a report on the future of the Australia–China economic relationship published with great fanfare in August 2016. Touted as 'the first major independent study' of the relationship, *Partnership for Change* was prepared jointly by the ANU's East Asian Bureau of Economic Research and the China Centre for International Economic Exchanges (CCIEE). Prime Minister Turnbull turned up to launch it (but pointedly did not endorse it).[13]

The report's 'co-editor' was Professor Peter Drysdale—an expert on Japan and for decades one of Australia's most enthusiastic free traders—who called for the economic and political relationship to be 'turbocharged' through larger flows of Chinese 'tourists, students, investors and migrants'.[14] He believes we could benefit from more Chinese competition in our 'sheltered industries' (even though Australia's import barriers are virtually non-existent while China's remain formidable).

The first premise of the report is that Australia must do nothing to jeopardise the bilateral relationship, a deeply entrenched belief that represents the most powerful lever wielded by Beijing in this country. The report reinforces the widespread, but exaggerated, belief that Australia's future prosperity depends above all on China's economic success,[15] To the extent that it is true, you would think we would want to diversify away from China rather than become more dependent on it, but no matter—Drysdale's report laments that the broader Australian community 'does not grasp the benefits of foreign investment' from China and calls for an end to unequal treatment of Chinese investors.[16] The claim that Chinese investment is just like any other investment, and should be just as free to enter, ignores the fact that, unlike Britain, the United States and Japan, China is a dictatorship that controls much of the economy and uses this control to pursue political influence and regional strategic dominance. The problem, the report implies, is not that in China important business decisions are often intimately tied to the interests and strategic aspirations of the party-state but that the Australian public is ignorant and often motivated by xenophobia.

As we will see in Chapter 9, the report's recommendation that Australia should give priority to unfettered Chinese investment in our most advanced scientific and technological research should be particularly worrying. The United States, Canada and the European Union are now recognising how dangerous this kind of Chinese investment can be, and in 2017 the United States launched an investigation into how to protect itself from predatory Chinese investment in high-tech sectors.

Echoing Beijing's displeasure at Australian rejections of a handful of strategic investments, the report bemoans the disincentive effect on Chinese investors, as if Australia has no national interests above and beyond maximising foreign trade and investment. While the report expresses vague hopes that China might open up its economy to foreign investment a bit more (many Western companies refuse to operate there because the government makes it too difficult to do business), it calls for the abolition of Australian restrictions on Chinese investment.

In 2014 Drysdale had noted that during the mining boom more Chinese investment came to Australia than anywhere else in the world, but the flow had slipped in part because of 'populist reactions', code for any concern about state-owned enterprises (SOEs) buying up assets like energy infrastructure and agricultural holdings.[17] He reassured us that SOEs are just like any other companies because they too have to obey Australian laws and regulations. Well, yes, but that doesn't change the fact that their CEOs are senior party members, appointed by the party and subject to the party's dictates.

So unashamedly does the report champion Beijing's economic ambitions and disdain any kind of Australian reservations about them that we could be forgiven for suspecting that the think tankers at the CCIEE in Beijing were messing with the heads of their ANU counterparts. The report notes: 'Australia's geopolitical and geo-economic position and its multicultural society are thus unique assets in shaping China's links with the West.' Indeed they are, but these are in fact the *weaknesses* of Australia that have been identified by the CCP's strategists for exploitation.

The true objectives are exposed by one who understands intimately how Beijing has targeted Australia, because for many years his job was to implement its strategy here. Chen Yonglin, the Chinese diplomat who defected to Australia, wrote in 2016 that, as the CCP sees it, Australia has three advantages as a testing ground for its expansion into the Western world. The first is our geopolitical position, which actually make us 'the weak link in the western camp'. The second is our very large community of ethnic Chinese, 'people who have intimate and diverse links with the PRC, have often been ideologically trained, and a majority of whom have a strong sense of Chinese chauvinism'. And the third is our multicultural policies, which permit Chinese loyal to Beijing to promote 'Chinese values and customs' as excuses for advancing the positions of the CCP.[18]

If the ANU economists were hoodwinked by their partners in Beijing, then that was always going to be the case. Beijing knew who they were partnering with. In 2009 Peter Drysdale berated Australia's political leaders who had 'performed like a bunch of clowns' in stopping Chinese conglomerate Chinalco from buying a large stake in Rio Tinto.

If only they, like him, 'had just had a round of intensive interaction with top players in the Chinese policy world', they'd get it.[19] It's painful to watch senior Australians come away from talks with 'top players' believing they have been taken into their confidence. Instead of grasping that there is a story told to Westerners and a real story, they are convinced that they have joined the select few who know how China ticks. Deploying a range of cheap rhetorical devices, Drysdale has ridiculed claims that the CCP is attempting to influence Australian politics.[20]

The political masters in Beijing could be certain the Chinese experts writing the 'independent' joint report would toe the party line. The CCIEE was established in 2009 'following the instructions of Premier Wen Jiabao … [to be] the highest level think tank established in China'.[21] Its first chair was former vice-premier Zeng Peiyan. The party had decided it needed some reliable think tanks. In 2016 President Xi explicitly called for the strengthening of think tanks as avenues for recruiting the leadership of the Communist Party.[22] National guidelines stipulate that think tanks 'should carry out activities for the purpose of serving the Party and government decision-making'.[23] A Brookings paper on China's think tanks tells us that they are never 'independent', and that the CCIEE 'operates under the guidance of the National Development and Reform Commission'. Its experts are de facto government officials with little latitude to think outside the party's parameters.[24]

The 'joint report' concludes that if its recommendations were adopted 'the Australia-China relationship will be taken to a wholly new level'.[25] That is undoubtedly true: the influence of the CCP over economic life in Australia would be complete and irreversible. Back in Beijing the cadres at the CCIEE must have been toasting their success. A joint report with a US think tank would never call for the abolition of all restrictions on Chinese investment or unfettered access of Chinese companies, state-owned or private, to America's advanced technology. The US is moving firmly the other way.

The ANU's media release announcing the new report carried a photo of a group of people waving large Australian and Chinese flags. No one seems to have noticed the symbolism of the image in which all of the flag-wavers are of Chinese heritage.

Norway and the Dalai Lama effect

When the dissident writer Liu Xiaobo was awarded the Nobel Peace Prize in 2010, the Chinese Communist Party was embarrassed and angry.[26] Although the Norwegian government played no role in the decision, Beijing retaliated by sharply cutting Norway's share of the Chinese salmon market.[27] Free trade talks were abandoned and diplomatic relations went into deep freeze. Other countries looking on got the message and began sidelining Liu Xiaobo.

Oslo was chastened. When the Dalai Lama visited Norway four years later the prime minister refused to meet him. Norway's foreign minister told reporters: 'The Dalai Lama has visited Norway roughly a dozen times since receiving the [Peace] prize in 1989—but things are different now. ... We need to focus on our relationship with China.'[28] Six years after the prize was awarded to Liu, the Norwegian government made what amounted to a grovelling apology to China.[29] Norway's reputation as a champion of human rights may never recover.

A study shows that a country's exports to China are liable to fall by eight per cent if its president or prime minister meets the Dalai Lama.[30] Around the world, leaders have come under intense pressure to snub the spiritual leader and many have succumbed, including John Howard in 2002, Kevin Rudd in 2008 and 2009 and Julia Gillard, who was 'acclaimed' by China's official media for her refusal in 2012.[31]

For the CCP, Tibetan independence is one of the 'five poisons' (the others are Taiwanese independence, Uyghur separatism, Falun Gong's existence and pro-democracy activism). The Dalai Lama is denounced as a 'wolf in monk's clothing' and an 'anti-China splittist'. (Somebody should tell the propaganda bureau that, after *Monty Python's Life of Brian*, accusing someone of being a 'splittist' sounds absurd to Western ears.) Beijing is relentless in its attempts to counter the Tibetan leader's enormous 'soft power' around the world. Among the many leaders reported to have been bullied into refusing to meet the Dalai Lama are those of South Africa, India, Denmark, Norway and Scotland. Under Chinese pressure, Pope Francis declined to meet him. Britain's prime minister, David Cameron, was rendered persona non grata in 2012 after he met with the Dalai Lama. In 2015 Cameron was still trying to make up with Beijing by refusing to meet the Tibetan leader, prompting the latter to lament: 'Money, money, money. That's what this is about. Where is morality?'[32] When in 2017 China imposed serious pressure on its fragile economy, Mongolia, where Tibetan Buddhism is widely practised, was forced to declare it would no longer welcome the revered spiritual leader. In a refreshing display of courage under intense pressure, in 2017 Botswana's president, Dr Ian Khama, agreed to meet the Dalai Lama, telling Beijing, 'We are not your colony'.[33]

China's geoeconomics

If you don't do what Beijing's political leaders want they will punish you economically. They put the economic vise on politicians around the world. They have been doing it for years and it works.

Shaun Rein, China Market Research Group, Shanghai[34]

To seek to dominate other countries by military means is costly and dangerous—just look at Iraq. For a modern state there are cheaper and less risky means of coercion, sometimes known as economic statecraft or geoeconomics. China has become the world's master practitioner. Geoeconomics can be defined as the deployment of economic punishments and rewards to coerce nations to adopt preferred policies. Robert Blackwill and Jennifer Harris, experts from the US Council on Foreign Relations, identify seven leading instruments: trade policy, investment policy, economic sanctions, the cybersphere, aid, monetary policy, and energy and commodity policy.[35]

It's tailor-made for a state that is economically powerful and heavily integrated into the global economic system and at the same time has the ability to exercise control over its own companies by rewarding them if they serve the state's strategic ambitions, and penalising them if they don't. And that means China. Beijing's control over the PRC economy is increasing rather than declining. Almost all of the 85 Chinese companies among the 2013 Fortune Global 500 were SOEs.[36] Although Beijing is expanding its armed forces, its real power comes from weaponising its economic entities.

Some of the more facile commentary argues that it is not in China's interests to cut iron ore imports from Australia or interfere in shipping routes in the South China Sea because China would suffer too.[37] It is yet another failure to understand the nature of China under CCP rule. China is far more willing than we are to absorb economic pain in pursuit of strategic goals. It has a higher pain threshold. While our political system is extremely vulnerable to industry lobbying, even by the small but vocal, in China companies do not complain if they want to remain in favour, and workers who take to the streets can expect retribution.

When Beijing pulls the geoeconomic levers to impose real economic pain, it usually denies that it is doing so. Beijing's coyness is partly because coercion that is too blatant is likely to elicit a backlash, and because most of its actions break the rules of the World Trade Organization. China wants power, but it also wants to be seen as a responsible global economic citizen.

China is not the only nation to use commercial pressure to achieve political and strategic ends. But today it is the most formidable. While the United States occasionally imposes economic sanctions—against North Korea and Iran, for example—their use is rare and specific to security threats. China, on the other hand, frequently aims to coerce its neighbours into submission using these weapons. And not only its neighbours. In their definitive account, Robert Blackwill and Jennifer Harris lament the fact that the US has withdrawn from its global engagement. It 'gives China free reign in vulnerable African and Latin American nations'.[38] Unease in some African countries has been build-ing for several years. As early as 2007 the opposition leader in Zambia, Michael Sata, was expressing it bluntly: 'We want the Chinese to leave and the old colonial rulers to return … [A]t least Western capitalism has a human face; the Chinese are only out to exploit us.'[39]

At times, China will abandon any pretence and apply as much pressure as it can as ruthlessly as it can. In March 2017, at the invita-tion of South Korea, the United States began to install the Terminal High Altitude Area Defense (THAAD) anti-ballistic missile system. It could shoot down missiles launched by an increasingly well-armed and aggressive North Korea. China objected strongly, fearing that THAAD's advanced radar system could be used to spy on it and neutralise a Chinese response to an attack.

China took forty-three retaliatory measures against South Korea in response to the THAAD decision. The South Korean conglomerate Lotte, which allowed some of its land to house part of the system, bore the brunt of the anger whipped up by the official Chinese media. The *Global Times*, for example, declared that South Korea must be punished and Chinese consumers should teach Seoul a lesson.[40] *Xinhua* warned that it 'could turn into a nightmare for Lotte', a prophecy fulfilled by its nationalist readers, who launched a violent campaign against Lotte's department stores in China, closing most of them.[41] (The consumer boycott and government retaliation did not let up and in September 2017 Lotte announced it would sell its stores in China and get out.) That was only the start. The PRC blocked imports of cosmetics and electronics and cancelled shows by K-Pop stars.[42] Korean tourists on Chinese streets were accosted. South Korean films, very popular in China, were banned from the Beijing International Film Festival. And in a display of childish pique, the face of pop star Psy, who was serving as a judge on a Chinese talent show, was blurred out.

The Korean tourism industry was thrown into panic when China banned group tours, causing tourist numbers to collapse.[43] In Seoul, tour operator Korea-China International Tourism reported an eighty-five per cent drop in tourists. An executive of one of the biggest Chinese travel companies admitted that 'tourism is part of diplomacy'.[44] All chartered flights from Korea were blocked before a major football match, forcing the Korean team to take a last-minute scheduled flight. (The team's exhaustion was said to have contributed to the short-priced favourite's loss to China.) Some top Chinese women's golfers planned to boycott a tournament in Hawaii sponsored by Lotte.

In June 2017 the new, more dovish, South Korean government suspended the installation of THAAD after the first two of six launchers had been installed and were operational. Some in the local community oppose it on security and environmental grounds. But the other four were installed in September after Kim Jong-un tested nuclear weapons, fired missiles over Japan and threatened to attack the US.

China has a unique advantage over nations like Australia and the United States: it can much more effectively use social pressure to mobilise its citizenry to boycott or otherwise penalise a foreign company. Boycotts and sanctions by China also cause pain to its own consumers and workers, but this 'only underscores Beijing's tolerance of pain when it comes to accepting domestic costs for its geoeconomics policies'.[45]

Analysts of China's use of economic coercion point to its 2010 shutdown of export to Japan of rare earth oxides, essential to the manufacture of various high-tech products, including components for Japan's exports. Japan had arrested a Chinese ship captain who'd rammed a Japanese coast guard vessel in a disputed maritime zone. China had by this time become a virtual monopoly supplier of rare earths, aided by the purchase by an SOE of a state-of-the-art processing plant in Indiana in 1995. It had to commit to operating the plant for at least five years, but the day after the five years were up the owners closed the plant, dismantled it and rebuilt it in China.[46] The US lost its rare earth production capacity and handed control of the essential material to China.

Under pressure, Japan soon released the captain. Blackwill and Harris noted that the rare earth ban was 'striking for its brazenness ... the first time China so boldly coerced a U.S. treaty ally'.[47] These incidents show that, for all of President Xi's claims that China must lead economic globalisation, China is willing to violate the rules-based global economic order when it suits its strategic interests.

In 2012, 150 containers of bananas were left to rot on Chinese wharfs because the Philippines objected to Chinese fishing boats encroaching on Scarborough Shoal. Around 200,000 banana workers were affected.[48] Beijing also made it plain to travel agents that tours to the Philippines should be suspended. Manila had to cave in. Vietnam, watching from the other side of the South China Sea, took a softer line on its territorial claims.[49]

The Philippines is especially vulnerable to Beijing's influence. Chinese-Filipinos are thought to own around half of the Philippines' market capital and they have outsized political influence for a group that makes up only 1.5 per cent of the population.[50] Moreover, in 2007 the Philippines government awarded management of the nation's entire electricity grid to China's State Grid Corporation. A Chinese SOE now has its hands on the nation's fuse box.[51]

During heightened Japan–China tensions, cyber attacks originating from China were launched against the Japanese parliament in 2011. They followed cyber theft of information on defence equipment and nuclear power plants.[52] Whether these attacks emanated from government units is hard to know, but 'Beijing's patriotic army of hackers has actively used cyber warfare to target the Taiwanese government and infrastructure networks'. Taiwan has been a special target, with China's cyber militia launching 'countless cyberattacks intended to harass, disrupt, or paralyze Taiwan's financial, transportation, shipping, military, and other networks'.[53]

Soon after Taiwan's new pro-independence president, Tsai Ing-wen, took office in May 2016, tourist numbers from mainland China plunged by thirty-six per cent, threatening the survival of an industry that had grown rapidly and largely on the back of the flow from the mainland.[54] Beijing had instructed mainland tour operators to slash their tours to Taiwan. Thousands of tourist industry operators and their staff marched in the streets of Taipei demanding the government appease the dragon by taking a more pro-Beijing position.[55] After the Beijing-induced crash it was forced to diversify and now limits the number of tourists from China.[56]

Beijing is believed to have deployed patriotic hackers in Australia. The Chinese government does not own up to using these methods, leaving those who displease China uncertain and nervous. As Blackwill and Harris observe: 'In fact, the arbitrariness of China's regulatory system is part of what makes Beijing so effective in its use of geoeconomics instruments.'[57] For a nation like Australia that operates by the rules, it's more difficult to use domestic regulations to penalise foreign imports or investments for geopolitical purposes.

Coercing Australia

It might be thought that Japan, Taiwan and South Korea belong to China's immediate strategic zone and Beijing would not try that kind of blackmail on a nation like Australia. But consider the case of Greece.

At the United Nations, no bloc has more firmly and consistently defended human rights than the European Union. When the United States wavered, the European Union could be relied on to raise its voice against states violating the rights embedded in the UN's charter, including the right to a fair trial, press freedom and LGBT rights. At least, that was the case until June 2017 when Greece vetoed a European Union resolution condemning China's persecution of activists and dissidents.[58] Greece's rogue action sent shock waves through the EU, with one diplomat describing it as 'dishonourable, to say the least'. Greece explained that it is more effective to raise human rights concerns in private meetings, succumbing to the classic PRC tactics of keeping everything critical out of the public eye and insisting on bilateral discussions behind closed doors.[59]

Why had Greece broken ranks? We do not have to look very far. In recent years China has poured billions into the Greek economy struggling under EU-imposed austerity measures. In 2016 China's biggest shipbuilding company, the state-owned China COSCO Shipping, bought a majority share in Greece's biggest port at Piraeus. Greek Prime Minister Alexis Tsipras was present at the sign-over ceremony to hear China's ambassador say, 'the agreement marks a historic milestone for Sino-Hellenic friendship'.[60] Greek ports are seen as vital to the OBOR initiative's access to Europe.

In addition, in 2016 China's State Grid Corporation bought a quarter share of Greece's electricity grid operator, after the EU bailout of Greece demanded privatisation of state assets. (State Grid's bid to buy Ausgrid in New South Wales was blocked by the federal government on security grounds.) Senior CCP officials have targeted Greece, crippled by its debts to European banks, with a view to developing a close strategic partnership and, in the words of one analyst, turning Greece into a kind of 'Chinese observer' at the EU.[61] Prime Minister Tsipras has been making pilgrimages to Beijing. The EU has unwittingly thrown Greece into the arms of China, which seems intent on using it as a beachhead into Europe.

Across the Aegean Sea, in August 2017 the Turkish government promised that it would stamp out all anti-China media reports.[62] China became annoyed with Turkey when in 2015 it had protested the mistreatment of Muslim Uyghurs in Xinjiang during Ramadan. Protests were staged outside the Chinese embassy in Ankara. But now the Turkish government had its eye on cash flows from the One Belt,

One Road initiative after President Erdoğan attended the big OBOR conference in Beijing three months earlier.

Australia has given way many times to Chinese threats of ill-defined economic retaliation. In 2016 the CCP's top leaders thought hard about punishing Australia for our stance on The Hague's ruling on China's illegal occupation of islands in the South China Sea. They held off, but it is only a matter of time before we receive the Taiwan or South Korea treatment. In January 2018 Beijing threatened Australia with economic harm via an article in the *Global Times*.[63] Ostensibly, our offence is to side with the United States over the South China Sea, although, as we'd done nothing different, the threat was more likely an expression of Beijing's fear of the Turnbull government's proposed new national security laws, which could sharply curtail the CCP's influence operations. Although the PRC has annexed disputed islands in violation of international law and turned them into heavily armed military bases, it is Australia, apparently, that is engaging in 'provocations' by allowing our navy ships to cross into the sea.

Punishments could include penalising Australian exporters with bogus quarantine or health claims, arresting staff of Australian firms on false charges, refusing visas to businesspeople, and launching cyber attacks by secret agencies or citizen hackers. Some industries have become far too dependent on markets in China—milk powder, complementary medicines, wine, certain food products. These could all be stopped on the wharves tomorrow.

But our greatest vulnerabilities to Chinese economic blackmail are education and the tourism sector, which in 2016 respectively generated $7 billion and $9.2 billion in revenue from China. Tourism is especially susceptible because it is expected to grow very rapidly ($13 billion by 2020) and the tap can be turned off quickly. (Students want to settle, while tourists can go to Thailand.) Moreover, the tourism industry has more political clout than universities. In an April 2013 meeting with then prime minister Julia Gillard, President Xi was already making veiled threats about the importance of Chinese tourists to Australia.[64] In late 2016 the federal government gave Chinese-owned airlines 'open access' to Australian skies, so they can ramp up the number of flights as much as they like. A fifth of Virgin Australia has been bought by the

Hainan-based HNA Aviation, a highly secretive and opaque company that is reported to be acting for the CCP.[65] (HNA is buying up pilot training schools at regional airports in Australia.[66] Some experts predict that pilot training in Australia will soon be entirely Chinese-owned.) The ACCC gave approval to Virgin, HNA and two other Chinese airlines to coordinate their operations to Australia. In short, Beijing can now turn off the tourist tap at will through the airlines it can control.

Yet the federal government seems oblivious, designating 2017 as the year of Chinese tourism. The Queensland government is investing heavily to attract a larger flow of Chinese tourists to Cairns, Brisbane and the Gold Coast, banking on a boom in regional tourism jobs.[67] While tourist numbers from other countries plateaued between 2011 and 2016, those from China nearly trebled, and Queensland reckons there is a long way up the curve still to travel.

In considering our exposure to tourist blackmail, various factors come into play. Beijing can more easily control the flow of tour groups booked through Chinese travel agents: independent travellers are less likely to be deterred; they spend more too. There has been a 'massive upsurge' in Chinese investment in the Australian tourism industry, accounting for forty per cent of the total in 2016.[68] Chinese investors are buying big hotels (Mercure, Sheraton, Hilton, Ibis, Sofitel),[69] snapping up distressed Queensland resorts (Daydream Island, Lindeman Island) and building new ones. Some have links to tour group agencies in China. Turning off the tourist tap will hurt them, but any complaints they may make would receive little sympathy in Beijing.

8

Spies old and new

Spying on ASIO

The sprawling Chinese embassy in Canberra and ASIO's glass-and-steel edifice sit on opposite sides of Lake Burley Griffin, around two kilometres apart as the crow flies. Between them, an intense struggle is taking place over the future of Australia. Worried about infiltration of Australia's institutions, in 2005 ASIO established a new counter-intelligence unit whose main task was to monitor and combat the escalating activity of Chinese spies. This followed the departure of ASIO director-general Dennis Richardson, who had effectively closed down the organisation's counter-intelligence capability in favour of counter-terrorism.[1]

ASIO is said to have been running hard to keep up ever since (providing a new career path for those Mandarin speakers whose loyalty to Australia can be assured). It believes that China has launched a 'full-court press' against Australia—that is, an all-out offensive. Along with its sister organisations, ASIO must try to resist the campaign coordinated out of the Chinese embassy across the lake. While ASIO cannot neglect its counter-terrorism function, its counter-intelligence and counter-subversion operations are arguably far more important to Australia's long-term future.

The construction of a new office complex for Australia's chief spy agency on the shores of Lake Burley Griffin provided an irresistible target for Chinese espionage. In 2013, as it was just being completed, the ABC reported that the building's blueprints, including floor plan, cable diagrams and even the location of its servers, had been stolen through a cyber intrusion emanating almost certainly from China.[2] ASIO denied its blueprints had been hacked but the shadow attorney-general, George Brandis, told parliament that intelligence sources had confirmed the report to him. The building could not be occupied until the communications systems had been reworked. Denying the claims in Beijing, a straight-faced foreign ministry spokesman declared that China opposes all forms of cyber attack.[3]

In 2015 journalists Primrose Riordan and Markus Mannheim revealed that a development site across the road from ASIO headquarters had been bought by a company controlled by a Chinese billionaire with links to the PLA.[4] Liang Guangwei has hosted top Chinese leaders, including former president Hu Jintao, at his company, Shenzhen Huaqiang. Until a month before SHL Development bought a block of land in Campbell (known as C5), whose corner is eighty metres from ASIO, Liang was a director of the Canberra development company. His wife, a Canberra resident, remains one of the three directors, but it is Liang's money that is now being heavily invested in Canberra's real estate, with two other large land acquisitions occurring in 2016 and 2017. At the auctions, other bidders were blown out of the water.[5]

A fifth-floor apartment eighty metres from ASIO would be a perfect spot to monitor vehicle traffic in and out of the building. No vetting or assessment was carried out before the prime block was sold to the PLA-linked company. Chief minister of the Australian Capital Territory Andrew Barr, who according to the local paper has never seen a development he did not like and accepted SHL's invitation to turn the first sod, said anyone questioning the sale is 'racist'.[6] And, he added, if there was a security problem then it was ASIO's fault for putting its HQ near a residential area.[7]

A thousand spies and informants

In a 2005 media interview after he had defected from the consulate in Sydney, Chen Yonglin claimed that there is a network of 'over 1000 Chinese secret agents and informants' operating in Australia.[8] It seemed like an extraordinary claim and was met by some with scepticism; after all, during the Cold War the Russians couldn't have had more than a few dozen spies and agents in this country. But Chinese intelligence gathering operates on a different model. In addition to traditional kinds of spying, China recruits large numbers of people of Chinese heritage to collect and pass on useful information, including commercial and military secrets and information on the activities of 'unpatriotic' groups like pro-democracy activists and Falun Gong. The embassy collates the information and sends it to Beijing or uses it in its own operations in-country.

One intelligence expert with ASIO connections put it like this: 'China's intelligence gathering is pervasive but not overtly intrusive and by and large not breaking any laws, but it is on an industrial scale.'[9] Chen's claim is consistent with China's much larger assault on the United States. A former FBI counter-intelligence officer described as 'a reasonable estimate' the claim that China has in place up to 25,000 intelligence officers and had recruited 15,000 informants already in the United States.[10]

As we will see, Chinese students in Australia monitor other students and academics and report any 'anti-China' speech and activities, such as criticising the CCP or watching a film about the Dalai Lama. Chinese-Australians with business links to China can be persuaded, through patriotism or blackmail, to report any intelligence they come across in their many conversations with Australian business leaders or officials. Those with access to valuable technological or scientific information will be asked to pass it on. It's been reported that ASIO is concerned that spies may be arriving as tourists.[11]

After reviewing the state of affairs, in 2016 Aaron Patrick wrote in the *Australian Financial Review*: 'Chinese security services are engaging in the most intense collection of intelligence by a foreign power Australia has ever seen.'[12] Intelligence expert Paul Monk says Chinese intelligence officers are 'having a field day', and that 'Chinese espionage right now is occurring on a scale that dwarfs what the Soviet Union accomplished during the height of the Cold War'.[13] In his comprehensive exposé, James To reports that overseas Chinese are recruited to gather low-grade intelligence by infiltrating or monitoring, among others, trade unions, women's groups, student associations and, for technology and business strategies, corporations.[14] ASIO, organised to monitor traditional forms of spying, is not equipped or resourced to keep abreast of this kind of 'decentralized micro-espionage'. I was told by a former analyst that even with rapidly expanding resources, 'the Chinese intelligence apparatus is just too big to defeat'.

Some in government are aware of the scale and seriousness of the threat, at least up to a point. But, unlike their counterparts in the United States and Canada, they have decided to stay silent about it. Cowed by the forceful and at times hysterical rebukes from Chinese leaders and media, they are afraid of Beijing's retribution and worried about provoking anti-Chinese sentiment. However, in his last public act as a public servant, in May 2017 the outgoing secretary of the defence department, Dennis Richardson, warned of Beijing's spying and influence operations.[15]

If the Australian populace—businesspeople, public servants and everyday citizens—were alert to the kinds of activities taking place, they could take measures to defend against this unprecedented campaign of civil society espionage. ASIO could be encouraged to provide much more explicit reports on the nature of the threat, rather than vague statements in its annual reports that don't mention China at all. If the evidence can be found, there should be, as in North America, prosecutions of Chinese spies. Government ministers could speak out about it, as they tentatively began to do in 2017.

It's worth remembering that many Chinese-Australians who, one way or another, help the PRC advance its objectives do so under pressure and are best seen as the victims of the CCP.

In 2016, after a long silence while he built his life in Australia, Chen Yonglin told the ABC that the number of spies and informants would have grown since he first suggested they number one thousand.[16]

Huawei and the NBN

It's well known that for some years the Chinese party-state has been using cyber espionage to intrude into our communications networks. In 2013 *Four Corners* reported that the most important government departments had been penetrated by China-based hackers, including the prime minister's department, the defence department, foreign affairs and the Australian overseas intelligence agency, the Australian Secret Intelligence Service. The first Chinese cyber infiltration of the foreign affairs department is thought to have occurred in 2001. The hacking reached a crescendo in 2007 and 2008, giving rise to 'a tremendous fear inside the intelligence community'.[17]

Attempts to penetrate Australia's communications networks are not confined to the activities of secret organisations operating from nondescript buildings in the suburbs of Shanghai, like the infamous Unit 61398.[18] It is suspected that Beijing may use state-owned and private companies to access communications, including classified ones, in Australia and elsewhere. And so in March 2012 the Gillard Labor government banned the giant Chinese telecommunications company Huawei from tendering to supply its equipment to the National Broadband Network (NBN). Our intelligence agencies had warned that there was 'credible evidence' that Huawei was linked to the Third Department of the PLA, the Chinese military's cyber-espionage arm.[19] The company's chairwoman admitted that it had been affiliated with the Ministry of State Security, the PRC's intelligence agency.[20]

In the meantime, Huawei had been spending up to create a public image of trustworthiness, including setting up an Australian board as a front. It appointed Liberal and Labor elders Alexander Downer and John Brumby, following up by employing retired rear admiral John Lord to chair it.[21] Lord said he had seen the company's R&D and was excited about it. He reassured cynics that, by appointing him to chair the board, Huawei was not aiming to 'crack the Australian military' but was interested in him because he knows his way around Canberra.[22]

Lawmakers in the United States had been looking more closely at Huawei, along with the other big Chinese telco equipment maker ZTE. In October 2012 the US Congress released a devastating report confirming fears about Huawei's close connections with the Chinese government and its intelligence agencies.[23] It concluded that the United States 'should view with suspicion the continued penetration of the U.S. telecommunications market' by these companies. All proposed acquisitions or mergers with American companies by Huawei, it suggested, should be blocked and all contractors to government systems should exclude Huawei equipment. The bottom line, it warned, is that Huawei and ZTE 'cannot be trusted to be free of foreign state influence and thus pose a security threat to the United States and to our systems'.

One of the more telling features of the Congressional investigation was the attempt to understand the relationship between Huawei (and ZTE) and the Chinese government. In China, Huawei is designated as belonging to a 'strategic sector' and receives special preferment. The investigators made numerous attempts to persuade Huawei to be straight with them but found the company and its executives to be evasive, shifty, obstructionist and, in the end, ready to lie. We know why: telling the truth would destroy the careful attempts by Huawei over many years to construct an image of a modern, independent, global company working solely for the benefit of its shareholders.

Although it is not a state-owned company, it would be naïve in the extreme to believe a company that with government support turned itself into the world's second biggest telecommunications equipment maker, with contracts to supply electronic equipment to communications networks around the world, did not have daily links with China's intelligence services. *The Economist* wrote that Huawei 'has stolen vast amounts of intellectual property and that it has been heavily subsidised in its expansion by the Chinese government, eager to use it as a Trojan horse with which to infiltrate itself into more and more foreign networks.'[24]

Huawei's linkages with the intelligence services were in place from its foundation by former PLA officer Ren Zhengfei. Ren was a director of the PLA's Information Engineering Academy, responsible for telecom research for the Chinese military and specifically '3PLA, China's signals intelligence division'.[25] According to a RAND Corporation report for the US Air Force, 'Huawei maintains deep ties with the Chinese military, which serves a multi-faceted role as an important customer, as well as Huawei's political patron and research and development partner.'[26] A 2011 CIA report fingered Huawei's chairwoman, Sun Yafang, as a former employee of the Ministry of State Security, the equivalent of the CIA itself.[27]

Despite this damning information, Huawei had powerful supporters in Australia. When the Gillard government banned the company from the NBN, Opposition finance spokesman Andrew Robb attacked the decision as 'the latest clumsy, offensive and unprofessional instalment of a truly dysfunctional government'.[28] That was not long after Robb had enjoyed an all-expenses-paid visit to Huawei's Shenzhen headquarters.[29] Kerry Stokes, who had used Huawei to help build a broadband network in Perth, said he had 'the utmost respect' for the company.[30] Alexander Downer laughed off the claims of the company's links to Chinese intelligence agencies. 'I don't know what's wrong with Australia,' said the Huawei Australia board member. 'It's not a John le Carré novel'.[31]

Downer had form. In 2004 he visited China as foreign minister where he told his Chinese counterparts that the ANZUS Treaty was only 'symbolic' and that Australia was not obliged to back the US in a conflict over Taiwan. He was sympathetic to a strategic realignment, collaborating with China on security and political issues, causing two commentators to conclude presciently: 'Mr Downer's talks in Beijing have shown how quickly the staunchly pro-US Government in Canberra is being turned by China's rising economic power and influence, to the point where it is distancing itself from a key US strategic posture.'[32] According to Chen Yonglin, 'Downer's stance immediately raised the interest of CCP leaders,' who saw an opening into which they could drive a wedge.[33]

In November 2013, after the Abbott government, acting on ASIO's advice, reaffirmed the ban on Huawei as an equipment supplier to the NBN, Huawei board chair John Lord wrote to the company's disappointed staff members: 'I want to make it crystal clear that Huawei has never been presented with any evidence that our company or technology poses any kind of security risk.'[34] His assurances came a year after the damning US Congressional report. The former fleet commander spoke of Huawei's excellent prospects, including its big contract to help build Optus' 4G network. He insisted that Huawei 'has nothing to hide', a judgement at odds with that of the US Congressional committee that found the company to be evasive in its testimony. (The committee also noted credible evidence that Huawei had violated immigration laws and engaged in bribery and corruption.[35])

In a strange twist, while banning Huawei the federal government allowed ZTE to tender to supply equipment to the NBN despite the

US Congressional committee bracketing the two as equally suspect. The decision was apparently endorsed by ASIO. In early 2017, ZTE was fined US$900 million for selling sensitive US-made technology to Iran, breaking US sanctions.[36] The conviction came after years of lying to federal investigators about the allegations. Afterwards, ZTE's CEO Zhao Xianming announced 'a new ZTE, compliant, healthy and trustworthy'.[37]

Some MPs had got the message about Huawei though. In 2016, when the federal infrastructure minister Paul Fletcher began wearing around Parliament House a Huawei smartwatch (a gift from the company), Senator Penny Wong grilled parliament's chief information officer. Is the watch connected to the building's network? The CIO didn't know; it wasn't her job to conduct a risk assessment of the device and she really didn't know much about Huawei.[38] Yet the parliamentary computer network had been hacked from China in 2011, giving that country's intelligence sources access to MPs emails for up to a year.[39] While the network was not used for classified communications, the hackers are likely to have compiled data on the personal relationships of current and future leaders, their real opinions on China and the United States, and gossip about their friends and enemies, all of which could prove very useful.

The head of our defence department in 2016, Dennis Richardson, was not unduly worried about all of this. In March 2012, while secretary of the Department of Foreign Affairs and Trade (DFAT) and a member of the board of the Canberra Raiders rugby league club, he took leave without pay from his job for half a day to help decide on a $1.7 million sponsorship agreement between the club and Huawei.[40] Huawei had never displayed any interest in rugby league—indeed, it was the first sports sponsorship the company had ever entered into.[41] Using a marketing budget to get close to influential figures is a tactic not unknown to Chinese (and other) companies. And who better to gain access to than Australia's foreign affairs boss, also the former director-general of ASIO, and soon to become defence secretary? Presumably, when the whistle later blew for kick-off at Canberra Stadium, Richardson stood shoulder to shoulder with Huawei executives, along with fellow Raiders board member Allan Hawke, formerly secretary of defence.

The careful cultivation of personal relationships with powerful people is a Chinese specialty, one that has been applied systematically and raised to a new level in Australia since 2005.

The Raiders were soon praising the benefits of the Huawei sponsorship, including the use of the company's 24/7 smartwatch monitoring of players, including their hydration, sleep, diet and wellness, as well as, with the help of Huawei's tablet computers, their location and movement speed.[12] Handy on a politician too. According to the club's marketing manager, the Raiders' corporate values of 'courage, respect, integrity and professionalism' are 'a good match for Huawei's own values'.

Huawei's reach

In its report on Huawei the US Congressional committee referred to the 'ongoing onslaught of sophisticated computer network intrusions that originate in China'. It concluded that 'China has the means, opportunity, and motives to use telecommunications companies for malicious purposes'.[43] Although its hardware was excluded from Australia's National Broadband Network, Huawei has successfully sold equipment to other communications networks, including those of Vodafone, Optus and Telstra,[44] aided by state subsidies that allow it to undercut the competition.[45] In 2014 the *South China Morning Post* reported that the Home Office in London had scrapped video conferencing equipment supplied by Huawei because of security concerns.[46] Acting on intelligence advice about the risks of eavesdropping, all departments were ordered to stop using Huawei equipment. No similar ban applies in Australian government departments.

Perhaps more worryingly, Huawei has a close commercial relationship with State Grid, the giant Chinese state-owned corporation that now owns a large portion of the electricity networks in Victoria and South Australia. State Grid, using Huawei's equipment, can collect massive amounts of data about power usage. If it has not already been installed, the effective operation of Australia's electricity network could depend on software installed in hardware made by Huawei.[47]

Perhaps this was a consideration that contributed to the blocking of the sale of the New South Wales distribution network Ausgrid to State

Grid in 2016. After all, the US Congressional committee expressed alarm at the fact that '[m]alicious implants in the components of critical infrastructure, such as power grids or financial networks, would … be a tremendous weapon in China's arsenal'.[48] Wade captures the broader concern with a rhetorical question:

> When a Chinese state-owned company with intimate links to the military and to China's intelligence activities gets the all-clear from the Foreign Investment Review Board to control major national infrastructure, and even to buy into the NSW electricity transmission network that carries optical-fibre communications between Australian government departments, the question must be asked: Are the processes of foreign investment consideration and approval in this country in need of revision?[49]

Huawei has been diligently building its brand and networks of influence in Australia, that is, beyond its links with a current and former defence secretary, a former rear admiral, a former foreign minister and a former state premier. Serving parliamentarians have been lavished with gifts and free travel. One target has been assistant treasurer Kelly O'Dwyer: the company paid for lion dancers at a Chinese New Year event in her electorate. Predictably, Sam Dastyari is in the frame, visiting Huawei's Shenzhen headquarters in 2013. The company flew News Corp journalist Greg Sheridan to China, after which he wrote an article gushing about the company's achievements, noting that all Chinese companies have CCP committees, telling us that 'nothing bad about Huawei has ever been proved' and suggesting the company had been innocently caught up in American anxieties about cyber hacking.[50] The scales have since fallen from Sheridan's eyes (as they have from mine).[51]

None of those who have availed themselves of Huawei's hospitality, or accepted its lucrative board positions, have done anything illegal. But who would doubt that they have used their positions and reputations to buff the company's veneer of respectability and so contribute to its successes?

In January 2018 the US telecom giant AT&T abandoned a deal to supply Huawei phones to its customers. The US Senate and House intelligence committee had written to the Federal Communications Commission reminding it of the evidence in the Congressional report on Huawei and noting that additional evidence had come to light.[52]

Honey traps

When Tony Abbott took his first trip to China as prime minister in 2014 he was accompanied by his chief of staff, Peta Credlin. They attended the high profile Boao Forum, reputed to be the 'most bugged' event in China. Officials and journalists had all been briefed on security by ASIO. Take a different phone. Don't put any phone in the charger supplied in your hotel room. Throw away USB sticks in any gift packs. Never leave your laptop in your room, even in the safe.

Credlin looked around when she first entered her hotel room.[53] She immediately pulled out the plug of her clock radio, and disconnected the TV set. Within minutes there was a knock on the door. 'Housekeeping.' The staff member entered, plugged the clock radio and TV back in, and left. Credlin unplugged them again and, sure enough, housekeeping came knocking. The devices were plugged back in. So to make a point, Credlin pulled out the clock radio and put it in the corridor outside her door. Then she covered the TV set with a towel. At the forum, the prime minister would tell the media that Australia was China's 'true friend'.[54]

Bugged clock radios are not the only danger for officials in Chinese hotel rooms. There are persistent stories of Australian political representatives on organised visits to China finding 'girls' in their hotel rooms. In the instances we hear of, the targets rush from their rooms to inform their group leaders. There must be others who have been ensnared by the honey trap and are forever owned. Intelligence expert Nigel Inkster writes that honey traps are being used more often by Chinese agents to recruit non-Chinese.[55] Australia's intelligence services are aware of 'numerous cases'. It may be mere rumour but I have been told a former senior Australian political leader was caught in such a trap and is now a reliable pro-Beijing commentator.

Fear of compromising photos with an escort is one kind of honey trap. The other exploits infatuation rather than fear. Love affairs, and even marriages, between men with access to valuable information and women of Chinese heritage working for Beijing are not unknown.

Besotted men do crazy things. In 2014 in Hawaii, a 27-year-old Chinese student seduced a 60-year-old former army officer and defence contractor. He was soon passing her classified information on US war plans and missile defence.[56] In another case, a Chinese-American FBI agent, Katrina Leung, a double agent for Beijing, had a sexual relationship with her FBI handler and the head of US Chinese counter-intelligence operations in Los Angeles. He fed her classified information for two decades.

It would be naïve to think that China's vast spying network was not working at recruiting Australian academics, experts and journalists to provide information, especially secret information. China's intelligence agents exploit vulnerabilities known as the 'four moral flaws': lust, revenge, fame and greed. Some of the techniques have been revealed in court documents arising from a series of espionage trials in the United States, but because Australia does not prosecute spies there is little information on how it works in this country.

In July 2017 Nate Thayer, an independent US journalist, wrote a detailed account of attempts by the Shanghai State Security Bureau, an intelligence agency within the Ministry of State Security, to recruit him to engage in espionage.[57] The bureau sometimes works through the Shanghai Academy of Social Sciences (SASS), which allows itself to be used as cover for recruiting foreign academics to spy for China. (The same is true of the Chinese Academy of Sciences.) Thayer notes that 'the FBI has assessed that the Shanghai State Security Bureau … has a close relationship with SASS and uses SASS employees as spotters and assessors'. Soon after Thayer's commentary appeared, a former CIA agent appeared in a Virginia court charged with espionage after he travelled to Shanghai to meet two men claiming to be employees of the Shanghai Academy of Social Sciences.[58]

I have seen no evidence that Australian academics, think tankers or journalists have been recruited in this way, although in 2008 journalist Philip Dorling reported that an ALP staffer had been recruited by Chinese agents. The staffer agreed to provide personal information on senior Labor Party figures and write background documents on internal party affairs, for which he was paid small sums.[59] With the 2007 election approaching (in which China's consulate in Sydney backed

Kevin Rudd), the staffer was urged to seek employment with a federal minister. When he learned that he would need a security clearance to work in a minister's office he broke off the relationship.

Thayer quotes an American specialist on Chinese intelligence activities: 'The FBI Washington Field Office has at least five counter-intelligence squads focused on China, covering think tanks, journalists, students, military attaches, diplomatic personnel, and declared MSS officers.' The US reports ought to ring alarm bells given the heavy traffic of academics, experts and journalists moving between Australia and China. For example, the Australia-China Council funds an Australian Studies Centre at the Shanghai Academy of Social Sciences, and the University of Sydney has an exchange agreement with it. It would be fair to assume that attempts have been made to recruit Australian academics visiting the SASS in Shanghai.

The Fitzgibbon–Liu affair

In 1963 Britain was captivated by a sensational scandal. It emerged that the minister for war, John Profumo, had been sharing a mistress, Christine Keeler, with a Russian military intelligence operative, Yevgeny Ivanov. The Profumo affair destabilised the government, almost brought down the prime minister, preoccupied the press for months, precipi-tated a wholesale security review and led to a dozen books and films. Andrew Lloyd Webber even wrote a musical about it. It was huge.

In 2009 Australia's minister for defence, Joel Fitzgibbon, was reported to have 'a very close' and long-standing friendship with a Chinese businesswoman, Helen Liu, who turned out to have close links to Chinese military intelligence.[60] She was also a wealthy property investor and a generous ALP donor. The journalists who broke the story—Richard Baker, Philip Dorling and Nick McKenzie—noted that when the minister was in Canberra he rented a townhouse owned by Liu's sister, Queena.

Defence intelligence officers carried out an unofficial, covert security assessment, uncovering Liu's links to the Second Department of the People's Liberation Army, responsible for collecting human intelligence on matters military, political and economic outside China.[61] Among the reasons for concern were two undeclared trips flying first-class to China by Fitzgibbon before he became the minister.[62] According to a senior defence intelligence official, when passed up the chain of command the unauthorised report into the issue was 'too much of a hot potato' and went nowhere. Then prime minister Kevin Rudd, who had reportedly dined with Ms Liu, did not ask for Fitzgibbon's resignation. Nor, as far as we know, were the pair subject to an ASIO assessment.

Helen Liu's connections with China's intelligence agencies went deeper. In 2017 it was revealed that one of her companies had made a large payment to a Hong Kong company believed to be a front for Chinese espionage. According to Baker, Dorling and McKenzie, the company's owner, Liu Chaoying, is or was a lieutenant colonel in the PLA and had been engaged in procuring missile and satellite technology.[63] She has also had close personal ties with Helen Liu. Liu Chaoying was well known to US authorities because she was intimately involved in 'Chinagate', the scandal in the mid-1990s that saw large sums of money funnelled into Bill Clinton's foundation that may have come from a Chinese intelligence agency as part of an influence operation. Helen Liu admits she knows Liu Chaoying but denies she knows anything of her intelligence connections. Meanwhile Helen Liu had been making large donations to the New South Wales Labor Party and Fitzgibbon's election fund. Baker, Dorling and McKenzie write: 'Fairfax Media is not suggesting Mr Fitzgibbon has received anything else from Ms Liu which he is required to declare.'

That this blatant security breach, in which the nation's defence minister was friendly with a Chinese intelligence operative, attracted so little scandal is a sign of the amazing naivety with which Australians view all things Chinese. Most journalists, editors, politicians and opinion makers took the view that China could not be so interested in Australia that it would plant spies. The whole affair was just a quirk deserving no further investigation. Senior politicians from both sides of politics lobbied Fairfax, publisher of *The Sydney Morning Herald* and *The Age*, to suppress the Fitzgibbon–Liu story, arguing it would damage our relationship with China and stir up anti-Chinese sentiment in Australia. They may have been right on both counts, but it is also true that both sides had deeper links with Ms Liu that they wanted kept in the shadows.

Helen Liu was a student in Sydney at the time of the Tiananmen Square massacre in 1989. According to pro-democracy activists, she attended anti-Beijing protests at around this time but then disappeared, reappearing a few years later as a wealthy businesswoman.[64] It soon became apparent that she was well connected in China—indeed, very well connected with senior party cadres. In the mid-2000s she was appointed an honorary chairman of the ACPPRC, along with Chau Chak Wing.

When the Fitzgibbon story broke in 2009, Bob Carr immediately came out to defend Helen Liu, branding as 'shameful' suggestions she was a security risk. As to claims she was a mystery woman, Carr said 'she's no more a mystery than any other woman'.[65] Carr and his wife, Helena, who is of Malaysian-Chinese descent, are close friends of Helen Liu.[66] At that stage her companies, part-owned by Chinese state corporations, had given more than $90,000 to the New South Wales ALP. Leaked documents indicate that, in reports back to Beijing through the Bank of China, Liu was saying she won Fitzgibbon over by paying him. 'The money we pay him is worthwhile,' she wrote.[67]

At the time of writing, the Department of Immigration is keen to speak with Helen Liu about the circumstances in which she obtained her Australian citizenship. It seems that while on a student visa in 1989 she obtained permanent residency fraudulently by making a sham marriage. One of those involved, a naïve young Australian woman who married Liu's Chinese boyfriend while her own boyfriend married Liu, confessed.[68] (Liu divorced her 'husband' a few years later. It's been suggested she did so after realising he may have been entitled to half of her newly made fortune.[69])

Questions about the legitimacy of Helen Liu's marriage were brought to the attention of the immigration department in 2012 by Opposition immigration spokesman Scott Morrison.[70] Journalists Baker, Dorling and McKenzie wrote that the department declined to release information about Liu's marriage after consulting the office of the minister, Chris Bowen.[71]

Hikvision

In September 2016 *The Times* of London splashed across its front page a story about the rapid penetration of the CCTV market by Hikvision, a company controlled by the Chinese government.[72] Hikvision's cameras had captured fourteen per cent of the British market and were installed in a range of government buildings as well as Stansted and Glasgow airports and the London Underground. Officials feared that if the CCTV cameras were internet-enabled then their data could be fed back to Beijing. *The Times* claimed Hikvision grew out of China's military surveillance organisation and had achieved rapid market share by undercutting competitors, a strategy made possible because of its cheap line of credit from state banks.

Hikvision is now the world's leading supplier of video surveillance equipment.[73] Hangzhou Hikvision Digital Technology is a state-owned enterprise founded in 2001, emerging out of a government research institute. It is controlled by a larger state-owned technology group, China Electronics Technology Group Corporation (CETC) (whose penetration of the University of Technology Sydney is discussed in Chapter 10).[74] The chair of its board also serves as the secretary of the Communist Party Committee of the company. He has exhorted members to realise the unity of the 'Hikvision Dream' and the 'China Dream'.[75] When in 2015 President Xi went on an inspection tour of Hangzhou he visited Hikvision's headquarters rather than that of the much more famous Alibaba. He was introduced to the company's head of research and development, Pu Shiliang, who is also reported to be the director of a technology laboratory within China's leading security agency, the Ministry of Public Security, which conducts a massive video surveillance program. The ministry is responsible for suppressing dissidents and for widespread abuse of human rights, including torture.[76]

Hikvision's most advanced cameras can recognise numberplates, even in fog, and can follow individuals using sophisticated face-recognition technology. In the United States, installation of the company's equipment in airports, prisons and schools, and a military base in Missouri, has led some industry experts to raise the alarm. One wrote to the US government: 'Every time one of their machines is plugged into the internet, it sends all your data to three servers in China. With that information, the Chinese government can log in to any camera system, anytime they want.'[77] While other industry leaders are less worried, a major video surveillance software company, Genetec, has said it will no longer service Hikvision (or Huawei) devices due to security concerns. For its part, Hikvision accuses its critics of a Cold War mentality.

Hikvision set up an Australian subsidiary in 2013. Since then it has won a large and growing market share for its 'incredibly cheap IP camera' (internet-enabled), in the words of one expert in Canberra's security industry.[78] It may be the largest supplier of video surveillance equipment in Australia. The same expert says that Hikvision's cameras, while very popular for monitoring commercial premises, schools, apartment blocks and the like, are not yet of sufficient quality for high-end uses like airports and secure government buildings (at least in Canberra).[79] Hikvision itself has said the gap between its cameras and the top brands is closing.[80] The cameras are always linked to servers, which are usually onsite, but the images could be rerouted to servers anywhere in the world.

One Australian supplier discontinued its relationship with Hikvision after trade magazines exposed the company's CCP links. Other industry experts I have spoken to are reluctant to say anything on the record but all are aware of the doubts about Hikvision. Even if retailers do not sell Hikvision cameras, most of the leading CCTV brands installed in Australia—including Swann and Honeywell—are actually devices manufactured by Hikvision in China and rebranded.[81] (Some brands will not reveal where their cameras are made.) One major national supplier of CCTVs, including Hikvision, told me that his customers are not aware of the risks of using Hikvision cameras, and that goes for government agencies too.[82] If it comes up, most dismiss the concerns as just another conspiracy theory. The security and surveillance expert has watched the Chinese penetration with growing alarm, describing Australians as 'sleeping zombies'.

In March 2017 experts discovered that Hikvision had inserted a 'backdoor' into its CCTV cameras allowing 'full admin access' to the devices. Hikvision categorically denied it, but the United States Department of Homeland Security (DHS) verified the reports and gave Hikvision cameras its worst possible score for security.[83] In May 2017 the DHS issued an alert warning of malicious intruders accessing sensitive information on networks by hacking into Hikvision cameras.[84] Hikvision cameras are seen as the weak link.

When I asked a senior security industry figure if the Chinese government could use a Hikvision camera to spy on the building where it's installed, he replied, 'Of course it could be used for spying.' After a series of investigative articles in 2016, the trade website *IPVM* concluded in 2016 that 'the rest of the world seriously needs to consider the risks of having a Chinese Communist Party controlled organization being their video surveillance provider'.[85] Yet Hikvision CCTV cameras are being installed all over Australia without any expression of official concern.

Cyber theft

In late 2015 the computer systems of the Australian Bureau of Meteorology were the victim of a 'massive' cyber assault, resulting in the installation of malicious software.[86] While most people thought not much damage could be done to a weather-forecasting organisation, in fact the bureau is better thought of as 'a broad-based environmental intelligence agency'.[87] Its work is at the cutting edge of scientific research on weather forecasting and climate change. Moreover, its supercomputers are linked to sensitive systems across government, including the defence department, which receives daily weather reports, not least in parts of the world where the armed forces are operating. If there were a conflict with China, disrupting our weather-forecasting capacity could be a significant strategic advantage. According to Peter Jennings, the bureau may be seen as 'the weakest link' to gain access to high-security agencies,[88] the kind targeted by top-secret PRC cyber agencies like Unit 61398. The 2015 cyber intrusion may take years to fix at a cost of hundreds of millions of dollars.

In late 2016 security concerns were raised when the Australian National University's cutting-edge National Computational Infrastructure (NCI) centre confirmed it would be installing hardware and software supplied by Chinese company Lenovo, in which the Chinese government has a stake.[89] The Pentagon has warned US military agencies against the use of Lenovo equipment.[90] The ANU facility is used by the Bureau of Meteorology, the CSIRO and Geoscience Australia, among others. A source at the NCI told me that 'the cat is out of the bag anyway', as Chinese equipment is used everywhere and experts like him always assume that their systems have been infiltrated.[91] All that can be done is to take measures to limit the intrusion to those users who have been hacked.

It is not often appreciated just how dependent China's remarkable economic growth has been on foreign technology, much of which has been acquired by devious means. As China makes the transition to a more high-tech economic future, this dependence is increasing. China's Thirteenth Five-Year Plan stresses this transition and devotes attention to how the needed technology can be acquired. Although China has invested huge amounts in science and technology education, Xi Jinping complains that China is still far too dependent on foreign technology.[92] The gap is so crucial that two experts writing on cyber security for a US think tank concluded that China's economic plans presuppose a huge program of state-sponsored theft.[93]

The dependence of China's future growth on Western technology was disclosed in an indiscreet 2013 interview in a Japanese newspaper with Jack Peng, a senior IT engineer and officer in the Silicon Valley Chinese Overseas Business Association (SCOBA), linking the technology hub with the PRC.

I think if we [overseas Chinese scholars] quit America and went entirely back to China, China's development would halt … China regards those of us living overseas as essential. It extends a hand to us to make the results of our research blossom on Chinese soil … Most of us serve as advisors to the Chinese government through the SCOBA organization … Everyone has entered into a system of full-scale cooperation.[94]

It's known that cyber theft is an enormous problem in Australia, as it is in every technologically advanced nation. The Russians do it better but the Chinese do it more. What makes China unique is the implementation over many years of a program of systematic theft of commercial information, a program planned, implemented and supported by the Chinese government. While theft of intellectual property has a long history in the United States and Australia, it is against the law for intelligence agencies to spy for companies, unlike in China. The PRC's explicit aim is to build the nation's technological and engineering capabilities on the back of research carried out in other nations.

The head of the US military's Cyber Command has described this rampant theft as 'the greatest transfer of wealth in history'.[95] One credible source estimates that IP theft costs the US economy $600 billion a year, with the PRC as the leading culprit.[96]

The former chief of cyber crime at the FBI gave the example of hackers who in one night stole all of the results of a $1 billion research program carried out by an American company over ten years. It's not only military and commercial information that's being stolen. In 2014–15 a PRC state-sponsored agency known as Deep Panda hacked healthcare providers, stealing patient records of some eighty million Americans, data that could be used to compile personal dossiers and blackmail persons of interest.[97] Another state-sponsored organisation, Axiom, has hacked, among others, energy companies, meteorological services, media outlets, NGOs and universities.[98] Sometimes the easiest route is to persuade a 'malicious individual' on the inside to do no more than open a zip file in an email, which then installs malware such as PoisonIvy or Hikit on the organisation's system.

While the United States has been upfront about the nature and scale of the cyber threat and its responses, until recently the Australian government has kept the Australian public in the dark. Now it is talking more, though without naming China. As always, the view seems to be that nothing should be said that might upset Beijing. The US government has prosecuted scores of people, mostly of Chinese ethnicity, for various kinds of industrial and military espionage. In Australia there have been no prosecutions, partly because our laws are weak and partly because there is no appetite. When the Bureau of Meteorology was hacked the government was reluctant to point the finger at China, even though it was almost certainly guilty.

Few companies are willing to expose the laxity of their cyber security or frighten their shareholders by publicising the theft of their intellectual property. An exception is Codan, an Adelaide-based communications and mining technology firm that manufactured a very effective metal detector sold around the world. That side of its business was booming until 2013–14 when, unaccountably, sales collapsed. It discovered that cheap copies of its product were being manufactured in China and sold in large numbers in Africa.[99]

A Codan executive visiting China in 2012 had had his laptop hacked while logged on to his hotel wifi. Malware was installed and he carried it back to Australia to infect the company's system. This had been used to steal the blueprints for its metal detector. (Government officials visiting China are now warned not only to avoid hotel wifi but also to leave their mobile phones at home and avoid using hotel room safes.) Codan was blissfully unaware until ASIO officers arrived to reveal that its computer system had been infiltrated.

One of the most disturbing aspects of the case was the Australian government's reaction. When Codan CEO Donald McGurk contacted the federal government to help him track down and prosecute the thieves, he was told 'you're on your own'.[100] The government was in the middle of negotiating the free trade agreement with China and did not want any dark element to disrupt the friendly atmospherics. Fear of offending Beijing is a constant theme in our government's dealings with China. Beijing and its various organs know when to turn on the histrionics and exploit this Australian cultural weakness. Codan was forced to pursue the culprits on its own, tracking them down with the assistance of a private investigative firm in China.

Codan makes military equipment as well as metal detectors. Its portable field radios can send encrypted messages over long distances and are widely used in training and operations by armed forces and border operations in the United States, Britain and Australia, which explains why ASIO came knocking at Codan's door. Every defence contractor in Australia is a high-value target. Listening in to the enemy's communication system has been of the highest military priority since the decommissioning of the last carrier pigeon (and attempts were made to intercept them too). Exports need a government permit. And it was design information about the field radios that the malware aimed to steal.[101] China's defence strategy relies heavily on an ability to degrade and disrupt the communications and surveillance capabilities of a superior American enemy.[102]

It's natural to think that spies target research in fields such as advanced materials, nanotechnology and so on, yet few sectors are immune, including agriculture. In 2016 the US government warned farmers to be alert to Chinese businessmen showing keen interest in genetically modified seeds.[103] A Beijing-sponsored espionage ring had been caught digging up seeds from Iowa farms to send to China.[104] US authorities treated it as a national security prosecution rather than a criminal case. There had been a spate of reported thefts of advanced food technology—after all, biotechnology is the subject of billion-dollar research programs. These warnings add a new dimension to the surge of Chinese investment in Australian agriculture, including joint ventures.

Racial profiling

Nervous about accusations of 'racial profiling', US authorities have had to tread carefully in their pursuit of Beijing's spies. Most are of Chinese heritage.[105] Beijing-linked organisations in the US have been quick to accuse US authorities of racial profiling, in the same way that their counterparts in Australia silence critics with the 'xenophobia' word. In the US there are examples of strong cases for prosecution being dropped because political authorities were nervous of this kind of accusation.[106] The irony is that the Chinese party-state bases its entire foreign outreach on ethnicity—that is, on racial profiling. What matters is not beliefs, as in the Cold War, but skin colour.

Of course, the PRC exploits Western liberal sensitivities wherever it can, encouraging its proxies and apologists to use accusations of racism and seizing on any wrongful accusation of espionage. Multiplying the ironies, the PRC security services launched their own public awareness campaign against spies, centred on a cartoon poster titled 'Dangerous Love', warning young female civil servants of the risks of being seduced by handsome Westerners such as visiting scholars.[107] Imagine the uproar if the Australian attorney-general launched a comic book warning public servants of the dangers of being seduced by women of Chinese heritage.

The Chinese embassy and consulates pull the strings of hundreds, perhaps thousands, of Chinese-Australians in sensitive positions. A Falun Gong practitioner in Canberra, interviewed by Alex Joske, said his wife's close friend had suddenly cut off contact with her. 'The friend later admitted that, despite being an Australian citizen and an employee of the Australian Public Service, she had been compelled by the Chinese government to do so.'[108] These Chinese-Australians are victims too.

Cyber warriors

In 2016 the federal government announced a new cyber-security strategy that would pour more resources, staff and determination into protecting Australia from cyber threats. The enhanced Australian Cyber Security Centre will be led by the top-secret Australian Signals Directorate (ASD). In addition to responding to cyber crime, in one of the most important defence initiatives in decades the government has begun a shake-up of the defence forces with the formation of a cyber-warfare division tasked with defending Australia from hostile attacks and having the ability to launch cyber offensives against enemies. The rank of the head of the division will be similar to those leading the three traditional services.

The new emphasis on cyber warfare is in large measure a response to China's commitment to achieve cyber superiority for its armed forces, announced in 2014. We cannot match China with troops and hardware, but one targeted cyber attack could wreak havoc. I am told that, as in the US, the who's who of cyber warfare in Australia are reading *Ghost Fleet*, a novel 'grounded in hardcore research' by Peter Singer (not the philosopher) in which the United States is defeated, and then occupied, because China's superior cyber capability allows it to cripple America's satellite systems and computer networks. It is believed that foreign intelligence agencies may already be planting malware for future sabotage.[109]

Although there is already a shortage of cyber skills in the civilian workforce, the new emphasis on cyber in the Australian Defence Force will require 100 cyber security specialists immediately, growing to 900 within ten years.[110] Where will they come from?

Deakin University, based in Geelong, runs one of Australia's few programs allowing both undergraduates and postgraduates to specialise in cyber security. Many graduates are expected to make their way into government agencies, scientific organisations like the CSIRO and the Australian Defence Force. The university's Centre for Cyber Security Research and Innovation (CSRI) 'works with industry and government through collaborative research projects to provide protection from major cyber security threats'.[111] It is dominated by researchers of Chinese heritage. Of the ten academic staff members listed on its website, six, including the centre's director, Professor Yang Xiang, are from China.

CSRI director Yang Xiang has a PhD from Deakin. He is also the director of the Network Security and Computing Laboratory (NSCLab) at Deakin, which is part-funded by the Australian Research Council (ARC). It names as a research partner the Australian Bureau of Meteorology, which, as indicated, was targeted in 2015 in a cyber attack believed to have been launched from China.[112] NSCLab's website lists the Cybersecurity Lab at the Australian Defence Force Academy (ADFA), run by professor of cyber security Hu Jiankun, as its sole 'friend lab', with which it shares data sets.[113]

Yang Xiang is closely connected to Xidian University. In May 2017 he received a Changjiang Scholar award from the Chinese government, which includes a professorship at Xidian University. His receipt of the award and the Xidian professorship are proudly advertised by the CSRI as a 'boost for cyber security collaboration'.[114] As we will see in the next chapter, Xidian University is closely connected to the People's Liberation Army and has shown a strong interest in expanding its overseas networks through its alumni association and academic exchanges. Xidian is one of China's top computer science and cryptography institutions and recently opened a school of cyber engineering.[115]

It's important to make the following point in reference to all of the scientists of Chinese heritage mentioned in this book and who work at Australian universities or research institutes, including Yang Xiang. They may have no intention of benefiting the PRC's military or intelligence capabilities at the expense of Australia. There is, however, a risk of benefiting the PRC to the detriment of Australia by the fact of collaborating with PLA and intelligence-linked researchers in China. Their collaboration with PLA researchers does not mean they are disloyal to Australia, as they may see it as being part of common scientific practice in an international scientific culture.

Yang Xiang has been a visiting professor at Xidian's State Key Laboratory of Integrated Services Networks since at least 2015.[116] The laboratory's academic committee is headed by Yu Quan, who has served as chief engineer of the PLA General Staff Headquarters 61st Research Institute,[117] described by US Army–backed experts as 'a major center of the PLA's information technology research'.[118] Yu has won six military technology progress prizes for his contributions to the PLA's technological development.[119] Gao Xinbo, the laboratory's director, has worked on three military armaments projects.[120] In 2016 he was awarded a highly prestigious second-place national science and technology prize.[121]

Yang Xiang is also a foreign expert at Xidian's Mobile Internet Security Innovation Talent Recruitment Base, also known as the National 111 Project for Mobile Internet Security, which falls under China's technology transfer and innovation program. The Xidian base is headed by Shen Changxiang, a leading communications and internet security expert. He is also a major general in the PLA Navy (PLAN).[122] He has been honoured by China's navy as a 'model science and technology worker' for his work, which includes seventeen military technology progress prizes and serving as a high-level engineer at the PLAN Classified Warship Technology Research Institute.[123] His research discoveries are described as seeing 'widespread use across the military'.[124]

When Deakin University's Xiang received his Xidian professorship, he said that he would actively offer his counsel and guidance in the areas of cyberspace security and talent cultivation, and strive to make newer and greater academic achievements at Xidian University.[125]

Eclipsing Deakin University as a training ground for Australia's future cyber warfare command is the Australian Defence Force Academy (ADFA), which offers more cyber security training than anywhere else in Australia. A large proportion of the new generation of Australia's cyber warfare experts will be trained there. In 2016 the academy began a new master's degree in Cyber Security, Strategy and Diplomacy, and another in Cyber Security (Advanced Tradecraft), hinting at careers in Australian spy agencies. The military academy also hosts the Australian Centre for Cyber Security, which trains doctoral students, including senior officers of the ADF, in the most sophisticated tools of cyber security. ADFA's cyber security research and teaching offer an obvious gateway to Australia's emerging cyber warfare capability and therefore represents an irresistible target for Chinese infiltration. For some years China has sent students to enrol in PhDs and to work as post-doctoral fellows, where they have access to the computer systems and, more importantly, can develop a network of contacts with the future leaders of Australia's armed forces and intelligence services.

In 2015 ADFA's Professor of Cybersecurity Hu Jiankun gave a tribute at the Chinese embassy to scholarship students, whose awards 'encourage them to return to China to work or serve the country through many channels'.[126] Professor Hu has worked together with experts from the Ministry of Public Security and the State Key Laboratory of Cryptology in Beijing.[127] He has also published many papers with researchers at Harbin Institute of Technology and Beihang University, both of which have been ranked in the top five 'most secretive and mysterious research universities in China'.[128]

When I visited ADFA, located adjacent to the Royal Military College at Duntroon near Canberra airport, I was surprised to see a group of PRC men in suits wandering around the campus taking photos. There was no security visible. As a campus of the University of New South Wales, ADFA is no more secure than any other Australian campus. I was told that the company that has the cleaning contract, including emptying the wastepaper baskets, is staffed by ethnic Chinese. While engaged in a conversation with an expert about PRC espionage in Australia, an ethnic Chinese cleaner entered the office to empty the bin. There is also a branch of the Chinese Students and Scholars Association (CSSA) at ADFA. In other parts of the world CSSAs have been accused of espionage.[129]

In *China's Espionage Dynasty*, James Scott and Drew Spaniel claim that Chinese graduate students working in science and technology labs may be pressured to install malware into the university system—or the research program's network—by plugging in an infected USB.[130] A 2011 FBI report on spying at American universities warned of foreign students (not only from China) being sent to collaborate with researchers and attain a position of trust before stealing information.[131] It gave the example of a member of a CSSA who defected to Belgium and revealed 'he had been coordinating industrial espionage agents throughout Europe for ten years'. A professor of interest may be identified then studied to find his or her 'motivations, weaknesses, politics, and ambitions'. They may then be befriended and recruited, sometimes naïvely offering up information. So concerned is the US State Department that in 2016 it proposed barring foreign students from research projects and classes covering areas such as defence technologies, energy engineering and aerospace.[132] ADFA appears to be oblivious.

9

'Malicious insiders' and scientific organisations

'Mobilising Ten Thousand Overseas Chinese'

At the highest level in China, directives for influence programs are formulated by the Politburo and passed down to the CCP's Central Committee. Responsibilities are there divided between the Overseas Chinese Affairs Office and the United Front Work Department.[1] They have different roles and functions but in Australia as elsewhere they are channelled and coordinated through the embassy and consulates. Through this structure the PRC reaches deeply into the Chinese diaspora in Australia, using it for the purposes of influence, control and espionage, including spying on the community itself. The essential fact to keep in mind is that the CCP uses the diaspora for recruiting informers, plants and spies as well as winning over or paying unwitting agents of influence. The whole structure serves as an effective tool of foreign policy.

Although it didn't name the country, ASIO's 2016–17 annual report was clear about the Chinese threat. 'We identified foreign powers clandestinely seeking to shape the opinions of members of the Australian public, media organisations and government officials in order to advance their country's own political objectives.'[2] It wrote that ethnic communities in Australia were the subject of covert influence operations aimed at shutting down criticism. In its previous report ASIO had warned of foreign interference in 'community groups, business and social associations', not least the 'monitoring, coercion or intimidation of diaspora communities'.[3] ASIO could be referring to only one country.

However, counter-terrorism work absorbs the lion's share of ASIO's resources, leaving little for counter-espionage, and for this new, third component of security protection that might be called 'counter-subversion'. While there has been extensive media attention on United Front work in Chinese social and business organisations, PRC control of Chinese professional organisations has gone unnoticed.[4] Yet they have become a vital conduit for PRC intelligence gathering and technology theft in Australia.

As we saw, the PRC openly declares that it regards all overseas Chinese, including those with foreign citizenship and even those born in other countries, as owing allegiance to the motherland. If you have Chinese heritage the CCP assumes it owns you. The essential purpose of the Overseas Chinese Affairs Office (OCAO) is to establish contact and develop relationships with 'overseas Chinese' (itself a loaded term) and align them with party objectives, both political ones like Taiwanese unification and commercial ones like technology transfer.

In March 2017, coinciding with the visit to Australia of PRC Premier Li Keqiang, the director of the OCAO, Qiu Yuanping, visited Sydney. She met with the most prominent and trusted community leaders, notably the wealthy political donors Chau Chak Wing, Zhu Minshen and Huang Xiangmo. Speaking to an audience including representatives of the Australian Council for the Promotion of Peaceful Reunification of China (ACPPRC), Qiu said that Premier Li's visit 'will powerfully promote the development of comprehensive strategic partner relations' between the two countries.[5] She told her audience that Chairman Xi Jinping and Premier Li Keqiang 'hold a special affection for overseas Chinese'. She then outlined the OCAO's planned development work for this year, 'hoping that everyone would energetically participate', invoking 'the overseas Chinese heart and the overseas Chinese strength, and exhorting them to support Xi's China Dream and the great rejuvenation of the Chinese nation'.

Qiu was formally thanked by Huang Xiangmo for bringing to Australia the ancestral nation's 'warmth and regards'. Despite his public battering in the Dastyari affair of 2016, Huang remained Beijing's chief operative for controlling the Chinese community in Australia. The event was a blunt reminder of the presumption in Beijing that overseas Chinese, no matter what kind of passport they hold, will naturally serve the motherland first. Those who attend these events voluntarily should be presumed to share that view.

In this light, a more interesting meeting (reported only in Chinese) took place the next day, on 24 March. Qiu Yuanping arrived at the University of Technology Sydney (UTS) for a 'leisurely chat' with over twenty senior Chinese scholars and researchers from the Sydney region.[6] Qiu talked about the implementation of the OCAO's newest policy, the 'Mobilising Ten Thousand Overseas Chinese for Innovation', which is explicitly about bringing 'overseas countrymen' back to China to advance innovation and technology. But it is also aimed at rallying those who serve the country from overseas.[7] The four million Chinese who have stayed abroad after their studies are 'one of the most valuable resources in implementing China's strategy for innovation development and drive'. Her organisation in Beijing, she said, 'is escorting you like an emperor'.

Among those reportedly soaking up the patriotic message were the executive director of UTS data science and deputy vice-chancellor, Professor Zhang Chengqi (who is also a member of the board of Bob Carr's ACRI), UTS professor of electrical engineering Zhu Jianguo (a member of the United Front organisation FOCSA, discussed later), professor of photonics at the University of New South Wales (UNSW) Peng Gang-Ding, UNSW professor of manufacturing engineering Wang Jun, Wollongong University engineering professor Jiang Zhengyi and Sydney University medical school associate professor Bao 'Bob' Shisan.

HUMINT (human intelligence)

Although the 'unseen enemy' of cyber hacking has received the most publicity, it is not the only, or necessarily the most effective, means of stealing information. In the United States the volume of China's cyber hacking reportedly declined in 2016 after an agreement between presidents Obama and Xi to refrain from cyber attacks for commercial purposes. Obama had threatened to retaliate with sanctions, so China has shifted to greater use of human rather than electronic infiltration.[8] The PRC has for some years pressured ethnic Chinese employees to steal confidential information and sensitive technology.[9] According to a Congressional report, in the United States it has been known for some time that scientists with access to valuable research data have been working for China.[10]

The PLA, which is responsible for the theft of a great deal of civilian data as well as for targetting military secrets, has a unit known as the Third Department that is responsible for a massive program of cyber attacks, hacking and exfiltration of data.[11] The Second Department is responsible for more conventional kinds of human intelligence gathering. In their *China's Espionage Dynasty*, James Scott and Drew Spaniel estimate that the Second Department has 30,000 to 50,000 human spies planted in organisations around the world whose aim is to collect information, confidential and otherwise, to be sent back to China. (It's believed that cyber attacks will at times be launched to cover the tracks of a human agent inside an organisation.[12])

While cyber theft can be conducted from anywhere in the world, HUMINT requires experts in positions of trust placed in Australian organisations. In its 2016–17 annual report ASIO made particular comment on 'malicious insiders', mainly government employees and contractors with privileged access to information including sensitive technology, who have been co-opted by a foreign intelligence service.[13]

In the United States, many stories of spies recruited by China have come to light, mostly through prosecutions.[14] One was the case of an American company, AMSC, that sold sophisticated 'electronic brains' for wind turbines to a Chinese company, Sinovel.[15] Having built its business supplying the specialised equipment, AMSC was suddenly cut off by Sinovel, with a truckload of parts turned away. It soon discovered that its technology had been stolen by Sinovel, which had bribed a Serbian software engineer who worked at AMSC's facility in Germany. (He was convicted and jailed.) Sinovel was founded by Han Junliang, who made his reputation working for the Dalian Heavy Industry Group, a giant state-owned enterprise. One of the investors in his company was princeling Wen Yunsong, son of China's Premier Wen Jiabao. Han was also close to the boss of the National Energy Administration, a relationship he used to turn Sinovel into the world's second largest wind turbine maker.

Another case is that of American Glenn Shriver, who, while studying Mandarin in China, was befriended by two men and a woman who turned out to be Ministry of State Security (MSS) officers.[16] They persuaded him to return to the US and make his way into sensitive areas of government service. Among a number of cash payments was one of $40,000 when he applied (unsuccessfully) for a job with the CIA. Shriver was caught and imprisoned for four years. His story shows that while espionage on behalf of the PRC is carried out predominantly by those of Chinese heritage, others are not immune to recruitment.

In Canada, the security agencies have for some years viewed China as the nation's most serious intelligence threat, operating mainly through the recruitment of Chinese-Canadians.[17] Visitors too can be suspect. The head of the Canadian Security Intelligence Service observed: 'It's surprising, sometimes, the number of hyperactive tourists we get here and where they come from.' A CSIS report noted as far back as 2004 that 'foreign students and scientists, business delegations and immigrants were among those recruited as informants'.[18] In 2013 a Chinese-Canadian engineer, Qing Quentin Huang, was arrested and charged with passing classified information about Canada's navy ship procurement strategy to China.[19]

Nanotechnology is seen by the Chinese government as the path to a 'great leap forward'.[20] In 2016 five Chinese nationals were charged with intellectual property theft from a Taiwanese nanotechnology company.[21] They planned to use the specialised technology to set up their own factory on the mainland. A case of suspected espionage at a CSIRO facility in 2013 (discussed later) also involved nanotechnology.

Although there have been no prosecutions of people of Chinese heritage engaged in commercial or government espionage in Australia, it would be naïve to believe that it is not happening. There can be little doubt that the Chinese government has built in Australia extensive networks for the theft of classified information and intellectual property to serve the development plans of China. Project 111, for example, offers generous inducements to overseas Chinese scientists to return home. According to Daniel Golden, who has written extensively about theft of IP from US universities, those recruited are encouraged not to come home empty-handed.[22]

The large and growing number of highly qualified Chinese-Australians now working in science and technology labs around the country provide fertile recruiting grounds. These Chinese-Australians are perfect targets for the PRC's finely tuned techniques of influence and coercion. Some have moved into senior management positions in companies, universities and government organisations with technical functions or at the heart of the nation's decision-making. Scientists, engineers, IT specialists and other professionals are drawn or pressured into a net of patriotic commitment to the motherland. Everyone born in China is regarded as a legitimate target by the Chinese party-state, expected to be ultimately loyal to the ancestral homeland.

Like so much else, this mirrors the pattern in the United States. In their book *Chinese Industrial Espionage*, William Hannas, James Mulvenon and Anna Puglisi detail an astonishingly dense network of associations of Chinese science and technology professionals operating within the United States, all with deep links to the Chinese state and with the goal of transferring sophisticated technology to China in order to support its goal of surpassing the United States.[23] There is a concentration of these organisations in Silicon Valley, where around one in ten high-tech workers is from mainland China.[24]

Professional associations

A parallel network of PRC-linked professional associations operates in Australia, often with names and objectives virtually identical to those in the United States. While these associations provide a venue for social networking and assistance with professional advancement, their members may be recruited to work for the PRC. The organisations are in some cases created at the suggestion of the Chinese state. Patriotic overtures are made but so are promises of 'extremely high' salaries on top of their legitimate salaries.[25]

James To—whose meticulously sourced work has not been questioned—discovered that the PLA and the Ministry of State Security identify candidates for intelligence gathering before they leave China: 'they are not necessarily asked to spy illegally, but simply invited to share information.'[26] Their handlers abroad cultivate warm relationships through dinners and events organised by cultural and professional associations. Carrots and sticks are deployed. The carrots are promises of good jobs and houses when they return to China. The sticks include refusing visas and threats to harm their families. Graduate students may become 'sleeper' agents, only activated if they find themselves in jobs with access to desirable information. According to James To, clandestine and aggressive methods are used mainly on those overseas Chinese who can provide information of scientific, technological and military value.

The Chinese Association for International Exchange of Personnel (CAIEP) keeps a very low profile and few people outside China have heard of it, even though its branches are active around the world.[27] Here it is known as the Australia-China Association for International Exchange of Personnel (ACAIEP). Its office is in Collins Street, Melbourne, and it maintains a permanent office in Beijing.[28] Its main task is to vacuum up high-tech information by forging links with Chinese-origin scientists working in research labs.

ACAIEP is one of a number of front organisations for the State Administration of Foreign Experts Affairs (SAFEA), which reports directly to the PRC State Council. Hannas, Mulvenon and Puglisi single out SAFEA as the foremost PRC-based technology transfer organisation.[29] In practice 'there is no distinction to be made between cooperating with' CAIEP and SAFEA.[30] In the United States, SAFEA (sometimes referred to as the Foreign Experts Bureau) was caught red-handed recruiting an engineer to supply to the PRC highly classified equipment designs for US stealth missiles.[31] The engineer was sentenced to thirty-two years in prison.

SAFEA's objective of recruiting spies to supply valuable information to the PRC is hinted at on its website, where its mission is to use 'many types of recruitment channels' and to do so by making 'full use of contacts with governments, exchanges with sister cities, international economic and trade negotiations, international conferences, and like opportunities' to recruit foreign experts.[32] SAFEA itself and its front organisations are active in Australia. In December 2016, SAFEA's director, Zhang Jianguo, toured Australia and New Zealand and met with officials from the Department of Immigration and Border Protection, presumably to remove obstacles to exchange visits.[33]

Developing institutional and personal relationships is a prelude to recruiting spies. ACAIEP acts as a facilitator, sometimes brokering cooperation agreements between Australian and Chinese universities, such as the one between Victoria University in Melbourne and the Chongqing Energy College, and the one between Victoria University, Liaoning University and the China Scholarship Council. The advantage of a front organisation like ACAIEP is that it conceals SAFEA's PRC links and 'insulates' universities in Australia from 'the stigma of supporting a foreign state whose goals are often inimical' to Australia's interests.[34]

Mirroring the United States, in Australia there are a number of science and technology professional associations for Chinese-Australian scientists, each with links to the PRC. These associations provide social contact and career advancement, but they also bring together scientists, engineers and others in ways that can be manipulated and directed by the embassy. Espionage experts Hannas, Mulvenon and Puglisi write that Beijing 'courts these associations and steers their activities using a mix of psychological pressure, political control, and financial incentives'.[35]

The peak body of these professional associations is the Federation of Chinese Scientists in Australia (FOCSA). It brings together thirteen associations and aims to 'represent Chinese scholars in Australia'.[36] In October 2004 the *People's Daily* celebrated the launch of FOCSA, noting that it began 'with the energetic support and aid of the Chinese Embassy in Australia's education office'.[37] China's ambassador in Australia, Fu Ying, was reported (in Chinese) as saying she 'hoped that the specialists and scholars would be able to transfer advanced technological achievements back to China.' The federation has held its meetings at the embassy education office in the Canberra suburb of O'Malley.

Looking back on its first five years, the Ministry of Education in Beijing noted with satisfaction that FOCSA had contributed towards the ancestral nation's scientific education. It had 'frequently through various methods encouraged members to participate in national service projects and events, actively organised and participated in the education office's "Spring Sunshine Plan", and constantly expanded opportunities (for Chinese scholars in Australia) to collaborate and exchange with Chinese colleagues. Many of the group's members maintain long-term stable cooperation with domestic research and higher education institutions.'[38]

One of FOCSA's vice-presidents is Professor Xinghuo Yu. He manages RMIT's scientific research programs and has been a member of Australian government bodies overseeing photonics and advanced manufacturing research.[39] The current president of FOCSA is Professor Lin Ye, a professor at the University of Sydney's Centre for Advanced Materials Technology where he works on nanotechnology, among other things. Ye graduated from the secretive Harbin Engineering University and the Beijing University of Aeronautics and Astronautics, respectively ranked second and fourth in China for military research.[40] He retains links with both. In 2014 he spoke at the Beijing University of Aeronautics and Astronautics. In 2016 he spoke at the Harbin Institute of Technology, which is ranked first for military research in China.

The Western Australia Chinese Scientists Association (WACSA) is very active. (Also active in the west are the Western Australia Chinese Engineers Association and the Western Australia Chinese Petroleum Association.) Founded in 2003, WACSA is open to 'professionals of Chinese ethnic background and with postgraduate qualifications'.[41] Its members are among the best scientists in their fields. Some work at senior levels in government. The president of WACSA is Guowei Ma, a professor of engineering at the University of Western Australia. Like other scientists of Chinese origin in Australia, Ma seems to carry out research solely with Chinese scientists, with almost no Western names among his scores of co-authors. WACSA's website links to the PRC's Perth consulate and the PRC embassy-sponsored FOCSA. In 2015 it welcomed the Perth consul general, who spoke about China's OBOR strategy. The consulate reported that the audience was 'full of confidence about the future of China's development and full of expectation about China-Australia cooperation'.[42] In February 2017 it held a major conference in Perth, opened by Australia's Minister for Foreign Affairs, Julie Bishop, and China's consul general.

Another prominent organisation is the Queensland Chinese Association of Scientists and Engineers (QCASE), which seems to have a close relationship with the PRC's Brisbane consulate and with institutions in China.[43] Brisbane consul general Sun Dali's address to a QCASE general meeting was reported by the Ministry of Foreign Affairs in Beijing in the following way: 'In this enthusiastic atmosphere, Consul General Sun used the Beijing spirit of "patriotism, innovation, inclusivity and virtue" to exhort everyone, and moreover wished the scientists a happy Chinese New Year.'[44]

The honorary chairman of QCASE since its foundation has been Max Lu (Chinese name Lu Gaoqing), a leading nanotechnology expert who worked his way into senior academic and administrative positions at the University of Queensland over two decades after completing his PhD there. His area of expertise, nanotechnology, is of great relevance to military, pharmaceutical and electronics applications, among others.

In 2004 Max Lu was the founding president of FOCSA. In 2011 he won a prize from the Ministry of Science and Technology in Beijing. He had been the 'core member' of the Chinese Academy of Sciences (CAS) Overseas Innovators Team—Shenyang Interface Materials Research Centre. CAS credits him with advancing its work in solar energy catalysis, energy storage and hydrogen storage.[45]

In 2017 Professor Lu was made an Officer of the Order of Australia for 'distinguished service to education, to national and international research in the fields of materials chemistry and nanotechnology, to engineering, and to Australia-China relations'. The citation lists his close connections with the Chinese state, including his membership of an Expert Consultative Committee of the ruling State Council.[46] According to a 2015 article by the All-China Federation of Returned Overseas Chinese, '[Max] Lu Gaoqing after so many years has never stopped being interested in China and his native land. Having worked for 28 years in foreign nations, Lu Gaoqing said that his feelings towards the ancestral nation and his native land have "never changed".'[47] Lu has been quoted by Xinhua News Agency speaking strongly in support of China's foreign policy.[48] At the same time he was serving on a number of influential Australian government advisory bodies.

In April 2016 Professor Lu took up a new position as president and vice-chancellor of the University of Surrey, 'the first Chinese to become the President of a top-ranking university in the western world'.[49]

Among the many professional associations for Chinese-Australians and Chinese in Australia, the Canberra Society of Chinese Scholars (CSCS) is of particular interest. The society has very close ties to the Chinese embassy, with its 2016 council and executive committee meeting held at the embassy's education office.[50] The meeting's agenda included a speech by education attaché Xu Xiao. The members of CSCS are drawn from the ANU, the CSIRO, the Australian Defence Force Academy and a number of federal government departments, including one who works in a federal intelligence organisation.[51] In early 2017 CSCS held a workshop entitled 'Overseas Chinese scholars returning home to serve'. Of the twenty-one on the attendance list, six were from the CSIRO.[52]

China's appetite for other countries' technology—obtained legally or otherwise—is satisfied by a number of means. One is to form companies in the West whose mission is to receive requests from Chinese companies needing a particular technology and then to search for possible suppliers among scientists or engineers of Chinese (or other) heritage in competitor companies.[53] Provinces and major cities also have their own recruitment programs linked directly to the United Front Work Department. In November 2016, the PRC-loyal Shenzhen Australia Community Association sponsored a Shenzhen (Australia) Overseas High-Level Talent Forum in Sydney to hold 'deep exchanges' with scholars from Sydney universities.[54] The meeting was addressed by two senior cadres from the United Front Work Department and the city's Overseas Chinese Federation, as well as the Sydney consulate's science and technology counsellor and SAFEA's chief representative in Australia. Huang Xiangmo spoke, as president of the Shenzhen Australia Community Association.

The Chinese-language *People's Daily* report of the event noted the presence of Western Sydney University (WSU) deputy vice-chancellor Professor Lan Yizhen.[55] Lan's title is actually Deputy Pro Vice-Chancellor (International) at WSU. He is closely tied to various United Front bodies, including serving as honorary adviser to the ACPPRC, run by

Huang Xiangmo, and the Australia China Economics, Trade and Culture Association (ACETCA).[56] Also present was Leo Mian Liu, described as 'the Executive Director of the UTS Australia-China Relations Institute' (see Chapter 5). Leo Mian Liu also serves as an honorary advisor to the United Front body ACPPRC.[57] Keeping Liu company from UTS was its deputy vice-chancellor, Professor Bill Purcell.

CSIRO

'I'm more worried about CSIRO than universities.' This comment was made to me by a public servant whose job is to manage classified research.[58] Universities in Australia, my interlocutor said, are driven by money, but the CSIRO is even more obsessed by it. When I asked how the organisation responds to the kinds of information about China's infiltration uncovered in this book, my interlocutor admitted: 'I try not to think about it, to be honest.'

In December 2013, CSIRO management called the Australian Federal Police (AFP) to report a suspected spy in its ranks. A Chinese scientist working at the Materials Science and Engineering labs in Melbourne had not turned up for work and was thought to have absconded with sensitive information.[59] Officers from the AFP's High Tech Crime Operations group called at his home but found only a CSIRO laptop. Eventually the AFP would seek the assistance of the French government because, it was reported, the fugitive had fled there.[60]

However, when the AFP tracked him down he refused to cooperate. Those who had worked with him reported they'd been concerned about his 'poor performance'; he had somehow obtained the job without suitable expertise.[61] Analysis of the computers he'd shared did not reveal evidence of espionage and the police dropped the case, although a senior manager emailed the police saying that the incident had been 'a wakeup call for the whole organisation'. When I phoned CSIRO headquarters to ask about the affair and its effect on the organisation I met a blank wall.

It's fair to assume that the results of every piece of scientific research carried out by the CSIRO become available free of charge in China. Logic suggests that the CSIRO is a prime target for Chinese espionage. Australia's premier scientific research organisation is engaged in a great deal of research of high commercial and strategic value to China, yet all of the indications are that the CSIRO has no understanding of the problem and does not care.

In 2015, 484 CSIRO staff members, close to ten per cent of its experts, were born in China.[62] For the Chinese embassy these men and women are an excellent recruiting ground for high-value informants channelling quality information to the PRC.

The CSIRO's director of China engagement and chief scientist for manufacturing and mining resources, Professor Wei Gang, is associated with the United Front group FOCSA, from which we learn of his work promoting the CSIRO's collaboration with China, particularly in nanotechnology. He concurrently holds various positions in China, including as overseas review expert for the Ministry of Education's Cheung Kong Scholars Programme, funded by 'patriotic businessman' Li Ka Shing in support of the 'best of the best' among Chinese researchers.[63] He is also director of the Yunnan Normal University board and a member of the expert advisory panel at the Shanghai Nanotechnology and Promotion Center, not to mention chair professor at the East China University of Science and Technology and a senior adviser to the government of Shenzhen. It is unclear whether these positions receive a salary, but Wei is clearly seen by Beijing as a loyal son of the motherland. (Professor Wei did not reply to an email requesting an interview.)

In the United States there is mounting concern that Chinese companies, with the encouragement of Beijing, are actively looking for investment opportunities in innovative American firms working on critical technologies like artificial intelligence, some with military applications.[64] A confidential Pentagon white paper covering the rush of Chinese money into Silicon Valley is ringing alarm bells in Washington. In August 2017 President Trump ordered an investigation of ways to stop the transfer of intellectual property to China through acquisition and outright theft.

In Australia, China has a more direct route to accessing sensitive technology—joint research programs with the CSIRO and universities. It's hard to know whether our research institutions have any awareness of the risks of technology theft, not least because for academics and researchers 'theft' may seem to be no more than traditional sharing of knowledge. But given the naivety of these institutions, it's unlikely they undertake any kind of serious due diligence to winnow out those collaborations that are innocent and mutually beneficial.

Data61

China has set about becoming the world leader in artificial intelligence (AI) by 2030. Artificial intelligence has many benign applications but is also central to the PRC's plans for enhanced domestic (and global) surveillance and internet censorship. One use in development is the capacity to identify 'criminals' before they have committed any crime.[65] It also has extensive military applications.

AI is attracting a great deal of attention in Australia too. Data61 is the CSIRO's high-profile research centre for data science, including AI. Claiming to be 'world leaders in data science research and engineering', it has a huge staff complement of 1100, plus over 400 resident PhD students. It's the hub of Australia's most advanced work on AI and a broad range of applications. For example, in collaboration with universities and other research centres it plays a crucial role in supporting Australia's cyber security. Among Data61's many collaborations is a $9.3 million partnership with the Defence Science and Technology Group (DST, formerly known as DSTO) 'to establish collaborative research projects with nine Australian universities around cyber security'.[66] It is also focusing on the data storage and transfer method known as blockchain.

A number of scientists at Data61 have co-authored papers with researchers at military institutions in China.

Chen Wang is a senior research scientist at Data61. He received his PhD from Nanjing University and researches cloud computing systems and energy services for the smart grid.[67] While at the CSIRO Chen Wang has collaborated with a number of researchers at the National University of Defense Technology (NUDT) in China, or, to give it its full title, the People's Liberation Army National University of Defense Science and Technology. NUDT is the top-ranked military academy in China and is led by the Central Military Commission, chaired by Xi Jinping. It is at the centre of China's ambitious push to modernise its armed forces with the most sophisticated weapons.

Among Chen Wang's recent co-authors are the following NUDT researchers:

- Liu Xiaocheng from the System Simulation Lab of NUDT's College of Mechatronics and Automation. He received his PhD on cloud simulation in 2015 from NUDT under the supervision of Professor Huang Kedi, the 'father' of China's Yinhe supercomputer.[68] Huang Kedi is a PLA major general[69] who has written on the use of simulation technology for warfare and joined military conferences on simulation technology.[70] Liu Xiaocheng's work includes collaboration with researchers from the PLA Unit 92941[71] and the PLA Navy Armaments Academy.[72]
- Chen Bin is also from the System Simulation Lab of NUDT's College of Mechatronics and Automation. He has collaborated with researchers from the PLA Unit 63892, the PLA Unit 95949, the PLA Air Force 1st Aeronautics Institute and the PLA Navy Armaments Academy.[73] Chen Bin has worked at NUDT's Research Center of Military Computational Experiments and Parallel Systems Technology and his research includes work on combat simulation.[74]
- Qiu Xiaogang works at NUDT's System Simulation Lab and has worked at NUDT's Research Center of Military Computational Experiments and Parallel Systems Technology.[75] A 2016 paper describes him as a researcher from both NUDT and the PLA Unit 31002.[76] He collaborated with a NUDT researcher who was at the same time also working for PLA Unit 77569, based in Lhasa.[77]

Given their secretive nature, there is almost no reliable information on any of the PLA units mentioned above. Based on their publications, however, the researchers' work has direct military applications.

There is no suggestion that Chen Wang has provided trade secrets or CSIRO intellectual property to his co-authors.

The revolving door and close-knit relationship between these three NUDT researchers and PLA research units indicates that the NUDT College of Mechatronics Engineering and Automation should be treated as a PLA research institute. The three NUDT researchers are involved in combat simulations and likely seek to use Chen Wang's knowledge of parallel systems and cloud computing, developed through his work at the CSIRO, to improve their combat simulations and thereby aid China's military.

Shiping Chen is a principal research scientist at Data61 and has worked at the CSIRO since 1999. He earned his bachelor's degree in 1985 from Harbin University of Science and Technology. He completed a master's degree at the Shenyang Institute of Automation in 1990, a state-run institution known for its work on robots and drones.[78] He stayed on at that institute to work there as a system engineer until 1995. In June 2017 the institute was named in an industrial espionage case in the United States in which a Chinese engineer, Yu Long, pleaded guilty to stealing highly sensitive documents containing military technology and passing them to the director of the Shenyang Institute.[79] Yu Long worked at an American military contractor supplying jet engines for F-22 Raptor and F-35 Lightning fighter aircraft. Australia has ordered a fleet of seventy-two F-35 fighters.[80]

Shiping Chen was awarded a PhD in computer science by UNSW in 2001.[81] There is no evidence that he has maintained ties with the Shenyang Institute of Automation.[82] However, since 2015 Chen has written three papers on networks and data science with a team at the State Key Lab of Networking and Switching Technology, Beijing University of Posts and Telecommunications.[83] The lab appears to be deeply involved in military research. A member of its academic committee is Major General Chen Zhijie of the Air Force Armaments Research Institute.[84] The head of the committee is Yu Quan from the PLA General Staff Headquarters 61st Research Institute. Yu Quan is a communications expert who is also connected to Yang Xiang, head of Deakin University's Centre for Cyber Security Research and Innovation. Yu heads the academic committee of Xidian's State Key Laboratory of Integrated Services Networks where Xiang holds a visiting professorship.

One of Shiping Chen's co-authors on the three papers is Chen Junliang, who has been involved in China's space program and communications networks research, including with and for the PLA.[85] He is credited with research that 'stopped the invasion of foreign intelligent network products' used in communications systems.[86]

There is no suggestion that Shiping Chen or Liming Zhu (see below) have provided trade secrets or CSIRO intellectual property to their co-authors or fellow researchers in China.

Liming Zhu is the research director for Data61's software and computational systems program, which includes research on big data, blockchain and cyber security. Among other projects, he leads Data61's team working with the Australian Treasury on the application of blockchain technology to financial transactions.[87] He's also a professor at UNSW, from where he obtained his PhD. Zhu does not appear to have formal links with institutions in China, but he does collaborate with PLA-linked researchers, publishing papers on data storage with researchers at PLA universities. One of his co-authors, Lu Kai, is a professor at the National University of Defense Technology, arguably the most important PLA university.[88] A leading Chinese computer scientist, Lu is intimately tied to China's military. He holds four national defence patents, which are typically classified, and has won three first-place 'military technology progress' prizes.[89] He has said that his work on supercomputers contributes to China's 'strong army dream'.[90]

10

'Engineering souls' at Australia's universities

Higher education is a forward battlefield in ideological work, and shoulders the important tasks of studying, researching and propagating Marxism, fostering and carrying forward the Socialist core value system, and providing talent guarantees and intelligent support for the realization of the Chinese Dream of the great rejuvenation of the Chinese nation.

State Council guidelines for higher education, 2015

In his 2016 presidential address to the Australian Academy of the Humanities, the eminent Sinologist John Fitzgerald pointed out that CCP leaders and university administrators across China see themselves as engaged in a war—a war against the free and open inquiry that we take for granted in Australia.[1] China, he said, 'is openly hostile to the idea of academic freedom'. Yet in case after case we can see Australia's university leaders sacrificing that freedom for Chinese lucre. As Fitzgerald bluntly puts it: 'Our university executives invite onto our campuses institutions and political representatives who profess to be at war with our values, including academic freedom.'

In a 2016 speech, Xi Jinping emphasised the need to place 'ideological work' and 'political work' at the heart of university education.

All teachers are obliged to believe in the 'core values of socialism' and become 'disseminators of advanced ideology'. They are entrusted with 'the sacred mission of engineering human souls'. Schools and universities are the primary centres for the party's 'thought work'.[2]

There is a tendency in the West to believe all of this is just a rhetorical legacy of Maoism. But Xi is deadly serious. An extensive program of enforcing ideological purity is underway across China. The Ministry of Education's guidelines, published in 2016, do not mince words: 'The illegal spread of harmful ideas and expressions in the classroom will be dealt with severely according to regulation and law.'[3] What are these harmful ideas? The banned thoughts were set out in a party communiqué forwarded in 2013 to university presidents. The 'Seven Prohibitions' include constitutional democracy, freedom of the press, and 'universal values', covering human rights and academic freedom. 'The few scholars who dare not to obey,' a 2014 US Congressional report warned, 'have been monitored, threatened, harassed, fined, beaten, indicted or imprisoned.'[4]

John Fitzgerald tells us that the communiqué was classified as a state secret, perhaps so as not to embarrass universities in countries like Australia that enter into partnerships with Chinese universities. The document was allegedly leaked to foreign reporters by a seventy-year-old Chinese journalist, Gao Yu, who was sentenced to seven years in prison for the crime. This is the reality of the system that Australian university executives and professors push from their minds as they exchange cheerful toasts of Maotai at banquets celebrating their latest joint venture with a Chinese university.

Thought management

To believe China's state agencies leave thought work at home when they go out into the world is to misunderstand the modern Chinese state at the most basic level. China's Ministry of Education has developed many ways of influencing and regulating what happens in Australia's universities in a way that advances President Xi's vision of higher education as a battlefield of ideas. It has, in Professor Fitzgerald's words, 'begun to export the style of interventionist academic policing it routinely practices at home'.

Nothing is too trivial to evade the purview of thought work. An Australian academic arrived at a Chinese university to deliver a marketing course to find that pages mentioning Taiwan and Hong Kong had been torn out of the textbook.[5] The policing goes beyond attempts by the CCP's ideological apparatus to control the thoughts of Chinese studying or working abroad. The CCP now aims to shape or silence the work and public statements of academics in Australia (including stopping the publication of what you are now reading). As prominent US China scholar Perry Link observes, the key is to persuade academics to censor themselves willingly. It does so by two main means.[6] The first is to blacklist 'unfriendly' scholars. In 2016 an ANU China scholar working on rights issues was barred from entering China to participate in a DFAT project there.[7] In March 2017, the 'detention' and questioning of UTS academic Feng Chongyi while undertaking fieldwork in Guangzhou sent a warning to anyone needing a visa to do academic work in China. (Professor Feng is an Australian permanent resident.)

During my discussions with them, China scholars in Australia typically begin to ruminate on how Beijing could punish them if they cross the line. And they all know where the line is. They express their views cautiously in public because they know they will be refused a visa, as a number of their American colleagues have been. For every scholar denied a visa, dozens resolve that it will not happen to them.

For academics who have invested ten or twenty years in acquiring their expertise, a prohibition on travelling to China would be a career-killer. One expert told me that since he is close to retirement he doesn't care any more and is free to tell Australians what is really going on. Some younger scholars interested in China steer their research into less politically sensitive areas, like cultural history. In researching this book I have noticed that China studies in Australian universities are pervaded by an atmosphere of caution, with scholars policing themselves so as to stay on the right side of the CCP's legion of watchers. Scholars from abroad who have made stronger criticisms of the CCP regime complain privately that they are not invited to speak at Australian universities. One of our best China observers, Rowan Callick, concluded that our universities 'have substantially withdrawn their capacity for sustained, genuinely independent analysis of contemporary China or of Chinese history'.[8]

If academics will not censor themselves, university administrators will do it for them, a baleful trend revealed again in May 2017 at Monash University. Teaching a course in human resources, lecturer Aaron Wijeratne gave his students a quiz taken from a widely used textbook. They were asked to complete the statement 'There is a common saying in China that government officials only speak truth when …'. The correct answer is when 'they are drunk or careless'. It is a common sentiment in China, but a Chinese student in the class, Gao Song, was offended and took to WeChat to complain. And Melbourne's Chinese consulate took notice.

A consular official phoned Monash's top brass, expressing concern and demanding that the university investigate the matter and 'seriously and appropriately manage it', warning that it would 'continue to monitor the situation'.[9] University authorities were aware that Monash had 4400 Chinese undergraduate students paying full fees.[10] And perhaps the consulate reminded them that in 2012 their university was granted the first licence in a decade for a foreign university to set up a campus in China, and that the Chinese government itself paid for the building to house its graduate school and research institute at China's Southeast University.[11]

Monash Business School deputy dean Robert Brooks moved fast. He suspended Wijeratne, had the quiz withdrawn, and said he would be reviewing the course. Soon after, he banned the 'commonly used' textbook from the school's courses.[12]

In China, news of the quiz set the internet abuzz after the *Global Times* reported on the victory: 'The change we can see here is that as China's power grows stronger … thoughtless remarks about China will die down.' In Australian universities, tolerance will no longer be shown towards 'thoughtless remarks'. When popular Chinese website 163.com republished the article it attracted almost half a million comments.[13] Nearer to home, *Sydney Today*, one of the largest Chinese-language news sources in Australia, stirred the pot. An article titled 'Rage! Monash University quiz publicly humiliates China!' lashed out at the lecturer: 'these [quiz] topics of yours are a mouthful of poisonous milk!'[14]

But not all readers of *Sydney Today* took the bait. Some criticised the Chinese media's take on the issue. One asked the editors whether they had actually had contact with Chinese officialdom. Others agreed with the quiz questions. 'It's a great truth, there's no defect here. China really is like this,' one wrote. But back at Monash University there is only one Chinese view that counts and the message to all university staff was loud and clear: 'China matters to us so don't do or say anything that might upset the consulate. We dance to its tune.'

Another kind of pressure to self-censor operates through financial linkages with universities, including Confucius Institutes and various kinds of joint projects between Australian and Chinese universities. In 2016 Australia's universities had almost 1100 formal research collaboration agreements with universities in China.[15] (The University of Sydney tops the list with 107 agreements.) There are hundreds of staff and student exchange agreements. They act as inducements to university administrators to act in a 'friendly' way towards China and keep critical scholars under pressure not to rock the boat.

It's not only China scholars who come under pressure. The 'red-hot patriots' abroad that President Xi has praised are on a hair-trigger looking for any infraction that 'hurts the feelings of the Chinese people'.[16] At the ANU a lecturer in an IT class, exasperated at the level of cheating, put up a message on the classroom screen: 'I will not tolerate students who cheat.'[17] A large proportion of his students were from China, and as he'd been told they may not be getting the message as their English was not very good, he included a translation in Chinese. The Chinese students had their 'feelings hurt'. The Chinese newspapers in Australia inflamed the issue. (The *People's Daily* reported the students' 'fury' and equated the lecturer's action to a neo-Nazi poster reading 'kill Chinese'.[18]) Under pressure, the lecturer made a grovelling apology for his 'poor decision', going on to praise the 'many excellent students in the class'.

At the University of Sydney, a lecturer hurt the feelings of Chinese students by using a map of the world that, when zoomed in, showed an Indian version of the disputed India–Bhutan–China borders. Some students left in protest. Others took to WeChat. A jingoistic Australia-based WeChat group calling themselves 'Australian Red Scarf' mounted a campaign, and the lecturer was forced to issue an apology.[19] Presumably, all maps covering disputed territory used at the University of Sydney must in future reflect the PRC's claims. Other nations' claims do not count. Reporting on the incident in China, the *Global Times* declared: 'The China-India border dispute broke out in Australia, and China won!' Yes, because the University of Sydney capitulated.[20]

The University of Sydney is surely the most supine in Australia. When the chief of the Group of Eight (a coalition of leading universities) was reported as acknowledging the problem of student intimidation of lecturers, albeit in the mildest and most inoffensive way, the university's vice chancellor Michael Spence issued a media release criticising her and declaring that Chinese officials in Australia 'respect the University's deep commitment to intellectual freedom', an apologia that does not pass the laugh test.[21]

At the University of Newcastle, a lecturer put up a chart he'd found listing Taiwan and Hong Kong as 'countries'. *Sydney Today* reported that students were 'seriously offended, very angry'.[22] They threatened that they could 'not rule out the possibility of implementing further measures to protect their rights'. The Sydney consulate complained to the university. The incident 'seriously hurt the feelings of Chinese students'.[23] (While appearing to share the students' anger, the Chinese authorities are always acting strategically.) To his credit, the lecturer said they should 'Learn to accept the reality of it'.

After years of having the history of humiliation drilled into them, some Chinese students react to the slightest offence as a way of demonstrating their jingoistic fervour. They are constantly on the lookout for evidence of discrimination, and feel aggrieved because they contribute so much money to their universities. The Chinese consulates amplify these feelings as a way of controlling the students and exerting pressure on Australians to see the world as the Communist Party does.

Here in Australia we walk on eggshells, terrified of doing anything to upset China, allowing ourselves to be bullied by the politics of denunciation, and sacrificing our self-respect as a result.

Many university administrators in Australia, and some academics, have only a vague understanding of academic freedom, and their haziness contributes to their lack of commitment to it. The hue and cry that some make about erosion of academic freedom seems to them an indulgence that can be sacrificed in the pragmatic interest of the institution.

Academic freedom is not only the 'moral foundation of the modern university'[24] but is at the very heart of free speech in Australian society. Unlike lobbyists and journalists, the public pays academics to become experts and expects them to use their expertise to enrich and inform our society. In China, many scholars have been persecuted for taking their academic freedom seriously—imprisoned or banished into obscurity because they dared to point to the historical and political distortions of CCP ideology. The CCP has become so confident in its power that it is brazenly attempting to silence scholars in the West whom it deems unfriendly. One might expect that Cambridge University Press (CUP) would be one of the fiercest defenders of academic freedom, yet in August 2017 it buckled to pressure from Beijing and blocked 300 online articles from its respected journal *China Quarterly*, articles red-flagged by the Chinese censors for dealing with issues like the Cultural Revolution and the Tiananmen Square massacre.[25] CUP wanted to maintain its journal's access to the Chinese market. After a storm of angry protests from China scholars, CUP reinstated the articles. Will the CCP stop there? No.

When an Australian university enters into a partnership with a Chinese university or state-owned enterprise it also enters into a partnership with the Chinese Communist Party. The party's program of 'thought management' sets the political and ideological rules that constrain the relationship, rules that no university in Australia would accept for its own staff and students. In these partnerships liberalism meets authoritarianism, and liberalism often gives way in order not to offend—and to keep the cash flowing.

Funding PLA upgrade[26]

In recent years, China's campaign to acquire by devious means the most proprietary and sensitive knowledge from technologically sophisticated countries has entered a new phase. Much of this research is carried out in Western universities and research institutes, most of them government-funded. As indicated, lured by Chinese money, but also consistent with the tradition of collaborative work among scientists, these Western research organisations have entered into hundreds of agreements with Chinese universities and research outfits.

For several years the Chinese party-state has been pursuing a coordinated program to acquire from abroad advanced military and industrial technology, and to do so by fair means or foul. As John Fitzgerald puts it:

China, rather than investing in open-ended critical inquiry and experimentation of the kind that stimulates innovation, invests strategically in national development and defence and then steals what it cannot discover or invent ... The strategy has paid huge dividends.[27]

It now emerges that beneath the radar Australian universities are helping to give China the technological leadership it craves.

The Australian Research Council (ARC) through its Linkage Program is funnelling Australian taxpayer funds into research with applications to China's advanced weapons capacity. The program aims to encourage national and international research collaborations between university researchers and partners in industry or other research centres, in this case with Chinese military scientists.

In 2016 the ARC awarded a three-year $400,000 grant to the University of Adelaide for a research partnership with the Beijing Institute of Aeronautical Materials, part of the Aviation Industry Corporation of China (AVIC).[28] AVIC is a state-owned enterprise and the main supplier of military aircraft to the People's Liberation Army Air Force, including the J-20 stealth fighter, the fifth-generation FC-31 stealth fighter and attack drones.[29] When the PLA unveiled its first aircraft carrier, the *Liaoning*, it was loaded with Shenyang J-15 fighter jets built by AVIC.[30]

AVIC's Beijing Institute of Aeronautical Materials describes itself as an 'important part of the national defence science and technology innovation system'.[31] The institute's president, Dai Shenglong, doubles as its Communist Party secretary.[32] In 2016 a Chinese consortium that included an AVIC subsidiary bought half of the UK-based global data storage company Global Switch. The Australian Department of Defence decided to terminate its contract with the local branch of the company, which stores highly sensitive data in its building in Ultimo.[33] Global Switch also has a partnership with Huawei.

According to the ARC project summary, the linkage project with the University of Adelaide is 'expected to make Australia capable of fabricating superior rubber-based materials and devices that are comfortable, quiet and energy efficient, for use in aircrafts [sic], automobiles and vessels'. It will also enhance the PLA Air Force's capacity to improve the performance of its most sophisticated warplanes.

The research team that put the linkage grant idea to the AVIC company and then lodged the application with the ARC is listed as Professor Qiao Shizhang, Dr Ma Tian-yi, Professor Zhengtao Su and Dr Wang Peng. Qiao Shizhang holds the chair of nanotechnology at the University of Adelaide and, among other appointments in China, is a visiting professor at Beijing University of Chemical Technology's College of Chemical Engineering, which hosts a State Key Laboratory that has taken up thirty-four national defence military-industrial projects.[34] Ma Tian-yi is a research fellow at the University of Adelaide and Wang Peng is a postdoctoral fellow there.[35]

The other senior member of the team, Professor Zhengtao Su, works at AVIC's Beijing Institute of Aeronautical Materials.[36] The bottom line of all this is that PLA-linked researchers, some at the University of Adelaide and one in China, are receiving funding from the Australian government to help enhance the effectiveness of China's military aircraft. This may not be their intention but it is an inevitable risk when funding AVIC research.

According to close observers, China has embarked on 'a deliberate, state-sponsored project to circumvent the costs of research, overcome cultural disadvantages, and "leapfrog" to the forefront by leveraging the creativity of other nations'. This is the warning made by William Hannas, James Mulvenon and Anna Puglisi in their definitive book *Chinese Industrial Espionage*.[37] Another expert, James McGregor, in a report for the US Chamber of Commerce, put it even more bluntly: China's high-tech research plan is a 'blueprint for technology theft on a scale the world has never seen before'.[38] So why would the Australian government be subsidising these ambitions, particularly when the technological advances are helping to build China's military might?

The AVIC link is not the only Australian government grant likely to assist China's military ambitions. In 2016 the ARC awarded $466,000 to a joint research project between researchers at the University of New South Wales, National Instruments Australia and Huawei, the giant Chinese telecommunications company. Australia's intelligence agencies believe Huawei is linked to the Third Department of the PLA, the military's cyber-espionage arm, which led the federal government to ban the use of Huawei equipment in Australia's National Broadband Network.

As we saw in Chapter 8, ASIO's assessment was influenced by a US Congressional report that judged Huawei to be an espionage risk. It concluded that Huawei (along with Chinese telco ZTE) 'cannot be trusted to be free of foreign state influence and thus pose a security threat to the United States and to our systems'. After trying and failing to get to the bottom of the company's links with Chinese government agencies, the report branded Huawei executives evasive and deceitful.

The purpose of the ARC project is to research 'massive connectivity and low latency machine-to-machine communications' and so contribute to a 'new type of world-class wireless infrastructure'— research with obvious military and espionage uses.[39]

'Make the foreign serve China'

John Fitzgerald lays down a challenge: Australians would do well to consider whether we share Xi Jinping's dream of the great rejuvenation of the Chinese people, and whether we want to help it by 'aligning the country's national research strategy too closely with China's'.[40] And yet, through hundreds of collaborative agreements with Chinese universities and research centres, we are in the middle of a major realignment of Australia's scientific and technological research so that it contributes to the Chinese Communist Party's ambitions.

The China Electronics Technology Group Corporation (CETC) is a state-owned military research organisation, 'one of China's ten official defense industry conglomerate-bureaucracies', according to one expert.[41] Its 'sacred mission' is to help to build a 'rich country, strong army'. At the same time it is collaborating closely with the University of Technology Sydney and benefiting from Australian government funding. (Danielle Cave and Brendan Thomas-Noone have also investigated these links.[42])

Many of the research institutes CETC operates were originally founded by and for the PLA and they continue to receive military funding and do military research. In 2010 its website described the organisation as 'the national squad for military-industrial electronics and the main force in the information industry'.[43]

The civilian use of some of its technologies means their military applications can be obscured.[44] But one expert, Matthew Luce, notes that while Huawei and ZTE deny any direct allegiance to the PLA, CETC is open about it, declaring that its purpose is 'leveraging civilian electronics for the gain of the PLA'.[45] Cave and Thomas-Noone note that as warfare 'becomes more information-oriented and networked, technologies that are critical to the civilian, military and security sectors continue to blur', and nowhere more so than within CETC's research.[46] It is likely that the PLA Navy ship that anchored itself off the coast of Australia in July 2017 to spy on US–Australian war games was packed with electronics supplied by CETC.

CETC has explored all avenues in its search for military technology—legal and illegal. In January 2011 a Massachusetts court sentenced Wei Yufeng to three years in prison, and her co-defendant Wu Zhen Zhou to eight years in prison, for conspiring to steal and export military electronics components and sensitive electronics used in military phased array radar, electronic warfare and missile systems. CETC was one of the organisations to be supplied with the stolen material.[47] In October 2010, York Yuan Chang and his wife, Leping Huang, were arrested in California on charges of conspiring to export restricted electronics technology to the PRC without a licence and making false statements. They had allegedly entered into contracts with the 24th Research Institute of CETC to design and transfer technology for the development of two types of high-performance analogue-to-digital converters.[48]

Apparently oblivious to all this, in April 2017 the University of Technology Sydney announced a partnership with CETC for a new joint centre on advanced research into big data technologies, metamaterials, advanced electronics and quantum computing and communications.[49] All of these have military or security applications. For example, China is investigating the use of metamaterials for the 'PLA's dream' of making 'invisible' stealth aircraft.[50] The Chinese state corporation is contributing $20 million to the UTS centre.

The new centre continues the university's previous work with CETC and follows an agreement signed with UTS vice-chancellor Attila Brungs to promote cooperation in technology research between the two institutions. The new joint research centre's work is expected to link with the CSIRO, which previously bought antennas from CETC's 54th Research Institute for the Square Kilometre Array. Cave and Thomas-Noone raise particular concerns about CSIRO's ten-year working relationship with CETC's 54th Research Institute, which is heavily engaged in military research.[51] In the United States, any proposed research with CETC 54 must obtain official sanction.

UTS's collaboration with CETC is not funded by the ARC. When I met with deputy vice-chancellors Glenn Wightwick and Bill Purcell they told me all of their research proposals, including those with CETC, comply with the Defence Trade Controls Act, which polices international collaborations on sensitive research topics. This suggests to me that the legislation no longer reflects the new technological and strategic circumstances. The defence department says it leaves it to universities to comply with the law, and the universities do so with apparent diligence.[52] But the uncovering of a deep network of linkages with China's top military researchers tells us the system is broken.

In 2016 UTS began a collaboration with CETC on research projects at the CETC Research Institute on Smart Cities,[53] whose work includes 'public security early warning preventative and supervisory abilities' and 'cyberspace control abilities'. A *Xinhua* report on CETC's work on smart cities notes that it 'integrates and connects civilian-military dual-use technologies'.[54] Looking past its slick public face, CETC technology assists the Chinese state to improve upon the world's most comprehensive and oppressive system of surveillance and control of its citizens.[55]

As if all of this were not astonishing enough, UTS's Global Big Data Technologies Centre (GBDTC)—which covers mobile sensing and communications, computer vision, cloud computing and data intensive systems, computational intelligence and brain computer interfaces— collaborates with CETC.[56] The collaboration includes 'cutting-edge wireless technologies for future telecommunications networks',[57] which might explain why Huawei has also partnered with the big data centre.[58]

These big data technologies are expected to 'transform defence intelligence analysis' and are of intense interest to both the US and Australian military and intelligence services. And of course the PLA, which has recommended 'leveraging the nation's big data project and the civil-military integration advanced development strategy to hasten the development of military big data'.[59]

UTS's big data centre claimed on its website that the Defence Science and Technology Group was one of its partners. DST is the premier Australian government organisation charged with developing advanced science and technology for Australia's armed forces.[60] Secrets held by DST and the CSIRO are believed to be among the 'top targets' for China's army of citizen spies.[61] In fact, DST has not been a partner with the big data centre, although researchers affiliated to it have taken up DST work. If DST's association with UTS has been minor in the past, DST expects to substantially increase its work with UTS as the latter shifts increasingly towards technology research.[62] A new Defence Science Institute, a venture between the New South Wales government and DST, is to be based at UTS, making the most compromised campus in the country a hub for Australian defence science research. However, DST insists that all of its work with universities is 'very early stage' in the research and development cycle and it urges publication of all results of the projects it supports. Because it does not have contracts with universities to do any classified research, DST takes no interest in the nationality of university employees. All classified research is carried out in DST's own facilities. The problem with this is stated concisely by Daniel Golden in his recent book *Spy Schools*: 'A foreign government may be eager to scoop up a fundamental breakthrough before its applications become so important that it's labelled secret'.[63]

More PLA collaboration

Eight scientists at UTS have connections with Xidian University, which emerged from the PLA's Military Electronic Engineering Institute and remains intimately linked with China's armed forces. Some of these

UTS academics have conducted research and authored papers with counterparts at Xidian University.

Xidian University's website boasts of its contributions to national defence technology, describing itself as 'standing out among the whole nation's tertiary institutions, with a superior position in national defence technology research', and claiming to be the alma mater of over 120 PLA generals.[64] When the university announced a new school of cyber engineering in 2015, China watchers interpreted it as beefing up China's defence, espionage and warfare capabilities.[65] One US expert noted that 'Xidian's close connection with the People's Liberation Army' suggests the civilian–military link on cyber research. Yet several UTS researchers collaborate with scientists at Xidian University.

UTS appears to have become an unofficial outpost of China's scientific research effort, some of which has direct application to advancing the PLA's fighting capability. Moreover, Australia's foremost scientific and technology organisations, including those with defence and intelligence responsibilities, are working hand-in-glove with researchers closely linked to PLA research centres. By blithely contributing to enhancing the sophistication of China's military and intelligence technology, there could be no better evidence of Australia's extraordinary naivety towards China and its methods than the activities of UTS.

President Xi Jinping declared in 2016 that the 'powerful engine of technological innovation' will drive the great rejuvenation of the Chinese people.[66] The PRC appears to have effectively mobilised some of Australia's most valuable intellectual resources, not to mention public funds, to help fuel that engine. Yet here in Australia we don't want to know.

Beijing is now investing huge sums towards giving the PRC a home-grown technological edge.[67] But the ambition, reaffirmed by Xi Jinping at the 19th Communist Party Congress in November 2017, to have the world's most technologically sophisticated military force means borrowing from wherever the knowledge is most advanced.[68] As Reuters reported, 'China is scouring the globe for know-how that can be coupled with domestic innovation to produce strategic weapons and equipment'.[69]

We've seen that Australian researchers are working with Chinese companies with links to the PLA. But the PLA is also benefiting from Australian expertise by sending its scientists here to be trained. The PLA's links appear to be most extensive with the ANU, UTS and the University of New South Wales (UNSW). Lieutenant General Yang Xuejun is a pivotal figure in this pattern of linkages into Australian universities. Xi Jinping recently appointed General Yang to preside over the PLA Academy of Military Science, the nation's foremost military research centre.

In Australia, one of General Yang's most prolific collaborators is Xue Jingling, Scientia Professor of Computing Science and Engineering at UNSW. Xue, among several other UNSW researchers, has extensive links with PLA's National University of Defense Technology (NUDT)—the nation's number-one military technology university—having published over two dozen papers with NUDT supercomputer experts. Some of this research has been funded by grants from the ARC worth over $2.3 million.

Close collaboration between Xue Jingling and Lieutenant General Yang Xuejun is only one part of a broader phenomenon. Other UNSW researchers have undertaken extensive research with NUDT in areas like autonomous underwater vehicles, optical fibres and navigation systems, including collaboration with PLA Senior Colonel Wang Feixue[70] and Major General Zhang Weihua.[71]

Wang Feixue, a 46-year-old professor at NUDT, is at the forefront of work on China's competitor to the US-controlled Global Positioning System, the Beidou satellite navigation system, which is expected to achieve global coverage by 2020.[72] The Beidou navigation system would be crucial for the Chinese military in the event of a conflict with the United States.[73] Working with NUDT experts, a number of UNSW scientists have contributed towards the development of the Beidou system, which has many civilian as well as military uses.[74] Of course, the PRC is fully entitled to develop its own global satellite navigation system, but should Australian expertise be used to enhance it?

Links between Australian and Chinese military universities run deeper than joint work resulting in journal publications. The flow of personnel from PLA institutions to Australian universities is also concerning. Two dozen NUDT-linked researchers have passed through UNSW as visiting scholars or PhD students in the last decade. A further fourteen have passed through ANU.

For example, one of Senior Colonel Wang's doctoral students, Li Min, visited UNSW for a practicum at the School of Surveying and Spatial Information Systems in 2008.[75] Her thesis lists six classified Chinese national defence projects relating to navigation systems that she worked on during her time as a doctoral student.[76] Having visited and studied at Australian institutions, these PLA researchers return to China with deep international networks, advanced training, access to research that is yet to be classified and, most importantly, the ideas of the future. In many cases, a clear connection can be drawn between work PLA personnel were doing in Australia and specific projects they undertook for the PLA.[77]

China recognises the valuable training and collaboration our universities can provide, and so does its military. As Senior Colonel Wang proclaimed at the 19th Communist Party Congress, at which he was a delegate, 'Science and technology are the core of fighting strength'.[78] The risky collaborations pursued by Australian universities can mostly be put down to naivety, and we might anticipate they will look much more closely at who they are aligning with now that it has been pointed out.

Some, however, are defensive. When asked about the collaborations between UTS researchers and scientists, companies and research institutes with close links to China's military, UTS deputy vice-chancellor Glenn Wightwick expressed complete satisfaction with the arrangements. He wrote to me that 'the alleged links with the PLA are not relevant as the work conducted will be dual-use, unclassified, and publicly available'.[79] Following an earlier email asking about the university's links with China's military, the response was to threaten legal action against me 'in the event that UTS or its staff members are unjustifiably denigrated'.[80] Professor Wightwick wrote that he was concerned that UTS academics may be 'intimidated' and that 'your academic freedom must be balanced against that of the UTS academics who may feature in your book.'

When I asked the universities and the ARC for responses to evidence of their links to China's military they typically wrote back saying they had abided by the legal requirements, pointing especially to their compliance with the Defence Trade Controls Act. Some said that if there is a problem then it is because the Department of Immigration or the security services approved visas.

The ARC and the minister for education Simon Birmingham attribute responsibility for any problems to the universities, saying that they are autonomous institutions and it's up to them to meet their legal obligations.[81] The laws and regulations governing these kinds of collaborations are inadequate and need to be rethought for a new environment where so much sophisticated military technology also has civilian uses, or grows out of them. And regardless of legislated requirements, universities have an obligation to consider whether they should be contributing to China's military power.

The commendable culture of open collaboration in the Australian science community is being exploited by the PRC, but attachment to it is also causing some scientists to ignore warnings to take a closer look at who they are working with. One senior scientist, when asked if he worried about collaborating with the PLA, said it does bother him. But his university insists that he find external funding for his work and China is where the money is. 'So what can I do?' he asked.[82]

Carrying the torch at UNSW

Beijing has been pouring huge amounts of capital into programs aimed at building the nation's science and technology infrastructure. They include the 973 Program for basic research and the 985 and 211 Projects aimed at university restructuring. The Torch program seeks to create high-tech commercial industries through foreign collaboration. It targets Western-trained Chinese scientists by recruiting them to return to China to work in the 150 or so national-level science and technology parks, or by asking them to 'serve in place' by staying abroad.[83]

The Torch program is embedded in China's Medium and Long-Term Plan for S&T Development (2006–20), which focuses on appropriating foreign technology and research. Rather than treating innovation as some sort of international scientific collaboration, it is more accurately described as a 'blueprint for technology theft', in the words of Hannes, Mulvenon and Puglisi in *China's Industrial Espionage*.[84] The National

Hi-Tech R&D Program, known as the 863 Program, predates Torch but is also aimed at enabling China to leapfrog the West, not only by pouring resources into domestic universities and research labs but also by stealing technology from abroad. In 2011, for example, a Chinese scientist in the United States was convicted of stealing industrial secrets to pass to the 863 Program in China.[85] The program 'provides funding and guidance for efforts to clandestinely acquire US technology and sensitive economic information', according to a 2011 report from the US Office of the National Counterintelligence Executive.[86]

The first overseas Torch program technology park is to be built at the University of New South Wales (UNSW). In April 2016 UNSW vice-chancellor Ian Jacobs signed a partnership with the Torch program at the Great Hall of the People in Beijing. As a sign of its high profile, Jacobs was flanked by Prime Minister Malcolm Turnbull and Premier Li Keqiang. The partnership came with $30 million in initial investments from eight Chinese companies, a sum expected to rise to $100 million by 2025 when the university will have built a whole new precinct next to its main Kensington campus in Sydney. A university media release claims that the Australian Torch Innovation Precinct at UNSW will contribute more than $1 billion to Australia's GDP in its first ten years.[87] The university says the number was generated by Deloitte Access Economics. It's the kind of number that ought to be treated sceptically; when I asked the university to provide me with a copy of the report it could not.

Ian Jacobs said he was 'thrilled' to be in Beijing's Great Hall of the People to sign the agreement. Back in Sydney the university threw a gala dinner. Jacobs was 'so excited' that his university would be part of China's plans to become 'the world's great technological innovator'.[88] The partnership is 'a global first and has the potential to reset the Australia-China bilateral relationship and boost the nation's innovation system'.[89] But which nation's innovation system? As the first Torch overseas partnership, the UNSW precinct spearheads China's drive to spur its own technological development by recruiting foreign research capacities. In recent years, China has increasingly emphasised the importance of 'indigenous innovation' but through relying on foreign technology and know-how, with the ultimate goal of making itself less reliant on foreign research. To this end, China's Ministry of Science and Technology has called on the government 'to encourage scientific research institutes, universities and overseas research and development institutions to establish joint laboratories or research and development centres'.[90]

Xinhuanet lauded the UNSW partnership as coming at an 'opportune moment' and went to the predictable ACRI deputy director, James Laurenceson, who, repeating a favourite party slogan, said it's a 'win-win situation for both countries'.[91]

Torch's technology park at UNSW is a major step forward in the commandeering of Australia's research resources to suit China's needs. UNSW's research chief Brian Boyle said that the program would allow the university to use the Chinese government as a facilitation mechanism. It would be the 'entry and identification point' in attracting Chinese investors, who would pursue China's research priorities.[92] He responded to a feature story by Anders Furze and Louisa Lim questioning the wisdom of the university's huge investment in its China-funded 'Torch technology park' by dismissing all of the evidence and suggesting the criticisms were motivated by xenophobia.[93]

Jacobs himself gave the game away when he told *The Australian*: 'We didn't want to keep going back, cap in hand, to Canberra asking for more. Instead, we went to China.' This 'new approach to bankrolling Australian research' represents UNSW taking 'its destiny into its own hands'.[94] This is head-shakingly naïve. What the university has done is to place its destiny in the hands of the Ministry of Science and Technology in Beijing.

How closely will UNSW conduct due diligence inquiries to weed out companies that have histories of corruption or links with military and intelligence organisations? Pro Vice-Chancellor (International) Laurie Pearcey, who has been heavily involved in the university's China engagement, told me that UNSW is 'very methodical' in checking out 'prospective partners'.[95] My guess is that companies whose corrupt practices are easily detectible will be weeded out but military linkages will not even be tested, although Pearcey says the company hired by the university to conduct due diligence does so.[96] Pearcey spoke highly of Huawei and could not see a problem collaborating with it. When I asked about collaborating with the Chinese government in the Torch program, Pearcey said that Australia enters into partnerships with all sorts of governments and there is no reason to single out China. Noting the US intervention in Iraq, he said: 'Let he who is without sin cast the first stone.'[97]

Ethnic enclaves

In recent years a trend has emerged in which certain university centres or departments have become enclaves of ethnic Chinese scholars. Non-Chinese academics are grumbling about ethnic discrimination, noting bias in staff recruitment, allocation of PhD scholarships and invitations to visitors, each of which goes against the spirit of multiculturalism.[98]

One consequence of the formation of these Chinese ethnic enclaves may be a shift in the academic culture to one that is less collegial, one where the supervisor speaks while others simply listen. Doctoral students may not absorb the Australian academic culture. This mono-ethnic clustering is readily apparent from the authorship of academic papers where it is not unusual to see eight or ten Chinese names of researchers from Australian and Chinese universities. A second generation is now emerging, formed from those who stay on in Australia after their PhDs, risking the perpetuation of an ethnic favouritism in hiring staff and doctoral student selection.

The ethnic enclave phenomenon is apparent at several universities, mainly in the faculties of engineering and information technology. For example, at Curtin University's Centre for Infrastructural Monitoring and Protection, seven of the eight academic staff are of Chinese heritage. All seven have worked previously with or for Professor Hao Hong, the centre's director. An expert in earthquake and blast engineering, Hao Hong is an adjunct professor at Tianjin University, from which he first graduated, and has received Chinese government grants. He has served as deputy president of the consulate-linked Western Australia Chinese Scientists Association (discussed in Chapter 9).

In recent years, a growing number of scholars of Chinese ethnicity have been appointed to the Australian Research Council (ARC) College of Experts, which allocates scarce funds to research projects. In 2016 the ARC published the names of the 176 members of the College of Experts but does not indicate to which of the four disciplinary groupings they belong. Assessment panels are drawn from these groupings. A little investigation, however, shows that several members of the college with expertise in engineering and IT are of Chinese heritage and have links with PRC military research.

To the extent that the growing number of scholars of Chinese heritage on the College of Experts reflects the rise in their number working in Australian universities, their presence is to be expected and welcomed. However, there are two grounds for concern. Firstly, if in their appointment practices senior Chinese academics are biased towards other Chinese-heritage academics then we can expect them to be similarly biased in their decisions over the allocation of research funds. I would expect that non-Chinese members of the College of Experts who might suspect their colleagues of bias would be extremely reluctant to say so because of xenophobia-phobia. The allegation would be impossible to prove and the accuser would immediately be accused of racism. The ARC ought to take a close look at this potential problem, although I suspect it would be too afraid to lift the lid.

The second, related, concern arises from the relationships between certain academics and Chinese military research institutions. The problem arises mainly in engineering, IT and related areas. We have seen already that the ARC has been allocating funds to research projects that have a distinct benefit to the People's Liberation Army and are conducted in conjunction with researchers associated with military-linked universities in China.

Some members of the ARC College of Experts have close links to Chinese military research. For example, Peng Shi is an engineering professor at both the University of Adelaide and Victoria University specialising in systems and control theory, computational intelligence and operational research.[99] He was a member of the ARC College of Experts between 2014 and 2016. He has been a member of teams receiving ARC grants worth $270,000 and $355,000 respectively.

Shi holds simultaneous professorships at Chinese universities undertaking military research. In 2016 he became a 'specially appointed' professor at Fujian University of Technology School of Information Science and Engineering after being recruited under the Thousand

Talents Plan, which uses generous funding to draw foreign experts into China.[100]

Since 2014 Peng Shi has been a professor at Harbin Engineering University, his alma mater, with whose experts he has collaborated for years.[101] He is located at Harbin's Marine Equipment and Control Technology Research Institute, which has a strong focus on military technology, specialising in intelligent dynamic control and driving systems for warships, and unmanned underwater vehicle systems and autonomous control technology.[102] For its many contributions to military technology, the institute was awarded the title of 'national defence science and technology innovation team' in 2008.[103] In 2014 the *People's Daily* praised one of its breakthroughs: 'In the field of dynamic positioning systems, Harbin Engineering University has already become an irreplaceably important technological force for our nation's navy and marine engineering fields.'[104]

For five years until 2004 Peng Shi was employed as a senior scientist at the Defence Science and Technology Organisation where he worked 'on a number of projects related to enhancing defence force capability.'[105] Shi's colleague and co-author at Adelaide University, Cheng-Chew Lim, has five former doctoral students who now work for DST.[106] Shi doesn't list the students he has supervised but it is likely that some of his former students also work for DST.

'Academic malware': Confucius Institutes

Confucius Institutes are 'an important part of China's overseas propaganda set-up'. So said China's propaganda boss Li Changchun.[107] Confucius Institutes are usually established in conjunction with overseas universities attracted by the prospect of hundreds of thousands of dollars from the Chinese government. Begun in 2004 by the PRC's Office of Chinese Language Council International, known as the Hanban, today there are over 500 Confucius Institutes around the world. Publicly, their tasks are to teach Chinese language, promote Chinese culture and encourage advanced China studies.

The Communist Party banned Confucianism as reactionary during the Cultural Revolution, and Red Guards levelled Confucius' tomb. But the sage has now been rehabilitated, not least as a means of promoting obedience to authority and national pride. While the institutes do indeed offer Chinese language training and promote Chinese culture, that is not all they do. As former CCP paramount leader Hu Jintao said, their purpose is 'to increase our Party's influence worldwide',[108] including their leverage over the organisations that host them.[109] Universities are told that the funding they receive for the institutes comes from the Chinese Ministry of Education. But the eminent US Sinologist David Shambaugh has pointed out that the money is actually provided by the CCP's External Propaganda Department and is 'laundered' through the Ministry of Education.[110]

At the Hanban's insistence, the contracts signed between Confucius Institutes and their Australian host universities are secret. Typically, each has a local director and one appointed by the Chinese government. The latter makes the important decisions. As they have spread they have tended to push out older, rival centres of language teaching and culture, centres less sympathetic to the CCP. As James To writes: 'The CCP's ultimate goal is to put Chinese language education under Beijing's complete domination.'[111]

Accordingly, Confucius Institutes have attracted persistent international criticism in response to allegations that they curtail academic freedom and serve China's surveillance and propaganda objectives. Some Australian university leaders are oblivious, or don't care, welcoming the money and the additional links to the economic giant.

There are fourteen Confucius Institutes at universities across Australia, including six of the prestigious Group of Eight. They have attracted controversy. An academic at UNSW revealed that staff at the Confucius Institute had been instructed not to comment on charges of censorship at the institute.[112] In 2013, the University of Sydney was accused of cancelling a visit by the Dalai Lama to avoid damaging its ties with China, including the funding it receives for its Confucius Institute.[113] When the event was pushed off-campus, and use of the university logo banned, vice-chancellor Michael Spence expressed relief, saying it was 'in the best interests of researchers across the university'.[114] It was another instance of a university becoming an institution 'whose interest lies in enforcing the Chinese government's implicit speech codes',[115] and so giving Beijing deniability.

Jocelyn Chey, a visiting professor at the University of Sydney, criticised the university's 2007 plan to incorporate its Chinese language program into a Confucius Institute. 'There's the question of academic freedom and the right of academics not just to teach but to research and publish in areas where they are not under the guidance or direction of anybody', Chey wrote.[116] She was told that the university's agreement with the Hanban would protect academic freedom, but the university refused to show her the document. In 2014 the Hanban's commitment to the free flow of information was sullied at a conference of the European Association of Chinese Studies in Portugal. Hanban chief Xu Lin, a top-ranking CCP official, instructed her staff to obtain all copies of the conference program and tear out a page advertising a Taiwanese scholarly exchange program.[117]

In a recent report on Confucius Institutes in the United States, the conservative National Association of Scholars (NAS) called for them all to be closed down.[118] It was echoing the conclusions of the American Association of Professors, which in 2014 characterised the institutes as 'an arm of the Chinese state', denouncing them as an arrangement that 'sacrificed the integrity of the university'. The Canadian Association of University Teachers agreed, urging colleges and universities to sever all ties. Several prominent scholars have testified to their pernicious influence.

The NAS report criticised the institutes for their erosion of academic freedom, the secrecy of their funding and operation, the biased presentation of Chinese culture and the pressure on the universities that host them 'to please China'. It reported many professors associated with the institutes speaking of 'immense pressure to stay on the good side of Confucius Institute directors and university administrators affiliated with the Confucius Institute'.[119] In his preface to the NAS report, president Peter Wood wrote that 'behind the appearance of a friendly and inviting form of diplomacy lies a grim authoritarian reality'. Faculty members in host universities believe the institutes to be bases for surveillance. Researchers have collected a number of off-the-record stories suggesting they are centres of 'threats and intimidation directed at Chinese nationals and Chinese Americans, and as cover for covert activities on the part of the Chinese government'.

The former China chief of the Canadian Security Intelligence Service has said that Western counter-intelligence agencies 'have identified Confucius Institutes as forms of spy agencies' used by the Chinese government.[120] He says it gets them close to important research centres in the West.[121]

Several universities have closed their institutes in response to these concerns, including the University of Chicago, Pennsylvania State University and a number in Canada. In 2014 education minister Christopher Pyne went to Peking University to say Australia welcomed the institutes.[122]

A 2014 report prepared by the Parliamentary Library noticed that Australian Confucius Institutes are often connected to individuals closely involved with the party and its objectives.[123] The vice chair of the University of Queensland's Confucius Institute, Liu Jianping, is the head of the Party Committee at Tianjin University. Zhu Minshen, who established a pro-CCP newspaper and came to public attention for his role in the Dastyari affair, is on the board of the University of Sydney's Confucius Institute.[124] William Chiu, for some years president of the United Front group Australian Council for the Promotion of the Peaceful Reunification of China, was on the board of UNSW's Confucius Institute.[125] Professor Fan Hong, director of the Confucius Institute at the University of Western Australia, spoke in China about the role of Confucius Institutes in advancing 'China's soft power'.[126]

In short, by welcoming a Confucius Institute onto campus, university administrators are abandoning foundational principles of university autonomy, both in setting curricula and making appointments on merit. They allow staff appointed by a foreign government to endorse or prevent use of certain teaching materials and accept that certain topics offensive to the CCP will not be broached. As John Fitzgerald writes, for China's education authorities each one represents the successful sidelining of the principles of autonomy and academic freedom and so 'marks a significant breach in the battlefront with Western liberal values'.[127]

This ought to be of concern to Peter Høj, vice-chancellor of the University of Queensland. In 2015 he was the recipient of the Hanban's Outstanding Individual of the Year Award. He serves as a senior consultant to the Hanban, apparently representing Oceania, and boasts of the extensive work done by the Confucius Institute at his own university, including taking the program into school classrooms.[128]

The party in our classrooms

Confucius Classrooms are also proliferating in Australian primary and high schools. There are sixty-seven of them, according to the Hanban.[129] In New South Wales the Department of Education was quick to warm to the idea. The Hanban (or, in reality, the CCP's Propaganda Department) provides Confucius Classrooms with US$10,000 as a start-up fund, an approved assistant teacher and other teaching resources.[130] To oversee the program the Department of Education actually established a Confucius Institute within the department.[131] Is there any other government department in Australia that would allow one of its units to be directed by a foreign state, let alone one renowned for its rigid censorship?

Sinologist Michael Churchman concluded that Confucius Institutes 'exist for the express purpose of letting foreigners understand China on terms acceptable to official China'.[132] After all, China's propaganda minister Liu Yunshan wrote in 2010 that China 'must make the requirements of the socialist core values system permeate every aspect of cultural undertakings.'[133] Senior New South Wales education officials conceded that certain topics would be banned in the classrooms. So as not to offend the donors it would be 'best not to engage in' discussions of issues like Tibet, the persecution of Falun Gong or the massacre in Tiananmen Square. 'There are so many other topics to discuss,' said a senior official. The purpose of the classrooms is for children 'to be learning Mandarin and to have a good understanding of how contemporary China works', which raises the question of what a 'good understanding' entails if the events of 1989 are suppressed.[134] If, as Louisa Lim argues, the CCP has succeeded in reformatting Chinese memory 'in an act of mass amnesia', then the New South Wales education department is happy to join in.[135]

But others could see what was at stake. A petition with over 10,000 signatures was received by the New South Wales parliament in October 2011. Confucius Institutes should be closed down, it said: 'The teaching of Chinese language and culture is welcome in NSW schools, but it should be available free from the influence of Chinese Communist Party doctrine and censorship.'[136] The petitioners were aware that Chinese diplomats had been pressuring schools with Confucius Classrooms to cancel plans to take their children to see a cultural performance associated with Falun Gong.[137]

As New South Wales Greens' spokesman David Shoebridge put it: 'These classes might be free to Treasury, but they are paid for by exposing children to a foreign government's propaganda machine.'[138] In 2016 it was reported that some parents on Sydney's north shore were boycotting schools with the classes. An online petition called on the New South Wales government to join with bodies like the Toronto district school board in closing the classrooms and replacing them with courses 'free from foreign censorship and propaganda'.

Patriotic students

In late 2015 a Chinese student at the Australian National University (ANU) walked into the busy campus pharmacy and began shouting at the pharmacist. 'Who authorised you to distribute this?' he demanded, pointing to a pile of *The Epoch Times*, the Falun Gong newspaper. The student, described by onlookers as enraged and aggressive, was identified as Tao Pinru, president of the Chinese Students and Scholars Association (CSSA) on campus. The pharmacist said she felt intimidated, and anxious about his threat of a boycott of the shop, and let him remove the offending newspapers. Tao threw them into a dumpster, she said.

The incident, uncovered and reported in the student newspaper *Woroni* by then student journalist Alex Joske, raises some worrying questions about what has been happening on our campuses.[139] How did the head of a Chinese student group acquire such a powerful sense of entitlement that he could storm into a university shop and demand that a newspaper be banished from the campus? No student of any other organisation could have felt such an entitlement, let alone succeeded in exercising it.

As we will see, Chinese student organisations function as an arm of the CCP. Writing about the campus pharmacy incident, three experienced China watchers at the *Australian Financial Review* commented: 'In the Chinese Communist Party's global effort to protect its grip on China, no battle appears too small. Aggression, threats, money and other favours are used by Beijing to influence public opinion in Australia, from campuses to the halls [of power].'[140]

Many will remember their own days at university when the campus hosted a wide range of political opinion expressed in newspapers, pamphlets and posters. Although they were mostly ignored, their existence contributed to our worldly education and was proof of the political vibrancy and tolerance of our universities. At a minimum they gave a voice to people with strong opinions. No one would have dreamed of attempting to ban the newspapers of the Socialist Workers Party or the Right to Life. Yet today, a fanatical group of students is allowed to censor political opinion on campuses.

What was most disturbing about the pharmacy incident was the reaction of ANU authorities. When asked about the incident they said they could do nothing as no one had called security, adding a vague criticism of Tao's action along the lines of 'tolerance of difference'. They didn't seem to care. Why did our foremost international university not investigate this incident and other instances of intimidation and silencing by the CSSA on campus? Why did it not at least issue a statement condemning such a blatant suppression of free speech? Why did the vice-chancellor not stock a pile of *Epoch Times* newspapers in the chancellery? The truth is that the ANU has a history of kowtowing to China.

In August 2016 the outgoing director of the ANU's Australian Centre on China in the World, Geremie Barmé, wrote to the university's vice-chancellor, Brian Schmidt, and chancellor Gareth Evans about the activities of a Chinese PhD student, Lei Xiying.[141] Lei had been accepted to research Australian media misrepresentations of China and anti-China activities at our universities. He had also been moonlighting as a Beijing propagandist, probably using the university's resources. In August 2016 he made an ultra-nationalist video with martial music and goose-stepping soldiers that went viral, attracting ten million viewers in twenty-four hours.[142] Noticed by Philip Wen, the video warned of hostile foreign forces fomenting a 'colour revolution' in China. Lei, who is linked to a number of CCP organisations and was rewarded for being an 'outstanding youth representative of online ideological construction',[143] believes Australia is a 'vassal of the United States'.

Lei has a history of posting scathingly anti-Australia messages on Weibo. In one he wrote: 'When I graduate I'm going to immediately leave dumb c*nt unsophisticated Australia. America's political running dog without even an ounce of capacity for independent thought.'[144] The phrase 'unsophisticated Australia' is a translation of 'Tu'ao' (土澳), a mocking expression used by some Chinese students implying that Australia is an uncivilised backwater.

When asked about Lei, the ANU's response was that he had 'the right to free speech' and took no action.[145] Sounds reasonable, but is it? Is it free speech, or is it virulently hostile propaganda targeting liberal values on behalf of a foreign government? Lei's video vilifies Chinese lawyers defending those whose human rights have been violated. The wave of arrests of human rights lawyers in 2015 was a direct assault on free speech and the rule of law.[146] Isn't Australia's commitment to free speech actually being exploited by Lei in support of a totalitarian state? Are we so soft as to defend everyone's right to free speech when their objective is to take away our free speech? The ANU is eager to maintain a harmonious relationship with China yet hosts state-sanctioned attacks on everything noble the West stands for.

Chinese students at the ANU were at the centre of the Olympic torch demonstration in Canberra in April 2008. Earlier in the month Beijing had picked out Australia, along with Japan, as dangerous destinations for the relay because of the activities of Tibetan and Falun Gong protesters.[147] They were especially worried about being outnumbered in Canberra and the embassy was instructed to formulate counter-measures. The president of the CSSA on the ANU campus, Zhang Rongan, confirmed that financial and organisational support was provided by the embassy. When the PRC was accused of using rent-a-crowds, Zhang began to deny any embassy support, removing previous admissions on websites and saying it was all done spontaneously by the students.[148]

It might be assumed that the display of patriotic anger by thousands of Chinese students at the torch relay would have given authorities in Australia pause for thought. But the flow of Chinese students filling the lecture halls (and coffers) of our universities has only accelerated.

The 131,000 in higher education in July 2017 was more than double the number in 2008.[149] Relative to population size, there are five times more Chinese students in Australia than in the United States. Around sixty per cent of ANU's international students are from China, mainly in the business, accounting and finance departments, contributing some fifteen per cent of its total income.[150] The university's chancellor, Gareth Evans, said that universities are 'totally dependent on those [Chinese] fees for their economic survival'.[151] He seemed to be agonising over whether anything could be done. In 2016 it emerged that ANU planned to reduce its dependence on Chinese students, but the idea seems to have gone nowhere.[152]

Parents in China closely follow published international rankings to select the most prestigious university for their child (although top Chinese universities are often preferred). Among the esteemed Group of Eight universities, the most dependent on Chinese students are ANU, the University of Sydney, the University of New South Wales and the University of Melbourne.

'Denounce and inform'

The trove of secret party documents discovered by James To revealed that the Chinese Students and Scholars Associations (CSSAs) were set up around the world after 1989 to manage and redirect the surge of hostility towards the CCP.[153] Since then, education attachés at embassies have coordinated their activities on campuses.[154] From the early 1990s the powerful Ministry of State Security, concerned about the spread of dissenting views among overseas students, has sent out agents posing as students, academics and businesspeople to monitor and report on student activities.[155] Today, after years of instruction under the protective umbrella of the Patriotic Education Campaign—described as an 'education in small-mindedness'[156]—most Chinese students who arrive in Australia have already been inoculated against possible infection by Western ideas. They are easily shepherded through their studies by the embassy and their proxies in the CSSAs.

One of Australia's foremost experts on the CCP, Gerry Groot, wrote of the expansion of United Front activity abroad under Xi Jinping, noting that the party-state has closely monitored the behaviour and speech of students.[157] CSSAs receive funding from the Chinese government and liaise with the local consulate or embassy.[158] For consulates, the student associations are a useful recruiting ground for new party members.[159] Ex-diplomat Chen Yonglin said that meetings of Sydney student associations are typically held inside the consulate, adding that 'the heads of the student organizations are usually hand picked by the Chinese consulate'.[160]

Each year the presidents of the CSSAs across Australia are flown at the embassy's expense to Canberra to a meeting held at its education office in the suburb of O'Malley. According to one former CSSA office holder, at these gatherings Chinese officials coordinate the activities of the various associations and instruct them on the latest party doctrines.[161] Student leaders are prolific in their output of pro-government statements.

In principle, all student organisations on Australian campuses are required to operate according to democratic principles, with free and fair elections, open meetings and transparent finances. CSSAs do none of these.[162] If a foreign government provides funding and appoints executives then secrecy is essential. No other student organisation would be permitted to operate this way. It was for these reasons that New York's prestigious Columbia University shut down its CSSA in 2015.[163] When the president of the CSSA at the University of Canberra, Lupin Lu, candidly admitted that the embassy provides guidance and financial help, the university seemed unconcerned that a foreign government was intervening in student affairs.[164]

Although at times they try to deny their links (as they did at the 2008 Olympic torch relay), one CSSA (at the University of Adelaide) describes itself on its website as 'an organisation under the direction of the education office of the embassy'. Guided and supported financially by the embassy, student leaders are in turn motivated by the promise of political connections and a head start to their careers, as well as patriotic pride. John Fitzgerald notes that Australian universities do not look after Chinese students and they 'feel they are being hosted by the Chinese government in Australia'.[165]

While providing social support for Chinese students, the associations also monitor and police the activities of students, trying to ensure they do not get involved in any corrupting activities. They are instructed, for instance, not to attend films that criticise the PRC. Their thoughts too are policed. If in class or among friends a Chinese student offers an opinion that may be construed as politically incorrect then he or she is likely to be reported to the embassy. In the ABC's 2017 *Four Corners* program 'Power and Influence', the president of the University of Canberra CSSA, Lupin Lu, said that 'for the safety of all ... students' she would report Chinese students organising a human rights protest to the embassy.[166] (Lu later took legal action against the ABC and Fairfax, claiming the program defamed her.) In some cases, parents back in China have been visited by state security to inform them of their child's dangerous activities in Australia and to warn them of the dire consequences should they persist. That happened to Anthony Chang's parents after he spoke at a pro-democracy rally in Brisbane.[167] Reading *The Epoch Times* or a book about the massacre at Tiananmen Square (which many students arriving in Australia have never heard of) could have long-term costs. One dissident student at the ANU said he keeps his views to himself and knows others who 'keep their opinions a secret' for fear of repercussions.[168]

In 2015 President Xi identified Chinese students studying overseas as 'a new focal point for the Communist Party's United Front Work'.[169] A brief prepared by the CIA on the expansion of the student informant system used on China's campuses describes a system of student-informants engaging in political spying and denunciation of professors and fellow students.[170] The 'denounce and inform' model is operating in Australia. A senior lecturer at an Australian university reported that he was interrogated four times in China after being denounced by someone who attended a seminar he gave on democracy at the University of New South Wales.[171] The system's purpose is to control debate and discussion on sensitive issues. The CIA warned of the spread to the West of a 'culture of denunciation'. When the Nobel committee announced on 8 October 2010 that dissident writer Liu Xiaobo would be awarded the Nobel Peace Prize, Peking University authorities investigated students whose facial expressions 'showed unusual happiness'. Those guilty of 'face crime' risked having their scholarships cancelled.

Through the CSSAs students can be mobilised to welcome VIPs from China or to drown out and intimidate any protesters. At times the students are organised with military precision. For example, during training sessions held on the ANU campus for the 2017 visit to Canberra of Premier Li Keqiang, embassy staff aided by the CSSA divided students into security squads and gave instructions like 'Male comrades must protect female comrades'.[172]

The Dalai Lama has not been invited onto an Australian campus for some years. If he were we could expect Chinese students, emboldened by China's growing power and their own patriotism, to respond in the same way that Chinese students did at the University of California, San Diego (UCSD) in early 2017. When it became known that the Tibetan spiritual leader had been invited to give the commencement address, Chinese students reacted with outrage and campaigned to have him disinvited. The UCSD CSSA warned that 'our association vows to take further measures to firmly resist the university's unreasonable behavior'.[173]

As in Australia, the Chinese students defended the party line by invoking the language of victimhood. They told the university that inviting the Dalai Lama to speak 'contravened the spirit of respect, tolerance, equality, and earnestness—the ethos upon which the university is built'. Others took to social media to argue that other students protested against Donald Trump because he does not respect women, Hispanics and LGBT people, yet now they disrespected Chinese students by inviting this 'secessionist' and 'terrorist' who masquerades as a spiritual leader.

In Australia, an exposé of the activities of the CSSA at the ANU was met with wounded appeals to 'inclusive discourse' and 'multicultural-ism' so that 'Chinese students at the ANU can study and live in an environment where they feel free to express their views'.[174] For a body that reports dissenters to the authorities at the embassy, which then harasses and punishes family members back in China, the hypocrisy is rank. Appeals to tolerance and respect by these Chinese students are all the more two-faced when their nationalist comrades back in China relish ridiculing what they call the 'white left' or *baizuo*, that is, those politically correct Westerners, often on campuses, who 'only care about topics such as immigration, minorities, LGBT and the environment'.[175] These patriotic netizens admire Donald Trump for his demonisation of the 'white left'.

The UCSD case immediately followed an attempt by the Chinese embassy in London to pressure students at Durham University to cancel a speech by a former Miss World Canada, Anastasia Lin. A Falun Gong practitioner, Lin was born in China but lived in Canada from an early age, and had spoken out against human rights abuses in China, including forced organ harvesting from Falun Gong prisoners. When she attempted to travel to China to compete as Canada's nominee in the Miss World final she was refused a visa. In recent years the Miss World competition has been sponsored largely or exclusively by Hainan-based interests, where the finals are now held.

The embassy told the Durham debating society students that the event could harm relations between the United Kingdom and China. The CSSA at Durham University complained that inviting Lin to speak was 'a violation of the belief and feelings of Chinese students'.[176] As Lin herself noted of the Chinese government: 'It's not enough for them to stifle their own citizens' voices, they are reaching beyond borders to try to silence us here in the West.' Chinese students on American and Australian campuses also say they are 'offended' and have their 'feelings hurt' when China's human rights abuses or the Dalai Lama are discussed. Perhaps universities could issue trigger warnings and provide 'safe spaces' on campus for Chinese students when there is a danger of their feelings being hurt by exposure to such distressing information. It would be more palatable than pressuring academics to curb their speech.

What to do?

Australian universities ought to be 'islands of freedom' where Chinese students and visiting Chinese scholars can practise the highest principles of free and open scholarship that are outlawed by China's one-party state.[177] Instead, by controlling Chinese students, facilitating links with Chinese universities and encouraging donations by wealthy Chinese businessmen, the CCP is using our campuses to wage its propaganda battles against critics like the Dalai Lama, Falun Gong and pro-democracy activists in exile. Apart from neutralising critics, Beijing's other aim is to cultivate friendly forces in Australia to advocate on its behalf, a strategy that's proved highly successful in Australia.

This chapter has only scratched the surface of what is happening in our universities. Much more could be said about how links with Chinese universities make our university administrators nervous about any criticism of Beijing that might emanate from their scholars or students. Nor have I examined the way universities compromise their principles in pursuit of donations from wealthy Chinese businessmen. (In June 2017 ASIO warned ANU to refuse a very large donation from a Chinese property developer because of his suspected links to the Chinese Communist Party.[178]) A full inquiry is needed to reveal the extent of PRC influence on campuses. Some universities are too compromised to conduct such an inquiry; they would need to choose between the traditions of free and open inquiry, on the one hand, and Chinese money and the kudos of association with the rising Asian power, on the other. Their senior executives have lost their ability to think independently. Only when a university has proven itself willing to sacrifice revenue to defend the principle of academic freedom can we feel confident it is not selling out.

Such an inquiry can only become more necessary as more and more scholars of Chinese heritage and dubious loyalties are recruited by Australian universities, and are promoted to professorships and senior management roles. As this happens, the pressure to close down independent scholarly work and frank debate on China, including the silencing of independently minded scholars of Chinese heritage, will intensify.

Our universities should be making a point of inviting dissident Chinese writers and intellectuals onto their campuses. They should invite the Dalai Lama. They should take steps to ensure that Chinese students are removed from their ideological ghettos by having them attend courses on human rights and democracy and encouraging an environment in which they can ask questions and find their own voices. All attempts to close down opinions that challenge the CCP should be called out and criticised. As undemocratic organisations controlled by a foreign government and operating in clandestine ways, CSSAs should be disbanded, and new organisations established by universities to support Chinese students. And the federal government should make it very clear that any Chinese student who engages in political agitation on behalf of Beijing will never be granted permanent residency in this country.

In these ways, Australia can welcome Chinese and all international students to places where, instead of being a mere slogan, intellectual freedom provides the environment in which a hundred flowers bloom and a hundred schools of thought contend.

11

Culture wars

Harry Wang was puzzled by complaints about his company's expansion plans from his south Gippsland farm neighbours. The boss of Ningbo Dairy Group offered them reassurance: 'It's strange in some ways because really milk is milk, and we will be producing it the same way in Australia as we do on our Chinese farms with all the same levels of cleanliness, hygiene and animal welfare standards.'[1]

Harry Wang, unlike the Australians who heard those words, was not thinking of the litany of pollution and food contamination stories plaguing Chinese agriculture, not least the scandal involving adulteration of milk with the industrial chemical melamine that saw 54,000 babies hospitalised and six die. Two more people later died as a result of the episode—a pair of milk company executives were executed for their roles in the adulteration.

Ningbo Dairy was not implicated in the melamine scandal. However (and apparently unknown to the authorities in Australia), it has a history of health and hygiene infractions. In April 2012 the company was sprung putting fake production dates on over 2000 bottles of yogurt.[2] Ten months later it was discovered that almost seventy per cent of its milk samples had high levels of coliform bacteria and beta lactamase (which prevents penicillin working). Ningbo contested the finding, but then apologised. And in April 2013 over 32,000 bottles of its milk were found with false production dates on them. The fine of around $70,000 suggests the company has friends in high places.

But not in Australia. After purchasing five farms in south Gippsland in 2015, Harry Wang planned to bring his farming methods to Australia. In China, Ningbo Dairy collects milk from cows kept in barns, their confinement allowing more milk to be extracted because they do not have to walk to and from the milking sheds. Not only could Ningbo extract fifty per cent more milk from each Gippsland cow, it could slash costs by bringing in 2000 Chinese farm workers, which Ningbo would be entitled to do under the China-Australia Free Trade Agreement. Moreover, the company would build its own bottling plant and fly all of the milk to China.

Canberra raised no objections to his plans, so what's the problem? wondered Harry Wang.

As public relations consultants Powell Tate drily remarked, 'the company's messaging needed work'.[3]

After 400 complaints flooded in—covering everything from animal welfare, effects on tourism, farm waste, truck movements and exploitation of workers—Bass Coast Shire Council saw fit to reject the development plan unanimously. Photographed standing in a windswept paddock on one of his farms, Harry Wang said he did not know what he was going to do now.[4]

Ningbo Dairy had been refused a social licence to operate. Luckily, Australia is not short of business advisers—and ex–prime ministers— offering advice to Chinese investors on how to get one. In March 2017 the boss of the Foreign Investment Review Board, Brian Wilson, advised a forum packed with Chinese investors to stay away from Australian 'icons', and to talk up the benefits of jobs and market growth.[5] In time, the chief regulator reassured them, Australians would get used to more Chinese ownership of assets here. Two weeks later former prime minister John Howard urged Chinese entrepreneurs to find an Australian partner if they want to avoid resistance.[6]

Powell Tate provides Chinese investors with a blueprint to obtain a social licence to operate in the Australian agricultural sector. The bottom line is that Chinese investors must observe cultural sensitivities and contribute to Australian society in some way rather than just attempting to maximise profits. This helpful advice may mollify a sceptical public, but it's not going to change any links the Chinese partner may have with the party-state apparatus.

It is true that many Chinese businesspeople do not understand the notion of a social licence to operate.[7] As they have grown up in a system in which the influence of money linked to powerful people prevails, why should they? For developers, progress has never depended on the permission of local communities to knock down and build, but only on the ability to exploit *guanxi*, and their skill at bribing the right officials. Some arrive in Australia expecting (not so unusually) to pay someone to get them access to politicians, perhaps by a political donation, preferably the federal treasurer because he 'owns the FIRB',[8] and Foreign Investment Review Board approval clears away every other obstacle.

When a $371 million bid by Shanghai Pengxin and Shanghai CRED for the vast Kidman estate (covering 2.5 per cent of the continent's agricultural land) was rejected by the federal government after a public outcry, Shanghai CRED entered a partnership with Gina Rinehart's Hancock Prospecting, creating a joint venture company called Australian Outback Beef. The company's bid of nearly $400 million for the Kidman properties was approved by the treasurer in December 2016.[9] The joint venture promised to keep the local management. But for how long? This kind of deal may do no more than put an Australian veneer over the purchase, without resolving the underlying tension. Down the track we can expect to see the Chinese company buy out its Australian partner when circumstances shift, such as the Australian partner wanting out and no other local firm wanting in, perhaps because the Chinese company makes it look unattractive.

Chinese voices

In China I met with a famous academic whose pro-government and nationalist arguments are well known. Over an hour of conversation, he presented a remarkably frank assessment of modern China and Australia's relationship to it. I was surprised at how much he knew about Australia. Because of his candour he asked to remain unnamed, but here are the most striking observations he made.

Australian anxieties about Chinese political interference are justified. I believe in what Confucius said: Don't do to others what you do not want others to do to you …

… [B]usinesspeople must get money out of China and are targeting health, nutrition, food security. Everywhere in China is polluted. So Australia is very important, especially for items like powdered milk, beef and fish. Iron ore exports are now declining after the end of China's building boom. Healthy food, like unpoisoned milk powder, is especially important for the rich (the poor have to use local produce).

Australia has a huge land area but doesn't make any money out of it.

Australians see many Chinese in their cities and they ask: 'Is this still Australia?' It's getting like London. And they read stories of Chinese being rude, like peeing on the grass and paying bribes. The Chinese will do it legally first but if that does not work then some will do it illegally …

Five million dollars is too cheap to get permanent residency in Australia.

[CH: 'Is much of the money used for these visas dirty money?'] Of course, but the Australian government doesn't care … So why does Australia allow so many millions to compete for your hospitals? How can you take so many people? Australia is so small. Some Chinese in Australia are pursuing their own interests. For instance, a daughter does a PhD at ANU and then gets PR [permanent residency]. Then she can bring her father.

I am first a Chinese citizen, then a global citizen. So I stick to the Confucius principle: Don't do to others what you don't want others to do to you. China has very restrictive immigration policies.

[On investment by state-owned enterprises overseas:] There needs to be a balance; it should benefit both. I believe in responsible globalisation—don't use your capital to change other countries' values. In Sydney, a rich Chinese wanted to knock down a heritage building. Reportedly he is a son of [a] former president's confidant. The local residents complained. They wanted to protect their culture. He offered to compensate them. For people like him nothing is non-tradable. They don't believe in the Confucius principle. They just want access to your resources to combine them with their resources, which is money.

The Communists have failed to educate people. They just tell them to become rich people ...

There are legitimate concerns that some wealthy Chinese-Australians have links to military intelligence. There is always a risk that foreign security might penetrate. The question is: How should the risk be managed? This is a big problem ...

It's a huge risk for Australia to take so many students. [CH: 'Do you think the president of the Chinese students' association at ANU was appointed or approved by the embassy?'] Without doubt. And the embassy would be giving the association money. The association needs money from the embassy for banquets, invited speakers and so on, and the Chinese government wants to manipulate students. So there is a convergence of interests of mutual benefit. But there is no contract, no one signed a deal. The leaders of the students' association understand the deal but other students don't know about it.

Columbia University has disallowed the biggest Chinese students' organisation because it violated the university's ethical code requiring transparency, fairness and democratic elections.

The Australian FBI [the Australian Federal Police] should intervene, talk to the embassy and caution it about its manipulation of students. And it should warn the student leaders, making it clear that their prospects for PR will be jeopardised if they engage in political activities. Make a law against politicking. Most Chinese students are self-interested. Most would not participate in student organisations if their PR were jeopardised.

[I noted that the ANU authorities did nothing in response to the incident in which the president of the CSSA demanded that copies of *The Epoch Times* be removed from the campus pharmacy.] They are selfish; they want Chinese student money. Who gave that Chinese student leader the right to behave as the police in Australia? Most Chinese are upset at the Dalai Lama, but who gives us the right to demand other countries not to welcome him? ... In China we do not have this freedom so why import it into Australia? Why import what is bad in China into other countries? What if Chinese in Australia began to use their numbers to elect Australia's leader? [CH: 'There are one million Chinese in Australia.'] We can send you twenty million.

Patriotism is fine. But biased patriotism is worse than no patriotism. If Chinese go to Australia we must obey your laws. Who gives us the right not to obey your laws? Many in China think: When I am patriotic I can do anything, anywhere. No, we can do it only on our territory. What is mutual respect? We must accept different ways and values. There is a danger of Chinese practising political and cultural imperialism on others' territories.

I left the meeting a little stunned at his blunt assessment of China–Australia relations.

Sally Zou's gold

Sally Zou has come to public attention for her extraordinary generosity. The owner of the gold mining company Aus Gold Mining Group, she donated $460,000 to the Liberal Party in 2015–16, making her easily the dominant donor in South Australia.[10]

When she is in Australia Ms Zou is a fiercely patriotic Australian. To prove it she took out a full-page newspaper advertisement to celebrate Australia Day. She even had her Rolls Royce painted over with the Australian flag. If this says something about the vulgarity of China's nouveaux riches, Sally Zou is not alone. In August 2017 some rich Chinese-Australians in Sydney drove through the city in a convoy of luxury cars emblazoned with Chinese flags and patriotic slogans. The excuse for this crude display of wealth was to protest against Indian incursions in Chinese territory (in fact, the PLA had occupied part of Bhutan). Next to a Bentley painted CCP red, a Porsche displayed a decal of the disputed Himalayan border region with the slogan 'China, Not An Inch Will Be Given Up', a slogan popularised by ANU student Lei Xiying.[11]

Aus Gold established an engineering scholarship at the University of Adelaide[12] and Zou became the largest benefactor of Port Adelaide

Football Club. She says she wants to help the club take Australian football to the world. In May 2017, with her financial backing, the club played the AFL's first overseas league match in Shanghai watched by 10,000 fans, most of whom had flown from Australia.[13] The idea of exporting a love of Aussie Rules to China is mere whimsy, so there must be another objective to Zou's investment.

When she is talking to the Chinese press Zou's patriotism changes hue. A 2011 story in *People's Daily* entitled 'Sally Zou: Devoting my wisdom to the Ancestral Nation from a foreign land' reported Zou saying that 'despite being a stranger in a strange land, she will continue to devote her wisdom and strength to the prosperous development of the Ancestral Nation'.[14] She had certainly done well in the Ancestral Nation, after being born into a wealthy steel-making family and setting up a Hong Kong company at age twenty-nine with a registered capital of HK$200 million.[15]

Sally Zou declared that she was 'willing to make her own company become a platform for Chinese enterprises to enter Australia,' while she also wanted to 'sell iron ore to Chinese enterprises at a lower price than Australian mining tycoons, to support the construction of the Ancestral Nation'. She ran into criticism when she struck a multibillion-dollar deal giving the huge state-owned China Gold Group exclusive rights to buy all gold produced by Aus Gold Mining.[16] Aus Gold later denied that any preferential deal had been made, stating that they 'would prefer to sell our gold to Australian buyers'. 'We are very loyal to the Australian community and Australian government', said a spokesperson. 'We are committed to Australia's future. We would like to make contributions back.'[17] In a March 2017 ceremony overseen by New South Wales energy and resources minister Don Harwin, China Gold Group signed an agreement underwriting Zou's Aus Gold.[18]

Perhaps Sally Zou's passion for both China and Australia only proves her commitment to bringing the two nations into a closer harmony. As evidence we might point to Sally's daughter, Gloria, whose eighth birthday Sally celebrated by spending around $50,000 on a full-page advertisement in *The Australian*.[19] Gloria is known to the *People's Daily* as the 'Little angel of Australia–China friendship'. Gloria may have been speaking for her mother when at a precious metals symposium she predicted that 'there will be a golden "Maritime Silk Road" between China and Australia and the coming "golden age of China-Australia relations" will have shining luster and long-term stability like gold and last for thousands of years maintaining beauty and firmness without changes'.[20]

Julie Bishop, whose West Australian branch of the Liberal Party has enjoyed a tsunami of Chinese cash, was so moved by these remarkably mature sentiments that she met with Gloria at a garden party where she heard another speech from the eight-year-old expressing her dream of 'China and Australia as one family'.[21] Sally had spread the love by setting up the Julie Bishop Glorious Foundation.[22] Addressing an incredulous Opposition in parliament, the foreign minister said she had never heard of it.

Real estate woes

Real estate has generated more anxiety than any other China-related issue. It's not surprising given its volume and visibility, and at a time of raging house price inflation. There's too much to say so I confine my comments to a few of the more salient points.

It's important to be clear upfront that Chinese-Australians are as entitled as any other Australian citizen to buy a house to live in. We should spare a thought for those Chinese-Australians who turn up to an auction to face Anglo frowns of disapproval, just as some do when they queue at the supermarket to buy infant formula. They are Australians being penalised for the sins of others.

Under federal law, foreigners may not buy established dwellings in Australia without approval from the Foreign Investment Review Board (FIRB), although it permits them to buy new ones. This law can be circumvented and for a long time was simply ignored. The FIRB did not bother regulating the flow of Chinese purchases of existing dwellings until a public outcry forced the hand of treasurer Joe Hockey in 2015. Dancing to another tune, Simon Henry, co-chief executive of Chinese real estate site Juwai, branded the law's enforcement 'racist'.[23]

Restrictions on foreign ownership have also been circumvented by asking family members to buy houses using funds transferred from abroad. As one real estate agent put it to me: 'The Chinese trust their family.' Alternatively, rich foreigners can buy Australian residency. Although it slowed in 2016, there was a surge in the number of Significant Investor visas granted, mostly to wealthy Chinese willing to invest $5 million in designated sectors.[24]

In 2016 overseas buyers, eighty per cent of them Chinese, snapped up twenty-five per cent of all new housing in New South Wales, and sixteen per cent in Victoria.[25] The percentages would be higher for Sydney and Melbourne. Approved foreign investment in Australia in 2016 reached $248 billion. This enormous flow was 'predominantly driven by increased investment in the real estate sector', according to the FIRB. Much of it was in apartments, which were sold to middle-class people in Beijing, Shanghai and Chengdu, sometimes without being advertised in Australia at all. Although overall growth in workers on 457 visas coming to Australia stopped in 2016, the occupation class with the fastest growth was real estate agents, mainly coming over from China to help flog property to Chinese buyers.[26]

Just why this is in Australia's national interest is hard to see, especially when cities around the world, led by Hong Kong and Vancouver, have taken measures to severely limit real estate investment from the Chinese mainland. In doing so they diverted more of the demand to Sydney and Melbourne.

The Property Council, surely the most brazenly self-interested lobby group in the country, insists that demand from China has no appreciable impact on house prices. It commissioned ACIL Allen Consulting (the coal industry's preferred modellers) to write a report that showed that Chinese demand is 'essential … [to] Australian economic DNA'.[27] Jobs, growth, tax revenue, you name it—without Chinese people buying Australian property, everything would suffer. In fact, said the council's chief executive, if foreign investment in commercial buildings fell by twenty per cent the loss in GDP 'would be akin to the loss of Australia's coal-fired electricity industry' (a bad thing).

Aspirational Chinese multimillionaires have targeted Sydney and Melbourne to buy up property so they can commute from China when they feel like it. According to one report, these 'migrant millionaires' are fuelling the property price bubbles in our two largest cities.[28] Real estate agents have been making a killing and defend the influx with ridiculous claims. Attracted by clean air, good schools and laws that are enforced, ultra-high-net-worth Chinese businessmen flying in and out 'want to contribute to Australian society', said one. Another suggested that '[i]t's a little bit like the country kids that used to go to boarding school and travelled back to far western NSW'.[29]

In March 2017 a police chief from Jinzhou City was sentenced to seventeen years in jail for embezzlement. He used the money to buy a large number of properties in Australia, including houses in Sydney for his two daughters.[30] Australia is a favoured destination for corrupt Chinese money, with a total of $3.36 billion of suspicious financial transactions investigated in 2015–16, with a third of it stashed in real estate.[31] By early 2017 the federal government's crackdown had forced rich foreigners, mainly Chinese, to sell $107 million worth of properties bought illegally,[32] but real estate agents on the ground claim that loopholes are used to get around the laws and illegal sales are greater than ever.[33]

In February 2017 Beijing's crackdown on capital flight was reported to have caused a sharp fall in Chinese demand for properties in Los Angeles, but no such decline seems to have affected Sydney.[34] The Australian newspapers were reporting Chinese developers 'roaring back into Melbourne' in the second half of 2016, with three-quarters of available development sites sold to mainland Chinese investors.[35] They are confident they can sell the apartments because they already have the buyers lined up back in China. That's what happens when a city is named the world's most liveable for six years in a row.

In an article headed 'World's biggest real estate frenzy is coming to a city near you', Bloomberg reports experts saying that what seems like a flood of Chinese investment into Australia is a mere 'trickle' compared with what is to come, if we allow it.[36] A 31-year-old owner of wheat farms in Jiangsu, for example, plans to buy six apartments in Sydney with a view to sending his children to high schools there sometime in the future.

Patriot writers

The Melbourne Writers Festival and Writers Victoria are respectable institutions on the literary scene, committed to helping authors find their voices and promoting a diversity of ideas. It seemed natural for them to support Chinese-language authors by entering a partnership with the Australian-Chinese Writers Association to organise the Chinese Writers Festival in August 2016. The Chinese Poets and Authors Society of Victoria and the Melbourne Chinese Writers Friendship Association were also involved.[37]

But what is the Australian-Chinese Writers Association? It's hard to find anything on the public record, but at an event celebrating its tenth anniversary in April 2016 the deputy consul general from the PRC's Melbourne consulate, Huang Guobin, praised the association as 'an important platform for spreading Chinese culture' and thanked the group for having 'always energetically supported and cooperated with the consulate's work'. In fact, the association had not always supported the consulate, but in recent years has been taken over by pro-Beijing forces.[38] From the consulate Huang was accompanied by Zhang Xiaohong, consul for Overseas Chinese Affairs, that is, for *qiaowu*.

A year earlier at the 2015 Chinese Writers Festival in Melbourne, the current president of the Chinese Writers Association (CWA), Tie Ning, was a prominent presence. Tie Ning is a well-respected author, but she is also a member of the 19th Central Committee of the Chinese Communist Party (and the 18th before that), one of the highest political bodies in China.[39] In the words of one astute observer: 'The relationship between the Chinese Writers Association and the Party is somewhat like a teenager and a dictator father … The Party doesn't require you to sing praise every day, but it makes sure that you don't write anything offensive, or worse, subversive.'[40] As China's peak literary body, the CWA is an important part of the CCP's overseas propaganda program and is the force behind the Melbourne Chinese Writers Festival. Authors arriving from China are selected by it.

The host of the tenth anniversary event of the Australian-Chinese Writers Association was the chair of the Australian Chinese Writers Festival, Hu Mei (May Hu). She arrived in Australia in 1988 and received permanent residency soon after the Tiananmen Square massacre. In 1992 she began work as the Head of Group Mandarin at SBS. In June 2017 she was awarded an Order of Australia medal for 'her service to broadcast media, women and the multicultural community of Victoria'.[41] Despite her continuing work at SBS, Hu was also involved with the World Indochinese Council for the Promotion of the Peaceful Reunification of China, a United Front group that held a press conference in March 2017 attacking Taiwanese independence.[42] Huang Huiyuan, president of the Melbourne Chinese Writers Association, also spoke at the press conference. Huang is deputy head of the pro-Beijing Chinese newspaper *Melbourne Daily*, in which role he has 'expressed his willingness to work hard to propagandise and promote China and Guangzhou'.[43]

The 2016 Chinese Writers Festival in Melbourne was enthusiastically reported in China, with chinaqw.com, a site affiliated with the Overseas Chinese Affairs Office, publishing an article promoting the festival and focusing on the event's keynote speaker, Lei Tao.[44] Lei Tao is party secretary of the Shaanxi Writers Association and a committee member of the party-approved China Writers Association. He previously worked as the director of the Shaanxi Provincial Party Committee's Propaganda Department. A loyal party member, he was editor-in-chief of the 'Shaanxi Propaganda Guide'.[45] Lei's profile published by Writers Victoria failed to mention any of this.

Comments by Lei at a press conference he held before departing for Australia emphasised the propaganda function of the Australian festival: 'through exchange with local Chinese writers and Australian writers, I will definitely expand the influence of Shaanxi's—and also China's—culture abroad, to let overseas writers understand the current creative situation in China.'[46] Of course, no Chinese writers critical of the CCP were invited.

The *People's Daily* published a long and detailed report on the 2016 festival itself, concluding that 'Australian-Chinese writers are gradually receiving the attention of mainstream society, and this closely reflects China's power and the increasing numbers of Chinese migrants'.[47] In truth, the consulates work hard to ensure that some Chinese writers receive no attention. Party secretary Lei Tao told the *People's Daily* that Australian-Chinese writers left a deep impression on him: 'even though their bodies are overseas, they are still firmly rooted in their ethnicity and with their cultural motherland, China'.[48]

Some Chinese-heritage writers in Australia left China to escape the party's intolerance of creative freedom. But they were not invited to the festival. Deputy consul general Huang told Chinese reporters that 'only by deeply understanding their own Ancestral Nation can overseas Chinese writers create high-quality works of literature'. In addition to partnering with the Chinese Writers Festival, the Melbourne Writers Festival features one or two Chinese writers at its annual event. All of these writers have been, from Beijing's point of view, safe. No dissident writers who would bring a quite different understanding of modern China have been given a platform.

In accord with their commitment to cultural openness, the Melbourne Writers Festival and Writers Victoria have been unwittingly collaborating with United Front bodies whose aim is to spread into Australian society the CCP worldview, one that is extremely intolerant of artistic licence and dissenting views. The cruel death of dissident writer Liu Xiaobo in a Chinese prison in 2017 reminded us of this. These worthy Australian organisations cannot be blamed for their naivety, for we are only beginning to understand the pervasiveness of the PRC's influence campaign in this country. But now they know. If they are to collaborate again with writers' associations close to the consulate, they should insist that dissident authors be invited and given a voice.

Let me finish with the story of one such writer. At age twenty, Qi Jiazhen was sentenced to thirteen years in a Sichuan prison, along with her father, for unspecified counter-revolutionary activities. There she was subjected to unrelenting propaganda. Eventually, she said, she was brainwashed, becoming the 'poster girl for successful rehabilitation'. She was allowed to come to Australia to study English in 1987. After the Tiananmen Square massacre in 1989 she gained permanent residency and eventually citizenship. 'I kept silent for seventeen years out of fear,' she told me. Now in her seventies, she is a fierce critic of the Communist Party and began to speak out through her books. She helped organise the 2016 Melbourne protest against the visiting *Red Detachment of Women* ballet performance.

When I met Qi Jiazhen in Melbourne she told me that in 2014, after she'd published a memoir about her tribulations in China, she was invited to speak at an event organised by the Chinese Writers Association. But between the issuing of the invitation and the day of the event the association had been taken over by pro-Beijing elements, probably with the help of the Melbourne consulate. Days before the event they asked someone else to be the main speaker, allocating only ten minutes to Qi Jiazhen and then interrupting her and closing the session before she could respond to questions. 'They can do here whatever they want,' she added matter-of-factly. 'How can the Communist Party be so powerful in Australia?' she asked me. I had no answer for her.

Co-opting God

Wherever overseas Chinese gather they become a potential target for influence and infiltration through *qiaowu* work, and that includes churches. The classified State Council reports read by James To adopt an 'ecumenical' approach, with no discrimination between Protestants and Catholics. They instruct cadres to monitor, infiltrate and 'sinify' overseas Chinese churches by actively promoting the CCP's concepts of Chineseness and 'spiritual love'.[49] For the CCP, nothing's sacred except fealty to the motherland and, of course, the party itself. The churches have added value for *qiaowu* cadres because they are linked into wider society through non-Chinese Christian networks. In addition, if the party can shape the messages coming from religious leaders, the faithful are more likely to believe them because they trust their pastors.

While Christian churches are being suppressed in China, the rapid growth of Chinese Christian churches in Australia provides an opportunity for *qiaowu* cooptation. Sydney alone boasts over a hundred Chinese churches, and Melbourne sixty.[50] In the older churches, sermons were mostly in Cantonese, but in the last decade more and more have congregations that speak Mandarin.

Across the Tasman, in 2001 the (Chinese) Presbyterian Church in New Zealand issued a statement on the Taiwan issue. Quoting Matthew 5:37, it called on the world to respect the feelings of Chinese Christians: 'Taiwan is an inalienable part of China. We are grateful for and cherish this gift bestowed by God.'[51] According to a 2014 article on the website of the Canberra Chinese Methodist Church: 'The awe-inspiring righteousness of Xi Jinping ... and the rise of a great nation that is modern China are part of God's plan, predestination and blessing'.[52] The author is Ms Zhang Xiaoyan, an Australian citizen and vice-president of the Chinese Writers Association of Sydney. Elsewhere she seems to endorse the prediction that a 'Red Brigade will be dispatched from China to stir up a huge wave, like a massive red tsunami, to rejuvenate Australia'.[53] Dr James Kwang, Bishop of the Chinese Methodist Church in Australia (CMCA), has made it clear that these are the personal views of one member of the church and that the CMCA does not support any regime or government 'as the sole purpose of the CMCA is to spread scriptural Christianity to all races in Australia and beyond'.

According to Chinese-Australian pastors I have spoken with, many parishioners believe that they have spies in their midst whose role is to report to the consulate any anti-party talk or activities. One pastor told me: 'There are lots of Communists in our church community.'[54] He guessed that around a quarter or a third are or have been Communists. Some join the church for the companionship, some for the social contacts; others are the consulate's assets.

Chinese Anzacs

Through its United Front organs and sympathetic individuals, the CCP is attempting to control how Chinese history is understood and to promote a certain narrative about China's place in Australia's pre- and post-settlement history. Although taking place behind the scenes, some of it can now be exposed. It should be stressed that for twenty to thirty years a number of Australian historians have been researching the long-neglected role of Chinese immigrants in Australia's colonial and modern history. In the last several years, however, some have become disturbed at the way Beijing is hijacking their work for its political and ideological purposes. This followed a decision around 2008 in Beijing to actively promote the history of overseas Chinese, with museums devoted to them springing up across China.[55] When Xi Jinping became president in 2013 there was renewed commitment by the State Council Information Office (also known as the Central Office of Foreign Propaganda) to 'telling a good Chinese story' to foreign audiences with a view to fostering warm feelings.[56]

In 2015 ASIO chief Duncan Lewis warned the organisational heads of the main political parties against accepting donations from the billionaire businessmen Chau Chak Wing and Huang Xiangmo. While their outsized political donations have attracted all of the attention, they have also been active in shaping Australian history and culture.

In September 2015 the Australian War Memorial (AWM) held a wreath-laying service in recognition of Chinese-Australian soldiers who served in the Australian Defence Force. Chau Chak Wing was conspicuous at the ceremony. He stood between the memorial's director, Brendan Nelson, and Returned Services League president Admiral Ken Doolan and laid the wreath on behalf of Chinese-Australians. Reporting on the AWM event, his company's website and the Chinese media described him as 'ACFEA chairman'. The Australia China Friendship and Exchange Association (ACFEA) is a United Front body responsible for organising a series of events attended by senior Communist Party officials.

Why was Chau given this prestigious role by the Australian War Memorial? How did this man become the representative of 'the Chinese-Australian community'? Inquiries revealed that he made no financial contribution to the event as it was one of the memorial's daily Last Post ceremonies. However, Dr Chau—his honorary 'doctorate of humane letters' was awarded by Keuka College, a little-known university in upstate New York—was well known to the AWM. His company funded and bought naming rights for an oral and audio-visual recording studio in the building, known as the Kingold Media Centre.[57] The centre was opened the same day, an event reported prominently in China.[58]

Chau had also made a donation to fund a study exploring the 'ethnic diversity of the Australian Imperial Force'. The burden of that project appears to have been to commission an academic at a Chinese university to write a history of Chinese-Australian soldiers. Chau's generosity is recognised by the inscription of his name on a stone inside the memorial's entrance, along with a very select group of the great and good of Australian philanthropy. (The AWM will not say how much he has donated.) After he laid the wreath for the 'sacrifice of Chinese origin soldiers', as *Xinhuanet* described them,[59] Dr Nelson and foreign minister Julie Bishop presented him with an 'Australian War Memorial Fellowship', which as far as I can tell is a framed certificate given to an elite of mega-donors. When I asked the memorial for more information, and whether due diligence had been carried out on Chau Chak Wing, I was told: 'These are matters of public record. We have nothing more to add.'[60]

The study Chau funded resulted in a book now on sale in the memorial's bookshop at the heavily subsidised price of $2.95 ($4.95 for the hardback). Titled *Quiet and Loyal Spirit: Commemorating Chinese Australian military service*, it was put together by historian Dr Sheng Fei of Sun Yat-Sen University in Guangdong and published by New Century Publications Fund in association with ACFEA.[61] The book is written in Chinese English, although some passages break into perfect English. The text is full of inaccuracies, at one point even referring to itself as *The Quite Loyal Spirit* and the AWM as the 'Australian National War Memorial'.

But it is the historical distortions in the book that are most worrying, beginning with its opening sentence: 'Chinese were among the first settlers as members of the first fleet in 1788.' Chinese convicts in England? Chinese marines? Seriously? There were no Chinese people on the First Fleet.[62] Absurd as it seems, this claim is now 'in the history books' and, going by experience, it's not fanciful to imagine it coming up in some future sovereignty claim.

The Second World War, which the book refers to as the Anti-Fascist War, is portrayed as the time China and Australia stood together to resist Japanese aggression, the point at which Australian society overcame its fear of Chinese invasion and the two nations formed a bond. The China-focused anti-communism that took Australia into conflicts in Malaya, Korea and Vietnam is not mentioned, and when the role of Chinese-Australian soldiers in the Korean and Vietnam wars comes up it is quickly passed over with no mention of the fact that Communist China backed Australia's enemies.

The role of Chinese-Australians in Australia's military history is deserving of proper study and full acknowledgement. But why would the Australian War Memorial entrust a Chinese academic with limited knowledge of Australia and no experience as a military historian to write this significant part of Australia's military history, and then promote it to visitors in its bookshop? PRC history books today are a mishmash of semi-fiction and official propaganda.[63] China is now described by a respected historian as 'a country that has … completely obliterated and then recreated its past'.[64] The CCP propagates a completely distorted picture of the role of Chinese soldiers and the Communist Party in the war against Japan.[65] Why does the memorial sell a book that is of risible production quality and presents to the public a distorted picture of this important part of the nation's history?

The gift-giving of Chinese billionaires follows a strategy of building legitimacy by donating to cultural, educational and medical causes.[66] If a PR company were asked by a foreign investor to recommend a strategy to ingratiate itself with the Australian public, it might (if it were sufficiently cynical) propose the client sprinkle itself with Anzac dust, and point out that the biggest bowl of Anzac dust is to be found at the Australian War Memorial. It goes without saying that the memorial is a sacred space for the nation and access to it should never be exploited by a foreign power.

Chau's Chinese Anzacs are not the only vehicle for co-opting Australian history. Friends of China are reinterpreting the place of Chinese immigrants in the nation's development. Important and under-valued as that history has been, these PRC sympathisers are attributing to them a much larger role than impartial historians do. The effect of these histories is to amplify the sense of grievance over the history of racism among Chinese-heritage people in Australia—and in China. It's not surprising to see a recent one, *Dragon & Kangaroo* by journalist Robert Macklin, praised in the Communist Party media.[67] The book was launched by Bob Carr.

Huang Xiangmo has offered to fund a book on Chinese immigrants in Australian history. Although some local historians, over-eager to demonstrate their respect for cultural diversity, have allowed themselves to be hoodwinked, others are alive to the dangers. When some Australian historians working in the area heard that Huang was behind the project, they withdrew their expressions of interest in contributing to the book.

In a similar show of caution, the Dragon Tails group of historians expressed interest in accepting an offer from the Australia-China Institute for Arts and Culture to host its biennial conference. When its committee became aware that Huang Xiangmo had funded the institute at Western Sydney University, it split over how it could protect the academic integrity of the conference. In the end it went ahead. Huang had donated $3.5 million to the university for the institute. Holly Huang, the general manager of Huang's Yuhu Group (Australia), was appointed to its board. Holly Huang's LinkedIn profile says she has a Master of Local Government degree from UTS.

The People's Liberation Army of Australia

In August 2015 the Australian Chinese Ex-Services Association established the 'Australian Eighth Corps', a unit made up of ex-PLA soldiers who had emigrated to Australia. A year later it staged a celebration at Hurstville Town Hall, its members dressed up in PLA fatigues, with caps, insignia and flags galore.[68] Photos of the event show surreal scenes. They sang patriotic army songs and recreated life in the barracks. These were not Chinese Anzacs who had fought for Australia, but ex-PLA who had served China. But in the minds of these patriots the difference is blurred. The event was a success and the PLA in Australia was back a year later, in Chatswood, singing 'The East Is Red'.[69]

> The Communist Party is like the sun,
> Wherever it shines, it is bright
> Wherever the Communist Party is
> Hurrah, the people are liberated!

The PLA has a long history of using song and dance troupes to deliver its message. It takes seriously Mao Zedong's dictum that an army with guns is not enough, 'we must also have a cultural army, which is absolutely indispensable for uniting our own ranks and defeating the enemy'.[70]

The organisers of the PLA in Australia are speaking directly to Chinese communities. The familiar uniforms and songs create a sense of belonging. Some Chinese-Australians are appalled at this militarisation of their community in support of the CCP. For others, the revolutionary nostalgia is attractive, keeping them emotionally, linguistically and culturally close to the PRC. While at one level these events are a piece of cultural theatre, they raise a challenging loyalty issue. If it comes to potential conflicts between Australia and China, with whom do these military veterans side?

The forerunner of the Australian Chinese Ex-Services Association was named the August 1st Brigade (the PLA was founded on that date). Its charter stipulates that 'all members must fervently love their motherland'.[71] In March 2017, members of the association took to the streets of Sydney to welcome visiting Premier Li Keqiang. Its president would go home to write: 'Today Chinese national flags subjugated Sydney! Thousands of Chinese people waited in the rain. The entire CBD was a sea of black hair, yellow skin and red national flags!'[72]

Digital totalitarianism

There's a KFC in Beijing where a machine uses facial recognition technology to suggest what you might want to order. According to a KFC spokesperson, 'The artificial intelligence-enabled system can recommend menu items based on a customer's estimated age and mood.'[73] While companies around the world keep electronic records of what we buy, KFC can now keep a record of your face. The machine remembers you next time. Asked about privacy, one customer responded, 'In China, you don't have any privacy anyway.'

The KFC outlet sounds like a novelty item, but the Chinese state and private tech companies are investing huge sums in facial recognition technology, big data and artificial intelligence to build a national system of surveillance and social control that would make George Orwell blanch. As a hint of what is to come, in Shenzhen a citizen who crosses a road against a red light may reach the other side to be confronted with a large video screen displaying her face, along with a warning from the police. Her infraction is logged on a computer somewhere, along with her other infractions. In a nation estimated to have 100 million CCTV cameras (one for every thirteen people) and growing,[74] it foreshadows a system of mass surveillance capable of tracking a face almost anywhere.

Jaywalking is only one small misdemeanour that will be logged by the 'social-credit system' being rolled out across China, described by one observer as 'the most ambitious attempt by any government in modern history to fuse technology with behavioural control'.[75]

Government agencies will award citizens points for good behaviour and deduct them for anti-social behaviour like being late with the rent and posting social media comments the authorities don't like. Under the system of reputation scores, if you perform well a promotion might be fast-tracked. *The Economist* reports a government official saying that by 2020 the emerging social credit system will 'allow the trustworthy to roam everywhere under heaven while making it hard for the discredited to take a single step'. It's hoped that it will allow better control of corruption and, of course, track criminal activity.

In this brave new world of 'digital totalitarianism' obedience to the state is rewarded and dissent punished.[76] China's paranoid one-party state is already deploying a sophisticated and highly effective form of political supervision, in a nation that already possesses an immense infrastructure devoted to policing the thoughts and actions of its citizens. Journalist and blogger Liu Hu, renowned for exposing corrupt officials, was charged with 'fabricating and spreading rumours' and fined by a court.[77] He was placed on a blacklist that prevents him from buying plane tickets and property and travelling on certain kinds of trains. There is no appeal system. The blacklist now has over seven million names, including a girl placed on it when she was two years old because she inherited a debt from her parents. A court had imposed a large fine on her father after he murdered his wife. He was then executed but his daughter inherited the fine.

In some cities, the ringback tone on the phone of blacklisted people is altered by the authorities so that callers are warned they are contacting a discredited person.

The social credit system will require a vast system of integrated data collection, storage, analysis and retrieval, which is precisely the objective of research into big data—that is, 'extremely large data sets that may be analysed computationally to reveal patterns, trends, and associations, especially relating to human behaviour and interactions'.[78] The social credit system still requires work before it can be rolled out across the country. However, with the backing of President Xi the state is determined to press ahead.

To predict an individual's potential for terrorist activity, China is now trialling a system that uses data on their employment history, bank records, consumption habits, friends and movements recorded through surveillance cameras. There's little doubt this emerging 'pre-crime' identification software will also be used against those proposing alternatives to CCP rule.[79]

The 'smart cities' program undertaken by the China Electronics Technology Group Corporation (CETC) is at the forefront of the social credit scheme. CETC is one of the Chinese state's top military research organisations, specialising in information and communications systems. It boasts that its integrated big data centre will 'support the modernisation of governance' of cities, improve the safety of cyberspace, and enhance cyberspace security and defence capabilities.[80] By creating a city's operational command centre, or 'brain', the smart-cities project integrates civilian–military dual-use technologies. There are plans to export it to other countries through the One Belt, One Road initiative.[81]

Australian taxpayers are helping to fund the development of the smart-cities program through an agreement between CETC and the University of Technology Sydney (UTS), as we saw in Chapter 10.[82] Along with its CETC collaboration on big data, UTS is contributing to the most sophisticated and oppressive system of surveillance and social control the world has seen, a kind of e-Stasi in which CCTV and AI take the place of neighbours and family members as informants.

China is not the only nation to develop facial recognition technology for social regulation. It's estimated that in the United States police departments already have the faces of half of the population logged on computers.[83] They have access to a 'virtual line-up' for tracking criminals. The extent of the US surveillance state revealed by the Snowden documents raises serious anxieties about the misuse of data. Yet in the US there are checks on police power. Laws provide some protection: police who misuse data can be prosecuted; the media investigate and report on abuses; citizens have the right to access their information. In short, there is a separation of powers. None of these apply in China. In fact, the new national security law passed in 2017 gives the authorities the legal right to access any personal data they deem necessary. Civil liberties activists in the West keep their governments honest. In China they are thrown in jail.

Beijing's Antarctic designs

Australia played an active role in the 1959 Antarctic Treaty. It indefinitely bans all mineral resource exploration, mining and drilling and includes strong protocols to protect the natural environment for the benefit of present and future generations. Military activities other than 'peaceful' ones are prohibited. The Australian Antarctic Territory covers forty-two per cent of Antarctica, the largest of any nation, and we have a long and proud history of scientific endeavour and wilderness protection. Six countries have recognised our claim to the Australian Antarctic Territory (AAT), although the rest of the world has not.

Over the last ten to fifteen years, the PRC has become heavily engaged in the Antarctic, building bases, laying down airstrips and acquiring ships fitted out for the purpose. Most of its activity is within the Australian sector. Building on its physical infrastructure, China maintains a permanent presence there and has been actively mapping out geographical sites. It is also establishing a base station for its Beidou satellite navigation system. The Antarctic base station will give any Chinese missile strike greater precision.[84]

Chinese-language sources reported by Anne-Marie Brady show that China is preparing the ground to enable it to mine resources in the vast pristine continent.[85] After concerns about China's intentions were raised in Western news media several years ago,[86] Chinese officials now use the language of environmental protection and scientific research embedded in the international discourse. When asked about its resource exploitation plans, the Chinese government denies it has any. Yet in materials aimed at Chinese audiences (uncovered by Anne-Marie Brady), Chinese polar officials clearly state the real goal. The internal newspaper of the Polar Research Institute of China, for example, writes that the main tasks of its new, fifth Antarctic base would be 'resource exploitation and climatic studies'.[87] The same institute describes the continent as 'a global treasure house of resources'. President Xi Jinping himself seemed to give the game away when, on a visit to Hobart, he said that the PRC would work with Australia and other nations 'to better understand, protect and exploit the Antarctic'.[88]

Beijing has been an energetic participant in international Antarctic processes culminating in the hosting in May 2017 of the preeminent

Antarctic Treaty Consultative Meeting. Australia and New Zealand have been actively assisting China to establish itself as a major Antarctic player. The PRC's main logistics base is in Hobart. It's not feasible to tell the history here, but in the Antarctic community of nations scientific research is power.[89] China has been spending big to acquire this power. China now spends more than any other nation on scientific research in the Antarctic.[90] In 2016 the CSIRO entered into a partnership with China to establish in Hobart a new centre for research into Southern Hemisphere oceans. China will contribute $20 million. CSIRO chief executive Larry Marshall, who in the same year was widely excoriated for slashing climate science research, was excited to announce the new collaboration.

Through its largesse and growing role in the Antarctic, China seems to have cultivated a cohort of scientific and policy boosters for its efforts. The director of the Australian Antarctic Division, Nick Gales, finds the growing collaboration 'incredibly exciting' and is enthusiastic about expanding the PRC's work in the Australian territory.[91] Nengye Liu, a law lecturer at the University of Adelaide, has taken a recent interest resulting in a string of articles praising Australia–China cooperation and describing the PRC as historically a rule-taker rather than a rule-maker (avoiding mention of instances where it is a rule-breaker).[92] China sees the Antarctic as resource-rich but, he reassures us, it will not start mining 'in the foreseeable future'.[93]

David Leary at UTS's law faculty believes that, while stories of future conflict make good newspaper copy, a 'sober analysis of international law' suggests a new era of cooperation. Just like other states, China's interests lie in strengthening international law.[94] Against all of the evidence, including the PRC's manifestly illegal annexation of territory in the South China Sea, Leary believes that 'China is no different to any other state'.[95]

Another lawyer, Julia Jabour from the University of Tasmania, lent support in an address to the Confucius Institute at the University of Adelaide.[96] She began by saying she had never heard of the Confucius Institute before but was happy to speak about China's intentions in Antarctica (and advise the Australian government accordingly). We demonise China because we don't understand it, she said, just as we did over its actions in the South China Sea. Her entire lecture was devoted to defending China against those who doubt the sincerity of its public posture. Because the PRC is 'legally bound by the rules of international law' those doubts are not justified, she said. Mining could only occur if all treaty parties agreed to overturn the ban, and that is not going to happen. In Jabour's world, what is not possible legally is not possible and 'provocative, dramatic headlines' about China's mining intentions are alarmist.

Australia's Antarctic policy wonks appear not to want to know what Chinese experts and officials are saying among themselves. The CCP regime has allowed the ruination of China's natural environment, and takes a cynical view of international law, ignoring it when convenient. It attacked the United Nations Convention on the Law of the Sea when an international tribunal deemed unlawful China's annexation of islands in the South China Sea. The decision was dismissed by China as 'nothing more than a piece of waste paper'.[97] It is violating the Hong Kong Basic Law guaranteeing the city political autonomy. And it is already ignoring the 1991 protocol banning mineral explorations.

Despite efforts by the major powers to welcome China into the international system as a 'responsible stakeholder', it must be evident that at bottom the PRC does not accept laws and norms that don't suit it. In Canada, *The Globe and Mail* editorialised, China 'plays along with the international system' but then acts as if it wants to overthrow it. 'What China wants, it gets.'[98] If the PRC has overridden the internationally endorsed sovereign claims of its neighbours to its west, south and east, why on earth would we believe it will respect international law in the Antarctic, where sovereignty claims are agreed only by convention? After all, the PRC regards the Antarctic Treaty as part of the world order created by the postwar powers, and it has said it wants to make a new global order. Brady argues that although the Antarctic Treaty will serve the PRC's interests for the next twenty to thirty years, it will seek to rewrite it when it comes up for review in 2048. By that point it will be fully prepared to begin extracting the continent's resources.

12

Friends of China

The China club

Spies, plants, informants, sympathisers and agents of influence—in Australia, the PRC has them all. Of equal value to China are the experts, commentators and business executives who take a public stance that serves Beijing's interests. We met some of them in Chapter 7's description of the fifth column and we will meet more soon. But behind the scenes another potent force has been operating that I have not yet mentioned: the China club.

Today's attitudes to China among Canberra's political-bureaucratic elite were formed during the Hawke–Keating years. Bob Hawke was prime minister between 1983 and 1991. Keating was Hawke's powerful treasurer and succeeded him as prime minister at the end of 1991, leading the nation until he lost the election in 1996. A cohort of advisers emerged in the Hawke–Keating era that would go on to dominate the central agencies of government for the next two decades, setting the agenda and nurturing the generation that followed. They persuaded Hawke and Keating that Australia's future lies in Asia and we should turn the nation to the north. It was a compelling case, but in the 2000s the 'Asia-only' view morphed into something else: the conviction that 'China is our destiny'.

Who were these advisers?

Dennis Richardson was Bob Hawke's chief of staff and went on to head the foreign affairs department, ASIO and the defence department until retiring in 2017. Allan Gyngell was foreign policy adviser to Keating and graduated to top positions in the prime minister's department, the department of foreign affairs and the Office of National Assessments. In later years he became a kind of éminence grise of foreign policy. Keating's economic adviser Ken Henry would rise quickly and head Treasury for a decade from 2001. Martin Parkinson was economic adviser to John Dawkins (the minister who did more than anyone else to corporatise Australia's universities), succeeding Henry as secretary of Treasury then running the prime minister's department. ANU economist Peter Drysdale was not a political staffer, but his free-market worldview and north Asian orientation were very influential in the 1980s, not least via his doctoral student Ross Garnaut.

Garnaut served as principal economic adviser to Hawke and then ambassador to China from 1985 to 1988. His landmark 1989 report, *Australia and the Northeast Asian Ascendency*, was the blueprint for the China club's new understanding of Australia's future. It argued that we must reorient our economy and our thinking towards northeast Asia, but between the lines was a deeper message, one that had swept through Canberra—economics *über alles*. When the Department of Foreign Affairs and the Department of Trade were merged in 1987 to become DFAT, no one doubted which of the distinct worldviews would prevail.

Once the ideas of the China club came to rule Canberra's central agencies, our economic relationship with China would begin to trump other considerations raised by Defence, intelligence agencies and, of course, those raised by human rights NGOs. By 2013 DFAT's China strategy was all about 'deepening and broadening' our partnership with China at every level, while respecting our 'different political systems and values'. There was no consideration of the risks and dangers; it might have been drafted by a think tank in Beijing. For DFAT the overriding consideration was that we should do nothing that might upset China's leaders.

The 2016 Drysdale report (considered in Chapter 7) is a pure product of the China club and ranks as perhaps the most dangerous advice an Australian government has ever received. Its key supporters are thanked for their contributions in the foreword, a roll call of China-boosters from Treasury (which supplied the cash), The Department of the Prime Minister and Cabinet (PM&C), DFAT and the ANU. Allan Gyngell, Martin Parkinson, Dennis Richardson and several second-generation members—Frances Adamson (DFAT), Geoff Raby (ex-DFAT), Ian Watt (ex-Treasury)—are all there. The effect of each one of the report's recommendations, which together amount to the removal of all restrictions on China's economic penetration of Australia, would be to give Beijing far greater economic and political leverage over Canberra in exchange for the promise of a fistful of dollars.

As for Hawke and Keating, when their political careers ended they went on to become reliable friends of China, shuttling between the two countries, mixing with the top cadres and tycoons. While Hawke's China links proved lucrative, Keating was more interested in influence.

The former Fairfax correspondent in Beijing, John Garnaut, suggested to me that 'China knows the vulnerabilities of our system better than we do'. Unregulated political donations are an obvious vulnerability in our open democracy. Another is our egalitarian culture. Former prime ministers can wander through an airport without anyone paying them too much attention. But spare a thought for those ex–prime ministers who move among their former constituents uttering a silent but desperate cry for the attention that was once heaped upon them. Hawke's attorney-general (and now ANU chancellor) Gareth Evans once named it 'relevance deprivation syndrome'.

Beijing understands that our former prime ministers and foreign ministers have walked the world stage, and feel they have important things to say. So when they travel to China they are fêted and fawned over. The people they once ruled may not give them their due, but the CCP knows how to honour a man of achievement, to restore the V and the I to the P. It has developed subtle techniques to stroke egos and has a whole apparatus to put them into practice. The process of forging close relationships with prominent figures from abroad who can be persuaded to disseminate Beijing's position is known as *liyong waili wei wo xuanchuan*, 'using foreign strength to promote China'.[1]

Through this program of flattery and royal treatment, involving all-expenses trips to China and meetings with top leaders, some of our former prime ministers, foreign ministers and state premiers have been turned into 'friends of China'. In addition to Bob Hawke and Paul Keating, Kevin Rudd, Bob Carr and John Brumby are frequent flyers to Beijing. Julia Gillard has resisted the Chinese sirens, probably because she is a more modest individual not driven by money or ego.

Guanxi is usually understood as the process of building personal networks for business purposes. But it is more than that. It is an 'intricate Chinese art of relationship management' that Westerners often blunder into.[2] The subtle (and at times not so subtle) process of trading favours 'binds the parties in a deal to a set of reciprocal obligations'. Westerners are prone to mistake this instrumental approach to business relationships for genuine 'friendship'. With their defences down, they become easy to manipulate.

Not every Australian influencer has been worked on by Beijing. Some just arrive at a view based on their own judgement that happens to suit the CCP's narrative. (Having done so they are likely to find important PRC people taking an interest in them, inviting them to events and having them quoted in the *People's Daily*.) But whatever the process of arriving at them, within our elites we can identify a number of positions sympathetic to Beijing's interests and which it therefore encourages.

The innocents
In response to the political donations scandal that broke out in Australia in August 2016, University of Melbourne legal academic Joo-Cheong Tham wrote an article—the bottom line of which was that foreigners have legitimate interests in donating to Australian political parties and that those who question Chinese donations are confused about the concept of 'Chinese' and fall into xenophobia of the Yellow Peril kind.[3] It is true that the scandal risked tarnishing all people of Chinese heritage with the same brush, but Professor Tham shows that he missed the essential point of the scandal when he poses the following rhetorical question: 'Why is ancestry or country of birth presumed to be significant among "Chinese" political donors but not among others?' I hope by now it will be obvious to the reader that the nature of the modern Chinese political regime is precisely that it makes ancestry significant. The CCP explicitly makes ethnicity an issue. This is the danger for

Australia, and we will be able to breathe easy about the large number of 'overseas Chinese' in Australia only when their ancestry matters no more than it does for immigrants from Italy, Indonesia or Chile.

Joo-Cheong Tham is but one of the many academics I have come across working on China who believe that China is essentially the same as any other country and any suggestion that it is not must be motivated by xenophobia. Even critics of the PRC who are fluent in Mandarin and have deep Chinese experience and connections (often familial) are whispered to be xenophobic so that their arguments can be dismissed. The racism charge is harder to make against ethnic Chinese critics of the PRC, so they are typically ignored. In truth, it is not the alleged xenophobia of the critics but the innocence and naivety of the sympathisers that stand out.

It might seem odd to place Bob Hawke, known as a wily politician, among the innocents. The money seems to have smoothed his path to the status of 'friend of China'. For well over a decade his main occupation has been facilitating business deals with Chinese firms and by the mid-2000s he had become 'seriously wealthy', with a fortune of some $50 million.[4] In 2012, National Party firebrand Barnaby Joyce denounced him for his (alleged) involvement 'in selling large parts of regional Australia to the Chinese'.[5]

The former prime minister has taken on the task of reassuring Australians concerned about China's intentions. He was one of the most vocal supporters of the free trade deal with China, going against calls by some in the Labor Party he once led for greater protections for Australian jobs.[6] In a 2012 opinion piece extolling the wonders of the return of the Middle Kingdom and its peaceful intentions, he assured his readers that he could see 'absolutely no grounds for apprehension' about China's rise.[7] He tells his nervous American friends that when China becomes the dominant economic power it 'will simply be occupying a position it has held for most of the past 2500 years'. Even if this claim were not a piece of historical revisionism (an ambit claim that with repetition must have washed over Hawke at all of those banquets), the suggestion that we should not be wary of China's dominance because that's how it was for 2500 years is hardly comforting.

The 'realists'

Paul Keating says he knows everything about China because he talks to the top leadership. An old China hand in Beijing repeated this to me with a wry grin: as if the CCP's leaders would confide their inner thoughts and plans to a foreigner. Keating chairs the International Advisory Council of the China Development Bank, which ostensibly provides strategic guidance but mainly provides the bank with well-paid champions. But the former prime minister believes he has access to the genuine sentiments of China's leaders.

Keating's been lecturing Australians on how we must change. We must tell the Americans that we will no longer be their 'client state'. Instead of our 'slavish devotion to American demands' we are going to forge an independent foreign policy. The US is finished as the dominant power, he says. He's a *realist*. 'The rise of China is entirely legitimate. It cannot be delegitimised to suit US strategic planners.'[8]

While the former prime minister believes the Chinese listen to him, in truth he is their unwitting mouthpiece. Like Bob Hawke echoing the party's nationalist propaganda, he tells us that 'China is returning to where it was before the industrial revolution. It's returning to be the primary economic state of the world.' Even if China were once the dominant economic state in the world (it wasn't), why Keating would accept this Han claim of entitlement to rule overall is a mystery. Nevertheless, for Keating, this is the new reality that must shape Australia's pivot to China. So, in words straight from the song sheet of the *People's Daily*, China's annexation of the South China Sea is not our concern. We must not provoke China. It's 'not our fight' and if the Americans want to send their navy to assert their freedom of navigation then that's up to them. Australia should not risk getting involved 'in another of their skirmishes'.

Chinese commentator Chang Ping describes the function of the post-1989 education system as one that 'deliberately blurs right and wrong'.[9] He reports the kinds of excuses Chinese students use abroad to defend totalitarianism at home: 'human rights are Western values', 'no society is all good' and 'every society has a skeleton in the closet'. The CCP insists that so-called universal values (like those enshrined in the UN Declaration of Human Rights) are Western values, and should not 'supplant the core values of Socialism' (in the words of the party's infamous Document 9).[10]

It's not surprising to hear these excuses for despotism from the mouths and keyboards of patriotic young Chinese abroad. But it's alarming to hear them parroted by influential voices in the West, and none more so in Australia than our former leaders. Here is Keating speaking at a public event at La Trobe University in April 2017 in which, with typical bravado, he wheels out five bits of Beijing propaganda in short order.

> Before the Industrial Revolution China was number one ... The idea that the Chinese state with its Communist Party that brought it together, and its general Confucian sense of itself, should in some way accommodate a set of broadly East Coast American values ... is a naïve view of how the world really works. We don't endorse abuse of human rights [but] ... [t]aking 600 million people out of poverty requires some means of central government and authority ... Or are we just hung up about the fact that some detainees don't get proper legal representation ... The Communist Party pulled the country together, after European imperialism had ripped it apart, and the Japanese had ripped it apart. That government of theirs has been the best government in the world in the last thirty years. Full stop.[11]

I am almost ashamed to reproduce Keating's contemptuous words, especially his scornful dismissal of human rights abuses as nothing more than a few detainees missing out on legal representation. Tell that to Liu Xiaobo. Even the CCP does not go as far as to dismiss the rights embedded in the United Nations Declaration as 'East Coast American values'. In 2016 China's foreign minister, Wang Yi, became enraged when a Canadian journalist asked about human rights in China. Foreigners have no right to ask about human rights, he fumed. 'Do you know that China has lifted more than 600 million people out of poverty?'[12]

It's worth commenting on the claim that 600 million were lifted out of poverty as it has become the most common reason cited by apologists to excuse the CCP's outrages. The Communist Party did not lift 600 million people out of poverty; it kept 600 million people in poverty.

It was only when the CCP lifted its foot off the neck of the Chinese people and permitted basic economic rights—the rights to own property, to set up a business, to move one's residence, to work for whoever one liked—that the Chinese people could lift themselves out of poverty.

Anne-Marie Brady, an expert on China's strategy for managing foreigners, tells us that for two decades the first objective of Chinese propaganda abroad has been to deflect criticism of torture and repression by highlighting the nation's extraordinary GDP growth, along with its political stability.[13] One of the means by which this propaganda effort is prosecuted is to recruit eminent figures, through flattery and money, to echo the Beijing line. Our former prime minister is the most influential antipodean figure sucked in by this strategy to excuse repression.

While projecting an air of worldly sophistication, Keating plays his role for Beijing guilelessly. He echoes the slogans of the CCP's more hawkish China Dreamers, buying into the party's recent exhumation of the idea of the Middle Kingdom's historical destiny. In 2016, at an exclusive meeting with China's core leader, he fell more deeply under the spell.[14] In words he repeated for our benefit, Xi Jinping told him: 'A strong country does not need to seek hegemony. Expansion and conflict is not in our DNA.' It's mystifying that anyone can accept this kind of rewriting of history from the leader of a nation that has colonised its neighbours and is annexing a vast marine territory to which it has no legitimate claim.[15] Yet, bewitched by his regal treatment and 'access', Keating is putty in CCP hands.

The capitulationists

Hugh White, Australia's most high-profile strategic analyst, believes we do not have to know much about the nature of the modern Chinese state in order to decide what kind of strategic stance we ought to adopt.[16] When we are dealing with great powers, the balance of power is all we need to know in order to craft a national strategy for dealing with it. In 2017 he spent an entire lecture speaking about China's rise, its intentions and its impact on Australia without mentioning the Chinese Communist Party, as if China is just China with what he calls 'Chinese values'.[17] The fact that it is ruled by an increasingly autocratic and aggressive one-party government has no bearing on how Australia should think about and respond to it, he claims.

White's argument hinges on a few big facts, viz: we have been 'relying on China to make us rich'; 'our future prosperity depends on' China; if China directed future investments away from Australia it would 'send our share market crashing'. Rory Medcalf, by deploying a few statistics, poured cold water over this kind of hyperbole.[18] Jonathan Fenby's 2017 book, *Will China Dominate the 21st Century?*, is a subtle assessment of the title's question.[19] He concludes in the negative. Fenby may or may not be right, but one thing is clear: White's assumption that the answer must be yes deserves careful scrutiny, especially if it forms the basis for arguing that Australia must sideline the US alliance and (as we'll see) set aside our democratic values.

For White, we have no choice but to back the economic winner, because if we don't then we will be forced to do so by China's sheer economic might. This is why he falls into the capitulationist camp. When White said the same thing in a 2010 essay his critics described it as 'a masterly statement of the case for appeasing the newest manifestation of the totalitarian challenge, the People's Republic of China'.[20]

The alternative view, that Australia together with the United States and Asian allies can do a great deal to circumscribe the political and strategic influence of China in other nations, is given short shrift by White. He aims to convince us that this option is not available because the only alternative to capitulation is *war*. For him the grand struggle can be reduced to the willingness of each party to go to war. The nation less willing to risk war will lose. Whether Australia must succumb to China depends on whether China's resolve is greater than the US's, and on that question White has no doubts. America will back down while 'we would be very unwise to underestimate China's resolve'.[21]

Here you'd think an understanding of the CCP, including its evolution under Xi Jinping, is indispensable, but no. Somehow being a 'realist' absolves one of the need to know any detail. All we need to know is the balance of economic and strategic power. If Australia sides with the United States in any kind of push back we would be on the wrong side of history and probably plunge ourselves into a war with China, quite possibly a nuclear one.

In this view, strategic analysis of world futures and the stance Australia should adopt is a kind of chess game played by great powers, in which pawns like Australia can be sacrificed. Assuming no one would be foolish enough to risk a nuclear war, a player's strength depends above all on economic power; China is becoming stronger and the United States weaker and so the logic of the situation leads to an inevitable outcome. So why would we align ourselves with the loser? The world is like a chicken coop, he suggests, in which harmony reigns when all the birds accept their place in the 'pecking order'.[22] Forget any commitment to 'arcane questions of international law'; it's all about 'pure power politics'.[23]

Like Keating, White believes that as a growing hegemonic power China needs breathing space and we should give it that space. But who has to lose breathing space in order for China to gain it? The United States, of course, but also Southeast Asian nations that have already been bullied out of traditional fishing grounds and whose territorial claims have been bulldozed. Yet by standing back while China fulfils its ambition to dominate Asia, are we not saying that the autonomy of the Philippines, Malaysia and even Vietnam has to be sacrificed? Maybe, say the hardheads. What about Papua New Guinea? Would we be comfortable with a Chinese naval base next to Port Moresby? (They already have one in Djibouti.)

In the actual world, the one 'realists' find too messy to think about, hegemonic powers understand, or soon come to learn, that using military superiority to subdue other states is a mug's game. There are much cheaper and more effective options, options perfected by the United States in Latin America. They involve cultivating a 'comprador class' (businesspeople who know their interests lie with the hegemon) and putting in place a domestic ruling party that acts on the hegemon's wishes. Essential to the long-term success of this strategy is disempowering the populace or shifting its worldview so that it comes to accept the inevitability and desirability of its own domination. In this task the hegemon recruits elites, including leading intellectuals.

So the world is not a chess game and Australia is not a pawn. The choice for Australia is not capitulation versus war. Weaker nations have always had strategies to avoid being ruled by more powerful ones.

They have various 'weapons' at their disposal. The CCP understands this well and, as the weaker power, has been using subtle strategies against the United States.[24]

Since the formalisation of the Australia–US alliance in 1951, Australia has not really needed US protection because there has been no direct threat to us. Now there is an emerging threat in the shape of a PRC that clearly wants to be the Asian hegemon. Yet powerful voices in this country are calling for us to weaken the US alliance and adopt 'an independent foreign policy'. But what does an independent foreign policy mean when an aggressive new power is determined to dominate the region in which we live?

Three of Hugh White's clearest conclusions make sense. The first is that 'we should never underestimate China's resolve to be the pre-eminent power in Asia'.[25] The second is that 'we are seeing the most fundamental transformation of Australia's strategic environment since British settlement'. And the third is that 'Australian politicians say we do not have to choose between the United States and China. But we do'.

For him, we must choose China because soon Asia will be 'without America'. The question of *what kind of Australia* we would live in if China were allowed to dominate in the way he believes it inevitably will is an awkward one for him. So whenever he gets close to issues like democracy, human rights and the rule of law, he tries to deflate their importance. Adopting a kind of postmodern moral relativism, he argues that one set of values is as good as the next.[26] We have yet to take China's 'moral standing' seriously enough, he believes. He writes as if 'China's values' can be found in the propaganda of the CCP, forgetting that the people of Taiwan might be thought to be living according to more authentic Chinese values, and are doing their best to resist having the CCP's version imposed on them.

Yet he tells us, seriously, that maybe the CCP's values would not be so bad for Australia. 'China's values are very different from ours,' he writes, but who is to say ours are better? After all, our values are 'hard to define' and we 'prefer to keep them vague'.[27] Moral choices, he tells us, are not black and white. Really? Are Australians in two minds about whether arbitrary arrests are desirable or not? What about judges who do what the party tells them to do? Are we undecided over whether electing our parliaments to make laws is a good thing?

White says we must be realistic: we are going to have to compromise our values so let's not get on our high horses. The values he will not name include freedom of speech, religious freedom, the rule of law, popularly elected government, and protections against arbitrary arrest and torture. Some of these, in Hugh White's realist worldview, will have to be compromised. The only questions, he concludes, 'are which ones we will compromise'.[28] That's just how the world is. To think otherwise is 'crude sloganeering'.

Isn't this just the sophistry of a philosopher, someone who does not believe he will ever be the one thrown in jail for his views or have his family members persecuted? The logic of White's position is that Australia has no choice but to live in China's shadow and bow to its influence. But rather than drawing such a conclusion with regret and foreboding, White engages in apologetics. We've been lucky so far, he writes, but now 'it's welcome to the real world'.[29] Maybe, if we 'think deeply enough' about it, such a state would not be such a bad thing. After all, our images of China remain 'very simplistic'.[30] So let's go with it, and see whether domination by the Chinese party-state is as uncomfortable as some fear.

The pragmatists
Writing in 2005, Richard Bullivant, a former intelligence analyst at the Office of National Assessments, made a provocative claim about the Department of Foreign Affairs and Trade.

> The Chinese intelligence service's most valued asset in Australia is DFAT and their opaque network of former diplomats, intelligence analysts, academics, Australia-Chinese consultants, all of whom reflect subtle but unremitting pro-Chinese and anti-U.S. sentiment.[31]

Geoff Raby was once Australia's ambassador in Beijing. Today, ensconced in the Chinese capital, he makes a lucrative living as an adviser and go-between for corporations wanting information on and networks into China. He is close to mining magnate Andrew Forrest. He had a seat on the board of Forrest's Fortescue Metals.[32] He was instrumental in setting up the Boao Forum where senior Chinese and Australian business leaders and politicians build their *guanxi*.

Raby is a frequent contributor to the opinion pages, arguing the 'pragmatist' position. He's keen for Australia to link its northern development plans to the One Belt, One Road initiative, highlighting the priority given to this link by Xi Jinping himself.[33] He believes Canberra is confused if it believes that the OBOR has an ulterior motive 'to impose a "Sino-centric" order on the world'.[34] He doesn't know what such a thing would even look like and can't identify any risks to us in Xi's grand program.

Some see Geoff Raby as a 'panda-hugger', but there is much more to him than that. Unlike Bob Carr, who doesn't know so much about China, Raby knows a great deal (more than he lets on) and understands how the system works (to the extent that any foreigner can). He justifies his position with a narrative that is superficially convincing. After two bibulous dinners with him in Beijing, I worked it out. Paraphrasing his words, it goes like this.

China is what it is. We must be pragmatic. Beijing has no strategy or strategic objectives for its future. The CCP's only goal is to keep the country growing so that the party can continue to survive. Look at all these middle-class Chinese [gesturing to the other diners]—they're happy, they're not complaining. [What about, I ask, forced organ removals from Falun Gong prisoners?] Some say that's happened; others say it hasn't. I don't know what the truth is.

China doesn't want to take over Australia. What we see in Australia is all down to a few corrupt businessmen. We just need to get along with China and adopt an independent foreign policy and stop tagging along behind the US. Australia's institutions are strong enough to resist any attempts by China to erode or corrupt them. [What about, I ask, the erosion of academic freedom, free speech, in universities?] That's only some universities; others are fine, so what's the problem? Besides, we have an independent media that exposes any problems as they arise.

The South China Sea is lost. There's no point protesting or resisting. China is not going to do anything with its military bases.

It wants free movement of trade more than anyone. Do you really think they are going to disrupt iron ore exports from Australia to China? The bases aren't a military threat to anyone. China knows the US could wipe them out with a missile at any time. China's armed forces are no match for the Americans, and Beijing knows it.

Australia should sign up to the OBOR initiative. And we should ratify the extradition treaty. People are completely wrong to say that OBOR has a strategic objective. There was no problem selling Darwin Port to a Chinese company, although we should have let the Americans know in advance. Canberra is becoming increasingly hawkish in its view of China, and that's a big mistake.

The former ambassador (whose name and face are used to sell bottles of Australian red wine in China) delivers his story with conviction. For cosmopolitan Westerners quaffing red in an upmarket restaurant in Beijing's ritzy Sanlitun district, it's hard to resist. Of course, it's the kind of pragmatism that suits Beijing's interests down to the ground. And so for the pragmatic Australian view Raby is the go-to man for official party newspapers. Behind this line of argument lies one sentiment: China is too big to resist, we can't change anything, so let's just go with it and not think about what the consequences might be.[35]

Dear friends

When eminent Australian Sinologist and founding director of Griffith University's Confucius Institute Colin Mackerras attended President Xi Jinping's speech to the Australian parliament in November 2014, he described it as 'one of the best and most meaningful experiences of my life'.[36] The speech, he wrote, 'was in all ways triumphantly successful'. Professor Mackerras had been visiting China since 1964 and he was 'bowled over' when Xi praised him for his 'tireless efforts to present a real China to Australia'. Xi may have been thinking especially of the professor's claim in the Chinese press that 'some western observers speak of the Tibetan people's culture suffering destruction or of China suppressing Tibetan Buddhism, but that is complete nonsense'.[37] The praise from the Communist Party leader was 'the crowning of my career'.

In a brief audience with the President at the official dinner, Mackerras was struck by the leader's charisma. When he discovered that in 2014 Xi had finally visited Tasmania and so every Australian state, Mackerras realised that *in precisely the same year* he too had visited the last of China's provinces, and this amazing coincidence made him feel 'an extra bond with him'. Leaving the dinner, he resolved that he would 'do more, much more, in the future' to improve Australia–China relations.[38]

While Colin Mackerras is at the end of his career, Callum Smith is at the beginning of his. An ANU graduate, in 2017 Smith was a research fellow at the Hunan Academy of Social Sciences International Relations Institute. He was in Shanghai as the Fairfax–ABC *Four Corners* investigation went to air. The 23-year-old typed out an opinion piece for the nationalist tabloid the *Global Times*, criticising Australian 'media phobia' of China and the 'malicious language' of the *Four Corners* program.[39] If the Chinese government controls ethnic media in Australia, so what? Fairfax too 'has its own political position'. If 'rational' Australians understood 'the true situation of China', instead of listening to 'pro-US' media like Fairfax and the ABC, then we would see 'the healthy development of Australia-China relations'.

If this sounds eerily similar to standard PRC propaganda, Smith later defended his views, attacking Fairfax and the ABC for their 'fearmongering'. As for the claim that wealthy businessmen Huang Xiangmo and Chau Chak Wing used their donations to influence our political parties, well, we should understand that 'building positive relationships' is common business practice in China. China does not have a 'sinister, secret agenda'; there is nothing secret about China's Australia policy, he assured us.

In a previous article for the *Global Times*, Smith had sided with Chinese patriots in their outrage at the slight to the nation's honour from the Olympic broadcast screw-up by Channel Seven, which he suggested was in fact a deliberate attempt to dishonour Chinese people because of the rise of xenophobia in Australia.[40] (If only he knew more about Channel Seven's owner, Kerry Stokes, of whom more below.) Defending the patriotic trolls who were savaging swimmer Mack Horton, he drew on Bob Carr as an authoritative voice representing

Australia's real interests and called on Australia to break its links with the United States and become 'independent'. And in September 2016 when the Hague court ruled against China's claims in the South China Sea, Smith borrowed from the Propaganda Bureau's hymn sheet to accuse Australia of 'brazen hypocrisy' because it has violated international law in its dealing with East Timor, as if this shameful episode somehow validated China's actions.[41]

China has found a dear friend in the up-and-coming China scholar and has probably been showing its appreciation while he resides there. When he returns to Australia, his employability will be enhanced by his deep personal connections with officials from across the party-state apparatus.

The appeasers

Naturally, there is no shortage in the business community of those who can find excuses to cover over the PRC's poor behaviour, or to tell us we need a more nuanced understanding. They take the high ground by leaping into print to attack all those who have succumbed to xenophobia, including those who question the benefits of Chinese investment in Australia. Andrew Parker is the head of the Asia desk at the mega-accounting firm PwC Australia (financially linked to Minshen Zhu's Top Education Institute). He complains that public debate about Chinese investment had become 'a fact-free zone', before launching into an encomium to the manifold benefits of foreign investment.[42] Those who worry about Chinese control of critical infrastructure 'hide behind a veil of defence and security'. Parker presents himself as one of the special few in possession of 'the facts', unclouded like the rest of us by 'populist alarm and misinformation'. He's a director of China Matters, Linda Jakobson's Sydney think tank that seems to have a monopoly on the truth.

Along with fellow West Australian billionaire Andrew Forrest, Kerry Stokes has been a powerful pro-Beijing voice in public and behind the scenes. 'Human rights have to be seen through China's eyes as well as our eyes,' he argues, adopting Beijing's moral relativism.[43] Our alliance with the United States undermines our relationship with China, he asserts; we should become 'the Switzerland of our region'. Stokes has plenty of opportunity to put his pro-Beijing views behind closed doors. He's very close to fellow West Australian and minister for foreign affairs Julie Bishop. Kevin Rudd and Tony Abbott were his mates. Most of Stokes' capital is invested not in media assets but in supplying equipment to the mining industry. His Caterpillar franchise in Western Australia (now sold) has been very lucrative and so too the one he has held in the northern provinces of China, covering Beijing.

Kerry Stokes is close to President Xi Jinping. Xi has dined at Stokes' Sydney residence a number of times.[44] He first got to know the future president when Xi was governor of Zhejiang in the early 2000s. The Stokes–Xi friendship was cemented in the lead-up to the 2008 Beijing Olympics, which in its later stages Xi oversaw. The Seven Network was the Australian broadcaster for the games so Stokes knew the lie of the land and had global contacts. He helped China win its bid for the Games.

Xi's short tenure as Shanghai party secretary in 2007 overlapped with Stokes' media venture in that city. Stokes entered a joint venture to operate the English-language *Shanghai Daily*, a highly unusual position for a foreigner. According to Xinhua News Agency, in a meeting with the head of the CCP's Propaganda Department, Liu Yunshan, the media mogul pledged greater cooperation between his Seven Network and Chinese state media.[45] The *Shanghai Daily* faithfully followed the party line, overseen by its in-house censors, which is to be expected. But the pledge seemed to have spilled over into the pages of Stokes' newspaper in Perth, *The West Australian*.

While I was researching China's spreading influence in this country, a number of journalists pointedly asked me: 'Have you seen what *The West Australian* is printing?' Stokes' newspaper has been a reliable cheerleader for Beijing. An editorial in November 2015, for instance, criticised the United States for its 'blatantly provocative' freedom of navigation exercises.[46] Echoing the party line, it told its readers that the dispute in the South China Sea 'has nothing to do with Australia'. We should stay out of it and devote ourselves solely to building our trade relationship with China.

One former journalist with the paper told me that Stokes had been 'allowing China to use the *West* as a billboard'.[47] The newspaper had turned over 'acreage' to Beijing's propaganda, like the opinion pieces from China's consuls general in Perth, and another solicited from the Chinese ambassador, Cheng Jingye, who tried to persuade readers that other nations were to blame for the dispute in the South China Sea and that China had acted with 'utmost restraint'.[48] In case we think that the Philippines, Vietnam and Malaysia have been bullied, the PRC ambassador assured us that China is opposed to all provocation and only wants peace.

The day after the ABC broadcast its *Four Corners* television program on China's infiltration of Australian institutions in June 2017, the Lowy Institute's East Asia Program director, Merriden Varrall, opined that she was not persuaded.[49] She suggested the program's claims of Beijing silencing dissent and interfering in our politics were jumping at shadows. Although she didn't have time to 'counter every claim in the *Four Corners* program', it's not true that the Chinese party-state is a 'communist behemoth'. Even so, it is legitimate, she implied, for the CCP to silence critics abroad because once Chinese, always Chinese, and being Chinese 'means loving China like one would love one's own father' and refraining from any public criticism. Chinese people (who in her view act as one) accept the 'social contract' under which they agree to stay out of politics in exchange for higher living standards.

For Dr Varrall, if we hear of Chinese students in Australia dobbing in fellow students to the Chinese authorities because they are overheard criticising the CCP or defending human rights, then we Australians should accept that this is 'how things work' in China. It's natural for students to continue to operate this way in Australia.[50] As for political donations, it's true that the past of billionaire Huang Xiangmo is unclear, and he does have Communist Party connections, but that does not mean there is anything wrong with his large donations to our political parties. If he withdrew his promised donation of $400,000 to the Labor Party when its shadow minister expressed a view on China's aggression in the South China Sea that Beijing did not like, well, so what? He just decided not to give money to an organisation that opposed his own beliefs.

In sum, nothing in the program persuaded Dr Varrall that China is trying to influence Australia or that the Chinese party-state is doing anything untoward in this country. If we were 'well-informed', 'realistic' and 'moderate', in the way she is, then we would reach the same conclusion.[51]

When at the end of 2017 public concern over PRC influence operations spiked, Varrall felt obliged to give the Chinese point of view.[52] Australians are ungrateful. Taxi drivers in Beijing are not as friendly to Australians. There's talk of retaliation. The way our political leaders criticise China's Influence is 'embarrassing'. When they imply that the proposed new security laws are aimed at China, CCP leaders become upset. In short, relations are strained not because of China's aggression in the South China Sea or because of its subversion activities in Australia; it's our fault and we need to change. This is the view now propagated by the Lowy Institute.

In the West, it's not often we come across such transparent apologetics for totalitarianism. More nuanced variations of Varrall's argument, however, are not uncommon in Australian academic and policy circles, where recognising the legitimacy of the PRC's aspirations and overlooking its methods of pursuing its ends frees one of the stain of 'xenophobia'. The academic arguments have a kind of seductive appeal, in the way Bob Carr's crude 'China-Whatever' arguments do not. Carr's own rejoinder to the *Four Corners* program was laughable for its misrepresentations and ropey arguments, and hardly worthy of a reply.[53] Nevertheless, ABC journalist Chris Uhlmann took up a rifle to blast away at the giant carp in the very small barrel, pointing out that, of the program's two billionaires, whom Carr could not bring himself to name, one gave him his job and the other provided a daughter to work in his office when he was premier of New South Wales.[54]

Australians against democracy

As I studied the views of the various 'friends of China' driving the debate in this country, one thing came as a shock to me: how little some value democracy. Many influential figures among our political, bureaucratic, media and academic elites seem to believe that democracy is a luxury, and is often a nuisance. Or they see it as a charade we engage in while knowing that it's the economy that really matters (just as in China). And when Australian citizens demand that governments respect human rights and follow the rule of law they might be shooting themselves in the foot. When Hugh White counsels, 'No more lecturing China about dissidents, Tibet or religious freedom,'[55] the advice is offered not because lecturing China about rights is ineffectual, but because rights and freedoms are trivial in the grand strategic game that is world history. When Geoff Raby complains that Australia is adopting an 'idealist approach' to China, too focused on values and human rights, he is telling us that a 'pragmatic approach aimed at boosting economic ties' is what really matters.[56]

In his joint report with a CCP-directed think tank, the prominent ANU economist Peter Drysdale signed off on the following justification for totalitarianism:

> Australia is a multi-party liberal democracy. China is governed as a one-party state. Australia has a freewheeling media [sic; not 'a free media']. China has a more controlled media environment [not 'a controlled media']. The Australian people provide input to their political system through regular representative elections. The Chinese people provide input to their political system through consultative mechanisms.[57]

One system is not better than the other; they are just different, and the differences 'need not be an obstacle to deeper trade or economic engagement'.[58]

If the Communist Party now defines 'Chinese values', then that is only one of the offensive elisions Drysdale accepts. He would soon be telling readers of the *Australian Financial Review* that the contrast between liberal democracy and totalitarianism is a 'false dichotomy'. In fact, China 'is becoming a critical defender of the rules-based order on which we rely for economic and political security'.[59]

We Australians have never had to fight to protect our democracy— not really, despite Japanese military overreach and Cold War fears of infiltration. We have never had to resist the looming threat of a powerful authoritarian neighbour, like the Baltic States in the decades after the war, or Latvia and the Ukraine today. Yet within the Australian community there are many who love our democratic institutions and the kind of daily life they permit. None feel more passionately than those Chinese-Australians who came here to find freedom, to escape the grip of the Chinese Communist Party. When they hear prominent Australians argue that there's not much difference between China's political system and ours, or that our freedoms can be traded off for economic benefits, or that the CCP represents 'Chinese values', they feel sick to the stomach.

13

The price of freedom

This book's message is succinctly captured in the words of an email I received from Professor Frank Dikötter, the eminent China historian and CCP scholar based at the University of Hong Kong.

> Three things matter. First, the CCP remains, structurally, a Leninist one-party state. Second, like all Leninist one-party states, it has both an organisation and a philosophy (propaganda) on how to undermine anything and everything opposed to it at home and abroad, namely the United Front. Finally, Leninist one-party states always make promises (or, phrased differently, lies) that can be discarded when no longer convenient; that is, very little it says should be taken at face value.
>
> To these three points should be added a qualifier: it is relentless. It relentlessly seeks to undermine any and all opposition to it both at home and abroad. In fact, there is no 'abroad' for people identified as PRC citizens by the CCP. All of this is so alien to the very nature of liberal democracies that it is hard for outsiders to comprehend. It's like a Boy Scout dealing with Don Corleone.[1]

We Australians like to think that we 'punch above our weight'. This is because we think of ourselves as a bantamweight when we ought to be a middleweight. Think about Russia, surely well above Australia in the weight divisions. It's militarily formidable, and not afraid of defending its interests. It keeps Europe nervous. The United States is furious with it because it may have changed the outcome of the presidential election. China treats Russia as a serious player in the global strategic game. Yet consider this fact. In 2016, the GDP of the Russian Federation stood at US$1.28 trillion. Australia's stood at US$1.20 trillion. By 2020 our economy will be bigger than Russia's. So why do we feel like a koala to Russia's bear?

More to the point, why are we so terrified of annoying China? Why have we allowed this increasingly bellicose power to spread its shadow over us? As this book argues, one factor dominates all others. Since the 1980s, we have set the economy before everything else and put power in the hands of those who tell us we must sacrifice everything to it, including our sovereignty as a free country.

When I began working on this book I believed that China's attempts to promote its position in Australia were ham-fisted and self-defeating. Its official spokespersons and media come across as strident and bullying, a throwback to the Cold War more likely to turn people off. But I slowly began to realise that the PRC's campaign to change Australian perceptions has been extremely effective. In addition to silencing most of its critics and winning over or intimidating the Chinese diaspora, the PRC has cultivated a highly influential cohort of pro-Beijing voices among this country's elites and opinion makers. In the media, and among business leaders and politicians, voices that are either pro-Beijing or urging appeasement are the loudest. Self-censorship among academics in our universities is rife. In the wider Australian community, PRC programs aimed at promoting a benign view of China have drawn in individuals and organisations attracted by the lure of Chinese friend-ship and money.

The subservience and self-interest of our elites provide the primary explanation for why we believe we are so powerless to resist the PRC takeover of Australia. There is a widespread view that China's rise is unstoppable, that our economy's fate is in Beijing's hands, and that China's size means it must dominate Asia. So it's best if we go along with this historical inevitability, because we don't really have any choice, and it won't be such a bad thing anyway. So we pursue 'friendship and cooperation', accept the flood of money, sell our assets, jump when China's diplomats shout, look the other way when our technology is funnelled offshore, recruit Beijing's agents into our political system, stay silent on human rights abuses, and sacrifice basic values like free and open inquiry in our universities. In the nation's post-settlement history, has there ever been a greater betrayal by our elites?

Protecting our freedom from the PRC's incursions will come at a price. We have seen that Beijing has made itself the master at pulling economic levers for political and strategic ends. As we begin to resist, Beijing will respond first with belligerent rhetoric and threats designed to scare us. In January 2018 the *Global Times* threatened 'strong countermeasures' if we continue to support the United States in its freedom-of-navigation exercises.[2] Then it will impose economic pressure at our weakest points, those sectors of our society most vulnerable to its blackmail and to which politicians are most sensitive. If we value our freedom, Australians will need to remain resolute and take the pain.

Experience shows, however, that Beijing backs off when others stand up to its economic bullying. Even so, it would be prudent to see past the self-interested or deluded demands of the China lobby and embark on sustained efforts to diversify our economy so that we become less reliant on China. In particular, forging stronger trade, investment, migration, student and tourist links with the other Asian giant, India, a democratic nation whose values mostly overlap with ours, would not only help insulate Australia against PRC coercion but contribute to India's emergence as a strategic counterweight to China.

At the same time, we could build a more balanced alliance with the United States by pursuing an Alliance of Asian Democracies, bringing together the democratic states of India, Japan, South Korea, Indonesia, New Zealand and Australia. The alliance would work towards reinforcing the freedoms of democratic governance across the region, countering the PRC's systematic program of undermining sovereignty, and forging strategic and military cooperation to the same end. Let's remember that resisting the PRC's influence in Australia is only one of many battles going on in a global war between democracy and the new totalitarianism. The re-emergence in late 2017 of the Quadrilateral Security Dialogue—an informal security partnership between the United States, India, Japan and Australia—could become an essential counterbalance to the PRC's attempts to gain strategic supremacy in Asia, as well as strengthening Australia's economic relations with India and Japan.[3]

When Australia pushes back, the CCP will apply pressure not only from outside through trade and investment. It will mobilise its forces already embedded in Australian society. PRC apologists will exploit our 'xenophobia-phobia', conflating the CCP with 'the Chinese people'. It's here that Chinese-Australians fearful of Beijing's growing influence are essential to any pushback. Organisations like the Australian Values Alliance send the message that many Chinese-Australians are *Australians* who see the danger and want to protect the freedoms they came here to live by. They are the ones best placed to counter the PRC's highly successful strategy of presenting its puppets in United Front organisations as the legitimate voice of overseas Chinese in Australia. After being lobbied and seduced by those puppets, politicians, journalists and leaders of all sorts of organisations across the country believe they are responding to the wishes of 'Chinese-Australians'. They are in fact dancing to the tune of the CCP.

Chinese-Australians who fear the creeping takeover of Australia by the PRC and watch in dismay as one independent institution after another falls under the sway of forces loyal to the Chinese Communist Party. Having lived under the CCP they understand its methods and its objectives. They also understand that when Australians begin to resist the growing influence of the CCP there is a danger that all Chinese-Australians will come under a pall of suspicion. They accept it's a risk they must take.

We shouldn't underestimate the lengths the CCP will go to. The Chinese embassy and consulates have organised street protests at which some Chinese-Australians and Chinese in Australia waved Chinese flags and chanted pro-Beijing slogans. This should give pause for thought, not least for Australia's security agencies. A military standoff or engagement between the United States and China is quite possible in the foreseeable future. It may be the only way to stop China annexing and controlling the entire South China Sea right down to the coast of Indonesia. A conflict in the East China Sea is perhaps even more likely, as China pushes its demand to incorporate Taiwan and take islands claimed by Japan. In these circumstances Australia would be under an obligation to back the United States.

Remembering that there are over one million people of Chinese heritage in Australia, we could expect some, citizens and non-citizens alike, to take to the streets to express their loyalty to Beijing—in other words, to Australia's enemy. This could create ongoing and potentially severe civil strife, unrest that would be orchestrated by the Chinese embassy in Canberra. The prospect of civil discord is not mere speculation. In an email to rally supporters, the organisers of the pro-Beijing protest in Melbourne in July 2016 actually threatened trouble should Australia continue to oppose China's claims in the South China Sea: 'As Chinese in Australia, we do not want to see Australia to fall into conflict and turmoil.'[4]

Civil strife would be only one of several forms of pressure China would apply to an Australian government in a conflict situation. Already Beijing sympathisers occupy positions of influence in leading institutions. Some are calling for the abandonment of the US alliance and an 'independent' foreign policy, or even one aligned with Beijing. They can be found in the media, think tanks, universities, businesses, business lobbies, the public service and, of course, parliaments. In a conflict, many of these fifth columnists would be calling for 'peaceful resolution', no matter how aggressively China had acted to precipitate the conflict.

I asked some of my Chinese-Australian friends in Sydney a difficult question: What proportion of the one million Chinese-Australians are loyal to Beijing first and what proportion are loyal to Australia first? And how many fall somewhere in between? It's impossible to answer with any accuracy, but we do need to have some idea. The immediate reply was: What do you mean by 'Chinese'? Do you include those from Hong Kong, Singapore, Malaysia? What about Tibetans—are they Chinese? Fair enough, let's confine it to Han Chinese born on the mainland.

One estimated those with strong pro-Beijing sentiments to be at twenty to thirty per cent. Perhaps another forty to fifty per cent are neutral; they are not anti-Beijing because of their 'patriotism', but they prefer to stay out of politics. That leaves around twenty to thirty per cent who are loyal to Australia first. Few of them, however, are willing to speak out because they fear retribution.

Another guessed differently. Those strongly 'pro-Communist' account for around ten per cent of Chinese-Australians, he said, while the same proportion are strongly anti-Communist. Perhaps twenty to thirty per cent are quiet supporters of the CCP regime. They all agreed that a large majority of the community supports Beijing's assertion of Chinese sovereignty in the South China Sea. And almost all Han Chinese believe Tibet and Taiwan belong to China.

Some of the China experts I have spoken to believe it's too late. In their assessment, the Chinese Communist Party and its offshoots have implanted themselves so deeply in the soil of Australia's institutions that we can no longer extract their roots. Others argue that we can do it, but that the process would take ten years. That seems about right to me. But it depends in the first instance on whether Australians *want* to rid our society of CCP influence. Today, few understand the dangers sufficiently to feel we need to begin taking steps to regain our independence, and keep at it despite the inevitable retaliation. Our naivety and our complacency are Beijing's strongest assets. Boy Scouts up against Don Corleone. But once Australians of all ethnic backgrounds understand the danger, we can begin to protect our freedoms from the new totalitarianism.

Acknowledgements

My largest debt is to Alex Joske for his excellent research support. His work opened up a wide array of invaluable information in Chinese-language sources in Australia and, especially, in China.

Since deciding to write this book, I have been surprised and gratified by the willingness of all kinds of people to help.

I am extremely grateful to Geoff Wade, who generously provided a series of leads and suggestions as well as advice on how to interpret much of the information, including a deeper grasp of what the CCP's objectives and methods are.

David Kelly and Philippa Jones in Beijing were exceptionally helpful in making contacts and allowing me to benefit from their deep knowledge of China.

John Garnaut has lent strong support and provided excellent advice throughout. John Fitzgerald has been a peerless source of knowledge and a pillar of support through the tribulations of publication. John Hu has been an invaluable source of information and links into the Chinese-Australian community.

Ye Fei, a brilliant and courageous Beijing political analyst, gave me extraordinary insights into China's politics and Beijing's international ambitions. I can name him because, tragically, he died three months after our last conversation.

Many of my interviewees in China and Australia cannot be named. The risk they face only increases my gratitude to them. Among those I am able to name, I would like to express my thanks to James Leibold, Greg Austin, Peter Jennings, Stephen Joske, Rory Medcalf, Phil Dorling, Chris Uhlmann, Qi Jiazhen, Jinping Cheng, Zhang Xiaogang, Frank Dikötter, Chen Yonglin, Nick McKenzie, Rowan Callick, Chris Buckley, Phil Wen, Greg McCarthy, Geoff Raby, Lucy Gao, Zhou Shixing, Feng Shuai, Angus Grigg, Bill Birtles, Zha Daojiong, Ma Tianjie, Anson Chan, Willy Lam, K.P. Chow, Hugh White, Børge Bakken, Feng Chongyi, Ying Yee, Kate Larsen, Jocelyn Chey, John Keane, Richard Baker, James Xiong, Kevin Jin, Anastasia Kapetas, Wu Lebao, Qin Jin, Paul Macgregor, Anne-Marie Brady, Lisa Dempster, Fergus Hanson, Tim Stephens, Jen Tsen Kwok, Fergus Ryan, Primrose Riordan, Chowai Cheung, Maree Ma and Warren Sun.

Of course, they hold a wide divergence of opinions about the topics discussed in this book and should not be held responsible for any of the views expressed in it.

Robert Manne kindly read the manuscript, alerting me to a number of potential problems and pressing me to think through more carefully some of the strategic implications.

My thanks lastly to Charles Sturt University for giving me the opportunity to pursue a project like this one.

Notes

Chapter 1 Dyeing Australia red

1   The account given here is based on: an author interview with Chen Yonglin on 1 March 2017; his comments quoted in a Chinese-language interview published in *The Epoch Times*, 25 June 2015 <www.epochtimes.com/gb/5/6/25/n965354.htm>; and an important article by Chen Yonglin, 'Australia is in the process of becoming China's backyard', first published in Chinese in *China in Perspective*, 31 August 2016.

2   Chen, 'Australia is in the process of becoming China's backyard'.

Chapter 2 How China sees itself in the world

1   Zheng Wang, *Never Forget National Humiliation: Historical memory in Chinese politics and foreign relations*, New York: Columbia University Press, 2012; Michael Pillsbury, *The Hundred-Year Marathon*, New York: St Martin's Griffin, 2016.

2   Here I am drawing heavily on Wang, *Never Forget National Humiliation*.

3   Wang, *Never Forget National Humiliation*, p. 104.

4   Geoffrey Crothall quoted by Wang, *Never Forget National Humiliation*, p. 116.

5   Wang, *Never Forget National Humiliation*, p. 116

6   'Chinese Education Minister: The Hostile Forces' First Choice for Penetration Is the Education System', originally published in *Sina*, 10 December 2016, <chinascope.org/archives/10801>.

7   Wang, *Never Forget National Humiliation*, pp. 111–12.

8   Wang, *Never Forget National Humiliation*, p. 115.

9   Quoted by Wang, *Never Forget National Humiliation*, p. 114.

10 Wang, *Never Forget National Humiliation*, p. 227.

11   Rachel Liu, 'A new definition of Chinese patriotism', *Foreign Policy*, 11 September 2014.

12   Wang, *Never Forget National Humiliation*, p. 125.

13   Liu Xiaobo, in *No Enemies, No Hatred: Selected essays and poems*, Perry Link, Tienchi Martin-Liao and Liu Xia (eds), Cambridge, Mass.: Belknap Press, 2012, p. 73.

14   Liu, *No Enemies, No Hatred*, pp. 74–5.

15   Liu, 'The Communist Party's "Olympic Gold Medal Syndrome"', in *No Enemies, No Hatred*, p. 251.

16   Liu, 'The Communist Party's "Olympic Gold Medal Syndrome"', p. 255.

17   Wang, *Never Forget National Humiliation*, pp. 150–2.

18   Lotus Ruan, 'The new face of Chinese nationalism', *Foreign Policy*, 25 August 2016.

19   Anon., 'Smug Aussie swimmer won't cloud Rio', *Global Times*, 8 August 2016.

20   Jennine Khalik, 'Rio Olympics 2016: CFMEU protests Channel Seven's coverage of China', *The Australian*, 9 August 2016.

21   James Jiann Hua To, *Qiaowu: Extra-territorial policies for the overseas Chinese*, Leiden: Koninklijke Brill, 2014, p. 44.

22   Wang, *Never Forget National Humiliation*, p. 154.

23   Lucy Hornby, 'China battles to control growing online nationalism', *Financial Times*, 8 January 2017.

24   Li Jing and He Huifeng, 'Anti-Japan protests turn violent in Shenzhen, Guangzhou and Qingdao', *South China Morning Post*, 17 September 2012.

25   Anon., 'Chinese state media condemns protests at KFC restaurants in wake of South China Sea ruling', *South China Morning Post*, 20 July 2016.

26   Jun Mai, 'China vows to nip patriotic protests in the bud to maintain stability', *South China Morning Post*, 13 January 2017.

27   Zheping Huang, 'Inside the Global Times, China's hawkish, belligerent state tabloid', *Quartz*, 9 August 2016.

28   Philip Wen, 'This is the deal: "In time, this world will be China's"', *The Sydney Morning Herald*, 10–11 September 2016.

29   Wang, *Never Forget National Humiliation*, pp. 129–32.

30   D.S. Rajan, 'China: Can Xi Jinping's "Chinese Dream" vision be realized?', *South Asia Analysis Group*, 3 January 2013.

31   Liu Mingfu, *The China Dream: Great power thinking and strategic posture in the post-American era*, New York: CN Times Books, 2015, back cover.

32   Quoted by Michael Pillsbury, *The Hundred-Year Marathon*, New York: St Martin's Griffin, 2016, p. 28.

33   William A. Callahan, 'Chinese visions of world order: Post-hegemonic or a new hegemony?', *International Studies Review*, 2008, no. 10, p. 753.

34   Pillsbury, *The Hundred-Year Marathon*, pp. 28, 12.

35   Zheng Wang, 'Not rising, but rejuvenating: The "Chinese Dream"', *The Diplomat*, 5 February 2013.

36 In case citizens are inclined to forget it, in 2017 the authorities instructed Chinese cinemas to screen four-minute patriotic propaganda videos, some featuring a fist-pumping Jackie Chan extolling President Xi's China Dream and core socialist values. See Huang Wan, 'Chinese cinemas to show patriotic trailer ahead of screenings', *Sixth Tone*, 30 June 2017.

37 Pillsbury, *The Hundred-Year Marathon*, p. 235.

38 Pillsbury, *The Hundred-Year Marathon*, p. 230.

39 Liu, *The China Dream*, p. 29.

40 <www.scio.gov.cn/m/zhzc/10/Document/1437648/1437648.htm>.

41 He Yafei's speech followed one in 2013 by Cai Mingzhao, director of the Foreign Propaganda Office, where he spoke of 'deepening foreign propaganda about the Chinese Dream', a dream that will benefit not only Chinese people but, because of the 'superiority of the Chinese nation', the 'people of the world' (Anon., 'China's foreign propaganda chief outlines external communication priorities', China Copyright and Media blog, 22 December 2014, translated from *People's Daily*).

42 Paul Keating, 'Australia must heed the shift in the US-China power balance', *The Australian*, 24 December 2016.

43 David Kelly, 'Winding back the China Solution', *The Interpreter*, Lowy Institute, 6 July 2017.

44 Liu, *The China Dream*, pp. 2, 4.

45 Jamil Anderlini, 'The dark side of China's national renewal', *Financial Times*, 21 June 2017.

46 Anon., 'Trump's Korea gaffe exposes hegemonic thinking in China', *Chosun*, 20 April 2017.

47 Bill Hayton, 'China's "historic rights" in the South China Sea: Made in America?', *The Diplomat*, 21 June 2016.

48 <pca-cpa.org/wp-content/uploads/sites/175/2016/07/PH-CN-20160712-Award.pdf>.

49 John Fitzgerald, 'Handing the initiative to China', *Inside Story*, 19 January 2017.

50 Hu Jintao, full text of speech, 24 October 2013 <www.smh.com.au/articles/2003/10/24/1066631618612.html>.

51 Geoff Wade, 'Popular History and Bunkum: The book "1421, The Year China Discovered America" is a fairytale & a fiction', posted at Maritime Asia <maritimeasia.ws/topic/1421bunkum.html>. See also <www.1421exposed.com/html/1421_and_all_that_junk.html>.

52 Quentin McDermott, 'Junk History', *Four Corners*, ABC TV, 31 July 2006 <www.abc.net.au/4corners/content/2006/s1699373.htm>.

53 Geoff Wade, 'The "Liu/Menzies" world map: A critique', *e-Perimetron*, Autumn 2007, vol. 2, no. 4, pp. 273–80.

54 Timothy Kendall, *Within China's Orbit?: China through the eyes of the Australian parliament*, Canberra: Parliamentary Library, 2008.

55 Kendall, *Within China's Orbit?*.

56 Fu Ying, speech to the National Press Club of Australia, as quoted in Geoffrey Barker, 'Diplomacy personified', *Australian Financial Review*, 10 June 2005, p. 20.

57 <www.china.com.cn/chinese/zhuanti/zhxxy/881212.htm>.

Chapter 3 *Qiaowu* and the Chinese diaspora

1 <www.scio.gov.cn/m/zhzc/10/Document/1437648/1437648.htm>.

2 Cheong Suk-Wai, 'Beijing's charm offensive: A challenge to test loyalty', *Straits Times*, 30 April 2017,

3 James Jiann Hua To, *Qiaowu: Extra-territorial policies for the overseas Chinese*, Leiden: Koninklijke Brill, 2014.

4 To, *Qiaowu*, p. 19.

5 To, *Qiaowu*, p. 47.

6 To, *Qiaowu*, p. 42.

7 To, *Qiaowu*, p. 254.

8 To, *Qiaowu*, p. 258.

9 To, *Qiaowu*, pp. 260, 261, 264.

10 To, *Qiaowu*, p. 257.

11 Hagar Cohen and Tiger Webb, 'Chinese nationals deported from Fiji were sex workers, not fraudsters: Source', *ABC News Online*, 6 October 2017.

12 Gabrielle Chan, 'Cabinet papers 1988-89: Bob Hawke acted alone in offering asylum to Chinese students', *The Guardian*, 1 January 2015.

13 To, *Qiaowu*, p. 27.

14 Quoted in Chan, 'Cabinet papers 1988-89'.

15 James To, 'Beijing's policies for managing Han and ethnic-minority Chinese communities abroad', *Journal of Current Chinese Affairs*, 2012, no. 4, p. 186.

16 To, *Qiaowu*, pp. 75, 78–9; To, 'Beijing's policies for managing Han', p. 186.

17 Anne-Marie Brady, 'China's foreign propaganda machine', *Journal of Democracy*, October 2015, vol. 26, no. 4, pp. 51–9.

18 James To explains that there are five major *qiaowu* organisations, two under the central government (the OCAO and the All-China Federation of Returned OC Association) and three party departments (the Propaganda Department, the International Department and the UFWD) (To, *Qiaowu*, pp. 73–80).

19 Marcel Angliviel de la Beaumelle, 'The United Front Work Department: "Magic weapon" at home and abroad', The Jamestown Foundation, *China Brief*, 6 July 2017, vol. 17, no. 9.

20 Anne-Marie Brady, 'Magic Weapons: China's political influence activities under Xi Jinping', Wilson Center, Washington, D.C., September 2017.

21 To, *Qiaowu*, p. 74. *Qiaowu* agencies are overseen by the CCP's International Department while organisations such as the ACPPRC are managed by the

United Front Work Department. However, they are coordinated by the embassy in Canberra and work closely together.

22 Rowan Callick, '"Non-profit" group linked to Chinese donors', *The Australian*, 5 September 2016.

23 To, *Qiaowu*, pp. 269–70.

24 <world.people.com.cn/n/2015/0527/c157278-27066031.html> 'Dr William Chiu, founder and chairman of the Australian Council for the Promotion of the Peaceful Reunification of China passes away', *People's Daily*, 27 May 2015.

25 To, *Qiaowu*, p. 268.

26 To, 'Beijing's policies for managing Han', p. 189.

27 Dylan Welch, 'Ernest Wong: Labor's go-to man for access to Chinese community', *7.30*, ABC TV, 19 September 2016.

28 Chris Bowen, accompanied by his wife, was flown to China in 2015 partly at the expense of the CCP and the Australian Guangdong Association, which Huang Xiangmo heads (Samantha Hutchinson and Ben Butler, 'Bowen on the Yuhu register as China doles out MP largesse', *The Australian*, 7 September 2016). In his memoir Bob Carr described a 'gloriously successful Labor fundraiser' at a Chinese New Year event organised by Sam Dastyari that raised $200,000, which was split between Labor head office and Chris Bowen's personal campaign (Rowan Callick and Sarah Martin, 'Dastyari's donor has party cell', *The Australian*, 7 September 2016). During the Dastyari affair, *The Australian* named the disgraced senator's 'allies and aides' as Carr, Huang Xiangmo, Eric Roozendaal, Chris Bowen, Minshen Zhu and Paul Yi-Wen Han.

29 <www.acpprc.org.au/schinese/jinqi/2015/jndhSep15.html>.

30 <world.people.com.cn/n1/2016/0207/c1002-28117190.html>.

31 To, *Qiaowu*, p. 268.

32 Julie Makinen, 'Beijing uses Chinese New Year to push China's soft power', *Los Angeles Times*, 18 February 2015.

33 Philip Wen, 'China's patriots among us: Beijing pulls new lever of influence in Australia', *The Sydney Morning Herald*, 28 April 2016.

34 <www.chinesenewyear.com.au/index.html>.

35 John Power, 'Pro-Beijing activism by ethnic Chinese in Australia stirs unease', *Asia Times*, 12 May 2016.

36 Rowan Callick, 'Australia's Chinese community: Inscrutable ties to another China', *The Australian*, 27 August 2016.

37 Wen, 'China's patriots among us'. Huang Xiangmo denied any connection between the group and the ACPPRC.

38 <www.xkb.com.au/html/cnc/shetuandongtai/2016/0414/168347.html>. See also *Sydney Today* <www.sydneytoday.com/content-1122194>, whose story was republished in *People's Daily* <australia.people.com.cn/n1/2016/0411/c364496-28265283.html>.

39 <www.bobning.com/fca/?page_id=37>.

40   <www.bobning.com/fca/?p=21>.

41   <www.facebook.com/philclearymayor/videos/1048116948618517>.

42   <www.sbs.com.au/yourlanguage/mandarin/zh-hans/content/su-jun-xi-jiang-jing-xuan-mo-er-ben-shi-fu-shi-chang?language=zh-hans>.

43   <world.people.com.cn/n1/2016/0723/c1002-28579502.html>.

44   <english.cri.cn/12394/2016/07/23/4001s935326.htm>.

45   Philip Wen and Daniel Flitton, 'South China Sea protests to come to Melbourne', *The Age*, 21 July 2016.

46   Naaman Zhou, 'Chinese ballet draws protests for "glorifying Red Army"', *The Guardian*, 18 February 2017.

47   Anon., 'Australian Chinese to boycott Chinese ballet "Red Detachment of Women"', *Duowei News*, 5 February 2017.

48   Rowan Callick, 'Rebel Chinese movement promotes "Australian values"', *The Australian*, 5 September 2016.

49   To, *Qiaowu*, p. 47.

50   To, *Qiaowu*, p. 122.

51   To, *Qiaowu*, p. 281.

52   To, *Qiaowu*, pp. 114–15.

53   Jamil Anderlini, 'The dark side of China's national renewal', *Financial Times*, 21 June 2017.

54   Email to the author, 23 October 2017.

55   Daniel A. Bell, 'Why anyone can be Chinese', *Wall Street Journal*, 14 July 2017.

56   <languagelog.ldc.upenn.edu/nll/?p=33412>.

57   Frank Ching, 'Does Chinese blood really lack the DNA for aggression?', *South China Morning Post*, 2 July 2017.

58   <world.huanqiu.com/exclusive/2017-06/10912308.html>.

59   To, *Qiaowu*, p. 116.

60   David Zweig and Stanley Rosen, 'How China trained a new generation abroad', *SciDev.Net*, 22 May 2013.

61   To, *Qiaowu*, pp. 123–4.

62   To, *Qiaowu*, p. 189.

63   <chinachange.org/2015/06/09/chinese-students-studying-abroad-a-new-focus-of-ccps-united-front-work/>. In *The End of History* (1989), Francis Fukuyama forecast that Chinese students would return from study abroad bringing transformational democratic norms, another instance of what might be called the 'Fukuyama Rule', where the influence of Fukuyama's predictions is in inverse proportion to their accuracy.

64   To, *Qiaowu*, p. 130.

65   To, *Qiaowu*, p. 189.

66   To, *Qiaowu*, p. 28.

67   Koh Gui Qing and John Shiffman, 'China's covert global radio network', Reuters, 2 November 2015; John Fitzgerald, 'How the ABC sold out

news values to get access to China' <www.abc.net.au/mediawatch/transcripts/1615_afr.pdf>.

68   To, *Qiaowu*, pp. 176–8.

69   <www.abc.net.au/mediawatch/transcripts/s4476824.htm>.

70   To, *Qiaowu*, pp. 179–80.

71   To, *Qiaowu*, p. 180.

72   Anon., 'Drive-by shooting won't stop Sunnybank-based Chinese-language newspaper Epoch Times, say staff', *Courier-Mail*, 3 November 2010; Kristian Silva, 'One Nation's Shan Ju Lin defends Pauline Hanson, says she fears Chinese Government will "take over"', *ABC News online*, 21 December 2016.

73   Qing and Shiffman, 'China's covert global radio network'.

74   Anne-Marie Brady, 'Magic Weapons: China's political influence activities under Xi Jinping', Wilson Center, Washington, D.C., September 2017.

75   Rowan Callick, 'Voice of China hits the Aussie airwaves', *News.com.au*, 17 August 2009.

76   Callick, 'Voice of China hits the Aussie airwaves'; <www.multicultural.vic.gov.au/images/stories/documents/2013/2002-12%20recipients%20-%20people.pdf>; <www.chinanews.com/hr/2011/09-19/3335774.shtml>.

77   See also Jia Gao, *Chinese Migrant Entrepreneurship in Australia from the 1990s*, Waltham, Mass.: Elsevier, 2015, Chapter 6.

78   <www.jl.xinhuanet.com/news/2004-07/16/content_2502263.htm>.

79   <en.people.cn/200503/14/eng20050314_176746.html>.

80   <en.people.cn/200503/14/eng20050314_176746.html>.

81   <www.oushinet.com/qj/qjnews/20160928/243581.html>.

82   John Fitzgerald, 'Beijing's *guoqing* versus Australia's way of life', *Inside Story*, 27 September 2016.

83   Fitzgerald, 'Beijing's *guoqing* versus Australia's way of life'.

84   Kelsey Munro and Philip Wen, 'Chinese language newspapers in Australia: Beijing controls messaging, propaganda in press', *The Sydney Morning Herald*, 10 July 2016.

85   Fitzgerald, 'Beijing's *guoqing* versus Australia's way of life'.

86   Munro and Wen, 'Chinese language newspapers in Australia'.

87   Wanning Sun, 'Chinese-language media in Australia: An opportunity for Australian soft power', *Australia-China Relations Institute*, 8 September 2016.

88   Fitzgerald, 'Beijing's *guoqing* versus Australia's way of life'.

89   <www.abc.net.au/mediawatch/transcripts/s4458872.htm>.

90   John Fitzgerald, 'How the ABC sold out news values to get access to China', <www.abc.net.au/mediawatch/transcripts/1615_afr.pdf>.

91   <http://www.acpprc.org.au/schinese/jinqi/2016/qwhOct16.html>.

92   <http://www.acpprc.org.au/schinese/jinqi/2016/qwhOct16.html>; <http://www.radioaustralia.net.au/chinese/our-people/1024564>.

93   Simon Denyer, 'The saga of Hong Kong's abducted booksellers takes a darker turn', *Washington Post*, 17 June 2016.

94   Will Koulouris, '20 years on, Hong Kong's return to China a resounding success: Former Aussie Victoria state premier', *Xinhuanet*, 18 July 2017.

95   Peter Hartcher, 'China's treatment of Hong Kong is a lesson for Australia', *The Sydney Morning Herald*, 11 October 2016.

96   Anon., 'New Zealand cancels meeting with Hong Kong pro-democracy advocates on "diplomatic" concerns', *ABC News Online*, 21 October 2016.

97   To, *Qiaowu*, p. 222.

98   Anne-Marie Brady, 'Magic Weapons: China's political influence activities under Xi Jinping', p. 13.

99   Philip Wen and John Garnaut, 'Chinese police chase corruption suspects in Australian suburbs', *The Sydney Morning Herald*, 15 April 2015.

100 To, *Qiaowu*, p. 193.

101 Anon, 'Businessman wrongly jailed pursues justice', *South China Morning Post*, 9 December 2004.

102 John Garnaut, 'China's rulers team up with notorious "White Wolf" of Taiwan', *The Sydney Morning Herald*, 11 July 2014; Anon., 'Triad member behind scuffles between pro-China and pro-independence protesters on Taiwan university campus', *Synglobe*, 25 September 2017; Anon., 'Zhang Anle, the Sunflower Movement and the China-Taiwan issue', *Synglobe*, 1 April 2014.

103 To, *Qiaowu*, p. 260.

104 To, *Qiaowu*, p. 261.

105 Bethany Allen-Ebrahimian, 'Interpol is helping to enforce China's political purges', *Foreign Policy*, 21 April 2017.

106 Philip Wen, 'Operation Fox Hunt: Law council says extradition treaty with China is "a joke"', *The Sydney Morning Herald*, 2 May 2016.

107 Primrose Riordan, 'China extradition treaty fatal, says freed academic', *The Australian*, 3 April 2017.

108 <www.aic.gov.au/publications/current%20series/facts/1-20/2014/4_courts.html>.

109 Anon., 'China's top court rejects judicial independence as "erroneous thought"', *The Guardian*, 26 February 2015.

110 Megan Palin, 'The reality of human organ harvesting in China', *News.com.au*, 14 November 2016.

111 Anon., 'Hospitals ban Chinese surgeon training', *The Sydney Morning Herald*, 5 December 2006.

112 David Hutt, 'The trouble with John Pilger's *The Coming War on China*', *The Diplomat*, 23 December 2016.

113 Fleur Anderson, 'Abbot-Turnbull clash jeopardises China link', *Australian Financial Review*, 1–2 April 2017.

114 Greg Sheridan, 'Desperately seeking someone to blame after China fiasco', *Weekend Australian*, 1–2 April 2017.

115 Wen and Garnaut, 'Chinese police chase corruption suspects in Australian suburbs'.

116 Wen and Garnaut, 'Chinese police chase corruption suspects in Australian suburbs'.

117 Minxin Pei, *China's Crony Capitalism: The dynamics of regime decay*, Cambridge, Mass.: Harvard University Press, 2016, p. 226.

118 Philip Wen, 'Operation Fox Hunt: Melbourne grandmother Zhou Shiqin prosecuted after return to China', *The Sydney Morning Herald*, 26 October 2016.

119 Rowan Callick, 'China tipped to give its spooks a licence to haunt foreign lands', *The Australian*, 4 July 2017.

120 Nigel Inkster, 'China's draft intelligence law', 26 May 2017 <www.iiss.org>.

121 To, *Qiaowu*, pp. 218–19.

122 To, *Qiaowu*, p. 280.

123 To, *Qiaowu*, p. 280.

124 Nick O'Malley and Alex Joske, 'Mysterious Bennelong letter urges Chinese Australians to "take down" the Turnbull government', *The Sydney Morning Herald*, 13 December 2017; Alex Joske, 'Bennelong byelection: The influential network targeting the Turnbull government in Bennelong', *The Sydney Morning Herald*, 15 December 2017.

125 O'Malley and Joske, 'Mysterious Bennelong letter urges Chinese Australians to "take down" the Turnbull government'.

126 Anthony Klan, 'China scare Labor's only success', *The Australian*, 18 December 2017.

127 Fitzgerald, 'Beijing's *guoqing* versus Australia's way of life'.

128 Fitzgerald, 'Beijing's *guoqing* versus Australia's way of life'.

Chapter 4   Dark Money

1   Primrose Riordan, 'China's local emperor Huang Xiangmo says politics just like sport', *Australian Financial Review*, 1 September 2016.

2   Anon., 'Honorary President Huang Xiangmo discusses the art of giving', *Shenzhen Chaozhou Chamber of Commerce Online*, 29 March 2013, <chaoshang.org/NewsView.asp?NewsID=327>.

3   Philip Wen and Lucy Macken, 'Chinese "King of the Mountain" brush with corruption scandal', *The Sydney Morning Herald*, 25 February 2016; Riordan, 'China's local emperor Huang Xiangmo says politics just like sport'.

4   <www.hurun.net/CN/HuList/Index?num=612C66A2F245>.

5   <finance.qq.com/a/20110729/006016.htm>.

6   Anon., 'Huang Xiangmo visits and expresses his sympathy for the pitiful masses', *Shenzhen Chaozhou Chamber of Commerce Online*, 4 March 2011 <chaoshang.org/NewsView.asp?NewsID=340>; Anon., 'Hurun publishes

2012 philanthropy list, 3 honorary presidents of our Chamber of Commerce in the first hundred', *Shenzhen Chaozhou Chamber of Commerce Online*, 25 March 2013 <chaoshang.org/NewsView.asp?NewsID=870>.

7 <finance.qq.com/a/20110401/004847.htm>.

8 <www.txcs88.cn/Essay_10410.html>.

9 Wen and Macken, 'Chinese "King of the Mountain" brush with corruption scandal'.

10 <epaper.qlwb.com.cn/qlwb/content/20141010/ArticelA06002FM.htm>.

11 <finance.sina.com.cn/360desktop/china/dfjj/20141010/121920503512.shtml>.

12 Michael Cole, 'Guangzhou party leader's fall tied to corrupt real estate deals', *Mingtiandi*, 15 July 2014.

13 Kirsty Needham, 'Chinese recipient of Huang Xiangmo political donation gets suspended death sentence', *The Sydney Morning Herald*, 7 June 2017.

14 Needham, 'Chinese recipient of Huang Xiangmo political donation gets suspended death sentence'.

15 Wen and Macken, 'Chinese "King of the Mountain" brush with corruption scandal'.

16 Minxin Pei, *China's Crony Capitalism: The dynamics of regime decay*, Cambridge, Mass.: Harvard University Press, 2016.

17 Pei, *China's Crony Capitalism*, pp. 1–2.

18 Pei, *China's Crony Capitalism*, pp. 2–3.

19 Pei, *China's Crony Capitalism*, p. 8.

20 Pei, *China's Crony Capitalism*, p. 243.

21 Pei, *China's Crony Capitalism*, pp. 247–8.

22 Pei, *China's Crony Capitalism*, p. 138.

23 Quoted by Pei, *China's Crony Capitalism*, p. 116.

24 Pei, *China's Crony Capitalism*, p. 117.

25 Pei, *China's Crony Capitalism*, p. 142.

26 Pei, *China's Crony Capitalism*, p. 133.

27 Pei, *China's Crony Capitalism*, p. 225.

28 Pei, *China's Crony Capitalism*, p. 226.

29 Joel Keep and Nila Liu, 'The defector', SBS Investigations, *SBS News Online*, 5 September 2016.

30 Pei, *China's Crony Capitalism*, pp. 82, 262.

31 Anon., 'China voice: catching 14 military "tigers"', *Xinhuanet*, 2 March 2015.

32 Pei, *China's Crony Capitalism*, pp. 6, 262.

33 Frank Fang, 'Former top Chinese military officer taken away for investigation', *The Epoch Times*, 12 February 2015.

34 Kenneth Allen, 'China announces reform of military ranks', *China Brief*, 30 January 2017.

35 Tania Branigan, 'China blocks Bloomberg for exposing financial affairs of Xi Jinping's family', *The Guardian*, 29 June 2012.

36 Li Lingpu and Larry Ong, 'China's Xi set to oust corrupt officials in Hong Kong', *The Epoch Times*, 1–7 December 2016.

37 Li and Ong, 'China's Xi set to oust corrupt officials in Hong Kong'. The Chinese People's Political Consultative Conference (CPPCC) is a prestigious body used to reward patriotic activists and businessmen. It has been described by senior leader Jia Qinglin as 'a patriotic united front organisation' (John Garnaut, 'Toeing the line', *The Sydney Morning Herald*, 13 April 2011).

38 Li and Ong, 'China's Xi set to oust corrupt officials in Hong Kong'. See also Pei, *China's Crony Capitalism*, p. 147.

39 <www.chinadaily.com.cn/china/2017-01/09/content_27894610.htm>.

40 Jamil Anderlini, 'The political price of Xi Jinping's anti-corruption campaign', *Financial Times*, 4 January 2017.

41 Anderlini, 'The political price of Xi Jinping's anti-corruption campaign'.

42 Pei, *China's Crony Capitalism*, p. 149.

43 Martin Wolf, 'Too big, too Leninist—a China crisis is a matter of time', *Financial Times*, 13 December 2016.

44 Riordan, 'China's local emperor Huang Xiangmo says politics just like sport'.

45 Gabrielle Chan, 'Dastyari's donations reveal a bigger story of links and largesse', *The Guardian*, 7 September 2016.

46 <www.yuhugroup.com.au/aboutus>.

47 See, for example, Rowan Callick, 'Non-profit group linked to Chinese donors', *The Australian*, 5 September 2016.

48 Huang has denied his Australian organisation is funded by Beijing (Primrose Riordan, 'Sam Dastyari linked political donor resigns from Bob Carr institute after major review', *Australian Financial Review*, 21 September 2016; see also Primrose Riordan and Lisa Murray, 'Sam Dastyari linked to Chinese patriotic force group', *Australian Financial Review*, 6 September 2016).

49 <www.chinanews.com/hr/2014/10-31/6738251.shtml>.

50 <www.acpprc.org.au/schinese/huizhang/ourchairman14.html>.

51 Brad Norrington, 'ALP branch accepts Shorten edict on donations from Chinese businessmen', *The Australian*, 21 July 2017; Sean Nicholls and Kate McClymont, 'Former NSW treasurer Eric Roozendaal joins Chinese firm that was a big donor to NSW political parties', *The Sydney Morning Herald*, 4 February 2014.

52 Chris Uhlmann and Andrew Greene, 'Chinese donors to Australian political parties: Who gave how much?', *ABC News Online*, 21 August 2016.

53 Gina McColl and Philip Wen, 'Foreign Minister Julie Bishop's links to Chinese political donors', *The Sydney Morning Herald*, 23 August 2016.

54 <https://www.linkedin.com/in/meijuan-anna-wu-751bb43a/>.

55 <periodicdisclosures.aec.gov.au/Returns/55/SWEQ6.pdf>.

56 Gina McColl, 'Chinese interests play increasing role in Australian political donations', *The Sydney Morning Herald*, 21 May 2016.

57   <www.yuhugroup.com/v2010/newsdetails.asp?id=364>.

58   Nicholls and McClymont, 'Former NSW treasurer Eric Roozendaal joins Chinese firm'.

59   Nicholls and McClymont, 'Former NSW treasurer Eric Roozendaal joins Chinese firm'.

60   Dylan Welch, 'Ernest Wong: Labor's go-to man for access to Chinese community', *7.30*, ABC TV, 19 September 2016.

61   <big5.xinhuanet.com/gate/big5/www.henan.xinhua.org/xhzt/2007-04/14/content_9789459.htm>.

62   <www.fjhk.org.au/cn/aboutus.html>; <http://www.acpprc.org.au/schinese/hen.asp>.

63   <http://www.theaustralian.com.au/national-affairs/state-politics/labors-biggest-individual-donor-cant-recall-his-contribution/news-story/02d77420334a6db3987b91b923964bf9>.

64   <www.yuhugroup.com.au/aboutus>.

65   <www.yuhugroup.com/v2010/newsdetails.asp?id=344>.

66   <www.yuhugroup.com/v2010/newsdetails.asp?id=345>.

67   <www.yuhugroup.com/v2010/newsdetails.asp?id=362>. Huang also founded and became chairman of the Australian Fellowship of China Guangdong Associations in October 2014, which combined a few pre-existing Guangdong Associations (<www.chinanews.com/hr/2014/10-31/6738251.shtml>).

68   Rowan Callick, 'Australia's Chinese community: Inscrutable ties to another China', *The Australian*, 27 August 2016.

69   Pei, *China's Crony Capitalism*, p. 260; Bruce J. Dickson, *Wealth into Power: The Communist Party's embrace of China's private sector*, Washington, D.C.: George Washington University, 2008.

70   <www.yuhugroup.com/v2010/newsdetails.asp?id=399>.

71   <www.yuhugroup.com/v2010/newsdetails.asp?id=403>.

72   <world.people.com.cn/n1/2016/0823/c1002-28659866.html>.

73   <www.yuhugroup.com/v2010/newsdetails.asp?id=407>.

74   Anne-Marie Brady, 'China's Foreign Propaganda Machine', Wilson Center, Washington, D.C., 26 October 2015, <https://wilsoncenter.org/article/magic-weapons-chinas-political-influence-activities-under-xi-jinping>, pp. 16–17. Huang has denied his Australian organisation is funded by Beijing.

75   <http://www.acpprc.org.au/schinese/jinqi/2016/hzhSep16.html>; <http://www.acpprc.org.au/english/7thtermlist.asp>.

76   <http://www.yuhugroup.com/v2010/newsdetails.asp?id=577>.

77   <http://www.gqb.gov.cn/news/2017/0324/42073.shtml>.

78   Kelsie Munro, 'Huang Xiangmo's pro-China group denies organising Premier Li rent-a-crowd', *The Sydney Morning Herald*, 24 March 2017.

79   <http://www.gqb.gov.cn>.

80   Bob Carr, 'Seven steps to tame fears over China', *The Australian*, 12 December 2017.

81 Australian Electoral Commission returns, from March 2012 to September 2016. Associates are William Chiu, Luo Chuangxiong, Eng Joo Ang and Peter Chen.

82 Sean Nicholls, 'Chinese property firm Yuhu hires ex-deputy premier Andrew Stoner', *The Sydney Morning Herald*, 18 November 2015.

83 <www.globaltimes.cn/content/1003731.shtml>.

84 <world.people.com.cn/n1/2017/0518/c1002-29285371.html>.

85 McColl and Wen, 'Foreign Minister Julie Bishop's links to Chinese political donors'.

86 <foreignminister.gov.au/speeches/Pages/2014/jb_sp_140516.aspx?w=tb1Ca GpkPX%2FlS0K%2Bg9ZKEg%3D%3D>.

87 <http://www.cnadc.com.cn/index.php?m=content&c=index&a=show&cati d=65&id=656>.

88 <trademinister.gov.au/speeches/Pages/2014/ar_sp_140915.aspx?w=O%2F% 2FeXE%2BIYc3HpsIRhVl0XA%3D%3D>.

89 <www.yuhugroup.com/v2010/newsdetails.asp?id=408>.

90 Michael Koziol, 'Union campaign against China FTA branded racist, short-sighted', *The Sydney Morning Herald*, 21 August 2015.

91 McColl and Wen, 'Foreign Minister Julie Bishop's links to Chinese political donors'.

92 Register of Members' Interests, 9 December 2013. See also Gina McColl, 'Chinese interests play increasing role in Australian political donations', *The Sydney Morning Herald*, 21 May 2016.

93 Dylan Welch, 'Political donations: Former NSW Labor powerbroker calls for an end to the funding arms race', *ABC News Online*, 19 September 2016.

94 Rowan Callick, 'Overseas Chinese political donors are mystery men in China', *The Australian*, 12 September 2016.

95 Huang Xiangmo, 'South China Sea: Australia would be rash to confront China', *Australian Financial Review*, 7 June 2016.

96 Zhou Bo, 'Duterte's genial tone on the South China Sea is just one of many signs of warmer Sino-Asean ties', *South China Morning Post*, 14 November 2016.

97 <http://www.theaustralian.com.au/news/inquirer/huang-xiangmo-and-dastyari-more-than-a-soap-opera/news-story/5138ad656beb2fc34b0e91246 f48764c>.

98 Primrose Riordan, 'Huang Xiangmo quits as head of pro-China advocacy group', *The Australian*, 27 November 2017.

99 <acetca.org.au/en/?dt_portfolio=04>. (Note the name in the title, Xue Shuihua, is incorrect. Shuihua is Shuihe's brother.)

100 ACETCA's PRC links are extensive. Among other activities, the association (which has an office in Sydney's Chinatown) has paid for students from Western Sydney University and Macquarie University to travel to China. It was the main organiser of the 2017 Chinese New Year celebrations in Sydney.

101 <acetca.org.au/?dt_portfolio=06>.

102 <www.dedeceblog.com/2011/02/03/the-mysterious-dr-chau/>.

103 <periodicdisclosures.aec.gov.au/Donor.aspx?SubmissionId=60&Client Id=20628&utm_source=TractionNext&utm_medium=Email&utm_ campaign=Insider-Subscribe-010217>.

104 Uhlmann and Greene, 'Chinese donors to Australian political parties'.

105 <periodicdisclosures.aec.gov.au/Donor.aspx?SubmissionId=60&Client Id=20628&utm_source=TractionNext&utm_medium=Email&utm_ campaign=Insider-Subscribe-010217>.

106 Macau casino billionaire Stanley Ho and his associates donated $1.6 million to the Labor Party in 2008–09, mostly to the New South Wales branch, but Labor was forced to give most of his money back after the ALP conducted a 'due diligence'. Labor would not give a clear reason but it was suggested at the time that Ho had his eye on the licence for Sydney's Star Casino, then up for renewal (Anon., 'Labor's mystery $200k donation', *New Matilda*, 12 April 2011; Anon., 'Was Stanley Ho hedging his bets with the Australian Labor Party?', *South China Morning Post*, 6 February 2009).

107 John Garnaut, 'Behind the mysterious Dr Chau', *The Sydney Morning Herald*, 4 July 2009.

108 <www.files.ethz.ch/isn/144769/cds_0606.pdf>, p. 27.

109 Garnaut, 'Behind the mysterious Dr Chau'.

110 Deborah Snow, Nic Christensen and John Garnaut, 'Chinese billionaire funding our MPs', *The Age*, 4 June 2009.

111 <list.juwai.com/news/2012/07/meet-the-chinese-billionaires-with-australia-in-their-sights>.

112 Email correspondence with John Garnaut, 29 September 2017.

113 <web.archive.org/web/20071201202445/http://www.aacfe.org:80/aboutus .aspx?id=99>.

114 The popular *Yangcheng Evening News* is not an official party organ but is subject to close supervision (<contemporary_chinese_culture.academic.ru/916/ Yangcheng_Evening_News>).

115 Garnaut, 'Behind the mysterious Dr Chau'.

116 John Garnaut, 'China spreads its watching web of surveillance across Australia', *The Sydney Morning Herald*, 26 April 2014.

117 <zhengxie.thnet.gov.cn/thzx/zxjg/200410/810fefa62cc24cb4b64f152680 7da366.shtmlohn>; John Garnaut, 'Toeing the line', *The Sydney Morning Herald*, 13 April 2011.

118 <sttzb.shantou.gov.cn/demeanor_s.asp?ID=78>.

119 Gerry Groot, 'The expansion of the United Front under Xi Jinping', *The China Story*, Yearbook 2015, Australian Centre on China in the World.

120 Statement of Claim, Chau Chak Wing v The Australian Broadcasting Corporation and ORS, Federal Court of Australia (NSW Registry), 5 July 2017.

121 Simon Benson, 'Chinese billionaire hits back at ASIO: I'm not a communist agent', *The Australian*, 27 June 2017.

122 Nick McKenzie and Richard Baker, 'Wikileaked: Billionaire Australian donor's Beijing links detailed in "sensitive" diplomatic cable', *The Sydney Morning Herald*, 16 July 2015.

123 John Garnaut, 'Are Chau Chak Wing's circles of influence in Australia-China ties built on hot air?', *The Sydney Morning Herald*, 16 October 2015.

124 <www.proversepublishing.com/authors/uren_roger>.

125 Liang Zhen, 'UN bribery scandal implicates CCP's Jiang faction', *The Epoch Times*, 31 March 2016.

126 <www.justice.gov/usao-sdny/pr/former-head-foundation-sentenced-20-months-prison-bribing-then-ambassador-and-president>.

127 Garnaut, 'Are Chau Chak Wing's circles of influence in Australia-China ties built on hot air?'.

128 Kaja Whitehouse, 'Troubled ex-UN official dies after barbell falls on his neck', *New York Post*, 23 June 2016.

129 Defence document lodged by the ABC, Fairfax Media and Nick McKenzie in the Federal Court of Australia, NSW District, 29 September 2017

130 Primrose Riordan, 'China backs Zhu's private Sydney college', *Australian Financial Review*, 15 April 2013.

131 <periodicdisclosures.aec.gov.au/Returns/60/VTEL6.pdf>.

132 Wendy Bacon and Ben Eltham write that other donations have been made in ways that need not be declared ('A top education?', *New Matilda*, 2 September 2016). In 2014–15 the ALP's returns initially listed Top Education Institute's address as 'Dr Minshen Zhu—CEO and Principal G01, 1 Central Ave, Australian Technology Park'. These were later amended to remove Zhu's name.

133 <www.chinaqw.com/node2/node116/node122/node174/userobject6ai3564.html>.

134 <www.chinaqw.com/node2/node116/node122/node174/userobject6ai3564.html>.

135 <www.citic.com/AboutUs/History>.

136 Gerry Groot, *Managing Transitions: The Chinese Communist Party, United Front Work, Corporatism and Hegemony*, Abingdon: Routledge, 2004, p. 108.

137 <www.chinaqw.com/node2/node116/node122/node174/userobject6ai3564.html>.

138 <www.cpaml.org/posting1.php?id=414>.

139 Lisa Murray and Primrose Riordan, 'China singled out Sam Dastyari as one of the country's key international supporters', *Australian Financial Review*, September 2016.

140 <www.fcm.chinanews.com.cn/2001-08-21/2/12.html>.

141 Madalina Hubert, 'Ex-envoy details Chinese regime's overseas scheme', *The Epoch Times*, 10 September 2015.

142 <www.fcm.chinanews.com.cn/2001-08-21/2/12.html>.

143 <www.chinaqw.com/node2/node116/node122/node174/userobject6ai3564.html>.

144 <www.fcm.chinanews.com.cn/2001-08-21/2/12.html>.

145 <http://www.acpprc.org.au/english/2ndtermlist.asp>.

146 Eryk Bagshaw, 'Top Education: Company at centre of donations furore a beneficiary of streamlined visa program', *The Sydney Morning Herald*, 10 September 2016.

147 <www.xzbu.com/7/view-2956207.htm>.

148 <en.people.cn/90001/90777/90856/6622207.html>,

149 <www.xzbu.com/7/view-2956207.htm>.

150 <www.top.edu.au/news/dr-minshen-zhu-of-top-education-attended-the-2nd-meeting-of-chinese-ministerial-consultative-committee-at-the-parliament-house-in-canberra>.

151 Latika Bourke, 'Labor Senator Sam Dastyari had Chinese interests foot the bill for travel entitlement repayment', *The Sydney Morning Herald*, 30 August 2016.

152 James Massola, 'Chinese donor the Yuhu Group steps in to help Sam Dastyari', *The Sydney Morning Herald*, 27 March 2015; Kelsey Monroe, 'Sam Dastyari donor steps down from university's China centre over "supposed Chinese influence"', *The Sydney Morning Herald*, 22 September 2016; Peter Martin, 'China's gifts, research, "special bonds" and Sam Dastyari's ghost from his past', *The Sydney Morning Herald*, 7 September 2016.

153 Some on the Labor Right have not discarded their anti-communism. Many on the Left have no sympathy for any kind of dictatorship and they are deeply concerned about the drift of the party under the influence of foreign money. Stephen Conroy, Kim Beazley and John Faulkner are reported to be among them.

154 Primrose Riordan, 'Sam Dastyari pledges to support China on South China Sea beside Labor donor', *Australian Financial Review*, 31 August 2016.

155 Riordan, 'Sam Dastyari pledges to support China on South China Sea beside Labor donor'.

156 Murray and Riordan, 'China singled out Sam Dastyari as one of the country's key international supporters'.

157 Sid Maher and Rosie Lewis, 'China sea conflict interested Labor senator Sam Dastyari', *The Australian*, 3 September 2016.

158 Quoted by Nick Bryant, 'Sam Dastyari tries to fix the ALP', *The Monthly*, July 2013.

159 Fergus Hunter, '"Cash for comment": Malcolm Turnbull questions Sam Dastyari over China money', *The Sydney Morning Herald*, 2 September 2016.

160 <www.abc.net.au/news/2017-06-05/asio-china-spy-raid/8589094>.

161 Rory Medcalf, 'Sam Dastyari's South China Sea support is a big deal and a timely warning', *Australian Financial Review*, 5 September 2016.

162 Nick McKenzie, James Massola and Richard Baker, 'Dastyari's bug warning', *The Age*, 29 November 2017.

163 Adam Gartrell, '"Whose side is he on?": Malcolm Turnbull says Sam Dastyari should be sacked', *The Sydney Morning Herald*, 29 November 2017.

164 Nick O'Malley, Philip Wen and Michael Koziol, 'Give and take', *The Sydney Morning Herald*, 10–11 September 2016.

165 Medcalf, 'Sam Dastyari's South China Sea support is a big deal and a timely warning'.

166 <www.globaltimes.cn/content/1004234.shtml>.

167 <www.globaltimes.cn/content/997320.shtml>.

168 A version of this section, written by Alex Joske and the author, was published as 'Political networking the Chinese way—a Sydney MP and his "community adviser"', *The Sydney Morning Herald*, 22 June 2017.

169 Primrose Riordan, 'NSW Labor leader echoes Chinese criticism of Australian media', *The Australian*, 27 September 2017.

170 Brad Norrington, 'NSW Labor rising star's wife, pro-Beijing staffer in China venture', *The Australian*, 15 June 2017.

171 Interview with Alex Joske, 19 June 2017.

172 <www.shyouth.net/html/zuzhibu/1_tjs_Lijie/2009-07-09/Detail_38416.htm>.

173 Interview with the author, 18 June 2017.

174 <www.aucnlinks.com/chairman.asp>.

175 PDF of Yang Dongdong's CV from <aucnlinks.com/chairman_detail.asp>, saved 30 November 2016.

176 PDF of Yang Dongdong's CV.

177 Yang Dongdong declined to answer questions when phoned by Alex Joske, saying he was too busy to speak.

178 PDF of Yang Dongdong's CV.

179 <www.chinaqw.com/hqhr/hrdt/200804/11/113213.shtml>.

180 <www.zhongguotongcuhui.org.cn/hnwtchdt/201506/t20150609_9990253.html>; <www.acpprc.org.au/schinese/jinqi/2009/rally09.html>.

181 <www.chinatown.com.au/news_59551.html>.

182 <localstats.com.au/demographics/federal-electorate/reid>.

183 <www.sydneytoday.com/content-833106>; <http://www.sbs.com.au/yourlanguage/mandarin/zh-hans/article/2016/07/04/jin-nian-da-xuan-hua-ren-zhi-yuan-zhc-zhu-xuan-xing-zhi-gao-zhang?language=zh-hans>.

184 Doug Hendrie, 'How a Chinese-language social media campaign hurt Labor's election chances', *The Guardian*, 9 July 2016.

185 <achina.com.au/bencandy.php?fid=41&id=8431>.

186 <achina.com.au/bencandy.php?fid=41&id=8810>; <www.mofcom.gov.cn/article/i/jyjl/l/201610/20161001406128.shtml>.

187 <mp.weixin.qq.com/s/uW2PCNK0xdSrafIvV0xo1w>.

188 <world.people.com.cn/n/2014/0307/c1002-24557722.html>.

189 <mp.weixin.qq.com/s/o7Qy38MI1HApmSYBqKIEGg>.

190 Latika Bourke, 'Clive Palmer apologises for China comments in which he referred to Chinese "mongrels"', *The Sydney Morning Herald*, 26 August 2014.

191 <www.aoweibang.com/view/31188756/>.

192 Fergus Hunter, 'Sam Dastyari contradicted Labor policy, backed China's position in sea dispute at event with donor', *The Sydney Morning Herald*, 1 September 2016.

193 James Robertson and Lisa Visentin, '"Adviser" with ties to Chinese communist lobbyist drops out of council race', *The Sydney Morning Herald*, 24 June 2017.

Chapter 5 'Beijing Bob'

1 Huang Xiangmo said that he 'personally appointed' Bob Carr to the ACRI post (Primrose Riordan, 'China's local emperor Huang Xiangmo says politics just like sport', *Australian Financial Review*, 1 September 2016). On 1 September 2017, in response to some emailed questions, Bob Carr wrote to the author that he was chosen and appointed by the university.

2 <www.yuhugroup.com/v2010/newsdetails.asp?id=414>.

3 <https://tinyurl.com/y78mcqcw>.

4 Primrose Riordan, 'Bob Carr's China research used to justify FTA, AIIB membership', *Australian Financial Review*, 5 September 2016.

5 Anon., 'Xi's speech at Belt & Road forum wins broad approval overseas', *Pakistan Observer*, May 2016.

6 Nick O'Malley, Philip Wen and Michael Koziol, 'Give and take', *The Sydney Morning Herald*, 10–11 September 2016.

7 Tony Stephens, 'Rally speakers decry fascism', *The Sydney Morning Herald*, 7 June 1989.

8 Bob Carr, *Diary of a Foreign Minister*, Sydney: NewSouth Publishing, 2014, p. 140.

9 Bob Carr, 'Australia needs a think tank that sees hope in partnership with China', *The Sydney Morning Herald*, 11 September 2016.

10 Anon., 'The influence of the People's Republic of China on Australian universities', Parliament House research, September 2017, and author conversations.

11 <www.uts.edu.au/sites/default/files/gsu-aboututs-pdf-annualreport-15-roo.pdf>, p. 34.

12 <www.alumni.uts.edu.au/news/tower/issue-11/the-new-silk-road>.

13 'The establishment of ACRI was made possible by the generous donations of Chinese philanthropists and entrepreneurs, Xiangmo Huang and Chulong Zhou' (<www.alumni.uts.edu.au/news/tower/issue-11/the-new-silk-road>. It adds: '"We share a vision to produce high-quality research that will have worthwhile results for both our countries' relationships in important business and societal spheres," said Mr Huang.'

14   Primrose Riordan, 'Sam Dastyari-linked political donor resigns from Bob Carr institute after major review', *Australian Financial Review*, 21 September 2016.

15   Riordan, 'China's local emperor Huang Xiangmo says politics just like sport'.

16   Louise Yaxley, 'Malcolm Turnbull questions Sam Dastyari's loyalty amid claims he passed security information to Chinese donor', *ABC News Online*, 29 November 2017.

17   Gerry Groot, 'The expansion of the United Front under Xi Jinping', *The China Story*, Yearbook 2015, Australian Centre on China in the World.

18   <www.australiachinarelations.org/about-us>.

19   In his emailed reply to the author, Carr says that ACRI has 'gone above and beyond standard obligations for an institution wholly housed within a university'.

20   Quoted by Matthew Knott and Heath Aston, 'Don't become "propaganda vehicles" for China: Universities warned over donations', *The Sydney Morning Herald*, 8 September 2016.

21   Riordan, 'Sam Dastyari-linked political donor resigns from Bob Carr institute after major review'.

22   <www.australiachinarelations.org/about-us>.

23   Email response to the author, 1 September 2017.

24   Philip Wen, 'Former foreign minister Bob Carr photograph "raised eyebrows"', *The Sydney Morning Herald*, 26 February 2016.

25   Stephen McDonnell, 'Carr's challenge on Tibet', The Drum, *ABC News Online*, 12 March 2012.

26   Email response to the author, 1 September 2017.

27   Email response to the author, 1 September 2017.

28   <www.uts.edu.au/sites/default/files/gsu-aboututs-pdf-annualreport-14-roo.pdf>.

29   Bob Carr mentions Huang and '15 Australian corporates' in a September 2016 opinion piece, but does not mention his second biggest benefactor (Carr, 'Australia needs a think tank that sees hope in partnership with China'). When I asked him about this he wrote that Mr Zhou has never asked that his name be kept out of the media.

30   <www.chinanews.com/gj/2014/05-16/6181200.shtml>.

31   Lucy Macken, 'Access all areas, bought via Beauty Point', *The Sydney Morning Herald*, 2 November 2013.

32   Philip Wen and Lucy Macken, 'Chinese "King of the Mountain" brush with corruption scandal', *The Sydney Morning Herald*, 25 February 2016.

33   Catherine Armitage, 'Falun Gong ban hits uni earnings', *The Australian*, 12 September 2005; Sarah Martin, 'Bob Carr's think tank "operating as Chinese propaganda arm"', *The Australian*, 9 September 2016.

34   Martin, 'Bob Carr's think tank "operating as Chinese propaganda arm"'.

35 Knott and Aston, 'Don't become "propaganda vehicles" for China: Universities warned over donations'.

36 John Fitzgerald, 'Accommodating China's interests in Australia business as usual', *The Australian*, 2 September 2016.

37 Hagar Cohen, 'Australian universities the latest battleground in Chinese soft power offensive', *Background Briefing*, ABC Radio, 14 October 2016.

38 Quoted by Knott and Aston, 'Don't become "propaganda vehicles" for China'.

39 Anon., 'Dim Sam won't stop Wong show', *The Australian*, 9 September 2016.

40 Kelsey Monroe, 'Sam Dastyari donor steps down from university's China centre over "supposed Chinese influence"', *The Sydney Morning Herald*, 22 September 2016

41 Riordan, 'Sam Dastyari-linked political donor resigns from Bob Carr institute after major review'.

42 <http://www.australiachinarelations.org/about-us>.

43 <https://www.uts.edu.au/staff/leo-mian.liu>.

44 <http://www.acpprc.org.au/english/events/youth2015.asp>. This suggests that ACRI may be managed like a Confucius Institute, each of which has a 'foreign director' and a 'Chinese director'. The foreign director is the public face and the Chinese director is the power behind the throne (<http://english.hanban.org/node_7877.htm>).

45 Interview with Alex Joske, 25 September 2017

46 <http://www.acpprc.org.au/schinese/jinqi/2015/YconMay15.html>.

47 <http://www.acpprc.org.au/schinese/jinqi/2015/YconMay15.html>.

48 <http://australia.people.com.cn/n1/2017/0402/c408038-29186436.html>.

49 <http://politics.people.com.cn/n/2015/0903/c1001-27544025.html>.

50 Interview with Elena Collinson, senior project and research officer at ACRI, 17 July 2017.

51 Emailed response to questions from the author, 1 September 2017.

52 <www.alumni.uts.edu.au/news/tower/issue-11/the-new-silk-road>.

53 Emailed response to questions from the author, 1 September 2017.

54 Anon., 'Former Australian FM hails new level in Sino-Australian ties', *China Daily*, 19 November 2014.

55 Anon., 'China-Australia relations', *Global Times*, 10 December 2016.

56 <world.people.com.cn/n1/2016/0813/c1002-28634074.html>.

57 <world.people.com.cn/n/2015/0102/c1002-26312099.html>.

58 <http://world.people.com.cn/n/2015/0102/c1002-26312099.html>.

59 Bob Carr, 'Why Australia is missing the strategic train in Asia', *Australian Financial Review*, 14 September 2017.

60 <world.people.com.cn/n/2014/0729/c1002-25363671-2.html>.

61 Bob Carr, 'Australia, China, and the lunacy of Trump's talk of trade war', *The Guardian*, 26 November 2016.

62 James Laurenceson, 'China isn't Australia's biggest trade problem: It's the US', *The Sydney Morning Herald*, 30 November 2016.

63   Primrose Riordan, 'Australia "slaughtered" without Beijing links under Trump, Huang Xiangmo warns', *Australian Financial Review*, 12 December 2016.

64   <world.people.com.cn/n/2015/0903/c1002-27543874.html>.

65   Carr, *Diary of a Foreign Minister*.

66   Dylan Welch, 'Ernest Wong: Labor's go-to man for access to Chinese community', *7.30*, ABC TV, 19 September 2016.

67   Jamie Smyth, 'China's $10bn propaganda push spreads Down Under', *Financial Times*, 9 June 2016.

68   Prashanth Parameswaran, 'Beware China's political warfare campaign against US, allies: Experts', *The Diplomat*, 10 October 2015. Liu Qibao has said: 'Experience has shown that it is better when China's cultural products are "sold out" rather than "sent out"', prompting China's state-owned cultural organisations to make strategic acquisitions of Western cultural enterprises. See further at: Anne-Marie Brady, 'China's foreign propaganda machine', Wilson Center, Washington, D.C., 26 October 2015 <www.wilsoncenter.org/article/chinas-foreign-propaganda-machine#sthash.LM2r2qad.dpuf>.

69   John Fitzgerald and Wanning Sun, 'Australian media deals are a victory for Chinese propaganda', *The Interpreter*, Lowy Institute, 31 May 2016.

70   Brady, 'China's Foreign Propaganda Machine'.

71   John Fitzgerald quoted in Smith, 'China's $10bn propaganda push spreads Down Under'.

72   Philip Wen, 'China's propaganda arms push soft power in Australian media deals', *The Sydney Morning Herald*, 31 May 2016.

73   Fitzgerald and Sun, 'Australian media deals are a victory for Chinese propaganda'.

74   <http://www.scio.gov.cn/zxbd/wz/Document/1456644/1456644.htm>.

75   Anon., 'China tells journalists to learn "Marxist news values"', Reuters, 30 August 2014.

76   Ross Gittins, 'Australia and China, a partnership facing massive change', *The Sydney Morning Herald*, 20 August 2016; Ross Gittins, 'Australia not part of China's Silk Road expansion of trade, for now', *The Sydney Morning Herald*, 31 July 2016; <www.rossgittins.com/2016/08/fast-moving-china-is-big-and-bold-we.html>; Ross Gittins, 'China will keep doing its own thing', *The Sydney Morning Herald*, 30 July 2016.

77   Andrew Clark, 'China: It's got so big it changes everything', *Australian Financial Review*, 15 August 2016; Andrew Clark, 'Australia will be buffeted as China makes a priority of looking after its own', *Australian Financial Review*, 21 July 2016; Andrew Clark, 'China and Australia's complicated security arrangement', *Australian Financial Review*, 25 August 2016; Andrew Clark, 'Xi Jinping's balancing act between the old and the new economy', *Australian Financial Review*, 30 July 2016.

78   Simon Denyer, 'Money can't buy happiness: Why a massive rise in wealth left Chinese people less happy', *Washington Post*, 23 March 2017.

79   Brian Toohey, 'A better way of going to war', *Australian Financial Review*, 21 July 2016. See also: Brian Toohey, 'China's private sector investing heavily in R&D', *Australian Financial Review*, 1 August 2016; Brian Toohey, 'Xi's technocratic crackdown risks China's growth', *Australian Financial Review*, 8 August 2016; Brian Toohey, 'Why suddenly so anxious about foreign capital?', *Australian Financial Review*, 22 August 2016; Brian Toohey, 'Ignore all the fearmongering on Beijing ties', *Australian Financial Review*, 6 September 2016; Brian Toohey, 'Ausgrid denies provision of "critical" service', *Australian Financial Review*, 15 August 2016; Brian Toohey, 'Ausgrid rejection displays disturbing ignorance', *Australian Finaancial Review*, 15 August 2016.

80   Glenda Korporaal, 'China warns Australia not to join US patrols in South China Sea', *The Australian*, 19 July 2016; Glenda Korporaal, 'Let's tread carefully on South China Sea ruling', *The Australian*, 27 July 2016; Glenda Korporaal, 'Bob Carr warns on alienating China over South China Sea patrols', *The Australian*, 26 July 2016.

81   Shane Wright, 'China warms on islands row', *The West Australian*, 20 July 2016.

82   <http://news.xinhuanet.com/zgjx/2016-08/11/c_135585550.htm>. ['Impressions from visiting China: Why were Australian journalists moved to say their "expectations were exceeded"', *All-China Journalists Association Online*, 11 August 2016.

83   John Wallace, 'What's good for Rupert Murdoch should be good for Chau Chak Wing', *Australian Financial Review*, 8 August 2017.

84   Malcolm Farr, 'Bob Carr's backroom manouevering ends Chinese nightmare for Sydney academic', *News.com.au*, 3 April 2017; Troy Bramston, 'Megaphone diplomacy with China will always fail: Bob Carr', *The Australian*, 7 April 2017.

85   <soundcloud.com/user-340830825/feng-chongyi-research-is-not-a-dinner-party>.

86   When an ABC reporter tweeted about the Feng Chongyi interview, Carr was indignant at the suggestion that he claimed to have secured Feng's release. He demanded an apology and complained to the director of ABC News.

Chapter 6   Trade, invest, control

1   Chinese political scientist Xie Guijua in 'THAAD can be halted under Moon govt', *Global Times*, 21 May 2017.

2   <data.worldbank.org/indicator/NE.EXP.GNFS.ZS>.

3   <fred.stlouisfed.org/series/B020RE1Q156NBEA>.

4   <TIN-How-dependent-are-Australian-exports-to-China.pdf>.

5   <TIN-How-dependent-are-Australian-exports-to-China.pdf>.

6   Rory Medcalf (ed.), 'China's economic leverage: Perception and reality', National Security College, ANU, Policy Options Paper no. 2, 2017.

7   <dfat.gov.au/trade/agreements/chafta/official-documents/documents/chafta-chapter-9-investment.pdf>.

8   <dfat.gov.au/trade/agreements/chafta/fact-sheets/pages/key-outcomes.aspx>.

9   KPMG, *Demystifying Chinese Investment in Australia*, report by KPMG and the University of Sydney, 2017.

10 KPMG, *Demystifying Chinese Investment in Australia*.

11 Australian Tax Office, 'Register of Foreign Ownership of Agricultural Land: Report of registrations as at 30 June 2017', Australian Tax Office, Canberra, 2017.

12 Anon., 'China's agricultural challenges: Roads to be travelled', Price waterhouseCoopers, London, November 2015.

13 Brad Thompson, 'Chinese lining up for Australian agriculture businesses: HSBC', *Australian Financial Review*, 17 December 2017.

14 US$7.1 billion in 2015–16 to US$16.2 billion (converted at an exchange of A$1=US$0.79). Greater China includes Hong Kong, Macau and Taiwan. Source: Mergermarket Infographic.

15 Glenda Korporaal, 'Find an Aussie partner, Howard tells potential Chinese investors', *The Australian*, 17 March 2017. The official Xinhua News Agency took up Howard's call with alacrity: <news.xinhuanet.com/english/2017-03/17/c_136135799.htm>.

16 Peter Drysdale, 'Chinese state-owned enterprise investment in Australia', *East Asia Forum*, 25 August 2014.

17 Linda Jakobson and Andrew Parker, 'High time for proper debate on Chinese investment', *The Australian*, 25 February 2016. They add: 'Having party connections is integral to the way Chinese society functions.'

18 See <http://chinamatters.org.au/our-supporters/>.

19 Geoff Wade, 'Chinese investment in Australia needs closer scrutiny', *The Australian*, 9 March 2016.

20 Greg Levesque, 'China's evolving economic statecraft', *The Diplomat*, 12 April 2017.

21 Against all this, James Reilly manages to argue—after setting out in some detail how China is uniquely able to apply economic coercion using tools no other nation possesses—that China's economic statecraft lacks coherence, and Australia has little to worry about (James Reilly, 'China's economic statecraft: Turning wealth into power', Lowy Institute, undated).

22 Drysdale, 'Chinese state-owned enterprise investment in Australia'.

23 Yi-Zheng Lian, 'China, the party-corporate complex', *The New York Times*, 12 February 2017 (emphasis added).

24 Lu Bingyang and Teng Jing Xuan, 'Train manufacturer merges jobs of chairman, party secretary', *Caixin*, 28 November 2016.

25 Wei Yu, 'Party control in China's listed firms', School of Accountancy, The Chinese University of Hong Kong, January 2009 (unpublished) <admin.darden.virginia.edu/emUpload/uploaded2009/party_secretary(yuwei)(full_version).pdf>.

26   <www.globaltimes.cn/content/1024360.shtml>. See also Lu and Teng, 'Train manufacturer merges jobs of chairman, party secretary'.

27   Gwynne Guilford, 'Jack Ma: Mowing down demonstrators in Tiananmen Square was the "correct decision"', *Quartz*, 17 July 2013.

28   Paul Keating believes that China is not interested in challenging American hegemony, but is relaxed about what he sees as China's plan to 'colonise' economically fifty or so states to its west. See Christian Edwards, 'Keating's China bank plans "economic colonisation"', *Australian Banking and Finance*, 2016.

29   John Garnaut, 'Chinese diplomats run rings around Australia', *The Sydney Morning Herald*, 27 March 2015

30   Quoted by Garnaut, 'Chinese diplomats run rings around Australia'.

31   John Garnaut, 'Chinese military woos big business', *The Sydney Morning Herald*, 25 May 2013.

32   Anon., 'Fact check: Does the China Free Trade Agreement threaten Australian jobs?', *ABC News Online*, 13 August 2015.

33   Primrose Riordan, 'Bob Carr's research used to justify FTA', *Australian Financial Review*, 5 September 2016.

34   Anon., 'Fact check'.

35   'A coup for Australia': ABC Radio National, *The World Today*, 10 November 2014. A bad idea: 'Why an Australian FTA with China has never stacked up', *The Conversation*, 22 October 2013.

36   Geoff Wade, 'Visa and industrial sector traps lurk in the ChAFTA', The Drum, *ABC News Online*, 1 December 2015.

37   <dfat.gov.au/trade/agreements/chafta/official-documents/Pages/official-documents.aspx>.

38   Nick McKenzie, Richard Baker and Chris Uhlmann, 'Liberal Andrew Robb took $880k China job as soon as he left parliament', *The Age*, 6 June 2017.

39   Ian Verrender, 'Australia's FTA experience backs up Treasurer's Ausgrid decision', *ABC News Online*, 15 August 2016.

40   Peter Martin, 'Free trade agreements "preferential" and dangerous, says Productivity Commission', *The Sydney Morning Herald*, 24 June 2015.

41   Geoff Wade, 'Are we fully aware of China's ChAFTA aspirations?', The Drum, *ABC News Online*, 1 December 2015.

42   Zheping Huang, 'Chinese president Xi Jinping has vowed to lead the "new world order"', *Quartz*, 22 February 2017.

43   <www.globaltimes.cn/content/927245.shtml>.

44   Eric Lorber, 'Economic coercion, with a Chinese twist', *Foreign Policy*, 28 February 2017; Anon., 'Ralls Corp's Oregon wind farms blocked by President Obama', *Huffington Post*, 28 November 2012.

45   Sarah Danckert, 'FIRB chairman Brian Wilson suspends himself as adviser to Carlyle investment house', *The Sydney Morning Herald*, 5 October 2016.

46 Extensive Chinese investment in health care also warrants attention. See, for example, <www.corrs.com.au/thinking/insights/chinese-investment-in-australia-the-rooster-crows-before-sunrise-breaks-the-dawn/>.

47 Chris Uhlmann, 'Chinese investment in Australia's power grid explained', *ABC News Online*, 21 August 2016; Phillip Coorey, 'Scott Morrison says Ausgrid sale to Chinese contrary to the national interest', *Australian Financial Review*, 11 August 2016.

48 Brett Foley, Perry Williams and Prudence Ho, 'Chow Tai Fook adds Australia power firm to property, jewelry', *Bloomberg*, 16 March 2017.

49 Peter Jennings, 'Security crucial when leasing assets to foreign companies', *The Australian*, 20 October 2015.

50 Joe Kelly, 'Ausgrid: Economic "populism behind decision", says Bob Carr', *The Australian*, 12 August 2016.

51 <news.xinhuanet.com/english/2016-08/12/c_135590666.htm>.

52 Jessica Gardner, 'DUET backs $74b takeover bid from Li Ka-shing's Cheung Kong Infrastructure', *Australian Financial Review*, 16 January 2017; Eric Ng, 'Cheung Kong Infrastructure's bid for Duet faces tough scrutiny in Canberra, say analysts', *South China Morning Post*, 7 December 2016.

53 Australian Cyber Security Centre, *2017 Threat Report*, Australian Cyber Security Centre, Canberra, 2017, p. 48.

54 John Kerin, 'Chinese hackers could shut down Australian power grid, warns former spy boss David Irvine', *Australian Financial Review*, 9 March 2015.

55 <i-hls.com/archives/61652>.

56 <www.energynetworks.com.au/about-us/board-of-directors>.

57 <www.energynetworks.com.au/sites/default/files/key_concepts_report_2016.pdf>.

58 For example, its chair from 2001–10, Qin Xiao, served as a party official in Beijing and is related through his sister to the princelings.

59 <www.northqueenslandregister.com.au/story/3365767/nq-trade-with-china-moves-forward/>.

60 <www.tiq.qld.gov.au/chinese-delegation-explore-opportunities-with-townsville-and-north-queensland/>.

61 <rajcairnsreport.wordpress.com/2013/03/19/another-labor-mayor-causing-problems-cox-and-hill-in-tit-for-tat-spat-townsville-bulletin-news/>.

62 Lisa Murray, 'China eyes new Sydney airport as part of "belt and road" plan', *Australian Financial Review*, 28 May 2017.

63 'A national fibreoptic backbone will be built for Pakistan not only for internet traffic … but also for terrestrial distribution of broadcast TV, which will cooperate with Chinese media in the "dissemination of Chinese culture".' <indianexpress.com/article/india/china-pakistan-economic-corridor-politics-security-risk-amid-sweeping-china-influence-4657511/>.

64 Anon., 'Backing Big Brother: Chinese facial recognition firms appeal to funds', Reuters, 13 November 2017.

65 One of the best sources, with an Australian focus, is Geoff Wade, 'China's "One Belt, One Road" initiative', Parliamentary Library briefing, Canberra, 2016, <https://www.aph.gov.au/About_Parliament/Parliamentary_Departments/Parliamentary_Library/pubs/BriefingBook45p/ChinasRoad>.

66 <www.youtube.com/watch?v=3W_vp3FKdIg>.

67 Ou Xiaoli, 'Laying the foundations for China's "One Belt, One Road"', *South China Morning Post*, 25 November 2015.

68 Wendy Wu, 'How the Communist Party controls China's state-owned industrial titans', *South China Morning Post*, 17 June 2017.

69 Christopher K. Johnson, 'President Xi Jinping's "Belt and Road" initiative: A practical assessment of the Chinese Communist Party's roadmap for China's global resurgence', Center for Strategic and International Studies, Washington, D.C., March 2016.

70 Anon., 'China offers wisdom in global governance', *Xinhuanet*, 6 October 2017.

71 Ben Blanchard and Elizabeth Piper, 'China invites Britain to attend new Silk Road summit: Sources', Reuters, 8 February 2017. Bloomberg notes that AIIB 'is central to President Xi Jinping's ambition to seek a bigger voice in global affairs and deeper economic integration with its neighbors' (<www.bloomberg.com/news/articles/2016-06-24/china-led-aiib-announces-first-loans-in-xi-push-for-influence>).

72 Wade, 'China's "One Belt, One Road" initiative'.

73 Wade Shepard, 'China's "New Silk Road" is derailed in Sri Lanka by political chaos and violent protests', *Forbes*, 21 February 2017.

74 Jessica Meyers, 'Sri Lankans who once embraced Chinese investment are now wary of Chinese domination', *Los Angeles Times*, 25 February 2017.

75 Bharatha Mallawarachi, 'Sri Lanka, China sign long-delayed $1.5 billion port deal', *Washington Post*, 29 July 2017.

76 Brahma Chellaney in <www.japantimes.co.jp/opinion/2015/03/09/commentary/world-commentary/the-silk-glove-for-chinas-iron-fist/#.WK0icBF0VhA>.

77 Michael Fumento, 'As the U.S. sleeps, China conquers Latin America', *Forbes*, 15 October 2015.

78 Andrea Ghiselli, 'The Belt, the Road and the PLA', *China Brief*, The Jamestown Foundation, vol. 15, no. 20, 19 October 2015.

79 Ghiselli, 'The Belt, the Road and the PLA'.

80 Andrew Erickson and Conor Kennedy, 'China's maritime militia', CNA Corporation, 7 March 2016.

81 Anon., 'Pentagon says China's PLA expanding its global footprint', *The Economic Times*, 13 June 2017 <economictimes.indiatimes.com/news/international/world-news/pentagon-says-chinas-pla-expanding-its-global-footprint/articleshow/59119655.cms>.

82 Geoff Wade, 'Landbridge, Darwin and the PRC', *The Strategist*, Australian Strategic Policy Institute, 9 November 2015.

83   Ghiselli, 'The Belt, the Road and the PLA'.

84   Michael Sainsbury, 'Australia stuck in the middle of China's latest attempt at "empire-building"', *Crikey*, 15 May 2017.

85   <news.xinhuanet.com/world/2014-11/17/c_1113285659_2.htm>.

86   <news.xinhuanet.com/english/2015-11/16/c_134822370.htm>.

87   <roll.sohu.com/20150814/n418857073.shtml>.

88   <au.china-embassy.org/eng/gdxw/t1289130.htm>.

89   Rowan Callick, 'One Belt, One Road China advisory group launches in Melbourne', *The Australian*, 27 May 2017.

90   Callick, 'One Belt, One Road China advisory group launches in Melbourne'.

91   <ciw.anu.edu.au/events/event_details.php?id=16356>.

92   <www.china-un.ch/eng/wjyw/t1437164.htm>.

93   Rowan Callick, 'Investor certainty pledge to China', *The Australian*, 21 February 2017.

94   Primrose Riordan, 'Andrew Robb under fire for pushing China's One Belt One Road policy', *Australian Financial Review*, 31 October 2016.

95   <http://www.australiachinaobor.org.au>.

96   Anne-Marie Brady, 'China's foreign propaganda machine', *Journal of Democracy*, vol. 26, no. 4, October 2015, pp. 39–40.

97   Henry Cook, 'Winston Peters says western world is too hard on China over freedom issues', *Stuff*, 5 December 2017; Fran O'Sullivan, 'Winston Peters works to keep China sweet', *New Zealand Herald*, 10 December 2017.

98   <english.cntv.cn/2015/07/07/ARTI1436223299326525.shtml>.

99   <news.xinhuanet.com/2016-12/11/c_1120095586.htm>.

100   <paper.people.com.cn/rmrb/html/2016-01/10/nw.D110000renmrb_20160110_2-03.htm>. The article extensively quotes Peter Cai, formerly of the Lowy Institute but now an adviser to the CEO of Virgin Australia. Virgin Australia is now partly owned by China's HNA Aviation Group.

101   Ana Swanson, 'Chinese propagandists are using adorable kids to take on Donald Trump', *Washington Post*, 18 May 2017.

102   Zheping Huang, 'China's craziest English-language propaganda videos are made by one mysterious studio', *Quartz*, 27 October 2015.

103   Nadia Daly, 'One Belt One Road: NT businesses welcome Chinese investment despite reluctance over "new Silk Road"', *ABC News Online*, 8 August 2017.

104   Jamie Smyth, 'Australia rejects China push on Silk Road strategy', *Financial Times*, 22 March 2017.

Chapter 7   Seduction and coercion

1   Tom Allard and John Garnaut, 'Gas boom as China signs $25bn deal', *The Sydney Morning Herald*, 9 August 2002, p. 5.

2   Anon., 'Gas contract avails ties with Australia', *People's Daily*, 17 September 2002.

3   Chen Yonglin, quoted in 25 June 2005 <www.epochtimes.com/gb/5/6/25/ n965354.htm> (in Chinese).

4   Kelly Burke, 'Howard stands firm on Dalai Lama meeting', *The Age*, 17 May 2002.

5   Anon., 'Gas contract avails ties with Australia'.

6   John Garnaut, 'Are Chau Chak Wing's circles of influence in Australia-China ties built on hot air?', *The Sydney Morning Herald*, 16 October 2015.

7   Rory Medcalf (ed.), 'China's economic leverage: Perception and reality', Policy Options Paper no. 2, National Security College, ANU, March 2017.

8   Linda Jakobson and Andrew Parker, 'High time for a proper debate on Chinese investments', *The Australian*, 25 February 2016.

9   Geoff Wade, 'Chinese investment in Australia needs closer scrutiny', *The Australian*, 9 March 2016.

10 Linda Jakobson and Bates Gill, *China Matters: Getting it right for Australia*, Melbourne: Black Inc., 2017.

11 Stephen FitzGerald, 'Managing Australian foreign policy in a Chinese world', *The Conversation*, 17 March 2017.

12 FitzGerald, 'Managing Australian foreign policy in a Chinese world'.

13 Paul Kelly, 'Friend or foe? Our China dilemma is our biggest test', *The Australian*, 17 August 2016. In his habitual practice of being the first to identify crises, landmarks and turning points in Australian, Asian and world history, Kelly describes the Drysdale report as 'audacious', 'a wake-up jolt', 'shattering delusions', 'confronting' and a 'watershed'. It sank like a stone.

14 East Asian Bureau of Economic Research and China Center for International Economic Exchanges, *Partnership for Change*, Australia–China Joint Economic Report, Canberra: ANU Press, 2016, p. 14.

15 *Partnership for Change*, p. 14.

16 *Partnership for Change*, p. 19.

17 Peter Drysdale, 'Chinese state-owned enterprise investment in Australia', *East Asia Forum*, 25 August 2014.

18 Chen Yonglin, 'Australia is in the process of becoming China's backyard', published in Chinese in *China in Perspective*, 31 August 2016 and translated into English by Chun Gwai lo.

19 Peter Drysdale, 'Australian needs to get its act together on China, and fast', *East Asia Forum*, 7 June 2009.

20 Peter Drysdale and John Denton, 'China's influence and how to use it to Australia's advantage', *Australian Financial Review*, 3 October 2017.

21 <www.china-un.org/eng/gyzg/t555926.htm>.

22 Cheng Li and Lucy Xu, 'Chinese thinks tanks: A new "revolving door" for elite recruitment', *Brookings*, 10 February 2017.

23 Anon., 'China to introduce dual-management on think tanks', *Xinhuanet*, 4 May 2017.

24 Li and Xu, 'Chinese think tanks'.

25 *Partnership for Change*, p. 19.

26 This section has benefited from the work of Robert Blackwill and Jennifer Harris, *War by Other Means: Geoeconomics and statecraft*, Cambridge, Mass.: Belknap Press, 2016, and of William Norris, *Chinese Economic Statecraft: Commercial actors, grand strategy, and state control*, Ithaca: Cornell University Press, 2016.

27 Blackwill and Harris, *War by Other Means*, p. 129; Tone Sutterud and Elisabeth Ulven, 'Norway criticised over snub to Dalai Lama during Nobel committee visit', *The Guardian*, 7 May 2014.

28 Quoted by Blackwill and Harris, *War by Other Means*, p. 129.

29 Sewell Chan, 'Norway and China restore ties, 6 years after Nobel prize dispute', *The New York Times*, 19 December 2016.

30 Blackwill and Harris, *War by Other Means*, p. 130.

31 Grant Holloway, 'Australia snubs Dalai Lama', *CNN.com*, 16 May 2002; Daniel Flitton, 'Praise for Dalai Lama snub', *The Sydney Morning Herald*, 29 June 2012.

32 Andrew Marszal, 'Dalai Lama criticises David Cameron for "money over morality" snub', *The Telegraph*, 23 September 2015.

33 Anon., 'Dalai Lama's visit: Botswana's President Dr Ian Khama tells China, "We are not your colony"', *The aPolitical*, 19 August 2017.

34 Quoted by Anon., 'Beijing's new weapon in economic war: Chinese tourists', *Inquirer.net*, 26 June 2017.

35 Blackwill and Harris, *War by Other Means*, p. 10.

36 James Reilly, 'China's economic statecraft: Turning wealth into power', Lowy Institute, 2013.

37 Stephen FitzGerald, 'Managing Australian foreign policy in a Chinese world', *The Conversation*, 17 March 2017.

38 Blackwill and Harris, *War by Other Means*, p. 3.

39 Quoted by Blackwill and Harris, *War by Other Means*, p. 129.

40 <www.globaltimes.cn/content/1035359.shtml>; <http://www.globaltimes.cn/content/1037529.shtml>.

41 Some relevant references here are: David Josef Volodzko, 'What a jet-lagged football team says about China-Korea relations', *South China Morning Post*, 2 April 2017; Cary Huang, 'Opinion: Why China's shadow boycott of South Korea is self-defeating', *South China Morning Post*, 2 April 2017; Peter Rutherford, 'Chinese women golfers may shun LPGA event amid China-South Korea tensions', Reuters, 30 March 2017.

42 Michael Holtz, 'China gets testier as South Korea advances its missile defense plans', *Christian Science Monitor*, 8 February 2017.

43 Brenda Goh and Muyu Zu, 'Playing favourites? Chinese tourism under scrutiny as Lunar New Year nears', *The Sydney Morning Herald*, 25 January, 2017.

44 Goh and Zu, 'Playing favourites?'.

45 Blackwill and Harris, *War by Other Means*, p. 109.
46 Michael Komesaroff, 'Make the foreign serve China', Center for Strategic and International Studies, paper no. 2, March 2017.
47 Blackwill and Harris, *War by Other Means*, p. 108.
48 Anders Corr and Priscilla Tacujan, 'Chinese political and economic influence in the Philippines: Implications for alliances and the South China Sea dispute', *Journal of Political Risk*, vol. 1, no. 3, July 2013.
49 Blackwill and Harris, *War by Other Means*, p. 113.
50 Corr and Tacujan, 'Chinese political and economic influence in the Philippines'.
51 Blackwill and Harris, *War by Other Means*, p. 116.
52 Martin Fackler, 'Virus infects computers in Japan's parliament', *The New York Times*, 25 October 2011; Blackwill and Harris, *War by Other Means*, p. 109.
53 Blackwill and Harris, *War by Other Means*, p. 101.
54 Goh and Zu, 'Playing favourites?'.
55 Chris Horton, 'China's attempt to punish Taiwan by throttling tourism has seriously backfired', *South China Morning Post*, 9 February 2017.
56 Horton, 'China's attempt to punish Taiwan by throttling tourism has seriously backfired'.
57 Blackwill and Harris, *War by Other Means*, p. 108.
58 Helena Smith, 'Greece blocks EU's criticism at UN of China's human rights record', *The Guardian*, 19 June 2017.
59 Nick Cumming-Bruce and Somini Senguptajune, 'In Greece, China finds an ally against human rights criticism', *The New York Times*, 19 June 2017.
60 <www.seatrade-maritime.com/news/europe/china-cosco-shipping-finally-gets-piraeus-port-majority-stake.html>.
61 Roie Yellinek, 'How can Greece pay back China?', BESA Center Perspectives Paper no. 523, 9 July 2017.
62 Anon., 'Turkey promises to eliminate anti-China media reports', Reuters, 3 August 2017.
63 Lindsay Murdoch, 'Beijing article warns Australia over South China Sea', *The Sydney Morning Herald*, 2 January 2018.
64 Bob Carr, *Diary of a Foreign Minister*, Sydney: NewSouth Publishing, 2014, p. 331.
65 Patrick Hatch, 'Who really owns this 19 per cent stake in Virgin Australia?', *The Sydney Morning Herald*, 7 August 2017; David Barboza, 'A Chinese giant is on a buying spree. Who is behind it?', *The New York Times*, 9 May 2017.
66 Eryk Bagshaw and Peter Hannam, 'Pilot shortage: Chinese-owned airport in Australia looks to increase its flights by 1000%', *The Sydney Morning Herald*, 27 December 2017.
67 <www.tiq.qld.gov.au/download/business-interest/invest/trade-investment-strategy-TIQ.pdf>.
68 Sue Williams, 'Chinese dominate in tourism investment', *The Sydney Morning Herald*, 27 January 2017.

69   Karen Wales, 'Chinese dominate in tourism investment', *Colliers Radar*, Colliers International, February 2017.

Chapter 8   Spies old and new

1   Brian Toohey, 'Enemies old and new', *Inside Story*, 2 November 2016.
2   Anon., 'China blamed after ASIO blueprints stolen in major cyber attack on Canberra HQ', *ABC News Online*, 28 May 2013.
3   Jonathan Kaiman, 'China calls Australian spy HQ plans hacking claims "groundless"', *The Guardian*, 29 May 2013.
4   Primrose Riordan and Markus Mannheim, 'ASIO's new neighbours' links to China's government', *Australian Financial Review*, 2 November 2015.
5   Kirsten Lawson, 'Failed bidders raise eyebrows at high price for Currong and Allawah flats', *Canberra Times*, 12 February 2016.
6   John Thistleton, 'Chief Minister Andrew Barr and developer Terry Shaw launch Campbell 5 units', *Canberra Times*, 21 September 2015.
7   Riordan and Mannheim, 'ASIO's new neighbours' links to China's government'.
8   Jewel Topsfield, 'Australia grants asylum to Chinese diplomat', *The Age*, 9 July 2005
9   Aaron Patrick, 'Australia is losing the battle against China's "citizen spies"', *Australian Financial Review*, 3–4 September 2016.
10   Bill Gertz, 'China's intelligence networks in United States include 25,000 spies', *Washington Free Beacon*, 11 July 2017.
11   Patrick, 'Australia is losing the battle against China's "citizen spies"'.
12   Patrick, 'Australia is losing the battle against China's "citizen spies"'.
13   Paul Monk, 'Chinese spies and our national interest', *Quadrant Online*, June 2012, <https://quadrant.org.au/magazine/2012/06/chinese-espionage-and-australia-s-national-interest/>.
14   James Jiann Hua To, *Qiaowu: Extra-territorial policies for the overseas Chinese*, Leiden: Koninklijke Brill, 2014, p. 44.
15   Andrew Greene, 'Chinese spies "very active" in Australia, departing defence secretary warns', *ABC News Online*, 12 May 2017.
16   Andrew Greene, 'Chinese spies in Australia on the rise, former diplomat Chen Yonglin says', *ABC News Online*, 20 November 2016.
17   Christopher Joye, 'Spy wars fuelled by territorial claims', *Australian Financial Review*, 28 April 2014.
18   <edition.cnn.com/2014/05/20/world/asia/china-unit-61398/>.
19   Paul Maley and Mitchell Bingemann, 'Spies feared China was hacking the NBN', *The Australian*, 28 March 2012.
20   US House of Representatives Permanent Select Committee of Intelligence, 'Investigative report on the US national security issues posed by Chinese telecommunications companies Huawei and ZTE', 8 October 2012 <https://intelligence.house.gov/sites/intelligence.house.gov/files/documents/huawei-zte%20investigative%20report%20(final).pdf>.

21 As premier of Victoria, Brumby had worked with Huawei to help establish an RMIT training centre (Michael Sainsbury, 'Huawei names John Brumby, Alexander Downer board members', *The Australian*, 6 June 2011). See also Maley and Bingemann, 'Spies feared China was hacking the NBN'.

22 Sainsbury, 'Huawei names John Brumby, Alexander Downer board members'.

23 'Investigative report on the US national security issues posed by Chinese telecommunications companies Huawei and ZTE'.

24 Anon., 'The company that spooked the world', *The Economist*, 4 August 2012.

25 'Investigative report on the US national security issues posed by Chinese telecommunications companies Huawei and ZTE', pp. 13–14.

26 Evan S. Medeiros, Roger Cliff, Keith Crane and James C. Mulvenon, 'A new direction for China's defense industry', RAND Corporation, 2005 <https://www.rand.org/content/dam/rand/pubs/monographs/2005/RAND_MG334.pdf>, p. 218.

27 Bill Gertz, 'Chinese telecom firm tied to spy ministry', *Washington Times*, 11 October 2011.

28 Phillip Coorey, 'ASIO not the target of my outburst, Robb explains', *The Sydney Morning Herald*, 28 March 2012.

29 Paul Osborne, 'Opposition slams NBN exclusion of Huawei', *The Australian*, 26 March 2012.

30 James Chessell, 'Kerry Stokes: Secrets to my China success', *Australian Financial Review*, 3 November 2012.

31 Maley and Bingemann, 'Spies feared China was hacking the NBN'.

32 Hamish McDonald and Mark Forbes, 'Downer flags China shift', *The Age*, 18 August 2004.

33 Chen Yonglin, at a press conference in a Chatswood club on the afternoon of 22 June 2005 and confirmed in correspondence with the author on 8 January 2018.

34 Peter Cai, 'Huawei "extremely disappointed" with NBN ban', *The Sydney Morning Herald*, 1 November 2013.

35 'Investigative report on the US national security issues posed by Chinese telecommunications companies Huawei and ZTE', pp. 34–5.

36 Paul Wiseman and Sadie Gurmin, 'Chinese cellphone giant ZTE to pay US almost $900M for breaking Iran sanctions', *The Mercury News*, 7 March 2017.

37 <http://www.zte.com.cn/global/about/press-center/news/201703ma/0307ma>.

38 Allie Coyne, 'Australian MPs still scared of Huawei', *iTnews*, 17 October 2016.

39 Christopher Joye and Aaron Patrick, 'Chinese spies may have read all MPs emails for a year', *Australian Financial Review*, 28 April 2014.

40 Chris Johnson and Chris Wilson, 'Ex-ASIO director helped Raiders', *The Canberra Times*, 31 March 2012.

41 Chris Wilson, 'Huawei is the real deal for Raiders', *The Sydney Morning Herald*, 31 March 2012. Huawei had also been negotiating with the ACT Brumbies rugby union team. When a journalist asked the club's chief executive, 'Are the Raiders a political pawn for Huawei to lobby the Federal Government?' he emphatically replied, 'Absolutely not.' With a preternatural insight into Huawei's motives, he added: 'In terms of his [Richardson's] ASIO links, it had absolutely nothing to do with getting the sponsor or not getting the sponsor. I can understand people making that inquiry, but absolutely not.'

42 Ray Shaw, 'Huawei and Canberra Raiders winning partnership', *iTWire Newsletter*, 29 March 2017.

43 'Investigative report on the US national security issues posed by Chinese telecommunications companies Huawei and ZTE', p. 2.

44 Ben Grubb, 'Telcos could face Huawei ban, Malcolm Turnbull confirms', *The Sydney Morning Herald*, 27 July 2015.

45 See anon., 'The company that spooked the world', and Medeiros, Cliff, Crane and Mulvenon, 'A new direction for China's defense industry', p. 218.

46 Peter Simpson, 'Huawei devices dropped amid security concerns', *South China Morning Post*, 14 January 2014. The story was originally published in a British Sunday newspaper. Nevertheless, Britain has allowed Huawei to supply equipment to British Telecom.

47 <e.huawei.com/mediafiles/MediaFiles/5/E/7/%7B5E763722-D55C-4813-A6A7-58079BC5C82A%7DState%20Grid%20of%20China%20Powers%20Up%20with%20Huawei%20Storage%20Solution.pdf>.

48 'Investigative report on the US national security issues posed by Chinese telecommunications companies Huawei and ZTE', p. 3.

49 Geoff Wade, 'The State Grid Corporation of China: Its Australian engagement and military links', *The Interpreter*, Lowy Institute, 17 December 2015 <www.lowyinstitute.org/the-interpreter/state-grid-corporation-china-its-australian-engagement-and-military-links>.

50 Greg Sheridan, 'A questionable risk to security—Huawei an extraordinary creation', *The Australian*, 18 May 2013.

51 Greg Sheridan, 'Turnbull government carefully tackles Chinese interference', *The Australian*, 17 June 2017.

52 Juro Osawa, 'AT&T deal collapse forces Huawei to rethink global plans', *The Information*, 9 January 2018.

53 As told to the author by one who heard it from Credlin.

54 Simon Benson, 'Tony Abbott says China visit is most important trip by Australian Prime Minister', *News.com.au*, 10 April 2014.

55 Nigel Inkster, 'China's draft intelligence law', International Institute for Strategic Studies, blog, 26 May 2017 <http://www.iiss.org/en/iiss%20voices/blogsections/iiss-voices-2017-adeb/may-8636/chinas-draft-intelligence-law-5b2e>.

56 John Schindler, 'The unpleasant truth about Chinese espionage', *The Observer*, 22 April 2016.

57 Nate Thayer, 'How the Chinese recruit American journalists as spies', *Asia Sentinel*, 4 July 2017.

58 Brandi Buchman, 'Bond revoked for ex-CIA agent charged with spying for China', *Courthouse News*, 10 July 2017.

59 Philip Dorling, 'China spies on top ALP figures', *The Canberra Times*, 11 July 2008.

60 Richard Baker, Philip Dorling and Nick McKenzie, 'Defence leaks dirt file on own minister', *The Sydney Morning Herald*, 26 March 2009. Liu was also a member of the ACPPRC.

61 Richard Baker and Philip Dorling, 'Defence "rejected" minister spy link concerns', *The Sydney Morning Herald*, 7 May 2009.

62 Richard Baker and Philip Dorling, 'Minister snared in row', *The Sydney Morning Herald*, 27 March 2009.

63 Richard Baker, Philip Dorling and Nick McKenzie, 'ALP donor Helen Liu had close ties with a senior Chinese military intelligence operative', *The Sydney Morning Herald*, 12 June 2017.

64 Baker and Dorling, 'Defence "rejected" minister spy link concerns'.

65 Richard Baker, Philip Dorling and Nick McKenzie, 'Secrets and lies', *The Sydney Morning Herald*, 20 April 2013.

66 Baker and Dorling, 'Minister snared in row'.

67 Richard Baker, Philip Dorling and Nick McKenzie, 'Secret payments to Labor MP listed in Liu files', *The Sydney Morning Herald*, 3 February 2010.

68 Richard Baker, Philip Dorling and Nick McKenzie, 'Immigration probes Helen Liu marriage', *The Sydney Morning Herald*, 18 September 2013.

69 Baker, Dorling and McKenzie, 'Immigration probes Helen Liu marriage'.

70 Baker, Dorling and McKenzie, 'Secrets and lies'.

71 Baker, Dorling and McKenzie, 'Secrets and lies'.

72 Alexi Mostrous and Billy Kenber, 'Fears over rise of Chinese CCTV', *The Times*, 16 September 2016.

73 <ipvm.com/reports/heres-what-really-sets-hikvision-apart>.

74 Xioa Yu, 'Is the world's biggest surveillance camera maker sending footage to China?', *VOA*, 21 November 2016; John Honovich, 'Hikvision CEO admits Hikvision China state-owned company', *IPVM*, 6 October 2016; John Honovich, 'Hikvision and the Chinese government', *IPVM*, 7 December 2016.

75 John Honovich, 'Hikvision exec simultaneously Chinese government security leader', *IPVM*, 27 April 2015; John Honovich, 'Hikvision and the China Communist Party', *IPVM*, 12 January 2016.

76 <ipvm.com/reports/hikvision-cetc-mps>.

77 Yu, 'Is the world's biggest surveillance camera maker sending footage to China?'.

78   Interview with the author, 6 March 2017.

79   Its cameras have been hacked (<ipvm.com/reports/the-hikvision-hacking-scandal-returns>).

80   <hznews.hangzhou.com.cn/jingji/content/2016-01/11/content_6039653.htm>.

81   <ipvm.com/reports/hik-oems-dir>.

82   Interview with the author, 3 August 2017.

83   <ipvm.com/reports/hik-backdoor>.

84   <ics-cert.us-cert.gov/advisories/ICSA-17-124-01>.

85   Honovich, 'Hikvision and the China Communist Party'.

86   Chris Uhlmann, 'China blamed for "massive" cyber attack on Bureau of Meteorology', *ABC News Online*, 2 December 2015; Andrew Greene, 'Bureau of Meteorology hacked by foreign spies in massive attack, report shows', *ABC News Online*, 12 October 2016.

87   Hamish Boland-Rudder, 'Capital the top spot for weather man', *The Canberra Times*, 30 August 2013.

88   Uhlmann, 'China blamed for "massive" cyber attack on Bureau of Meteorology'.

89   Andrew Greene, 'Chinese technology on Australian supercomputer sparks security concerns', *ABC News Online*, 19 November 2016.

90   Bill Gertz, 'Military warns Chinese computer gear poses cyber spy threat', *Washington Free Beacon*, 24 October 2016.

91   Interview with the author, 15 March 2017.

92   John Lee, 'Innovation in China: More than a fast follower?', *The Diplomat*, 9 June 2016.

93   James Scott and Drew Spaniel, *China's Espionage Dynasty*, Institute for Critical Infrastructure Technology, 2016, pp. 10–11.

94   Quoted by William Hannas, James Mulvenon and Anna Puglisi, *Chinese Industrial Espionage*, London: Routledge, 2013, p. 126.

95   Richard A. Clarke, 'How China steals our secrets', *The New York Times*, 2 April 2012.

96   Erin Ailworth, 'Trial over theft of wind technology spotlights U.S.-China Tensions', *The Wall Street Journal*, 6 January 2018.

97   Scott and Spaniel, *China's Espionage Dynasty*, p. 15.

98   Scott and Spaniel, *China's Espionage Dynasty*, p. 18.

99   Andrew Fowler and Peter Cronau, 'Hacked!', *Four Corners*, ABC TV, online transcript, 29 May 2013; Anon., '"You're on your own": Codan fights back after Chinese hacking attack', *The Sydney Morning Herald*, 25 June 2015.

100 Anon., '"You're on your own": Codan fights back after Chinese hacking attack'.

101 Isaac Leung, 'Codan network hacked by Chinese', *Electronics News*, 29 May 2013.

102 Des Ball speaking to Fowler and Cronau, 'Hacked!', *Four Corners*.

103 John Schindler, 'The unpleasant truth about Chinese espionage', *The Observer*, 22 April 2016.

104 Josh Kenworthy, 'In a Midwestern cornfield, a scene of Chinese theft and espionage', *Christian Science Monitor*, 11 April 2016.

105 Schindler, 'The unpleasant truth about Chinese espionage'.

106 Schindler, 'The unpleasant truth about Chinese espionage'.

107 Anon., 'China warns women off handsome foreign spies in "Dangerous Love" comic', *ABC News Online*, 21 April 2016.

108 Alex Joske, 'Incident at university pharmacy highlights a divided Chinese community, *Woroni*, 28 August 2016.

109 Pavel Polityuk and Eric Auchard, 'Petya attack "likely cover" for malware installation in Ukraine', *iTnews*, 30 June 2017.

110 Allie Coyne, 'Australia has created a cyber warfare unit', *iTnews*, 30 June 2017.

111 <http://www.deakin.edu.au/research/research-news/articles/boost-for-cyber-security-collaboration>.

112 Chris Uhlmann, 'China blamed for "massive" cyber attack on Bureau of Meteorology computer', *ABC News Online*, 2 December 2015.

113 <nsclab.org/nsclab/collaboration.html>.

114 <www.deakin.edu.au/research/research-news/articles/boost-for-cyber-security-collaboration>.

115 <sinosphere.blogs.nytimes.com/2015/01/06/university-in-xian-opens-school-of-cyberengineering/?_r=0>.

116 <news.xidian.edu.cn/info/1004/5824.htm>.

117 <xyh.xidian.edu.cn/info/1020/1890.htm>.

118 <escholarship.org/uc/item/6f26w11m#page-4>.

119 <renshichu.bit.edu.cn/mxms/lyys/89142.htm>.

120 <www.xidian.edu.cn/info/1020/3374.htm>.

121 <news.xidian.edu.cn/info/2106/195863.htm>.

122 <www.weihai.gov.cn/art/2016/11/10/art_16616_785996.html>.

123 <www.81.cn/2016hjcllqzn/2016-04/21/content_7017010.htm>.

124 <mis.xidian.edu.cn/html/team/domestic/2017/0306/20.html>.

125 <info.xidian.edu.cn/info/1010/11236.htm>.

126 <http://www.edu-australia.org/publish/portal72/tab5536/info116240.htm>.

127 <http://ieeexplore.ieee.org/document/7116415/>; <http://ieeexplore.ieee.org/document/7802648/>.

128 Stephen Chen, 'Top 5 most secretive and mysterious research universities in China', *South China Morning Post*, 19 April 2015.

129 Anders Corr, 'Ban official Chinese student organizations abroad', *Forbes*, 4 June 2017.

130 Scott and Spaniel, *China's Espionage Dynasty*, p. 34.

131 US Department of Justice, Federal Bureau of Investigation, 'Higher education and national security: The targeting of sensitive, proprietary and classified

information on campuses of higher education', April 2011, p. 9 <https://www.fbi.gov/file-repository/higher-education-national-security.pdf/view>.
132 Scott and Spaniel, *China's Espionage Dynasty*, p. 37.

Chapter 9 'Malicious insiders' and scientific organisations

1   James Jiann Hua To, *Qiaowu: Extra-territorial policies for the overseas Chinese*, Leiden: Koninklijke Brill, 2014, p. 73ff.
2   ASIO, *ASIO Annual Report 2016–17*, ASIO, 2017.
3   ASIO, *ASIO Annual Report 2015–16*, ASIO, 2016.
4   In 2007 the former diplomat Chen Yonglin revealed that Chinese missions often play the leading role in setting up Chinese professionals groups in an effort to use them to influence the mainstream. See Madalina Hubert, 'Ex-envoy details Chinese regime's overseas scheme', *The Epoch Times*, 7 June 2007 <www.theepochtimes.com/n3/1749162-ex-envoy-details-chinese-regimes-overseas-scheme/>.
5   <www.gqb.gov.cn/news/2017/0324/42073.shtml>.
6   <https://taschinese.com/thread-189619-1-1.html>.
7   <news.xinhuanet.com/2016-09/05/c_1119513745.htm>.
8   Scott Harold, 'The U.S.-China cyber agreement: A good first step', *The Cypher Brief*, 31 July 2016.
9   To, *Qiaowu*, p. 43.
10 To, *Qiaowu*, pp. 43–4.
11 James Scott and Drew Spaniel, *China's Espionage Dynasty*, Institute for Critical Infrastructure Technology, 2016, pp. 10–11.
12 Joshua Philipp, 'Rash of Chinese spy cases shows a silent national emergency', *The Epoch Times*, 25 April 2016.
13 ASIO, *ASIO Annual Report 2016–17*, ASIO, 2017, p. 5. See also ASIO, *ASIO Annual Report 2015–16*, ASIO, 2016, pp. 25–6.
14 Four cases came to light in April 2016 alone. See Philipp, 'Rash of Chinese spy cases shows a silent national emergency'.
15 Michael Riley and Ashlee Vance, 'Inside the Chinese boom in corporate espionage', *Bloomberg*, 16 March 2012.
16 US Department of Justice, 'Michigan man sentenced 48 months for attempting to spy for the People's Republic of China', media release, 21 January 2011.
17 Anon., 'China tops spy list: CSIS', *The Star*, 30 April 2007.
18 Anon., 'China tops spy list'.
19 Anon., 'Beijing rejects claims Canadian engineer is Chinese spy, *ABC News Online*, 2 December 2013.
20 Haiyan Dong, Yu Gao, Patrick J. Sinko, Zaisheng Wu, Jianguo Xu and Lee Jia, 'The nanotechnology race between China and USA', *Materials Today*, 12 April 2016.

21 Jason Pan, 'Prosecutors charge five with nanotechnology theft', *Taipei Times*, 28 July 2016.
22 Daniel Golden, *Spy Schools: How the CIA, FBI, and Foreign Intelligence secretly exploit America's universities*, New York: Henry Holt, 2017, p. 17.
23 William Hannas, James Mulvenon and Anna Puglisi, *Chinese Industrial Espionage*, London: Routledge, 2013, Chapter 5.
24 Hannas, Mulvenon and Puglisi, *Chinese Industrial Espionage*, pp. 122–3.
25 Interview with Chen Yonglin, 1 February 2017. Chen says some scientists are given very large bonuses for supplying information to the PRC (payments the ATO does not hear about).
26 To, *Qiaowu*, pp. 45–6.
27 Interview with Chen Yonglin, 1 February 2017.
28 The director of ACAIEP is Ms Guixia Gao.
29 Hannas, Mulvenon and Puglisi, *Chinese Industrial Espionage*, pp. 78–80.
30 Hannas, Mulvenon and Puglisi, *Chinese Industrial Espionage*, p. 96.
31 For the case of Noshir Gowadia see <web.archive.org/web/200705231 75209/>; <honolulu.fbi.gov/dojpressrel/pressrel06/defensesecrets110906 .htm>; and <www.justice.gov/opa/pr/hawaii-man-sentenced-32-years-prison-providing-defense-information-and-services-people-s>.
32 Hannas, Mulvenon and Puglisi, *Chinese Industrial Espionage*, pp. 79–80.
33 <www.gov.cn/xinwen/2016-12/01/content_5141607.htm>.
34 Hannas, Mulvenon and Puglisi, *Chinese Industrial Espionage*, p. 110.
35 Hannas, Mulvenon and Puglisi, *Chinese Industrial Espionage*, p. 114.
36 <www.focsa.org.au/aboutus.html>.
37 <www.people.com.cn/GB/guoji/14553/2907862.html>.
38 <2007.chisa.edu.cn/szxrzz/qikan/2009no10/200910/t20091020_123750.html>.
39 <www1.rmit.edu.au/staff/xinghuo-yu>.
40 Stephen Chen, 'Top 5 most secretive and mysterious research universities in China', *South China Morning Post*, 19 April 2015.
41 <www.wacsa.com/conference-zh/welcome/>.
42 <perth.chineseconsulate.org/chn/zlsgxw/t1297108.htm>.
43 <www.qcase.org.au/en/>; <www.mfa.gov.cn/chn//pds/gjhdq/gj/dyz/1206/ 1206x2/t1419700.htm>; <www.fmprc.gov.cn/ce/cgbrsb/chn/zlgxw/t1014449 .htm>; and <www.cnzsyz.com/aozhou/359263.html>.
44 <www.fmprc.gov.cn/ce/cgbrsb/chn/zlgxw/t1014449.htm>.
45 <www.most.gov.cn/cxfw/kjjlcx/kjjl2011/201202/t20120217_92526.htm>.
46 <www.gg.gov.au/sites/default/files/files/honours/ad/ad2017/slkh83xzcb/AO Final Media Notes.pdf>.
47 <www.chinaql.org/c/2015-12-14/485805.shtml>.
48 <news.xinhuanet.com/fortune/2010-09/14/c_12551099.htm>.
49 <www.qcase.org.au/en/professor-max-lu-was-appointed-as-president-and-vice-chancellor-of-the-university-of-surrey-the-united-kingdom-uk/>.

50 <www.cscs.org.au/wp-content/uploads/2016/12/2016-2018-Council-Meeting-Agenda.pdf>.

51 <www.cscs.org.au/wp-content/uploads/2016/12/2016-2018-Council-Name-List1.pdf>; <www.cscs.org.au/?page_id=10>.

52 <www.cscs.org.au/wp-content/uploads/2017/03/CSCS_Attendee_List.pdf>.

53 Hannas, Mulvenon and Puglisi, *Chinese Industrial Espionage*, pp. 116–17.

54 <www.sydneytoday.com/au-news/1589112?flag=1>.

55 <australia.people.com.cn/n1/2016/1115/c408038-28862609.html>.

56 <acetca.org.au/en/?dt_portfolio=professor-yi-chen-lan>.

57 <www.acpprc.org.au/english/7thtermlist.asp>.

58 Interview with the author, 3 August 2017.

59 Richard Baker and Nick McKenzie, 'Chinese's [sic] scientist absence exposed alleged spying activities at CSIRO', *The Sydney Morning Herald*, 5 December 2013.

60 Unnamed journalist quoted by AFP in email dated 10 September 2015 released under freedom of information.

61 Documents released under freedom of information.

62 <www.csiro.au/china/>; <https://www.csiro.au/en/About/We-are-CSIRO>.

63 <www.lksf.org/the-5th-cheung-kong-scholars-award-ceremony-held-in-beijing/>.

64 Paul Mozur and Jane Perlez, 'China bets on sensitive US start-ups, worrying the Pentagon', *The New York Times*, 22 March 2017.

65 Paul Mozur, 'Beijing wants AI to be made in China by 2030', *The New York Times*, 20 July 2017.

66 <www.csiro.au/en/News/News-releases/2017/CSIROs-Data61-strengthening-Australias-cyber-security>.

67 <people.csiro.au/w/c/Chen-Wang>.

68 <xwb.hnedu.cn/chuangxin/UploadFiles_1600/201507/2015070717485119.xls>; <mil.cnr.cn/ztl/gfkdrc/xwbd/201309/t20130926_513699890.html>.

69 <www.huang123.cn/show.php?pid=1010>.

70 <wenku.baidu.com/view/43d5ee49bcd126fff7050bc0.html>; <http://www.defence.org.cn/article-2-28113.html>.

71 <www.cnki.com.cn/Article/CJFDTOTAL-XTFZ201105018.htm>.

72 <xueshu.baidu.com/scholarID/CN-BS74SKWJ>.

73 Ao Fu-jiang, Qi Zong-feng, Chen Bin and Huang Ke-di, 'Data stream mining techniques and its application in simulation systems,' *Computer Science,* issue 03, 2009 (in Chinese); Chen Bin, Ju Ru-sheng, Jiang Zhao-jin and Huang Ke-di, 'Web-based situation display method in combat simulation', *Journal of System Simulation*, issue 24, 2009 (in Chinese); Yang, Lun, Chen Bin, Huang Jian and Huang Ke-di, 'Research of general 2-dimension view display system in combat simulation, *Ordnance Industry Automation*, issue 12, 2007 (in Chinese); Yang Lun, Chen Bin, Huang Jian and Huang Ke-di, 'Model

development and management in the computational experiment oriented to emergency management', *Journal of National University of Defense Technology*, issue 03, 2015 (in Chinese).

74 <www.cqvip.com/qk/96569x/201108/38633287.html>; <www.cqvip.com/qk/95956x/200712/26266402.html>.

75 <www.cqvip.com/qk/96569x/201108/38633290.html>.

76 <www.cssn.cn/jsx/201611/t20161128_3291681.shtml>.

77 Hu Peng, Qiu Xiao-gang and Meng Rong-qing, 'Resource Description in Remote Sensing Satellite Simulation Integrated Environment', *Computer Simulation*, issue 07, 2011 (in Chinese).

78 <www.sia.cn/gkjj/lsyg/>.

79 <www.militarytimes.com/news/pentagon-congress/2017/06/23/scientist-gets-time-served-for-theft-of-military-documents/>.

80 Prosecutors alleged Long, desiring to return to China, promised to provide stolen aircraft technology to the Shenyang Institute and the Chinese Academy of Sciences if they offered him employment. They did and he returned to China carrying 'voluminous' secret documents. In an email, Long outlined his American work experience before concluding, 'I believe my efforts will help China to mature its own aircraft engines' (<www.justice.gov/usao-ct/pr/chinese-national-admits-stealing-sensitive-military-program-documents-united-technologies>).

81 He also holds an adjunct professorship at the University of Sydney (<people.csiro.au/C/S/Shiping-Chen>).

82 He visited the China University of Petroleum in June 2017 to talk about blockchain technology (<computer.upc.edu.cn/s/120/t/572/20/dc/info139484.htm>). He also visited Harbin Institute of Technology's Weihai campus to discuss research collaboration with the institute's president and the head of the campus's computer science and technology school (<today.hitwh.edu.cn/news_show.asp?id=27444>).

83 <ieeexplore.ieee.org.virtual.anu.edu.au/document/7983451/>; <ieeexplore.ieee.org.virtual.anu.edu.au/document/7207357/>; <ieeexplore.ieee.org.virtual.anu.edu.au/document/7557479/>.

84 <sklnst.bupt.edu.cn/content/content.php?p=2_8_4>.

85 <https://tinyurl.com/y8nhrjg9>.

86 <www.ixueshu.com/document/f6efe1550ca0d51e318947a18e7f9386.html>.

87 <www.csiro.au/en/News/News-releases/2016/Data61-and-Treasury-to-examine-blockchain-technology-potential>.

88 Another is Fu Yinjin of the People's Liberation Army University of Science and Technology.

89 <www.ccf.org.cn/c/2017-05-11/594599.shtml>.

90 <zqb.cyol.com/html/2013-08/30/nw.D110000zgqnb_20130830_5-06.htm>.

Chapter 10   'Engineering souls' in Australia's universities

1   John Fitzgerald, 'Academic freedom and the contemporary university: Lessons from China', *Humanities Australia*, 2017, 8, pp. 8–22.

2   John Fitzgerald, 'Academic freedom and the contemporary university'.

3   Quoted by Fitzgerald, 'Academic freedom and the contemporary university'.

4   Perry Link, testimony to Committee on Foreign Affairs, House of Representatives, 'Is academic freedom threatened by China's influence on US universities?', Washington, D.C.: US Government Printing Office, 4 December 2014, p. 3.

5   Interview with the author, 10 May 2017.

6   Perry Link, testimony to Committee on Foreign Affairs, House of Representatives, 'Is academic freedom threatened by China's influence on US universities?', p. 11.

7   Interview with the author, 10 May 2017.

8   Rowan Callick, 'Traps for old players, the People's Republic of China way', *The Australian*, 9 September 2016.

9   <world.huanqiu.com/exclusive/2017-05/10701945.html>.

10   Kirsty Needham, 'China's internet erupts over Monash University's drunk officials quiz question', *The Sydney Morning Herald*, 22 May 2017.

11   Primrose Riordan, 'Monash University suspends lecturer over quiz question', *The Australian*, 22 May 2017.

12   Primrose Riordan, 'Monash throws out the textbook over Chinese student complaints', *The Australian*, 30 May 2017; Riordan, 'Monash University suspends lecturer over quiz question'.

13   <news.163.com/17/0520/06/CKS0O4CL0001899N.html>.

14   <www.sydneytoday.com/content-101720255970006>.

15   <https://www.universitiesaustralia.edu.au/global-engagement/international-collaboration/international-links/Link-Maps/Australian-universities-formal-agreements-by-country>.

16   John Garnaut, 'Our universities are a frontline in China's ideological wars', *Australian Financial Review*, 30 August 2017.

17   Emma Reynolds, 'Tensions rise as Chinese government's influence infiltrates Aussie universities', *News.com.au*, 1 September 2017.

18   <http://en.people.cn/n3/2017/0811/c90000-9254290.html>.

19   Andrea Booth, 'Chinese students left fuming after Sydney uni lecturer uses contested map of China-India border', *SBS News Online*, 22 August 2017.

20   Rowan Callick, 'Chinese students taught to "snitch" on politically incorrect lecturers', *The Australian*, 1 September 2017.

21   Primrose Riordan, 'Top unis admit China influence, Go8 fears backlash', *The Australian*, 23 September 2017; <https://sydney.edu.au/news-opinion/news/2017/09/25/university-of-sydney-engagement-with-china--statement.html>.

22   <sydney.jinriaozhou.com/content-101734356533003>.

23   Primrose Riordan and Rowan Callick, 'China consulate involved in Newcastle Uni Taiwan row', *The Australian*, 28 August 2017.

24   Thomas Cushman, testimony to Committee on Foreign Affairs, House of Representatives, 'Is academic freedom threatened by China's influence on US universities?', p. 16.

25   Maev Kennedy and Tom Phillips, 'Cambridge University Press backs down over China censorship', *The Guardian*, 22 August 2017.

26   For the material on UTS and CETC I owe a large debt to Geoff Wade, and the detailed investigation of Chinese-language sources by Alex Joske.

27   John Fitzgerald, 'China's scientists trapped', *Australian Financial Review*, 3 October 2013.

28   <rms.arc.gov.au/RMS/Report/Download/Report/a3f6be6e-33f7-4fb5-98a6-7526aaa184cf/70>.

29   <www.forbes.com/sites/anderscorr/2016/06/22/chinas-aerospace-defense-industry-sacks-us-military-technology/#49a64c595aae>.

30   <www.scmp.com/news/china/diplomacy-defence/article/2058888/j-15-fighter-jets-chinas-liaoning-aircraft-carrier-make>; <mil.news.sina.com.cn/china/2016-11-29/doc-ifxyawmm3819629.shtml>.

31   <www.biam.ac.cn/tabid/87/Default.aspx>.

32   <www.bloomberg.com/research/stocks/private/person.asp?personId=273713617&privcapId=273591866>.

33   Chris Uhlmann, 'Australian Defence files to be moved out of privately owned data hub after Chinese buy-in', *ABC News Online*, 20 June 2017.

34   <www.adelaide.edu.au/directory/s.qiao>; <news.buct.edu.cn/kxyj/49393.htm>; <http://www.oic.buct.edu.cn/sysgk/index.htm>.

35   <chemeng.adelaide.edu.au/qiao/members/tianyi-ma/>.

36   <www.biam.ac.cn/tabid/86/InfoID/3168/frtid/209/Default.aspx>.

37   William Hannas, James Mulvenon and Anna Puglisi, *Chinese Industrial Espionage*, London: Routledge, 2013, p. 259.

38   <www.uschamber.com/report/china's-drive-indigenous-innovation-web-industrial-policies>.

39   <https://tinyurl.com/y9per3ct>.

40   Fitzgerald, 'China's scientists trapped'.

41   Matthew Luce, 'A model company: CETC celebrates 10 years of civil-military integration', *China Brief*, The Jamestown Foundation, vol. 12, no. 4, 2012.

42   Danielle Cave and Brendan Thomas-Noone, 'CSIRO cooperation with Chinese defence contractor should raise questions', *The Guardian*, 3 June 2017.

43   <web.archive.org/web/20101029184346/http://www.cetc.com.cn:80/Article_List.aspx?columnID=1>.

44   <jamestown.org/program/a-model-company-cetc-celebrates-10-years-of-civil-military-integration/>.

45   Luce, 'A model company'.

46 Cave and Thomas-Noone, 'CSIRO cooperation with Chinese defence contractor should raise questions'.

47 Hannas, Mulvenon and Puglisi, *Chinese Industrial Espionage*, p. 259.

48 Hannas, Mulvenon and Puglisi, *Chinese Industrial Espionage*, pp. 259–60.

49 <www.uts.edu.au/about/faculty-engineering-and-information-technology/news/joint-iet-research-centre-china>.

50 <en.yibada.com/articles/55692/20150820/chinese-researchers-hopeful-metamaterials-key-unlocking-invisible-planes.htm>.

51 Cave and Thomas-Noone, 'CSIRO cooperation with Chinese defence contractor should raise questions'.

52 Tom Igguldon, 'Australian universities accused of sharing military technology with China', *ABC News Online*, 15 December 2017.

53 <newsroom.uts.edu.au/news/2016/12/uts-launch-centre-china-promote-research-and-commercialisation>.

54 <news.xinhuanet.com/info/2016-11/17/c_135835124.htm>.

55 <www.cetccity.com/home>.

56 <www.uts.edu.au/about/faculty-engineering-and-information-technology/news/new-uts-centre-driving-big-data>.

57 <www.uts.edu.au/about/faculty-engineering-and-information-technology/news/joint-iet-research-centre-china>.

58 <www.uts.edu.au/research-and-teaching/our-research/global-big-data-technologies-centre>.

59 <news.xinhuanet.com/mil/2017-03/15/c_129509791.htm>; <ndupress.ndu.edu/Media/News/News-Article-View/Article/621113/defense-intelligence-analysis-in-the-age-of-big-data/>.

60 <web.archive.org/web/20160530101219/http://www.uts.edu.au/research-and-teaching/our-research/global-big-data-technologies-centre/working-us/our-partners>.

61 Aaron Patrick, 'China's citizen spies', *Australian Financial Review*, 3–4 September 2016.

62 Interview with senior officer managing university engagement, DST Group, 3 August 2017.

63 Daniel Golden, *Spy Schools: How the CIA, FBI, and Foreign Intelligence secretly exploit America's universities*, New York: Henry Holt, 2017, p. 7.

64 <www.xidian.edu.cn/xxgk/xxjj.htm>.

65 Edward Wong, 'University in Xi'an opens school of cyberengineering', *The New York Times*, 7 January 2015.

66 <news.ifeng.com/a/20160531/48886124_0.shtml>.

67 The rest of this section was written with Alex Joske, who also did most of the research for this section.

68 Minnie Chan, 'Xi Jinping tells Chinese defence firms to aim higher and catch up on weapons technology', *South China Morning Post*, 4 October 2017;

Charlotte Gao, '3 Major Takeaways from Xi Jinping's Speech at the 19th Party Congress', *The Diplomat*, 18 October 2017.

69 David Lague, 'In satellite tech race, China hitched a ride from Europe', Reuters, 23 December 2013.

70 <https://link.springer.com/article/10.1007/s10291-010-0165-9>.

71 Zhang Weihua with UNSW researchers: <http://www.sciencedirect.com/science/article/pii/S1874490714000020>; Zhang Weihua is a major general: <http://www.gzht.casic.cn/n1377750/n1377781/c1802727/content.html>.

72 <http://eng.chinamil.com.cn/news-channels/china-military-news/2015-06/26/content_6556886.htm>; <http://news.xinhuanet.com/mil/2015-06/25/c_127950466.htm>.

73 <https://www.uscc.gov/sites/default/files/Research/Staff%20Report_China%27s%20Alternative%20to%20GPS%20and%20Implications%20for%20the%20United%20States.pdf>.

74 <http://www.sciencedirect.com/science/article/pii/S0273117712005777>; <http://ieeexplore.ieee.org/document/7809968/>.

75 <http://citeseerx.ist.psu.edu/viewdoc/download?doi=10.1.1.156.9303&rep=rep1&type=pdf>;<https://wenku.baidu.com/view/4ee98410227916888486d73f.html?re=view>.

76 <http://www.wendangku.net/doc/e1ba346fff00bed5b9f31dd3-134.html>.

77 Clive Hamilton and Alex Joske, 'Australian universities are helping China's military surpass the United States', *The Sydney Morning Herald*, 28 October 2017.

78 <http://news.xinhuanet.com/politics/19cpcnc/2017-10/22/c_129724787.htm>.

79 Emailed responses to the author, 14 November 2017.

80 Email to the author, 25 July 2017.

81 Emailed responses to the author, 27 October 2017.

82 Conversation with Alex Joske, 8 November 2017.

83 <www.ctp.gov.cn/hjjh/index.shtml>; <http://www.gov.cn/xinwen/2017-03/24/content_5180907.htm>.

84 Hannas, Mulvenon and Puglisi, *Chinese Industrial Espionage*.

85 Anon., 'Chinese scientist Huang Kexue jailed for trade theft', *BBC News*, 22 December 2011.

86 <www.freerepublic.com/focus/news/3229656/posts>.

87 <newsroom.unsw.edu.au/news/general/unsw-partners-china-100-million-innovation-precinct>.

88 <http://www.president.unsw.edu.au/speeches/torch-gala-dinner-speech-address-professor-ian-jacobs-unsw-sydney-16-august-2016>.

89 <https://newsroom.unsw.edu.au/news/general/unsw-partners-china-100-million-innovation-precinct>.

90 Quoted by Hannas, Mulvenon and Puglisi, *Chinese Industrial Espionage*, p. 63.

91   <news.xinhuanet.com/world/2017-03/24/c_1120688273.htm>.

92   John Ross, 'Torch precinct lights the way for UNSW innovators', *The Australian*, 7 May 2016.

93   Anders Furze and Louisa Lim, '"Faustian bargain": Defence fears over Australian university's $100m China partnership', *The Guardian*, 19 September 2017; Brian Boyle, 'Chinese partnerships are vital for universities and global research', *Australian Financial Review*, 30 October 2017.

94   Ross, 'Torch precinct lights the way for UNSW innovators'.

95   Interview with Laurie Pearcey, 2 August 2017.

96   '… we do extensive due diligence on all of our prospective partners and this is conducted by an expert independent third party. This involves consideration against a range of criteria including corporate beneficial ownership information as well as sanctions/regulatory/exclusion lists and so through this process we absolutely do look at military linkages as part of our considerations.' Email to the author, 5 October 2017. On 17 October Pearsey emailed as follows: 'All of our research contracts with overseas partners go through a rigorous due diligence process and this includes ensuring that all contracts are compliant with Defence Trade Controls.'

97   Laurie Pearcey seems sympathetic to the goals of the Communist Party regime, variously arguing that: once the elitist demands for democracy fade, Hong Kongers will realise that their destiny has always been as part of China ('Beyond the fog of tear gas, Hong Kong's future remains with China', *The Conversation*, 2 October 2014); that the One Belt, One Road initiative will save Australia from 'splendid isolation' ('China's Belt and Road initiative counters isolationist sentiment: Australian academics', *Xinhuanet*, 23 November 2016); and that Australian universities must suspend their parochialism and take the 'bold first step along the new Silk Road' ('Scholar urges bold step for Australia's higher education along new Silk Road', *Global Times*, 26 May 2015). His views are regularly trumpeted by China's official media. He is the director of UNSW's Confucius Institute.

98   This topic is sensitive and no studies have been carried out. The existence of enclaves is easy to see from university staff lists for certain departments and centres. The possible impacts on academic culture are here speculations based on anecdote.

99   University of Adelaide: <www.adelaide.edu.au/directory/peng.shi>; Victoria University: <www.vu.edu.au/contact-us/peng-shi>.

100 <www.fjut.edu.cn/e3/56/c467a58198/page.htm>.

101 <www1.hrbust.edu.cn/xueyuan/zidonghua/shownews.asp?id=97>.

102 <heuac.hrbeu.edu.cn/2016/0530/c1467a34057/page.htm>; <heuac.hrbeu.edu.cn/1540/list.htm>.

103 <heuac.hrbeu.edu.cn/1478/list.htm>.

104 <military.people.com.cn/n/2014/1020/c1011-25868325.html>.

105 <www.fjut.edu.cn/e3/56/c467a58198/page.htm>; <www.vu.edu.au/contact-us/peng-shi>.

106 <www.eleceng.adelaide.edu.au/Personal/cclim/research/pgstudents.html>.

107 Anon., 'A message from Confucius', *The Economist*, 22 October 2009.

108 Omid Ghoreishi, 'Beijing uses Confucius Institutes for espionage, says Canadian intelligence veteran', *The Epoch Times*, 14 October 2014.

109 <english.hanban.org/node_10971.htm>.

110 David Shambaugh, 'China's propaganda system: Institutions, processes and efficacy', *The China Journal*, no. 57, January 2007.

111 James Jiann Hua To, *Qiaowu: Extra-territorial policies for the overseas Chinese*, Leiden: Koninklijke Brill, 2014, p. 146.

112 Rachelle Petersen, *Outsourced to China: Confucius Institutes and soft power in American higher education*, New York: National Association of Scholars, 2017, p. 80.

113 Anon., 'Sydney University criticised for blocking Dalai Lama visit', *The Guardian*, 18 April 2013.

114 Adam Harvey, 'Uni under fire for pulling pin on Dalai Lama event', *ABC News Online*, 18 April 2013.

115 Petersen, *Outsourced to China*, p. 83.

116 Hagar Cohen, 'Australian universities the latest battleground in Chinese soft power offensive', *ABC News Online*, 14 October 2016.

117 Zhiqun Zhu, 'The undoing of China's soft power', *The Diplomat*, 8 August 2014.

118 Petersen, *Outsourced to China*.

119 Petersen, *Outsourced to China*, p. 88.

120 Ghoreishi, 'Beijing uses Confucius Institutes for espionage, says Canadian intelligence veteran'.

121 Raffy Boudjikanian, 'Local Chinese school visited by CSIS, director says', *CBC News*, 8 September 2014.

122 <pkuasc.fasic.org.au/australian-minister-of-education-the-hon-christopher-pyne-visits-peking-university/>.

123 Geoff Wade, 'Confucius Institutes and Chinese soft power in Australia', Canberra: Parliamentary Library, 24 November 2014.

124 <sydney.edu.au/confucius_institute/about/profiles.shtml>.

125 <web.archive.org/web/20140301220106/http://confuciusinstitute.unsw.edu.au/about-us/our-people/>.

126 Wade, 'Confucius Institutes and Chinese soft power in Australia'.

127 John Fitzgerald, 'Academic freedom and the contemporary university—lessons from China', *Humanities Australia*, 2017.

128 <www.uq.edu.au/news/article/2015/12/uq-vice-chancellor-receives-confucian-award-china's-vice-premier>.

129 <english.hanban.org/node_10971.htm>.

130 <schoolsequella.det.nsw.edu.au/file/33b88803-c07c-46dc-8c43-eccf bae5f80c/1/mcc-nsw.pdf>.

131 Justin Norrie, 'Confucius says school's in, but don't mention democracy', *The Sydney Morning Herald*, 20 February 2011.

132 Michael Churchman, 'Confucius Institutes and controlling Chinese languages', *China Heritage Quarterly*, ANU, no. 26, June 2011.

133 <theory.people.com.cn/GB/12650342.html>.

134 Norrie, 'Confucius says school's in, but don't mention democracy'.

135 Louisa Lim, *The People's Republic of Amnesia: Tiananmen revisited*, Oxford: Oxford University Press, 2014.

136 <www.parliament.nsw.gov.au/la/papers/DBAssets/tabledpaper/web Attachments/27820/10,000%20%2B%20petition%20on%20Confucius %20Classrooms.pdf>.

137 Tom Cowie, 'Theatre group raises questions about Chinese Consulate intimidating schools', *Crikey*, 23 February 2011.

138 Kelsie Munro and Hannah Francis, 'Confucius Classrooms: Chinese government agency teaching Victorian kids', *The Age*, 29 May 2016.

139 Alex Joske and Philip Wen, 'The "patriotic education" of Chinese students at Australian universities', *The Sydney Morning Herald*, 7 October 2016.

140 Angus Grigg, Lisa Murray and Primrose Riordan, 'Canberra pharmacy at front line of China's push for global influence', *Australian Financial Review*, 1 September 2016. Note: the words 'of power' were accidentally omitted from the published story.

141 Open letter from Geremie Barmé to ANU vice-chancellor Brian Schmidt and chancellor Gareth Evans, 15 August 2016. Note: In May 2017 Professor William Maley confirmed to me that Lei Xiying was continuing his doctoral studies at the ANU.

142 Philip Wen, 'The Australian connection behind China's ultra-nationalist viral video', *The Sydney Morning Herald*, 4 August 2016.

143 Andrew Chubb, 'Are China's most extreme nationalists actually foreign stooges?', *Foreign Policy*, 26 July 2016.

144 <weibo.com/1634365454/DEOLuCkNR?from=page_1005051634365454 _profile&wvr=6&mod=weibotime&type=comment>.

145 Open letter from Barmé to Schmidt and Evans.

146 Alex W. Palmer, 'The lonely crusade of China's human rights lawyers', *The New York Times Magazine*, 25 July 2017.

147 To, *Qiaowu*, p. 31.

148 To, *Qiaowu*, pp. 32–4.

149 <https://internationaleducation.gov.au/research/International-Student-Data/ Pages/InternationalStudentData2017.aspx>.

150 Ross Peake, 'Overseas students are good for Canberra – and vice versa', *Canberra Times*, 4 September 2015.

151 Anon., 'Protect uni students from foreign spies, says Gareth Evans', *The Australian*, 4 October 2017.

152 Alexander Joske, Kelsey Munro and Philip Wen, 'Australia's top-ranked global university moves to lower share of Chinese students', *The Sydney Morning Herald*, 5 October 2017.

153 James To, 'Beijing's policies for managing Han and ethnic-minority Chinese communities abroad', *Journal of Current Chinese Affairs*, no. 4, 2012, pp. 183–221, 205–6.

154 To, *Qiaowu*, p. 29.

155 To, *Qiaowu*, p. 218.

156 Chang Ping, 'Chinese students studying abroad a new focus of CCP's "United Front work"', *China Change*, 9 June 2015.

157 Gerry Groot, 'The expansion of the United Front under Xi Jinping', *China Story Yearbook*, Canberra: Australian Centre for China in the World, 2015.

158 James Scott and Drew Spaniel, *China's Espionage Dynasty*, Institute for Critical Infrastructure Technology, 2016, p. 34.

159 Madalina Hubert, 'Ex-envoy details Chinese regime's overseas scheme', *The Epoch Times*, 10 September 2015.

160 Hubert, 'Ex-envoy details Chinese regime's overseas scheme'.

161 Joske and Wen, 'The "patriotic education" of Chinese students at Australian universities'.

162 At an unadvertised meeting in 2017, Guo Xiaohang was elected president of the ANU/ACT CSSA 'unanimously' (<hmp.weixin.qq.com/s/7wYwZYtpM2X9pVTXT7GCfQ>).

163 Matthew Robertson, 'Columbia University closes Chinese students group', *The Epoch Times*, 24 March 2015.

164 Nick McKenzie, Sashka Koloff and Anne Davies, 'Power and influence', *Four Corners*, ABC TV, 6 June 2017.

165 John Garnaut, 'Chinese spies at Sydney University', *The Sydney Morning Herald*, 21 April 2014.

166 McKenzie, Koloff and Davies, 'Power and influence', *Four Corners*. Lupin Lu, a young Chinese student temporarily living in Australia, launched a defamation action against the ABC and Fairfax Media in the Supreme Court of Victoria claiming that the program implied that she is, inter alia, a spy or a proxy for the Chinese Communist Party in Australia and that, as a result of the program and subsequent news reports, her reputation has been severely injured. Against the defendants Lu is claiming damages, aggravated damages, injunctions against further publication, interest on the damages, legal costs and 'such further or other relief as the Court considers appropriate' (Ping (Lupin) Lu Statement of Claim lodged at the Supreme Court of Victoria on 29 November 2017).

167 McKenzie, Koloff and Davies, 'Power and influence', *Four Corners*.

168 Grigg, Murray and Riordan, 'Canberra pharmacy at front line of China's push for global influence'.

169 Chang Ping, 'Chinese students studying abroad a new focus of CCP's "United Front work"', *China Change*, 9 June 2015.

170 Central Intelligence Agency, 'China: Student informant system to expand, limiting school autonomy, free expression', Washington, D.C.: Directorate of Intelligence, 23 November 2010, <https://fas.org/irp/world/china/docs/cia-sis.pdf>.

171 Garnaut, 'Chinese spies at Sydney University'.

172 Alex Joske, personal communication, 30 March 2017.

173 John Horwitz, 'Chinese students in the US are using "inclusion" and "diversity" to oppose a Dalai Lama graduation speech', *Quartz*, 15 February 2017.

174 Zhang Xunchao (CSSA member and Ostar employee), 'Open letter to Woroni regarding the ANU Chinese student community', *Facebook* post, 1 September 2016.

175 Chenchen Zhang, 'The curious rise of the "white left" as a Chinese internet insult', *Open Democracy*, 11 May 2017.

176 Jim Waterson, 'The Chinese Embassy told Durham University's debating society not to let this former Miss World contestant to speak at a debate', *Buzzfeed*, 11 February 2017 <https://www.buzzfeed.com/jimwaterson/the-chinese-embassy-told-durham-universitys-debating-society?utm_term=.gix2qE5NR#.iekolLEOn>.

177 Committee on Foreign Affairs, House of Representatives, 'Is academic freedom threatened by China's influence on US universities?', Washington, D.C.: US Government Printing Office, 4 December 2014.

178 Chris Uhlmann, 'ASIO warned ANU of donor links to Chinese Communist party, Opposition ramps up inquiry call', *ABC News Online*, 13 June 2017.

Chapter 11   Culture wars

1   Sue Neales, 'China's Ningbo Dairy Group looks to greener Australian pastures', *The Australian*, 4 April 2015.

2   <finance.sina.com.cn/consume/puguangtai/20130504/123015349344.shtml>; <news.ifeng.com/gundong/detail_2013_02/27/22524284_0.shtml>; <news.ifeng.com/gundong/detail_2013_03/01/22609837_0.shtml>.

3   Powell Tate, 'The licence that matters: Beyond Foreign Investment Review Board approval', report by Powell Tate, 2017, p. 46.

4   Sue Neales, 'Dreams blocked as council cries over milk spilling to China', *The Australian*, 5 September 2015.

5   Sue Neales and Primrose Riordan, 'Avoid Aussie icons: FIRB boss's tips for China on investment', *The Australian*, 1 March 2017.

6   Glenda Korporaal, 'Find an Aussie partner, Howard tells potential Chinese investors', *The Australian*, 17 March 2017.

7   Powell Tate, 'The licence that matters', p. 30.

8   Powell Tate, 'The licence that matters', p. 48.

9   Dominique Schwartz, Anna Vidot and Clint Jasper, 'S Kidman and Co: Scott Morrison approves sale of cattle empire to Gina Rinehart, Chinese company', *ABC News Online*, 10 December 2016.

10   Cameron England and Tory Shepherd, 'Chinese mining magnate Sally Zou is SA Libs' largest donor as PM Malcolm Turnbull reveals his $1.75m donation', *Adelaide Now*, 2 February 2017.

11   <www.sbs.com.au/yourlanguage/cantonese/zh-hant/article/2017/08/15/chinese-ferrari-protesting-sydney-towards-india?language=zh-hant>; <www.sydneytoday.com/content-1017332410100010>

12   <scholarships.adelaide.edu.au/scholarship/ug/ecms/ausgold-mining-engineering-scholarship>.

13   <www.portadelaidefc.com.au/news/2016-10-26/ausgold-joins-port-as-world-program-backer>. For good measure, Zou also backs Adelaide United football team (<www.adelaideunited.com.au/article/adelaide-united-and-ausgold-join-forces-for-afc-champions-league/1r7qsivp77mwe1wowegfucy87u>). Gui Guojie, the property developer boss of Shanghai CRED and business partner of Gina Rinehart, is a major funder of Port Adelaide AFL Club (Brad Thompson, 'Kidman owner wins with AFL in Shanghai', *Australian Financial Review*, 25 October 2017).

14   <culture.people.com.cn/GB/40494/40496/13836208.html>.

15   <zqb.cyol.com/content/2006-10/19/content_1543581.htm>.

16   <www.xwtoutiao.cn/p/ict8k50s/>.

17   Primrose Riordan, 'Sally Zou denies billion-dollar deal with Chinese state-owned company', *The Australian*, 17 May 2017.

18   <www.xwtoutiao.cn/p/ict8k50s/>.

19   Anon., 'Tips and rumours: Who is Gloria and why did she take out a full page ad in The Oz?', *Crikey*, 19 March 2015.

20   <en.people.cn/n/2015/1027/c90000-8967567.html>.

21   <australia.people.com.cn/n/2015/1124/c364496-27850484.html>.

22   When in June 2017 the Labor Party attempted to put Bishop on the spot by asking about the Julie Bishop Glorious Foundation in parliament, the government returned fire by attacking Labor for taking money from dodgy gold dealer Simon Zhou, even putting him on its Senate ticket. Labor retaliated by bringing up Andrew Robb's Chinese deals, and the government lobbed back accusations against 'Shanghai Sam' Dastyari and Joel Fitzgibbon. The exchange was vicious and exposed just how deeply both major parties have been corrupted by Chinese money and why both feel so obligated that they have been unwilling to crack down on it, at least until Prime Minister Turnbull introduced in December 2017 new national security legislation, a very important move. (For the parliamentary exchange, see Louise Yaxley, 'Julie Bishop denies knowledge of Chinese donor setting up company bearing her name', *ABC News Online*, 14 June 2017.)

23 Sally Rose, 'FIRB Chinese real estate buyer crackdown called "racist" as Ray White urges calm', *The Sydney Morning Herald*, 26 March 2015.

24 Lucy Macken, 'Cashed-up Chinese find the sweet spot', *The Sydney Morning Herald*, 23–24 August 2014.

25 Elizabeth Redman, 'Foreigners spending $8bn a year on new housing in NSW and Victoria', *The Australian*, 24 March 2017.

26 Jackson Gothe-Snape, 'Property sector scrambling to recruit Chinese real estate agents on 457 visas', *SBS Online*, 10 April 2017.

27 Property Council of Australia, 'New report demonstrates value to the Australian economy from foreign investment in real estate', media release, 30 May 2017.

28 Sarah Martin, '"Migrant millionaires" fuel property boom', *The Australian*, 26 April 2017.

29 Martin, '"Migrant millionaires" fuel property boom'.

30 Kirsty Needham, 'Chinese police chief Wang Jun Ren jailed for buying Australian real estate with corrupt money', *The Sydney Morning Herald*, 18 March 2017; Angus Grigg and Lisa Murray, 'Corrupt Chinese payments fund education, housing and holidays in Australia', *Australian Financial Review*, 2 March 2016.

31 Paul Maley, 'China's dodgy $1bn in property', *The Australian*, 30 January 2017.

32 Miles Godfrey, 'Foreign buyers cash out', *Daily Telegraph*, 6 February 2017.

33 Larry Schlesinger, 'Foreign investor crackdown dismissed as "farce"', *Australian Financial Review*, 11 August 2015.

34 David Pierson, 'Mega-mansions in this LA suburb used to sell to Chinese buyers in days. Now they're sitting empty for months', *Los Angeles Times*, 23 February 2017.

35 Larry Schlesinger, 'Chinese developers surge back into Melbourne', *Australian Financial Review*, 18 January 2017.

36 Anon., 'World's biggest real estate frenzy is coming to a city near you', *Bloomberg News*, 15 November 2016.

37 <writersvictoria.org.au/civicrm/event/info?id=120&reset=1>.

38 Its website hosts nineteen articles by Yang Dongdong, described as a member of a New South Wales government minister's advisory committee and discussed in Chapter 4, on themes like 'Listening to Chairman Xi speak at Parliament House' (<www.aucnln.com/>).

39 <chinavitae.com/biography/Tie_Ning%7C3506>; <https://en.wikipedia.org/wiki/19th_Central_Committee_of_the_Communist_Party_of_China>.

40 Yaxue Cao, 'Mo Yan, according to you—part two', *China Change*, October 2012, <chinachange.org/2012/10/23/mo-yan-according-to-you-part-two/>.

41 <www.sbs.com.au/news/article/2017/06/12/sbs-mandarin-broadcaster-may-hu-honoured-order-australia-medal>.

42 <www.aucnln.com/article_12782.htm>.

43 <www.gzqw.gov.cn/site6/sqqw/10/57335.shtml>; <http://www.aucnln.com/article_867.htm>.

44 <www.chinaqw.com/m/zhwh/2016/08-11/98769.shtml>.

45 <www.chinawriter.com.cn/zxhy/member/1907.shtml>.

46 <sn.xinhuanet.com/snnews2/20160824/3399533_c.html>.

47 <world.people.com.cn/n1/2016/0830/c1002-28677567.html>.

48 <world.people.com.cn/n1/2016/0830/c1002-28677567.html>.

49 James Jiann Hua To, *Qiaowu: Extra-territorial policies for the overseas Chinese*, Leiden: Koninklijke Brill, 2014, p. 150.

50 <www.cccowe.org/content_pub.php?id=catw200507-8>.

51 <web.archive.org-Presbyterian Church of Aotearoa New Zealand (1).pdf>.

52 <http://www.achina.com.au> (screenshot saved).

53 <http://blog.ccmchurch.com.au/archives/18913/comment-page-1>.

54 Interview with author, 6 June 2017.

55 Hong Liu and Els van Dongen, 'China's Diaspora policies as a new mode of transnational governance', *Journal of Contemporary China*, vol. 25, no. 102, 2016.

56 Anne-Marie Brady, 'China's foreign propaganda machine', *Journal of Democracy*, vol. 26, no. 4, October 2015, pp. 51–9.

57 Email to the author from Greg Kimball, media relations manager, Australian War Memorial, 10 July 2017.

58 <news.xinhuanet.com/english/photo/2015-09/17/c_134633608_5.htm>; <news.xinhuanet.com/world/2015-09/17/c_1116592509.htm>.

59 <news.xinhuanet.com/english/photo/2015-09/17/c_134633608_5.htm>; <news.xinhuanet.com/world/2015-09/17/c_1116592509.htm>.

60 Email to the author from Greg Kimball, media relations manager, Australian War Memorial, 18 July 2017.

61 Sheng Fei (ed.), *Quiet and Loyal Spirit: Commemorating Chinese Australian military service*, New Century Publications Fund, 2015.

62 With thanks to First Fleet historian Cathy Dunn for confirming this. According to historian Shirley Fitzgerald: 'The earliest documented Chinese settler was Mak Sai Ying, who arrived in 1818, and purchased land in Parramatta' (<dictionaryofsydney.org/entry/chinese>). However, Fitzgerald repeats the erroneous claim that 'Chinese contact with the east coast of Australia almost certainly occurred by the time of the Han Dynasty (202 BC–220 AD), and may date further back to the undocumented past'.

63 Howard French, 'China's textbooks twist and omit history', *The New York Times*, 6 December 2004.

64 Ian Johnson, 'China's memory manipulators', *The Guardian*, 8 June 2016.

65 The CCP claims that it was the PLA that defeated the Japanese aggressors, whereas in truth the CCP withdrew and left most of the fighting to their nationalist opponents, the Kuomintang.

66 The strategy is applied to the Koch brothers in the United States, according to David L. Levy ('It's the real thing', *ClimateInc*, 8 September 2010).

67 Karl Wilson, 'Exploring a shared history', *China Daily*, 11–17 December 2017. See Robert Macklin, *Dragon & Kangaroo: Australia and China's shared history from the goldfields to the present day*, Sydney: Hachette, 2017.

68 <www.yeeyi.com/news/index.php?app=home&act=article&aid=149963>; <au.fjsen.com/2016-08/25/content_18366654.htm>.

69 <mayt.com.au/2017/01/tw/>.

70 Mao Tse-tung, 'Talks at the Yenan Forum on Literature and Art' (May 1942) in *Selected Works of Mao Tse-tung*, Peking: Foreign Languages Press, 1967.

71 <www.cyberctm.com/zh_TW/news/detail/873395#.WaeyfMZjKi4>.

72 <www.meipian.cn/gkpajr3>.

73 Amy Hawkins, 'KFC China is using facial recognition tech to serve customers—but are they buying it?', *The Guardian*, 11 January 2017.

74 James T. Areddy, 'One legacy of Tiananmen: China's 100 million surveillance cameras', *Wall Street Journal*, 5 June 2104.

75 Nathan Vanderklippe, 'Chinese blacklist an early glimpse of sweeping new social credit control', *The Globe and Mail*, 3 January 2018.

76 Anon., 'China invents the digital totalitarian state', *The Economist*, 17 December 2016.

77 Nathan Vanderklippe, 'Chinese blacklist an early glimpse of sweeping new social credit control', *The Globe and Mail*, 3 January 2018.

78 <https://en.oxforddictionaries.com/definition/big_data>

79 Anon., 'China invents the digital totalitarian state'. US tech researchers are now developing ways for people to protect themselves from having their faces logged. One promising method is the wearing of spectacles with zany patterns on the frames to confuse image capture (<www.theguardian.com/technology/2016/nov/03/how-funky-tortoiseshell-glasses-can-beat-facial-recognition>).

80 <news.xinhuanet.com/info/2016-11/17/c_135835124.htm>.

81 <en.cetc.com.cn/enzgdzkj/news/408468/index.html>.

82 <newsroom.uts.edu.au/news/2016/12/uts-launch-centre-china-promote-research-and-commercialisation>.

83 Sam Levin, 'Half of US adults are recorded in police facial recognition databases, study says', *The Guardian*, 18 October 2016.

84 Geoff Wade, 'Beidou: China's new satellite navigation system', post on website of the Parliamentary Library, Canberra, 26 February 2015 <http://www.aph.gov.au/About_Parliament/Parliamentary_Departments/Parliamentary_Library/FlagPost/2015/February/Beidou_China_new_satellite_navigation_system>.

85 Anne-Marie Brady, 'China's expanding Antarctic interests: Implications for Australia', Australian Strategic Policy Institute, Canberra, August 2017; Anne-Marie Brady, 'China's expanding Antarctic interests: Implications for New Zealand', paper presented at the conference Small States and the Changing Global Order: New Zealand Faces the Future, University of

Canterbury, Christchurch, New Zealand, June 2017 <http://www.arts. canterbury.ac.nz/political/documents/ssanse2017_documents/Anne-Marie_ Brady_policybrief.pdf>.

86 Nicola Davison, 'China eyes Antarctica's resource bounty', *China Dialogue*, 19 November 2013; Jo Chandler, 'Chinese resources chief eyes Antarctica minerals', *The Sydney Morning Herald*, 7 January 2010.

87 Brady, 'China's expanding Antarctic interests'.

88 <www.fmprc.gov.cn/mfa_eng/topics_665678/xjpzxcxesgjtldrdjcfhdadl yxxlfjjxgsfwbttpyjjdgldrhw/t1212943.shtml>.

89 With thanks to Tim Stephens of the University of Sydney Law School for making this point.

90 Brady, 'China's expanding Antarctic interests: Implications for Australia', Table 1.

91 Will Koulouris, 'Interview: Australia-China collaboration in Antarctica a shining example of great relationship', *Xinhuanet*, 15 September 2017.

92 Nengye Liu, 'How China came in from the cold to help set up Antarctica's vast new marine park', *The Conversation*, 1 November 2016 <theconversation .com/how-china-came-in-from-the-cold-to-help-set-up-antarcticas-vast- new-marine-park-67911>.

93 Nengye Liu, 'Demystifying China in Antarctica', *The Diplomat*, 9 June 2017 <thediplomat.com/2017/06/demystifying-china-in-antarctica/>.

94 David Leary, 'The future of Antarctica: Conflict or consensus?', blog post, 14 January 2016 <www.uts.edu.au/about/faculty-law/news/future- antarctica-conflict-or-consensus>.

95 Dr Tony Press, who for many years headed the Australian Antarctic Division and who remains a central player, also believes that China's membership of the treaty regime ensures that its commitment to the mining ban will be honoured (Nick Rowley, 'In Conversation on Antarctic sovereignty: full discussion', *The Conversation*, 3 July 2014 <theconversation.com/in- conversation-on-antarctic-sovereignty-full-discussion-28600>).

96 <blogs.adelaide.edu.au/confucius/2016/10/05/china-joining-the-polar-club/>.

97 Thomas Kellogg, 'The South China Sea ruling: China's international law dilemma', *The Diplomat*, 14 July 2016 <thediplomat.com/2016/07/the- south-china-sea-ruling-chinas-international-law-dilemma/>.

98 Anon., 'China's international law problem is as wide as the sea', *The Globe and Mail*, 12 July 2016.

Chapter 12   Friends of China

1 Anne-Marie Brady, 'China's foreign propaganda machine', in Larry Diamond, Marc Plattner and Christopher Walker (eds), *Authoritarianism Goes Global*, Baltimore: Johns Hopkins University Press, 2016, p. 190.

2 Jiayang Fan, 'Trump, Confucius, and China's vision', *The New Yorker*, 19 May 2017.

3   Joo-Cheong Tham, 'Of aliens, money and politics: Should foreign political donations be banned?', *King's Law Journal*, 2017, vol. 28, no. 2, pp. 1–17.

4   <www.newworldencyclopedia.org/entry/Bob_Hawke>.

5   Sue Neales, 'Labor backing China bid for Kimberley land, says Barnaby Joyce', *The Australian*, 1 June 2012.

6   Anon., 'Tony Abbott says Labor "should listen to Bob Hawke" over China trade deal', *The Guardian*, 28 August 2015.

7   Bob Hawke, 'Forging an iron bond of friendship with China', *Australian Financial Review*, 19 December 2012.

8   Paul Kelly, 'Australia must heed the shift in the US-China power balance: Keating', *The Australian*, 24 December 2016.

9   Chang Ping, 'Chinese students studying abroad a new focus of CCP's "United Front work"', *China Change*, 9 June 2015.

10   <www.chinafile.com/document-9-chinafile-translation#start>.

11   <www.latrobe.edu.au/news/ideas-and-society/the-hon.-paul-keating-on-our-role-in-asia-in-the-trump-era>. From minute 33.00 to minute 36.35.

12   Philip Wen, 'Chinese foreign minister Wang Yi flies off the handle on video', *The Sydney Morning Herald*, 2 June 2016.

13   Brady, 'China's foreign propaganda machine', p. 189.

14   Kelly, 'Australia must heed the shift in the US-China power balance'.

15   At other times, Keating does not echo the CCP's absurd claim but contradicts it. But he presents PRC colonisation as somehow natural. With its One Belt, One Road initiative, he said, China plans the 'economic colonisation of the 50-odd states between the western border of China up to at least western Europe' (<www.rfigroup.com/australian-banking-and-finance/news/keatings-china-bank-plans-economic-colonisation>).

16   Hugh White, 'China's power and the future of Australia', Annual lecture, Centre on China in the World, Australian National University, 11 April 2017 <http://ciw.anu.edu.au/lectures_seminars/2017.php>. This section is drawn largely from: Clive Hamilton, 'China capitulationism: What's missing from Hugh White's China calculus', *policyforum.net*, 28 April 2017 <https://www.policyforum.net/china-capitulationism/>. Hugh White replied: 'We need to talk about China', *policyforum.net*, 4 May 2017 <https://www.policyforum.net/need-talk-china/>.

17   White, 'China's Power and the Future of Australia'.

18   Rory Medcalf (ed.), 'China's economic leverage: Perception and reality', National Security College, ANU, Policy Options Paper no. 2, 2017.

19   Jonathan Fenby, *Will China Dominate the 21st Century?*, Cambridge, U.K.: Polity Press, 2017.

20   Michael Danby, Carl Ungerer and Peter Khalil, 'No winners by appeasing China', *The Australian*, 16 September 2010.

21   White, 'China's power and the future of Australia'. See also Hugh White, *Without America: Australia in the New Asia*, Quarterly Essay, issue 68, 2017,

Melbourne: Black Inc. Books. While for White the only options are choose China or go to war, two US strategic analysts consider a wider range of options for responding to China's aggressive expansion—see Hal Brands and Zack Cooper, 'Getting serious about strategy in the South China Sea', *Naval War College Review*, Winter 2018, vol. 71, no. 1.

22 White, *Without America*, p. 9.

23 White, *Without America*, pp. 11, 12.

24 Michael Pillsbury, *The Hundred-Year Marathon*, New York: St Martin's Griffin, 2016, Chapter 7.

25 Speaking at a forum hosted by the Australia-China Relations Institute, 'South China Sea: What next?', held at the National Library of Australia, 23 November 2016.

26 White, 'China's power and the future of Australia'.

27 White, 'China's power and the future of Australia'.

28 White, 'China's power and the future of Australia'.

29 White, *Without America*, p. 69.

30 White, 'China's power and the future of Australia'.

31 Richard Bullivant, 'Chinese defectors reveal Chinese strategy and agents in Australia', *National Observer*, Spring 2005, no. 66, pp. 43–8.

32 In his memoir, Bob Carr wrote that Andrew Forrest says of the Chinese: 'I think they want humility from us' (Bob Carr, *Diary of a Foreign Minister*, Sydney: NewSouth Publishing, 2014).

33 Geoff Raby, 'Northern Australia takes its place on Xi Jinping's new silk road map', *Australian Financial Review*, 11 May 2016.

34 Geoff Raby, 'Xi Jinping's One Belt, One Road triumph and Australia's Sino confusion', *The Australian*, 17 May 2017.

35 In 2017 the winds in Canberra began to blow in a new direction. The government began to push back, verbally at least, against the PRC's inter-ference in Australian politics and society. Geoff Raby seemed to shift too, writing in October that President Xi Jinping is centralising too much power in himself. This overreach is making China less stable and multiplying economic risks for western countries. Geoff Raby, 'A stronger Xi Jingping (sic) means a more brittle Chinese state', *Australian Financial Review*, 30 October 2017.

36 <https://www.griffith.edu.au/__data/assets/word_doc/.../Xi-Jinping Mackerras-1.docx>.

37 <www.chinanews.com/cul/2016/08-04/7962178.shtml>.

38 <https://www.griffith.edu.au/__data/assets/word_doc/.../Xi-Jinping Mackerras-1.docx>.

39 Callum Smith, 'Fears of Chinese infiltration of Australia overblown', *Global Times*, 8 June 2017.

40 Callum Smith, 'No room for fear, greed in Sino-Australian ties', *Global Times*, 11 August 2016.

41 Callum Smith, 'Australian hypocrisy on full view in UNCLOS case', *Global Times*, 7 September 2016.

42 Andrew Parker, 'Populist alarm skews Chinese investment debate', *The Australian*, 1 May 2017.

43 <resources.news.com.au/files/2012/09/18/1226476/658338-full-transcript-australia-in-chinas-century-conference.pdf>.

44 Interview with former associate, 4 May 2017.

45 Ben Butler, 'Seven in China media ties', *Herald Sun*, 6 May 2010.

46 Editorial, 'Australia must not get sucked into dangerous US power play', *The West Australian*, 5 November 2015.

47 Interview with former journalist, 4 May 2017.

48 Cheng Jingye, 'China seeks peaceful solution to sea dispute', *The West Australian*, 17 June 2016.

49 Merriden Varrall, 'Four Corners sees the Party-state in all the shadows', *The Reporter*, Lowy Institute, 6 June 2017.

50 Between 6 June and 31 July 2017 Dr Varrall (temporarily) changed her tune, writing in *The New York Times* that Chinese students in Australia should not have their views closed down, a 'threat to debate and openness' that universities need to deal with (Merriden Varrall, 'A Chinese threat to Australian openness', *The New York Times*, 31 July 2017).

51 A week after the death of imprisoned writer Liu Xiaobo, Merriden Varrall's contribution was to report sympathetically the reactions of Chinese nationalists, who blamed the West for Liu's death rather than his jailers in China. Her article was a rebuke to the outpouring of grief in the West, including from Chinese writers and dissidents. (Merriden Varrall, 'China sees the West behind Liu Xiaobo', *The Interpreter*, Lowy Institute, 18 August 2017). Elsewhere, Varrall misinterpreted the results of a Lowy Institute poll of public opinion by making out Australians are 'confused' because their growing anxiety about the military threat China poses was construed by her as conflicting with their belief that China is more economically important to us. The article aims to make the case that if only Australians were better informed they would be less worried and more friendly towards China.

52 Merriden Varrall, 'Why Australia needs a smarter China policy', *South China Morning Post*, 17 December 2017.

53 Bob Carr, 'One Chinese political donation does not a scandal make', *The Australian*, 10 June 2017.

54 Chris Uhlmann, 'Bob Carr fascinates with sins of omission on Chinese influence', *The Australian*, 12 June 2017.

55 Michael Danby, Carl Ungerer and Peter Khalil, 'No winners by appeasing China', *The Australian*, 16 September 2010.

56 Jamie Smyth, 'Australia rejects China push on Silk Road strategy', *Financial Times*, 22 March 2017.

57 East Asian Bureau of Economic Research and China Center for International Economic Exchanges, *Partnership for Change*, Australia-China Joint Economic Report, Canberra: ANU Press, 2016, p. 181.

58 *Partnership for Change*, p. 183.

59 Peter Drysdale and John Denton, 'Chinese influence and how to use it to Australia's advantage', *Australian Financial Review*, 3 October 2017.

Chapter 13   The price of freedom

1   Email correspondence, 17 April 2017.

2   Lindsay Murdoch, 'Beijing article warns Australia over South China Sea', *The Sydney Morning Herald*, 2 January 2017.

3   Grant Wyeth, 'Why has Australia shifted back to the Quad?', *The Diplomat*, 16 November 2017.

4   Philip Wen and Daniel Flitton, 'South China Sea protests to come to Melbourne', *The Age*, 21 July 2016.

Index

Note: Chinese names are shown with surname first and personal name second. Where the owner of the name reverses the order, a comma appears after the surname. Most Chinese names are also given in Chinese characters to avoid ambiguities.